The Noé Jitrik Reader

A book in the series

Latin America in Translation/En Traducción/Em Tradução

Sponsored by the Duke–University of North Carolina

Joint Program in Latin American Studies

by Noé Jitrik

edited by Daniel Balderston

translated by Susan Benner

The Noé Jitrik Reader

Selected Essays on Latin American Literature

Duke University Press   Durham and London   2005

© 2005 Duke University Press

All rights reserved

Printed in the United States of America on acid-free paper ∞

Typeset in Minion by Keystone Typesetting, Inc.

Library of Congress Cataloging-in-Publication Data appear on

the last printed page of this book.

Contents

Editor's Preface

Suspending Belief

Noé Jitrik is one of Latin America's foremost literary critics, with almost a half-century of critical production. He has influenced many younger scholars, directed major literary projects, and been central to the professionalization of literary criticism in the continent, a role similar to that played by Antônio Cândido in Brazil and by the late Angel Rama of Uruguay. He is also the author of a solid body of work on literary theory and of numerous works of fiction and poetry. This volume will show something of the range and depth of his literary essays, focusing on his work on Argentine and more broadly on Spanish American literature.

Jitrik was born in 1928 in Rivera, on the western edge of the province of Buenos Aires, in a town that was then largely Jewish, in keeping with the initial emphasis (by Baron Hirsch and other organizers of the emigration of Jews from eastern Europe to Argentina and southern Brazil) on rural and small-town settlements. He studied at the University of Buenos Aires and began his teaching career at the university level in Córdoba, the third city of Argentina and a provincial capital. Involved with the polemical cultural journal *Contorno* in the 1950s (led by David and Ismael Viñas, with participation by such others as Ramón Alcalde, Adolfo Prieto, and Tulio Halperín Donghi), he published his first articles there and was a member of its editorial board in 1958–1959. Subsequently he devoted himself to university teaching, first at the University of Córdoba (from 1960 to 1966), then for a few months at the University of Buenos Aires in 1966 before his teaching career (like that of many others) was interrupted by General Onganía's military dictatorship and its sharp consequences for the institutions of higher education in Argentina. From 1967 to 1970 he taught at the University of Besançon in France, then was back briefly at the University of Buenos Aires before his longest period of exile, in Mexico. In Mexico City Jitrik taught at the Colegio de México from 1974 to 1980 and at the UNAM (the National University of Mexico) from 1981 to 1992. In 1987 he began dividing his time between Mexico and the University of Buenos Aires, eventually becoming director of the Instituto de Literatura Hispanoamericana of that institution. In addition, he has taught as a visiting professor in countless universities in Argentina, as well as in Mexico, the United States (Indiana University and the University of California, Irvine), Puerto Rico, France, and Venezuela.

With his wife, Tununa Mercado (a noted fiction writer, one of whose books is available in English translation from the University of Nebraska Press), and their two children, Jitrik spent intense and productive years in exile in Mexico. This period is crucial to an understanding of Jitrik's critical production; up to then his critical writing had focused largely on Argentine literature, but his writing of the Mexican period and subsequently was more broadly concerned with the literature of Spanish America. Essays on García Márquez, Carpentier, Neruda, Lezama Lima, and numerous Mexican writers are examples of this interest. Few Argentine critics of his generation have ranged as widely in their writings.

Jitrik's first book was a polemical discussion of Leopoldo Lugones (1874–1938), considered the national poet of Argentina in the first decades of the twentieth century; it was provocatively titled *Leopoldo Lugones, mito nacional* (Leopoldo Lugones, A National Myth; 1960). Also from 1960 is a book on Horacio Quiroga (1878–1937), the writer (born in Uruguay but who lived for much of his life in Argentina) best known for his stories of life in the jungle of the province of Misiones. Other books from the 1960s include monographic studies of Esteban Echeverría and of Sarmiento's *Facundo*, the important collection of essays *Escritores argentinos, dependencia o libertad* (Argentine Writers: Dependency or Freedom; 1967), and an anthology of writings of the Argentine generation of 1880 (1968). This period of Jitrik's writing, focused on the nineteenth-century period of national consolidation in Argentina, makes frequent use of models from dependency theory and other elements of Marxist analysis.

The 1970s, the period of Jitrik's most intense engagement with French new criticism, saw the publication of his monographic studies of José Hernández, Sarmiento, and José Martí (all 1971), and the important collections *Ensayos y estudios de literatura argentina* (Studies on Argentine Literature) and *El fuego de la especie* (The Fire of the Species) (also both 1971); from the latter collection we have included the essays on Cortázar's *Bestiario* (*Bestiary*) and on Echeverría's "El matadero" (The Slaugher House), widely considered the first short story in Spanish American literature. In 1973 he published an important study of the Argentine avant-garde writer-philosopher Macedonio Fernández (later the pretext for an extended essay on character in narrative, *El no existente caballero* (The Non-Existent Gentleman; 1975), and in 1975 the collection *Producción literaria y producción social* (Literary Production and Social Production) whose title again indicates the influence of Marxist thought and dependency theory, though this model is now conjoined to methods drawn from semiotics and French structuralism. His final major work of the 1970s was *Las contradicciones del modernismo* (The Contradictions of Modernism; 2nd ed., 2000), a significant contribution to criticism of Spanish American *modernismo*, the fin de siècle movement led by Rubén Darío (and exemplified most importantly by Leopoldo Lugones in Argentina); in this book Jitrik, basing himself on a close reading of a few poems, examines the movement's transnational character, the ways in which it was important to the emergence of autonomous intellectual voices, and its relations and conflicts with bourgeois national projects of the time.

The 1980s saw the publication of *La memoria compartida* (Shared Memory; 1982), a collection of long critical essays that range widely across Spanish American literature (Neruda and Carpentier) as well as Argentine literature (Sarmiento and Arlt). Also from this decade are *La lectura como actividad* (Reading as an Activity; 1982), Jitrik's first attempt to systematize his thinking about theories of critical production, and a book of essays on the writings of Christopher Columbus, *Los dos ejes de la cruz* (The Two Axes of the Cross; 1983). In 1984 he published *Las armas y las razones* (Arms and Reasons), a collection mostly of political essays that set forth a critique of Argentine populist thought, particularly of Peronism. Another major collection is the 1987 *La vibración del presente* (The Vibration of the Present), from which I have drawn essays on Borges, José María Arguedas, and the avant-garde; it also includes essays on José Lezama Lima, Juan Rulfo, Juan José Saer, and others. In 1987 he published two more books on literary theory. The last major collection of that decade is *El balcón barroco* (The Baroque Balcony), from which I have selected two essays; it also includes studies of José Vasconcelos, Alfonso Reyes, and several essays on literary semiotics (including the semiotics of theater).

Recent books include *La selva luminosa* (The Bright Forest; 1993), *El ejemplo de la familia* (The Example of the Family; a 1998 anthology of his essays on Argentine literature), and *Suspender toda certeza* (Suspending All Certainty), a 1997 anthology of his critical essays edited by Gonzalo Aguilar and Gustavo Lespada, with a critical introduction by the editors that is the best study of Jitrik's thought to date. In addition to the essays collected in his many books, he is the author of at least eighty uncollected essays.

His reflection on literary theory includes *Procedimiento y mensaje de la novela* (Process and Message of the Novel; 1962) on point of view and narration; *El no existente caballero* (1975) on fictional character; *La lectura como actividad* (1982) on reading; *Temas de teoría: el trabajo crítico y la teoría literaria* (Theoretical Topics: Critical Work and Literary Theory; 1987), his most systematic presentation of his ideas on "critical work"; *Lectura y cultura* (Reading and Culture; 1987), further thoughts on reading; *Historia e imaginación literaria* (History and Literary Imagination; 1995) on the historical novel; and *Los grados de la escritura* (Degrees of Writing; 2000), a series of semiotic reflections on the activity of writing, stemming from such familiar concepts as correction, drafts, beginnings, developments, and endings. Jitrik is also the author of more than a dozen books of poetry and fiction, including the recent novels *Mares del sur* (The Southern Seas; 1997) and *El Evaluador* (The Examiner; 2002).

Honored by the Modern Language Association as an honorary fellow and by the University of Puebla in Mexico with an honorary doctorate, Jitrik is widely recognized, though little of his work has been translated. His current major project is editing a twelve-volume history of Argentine literature (with five volumes published to date).

Jitrik in his theoretical writings establishes a distinction between "crítica literaria" (literary criticism) and the option that he prefers, "trabajo crítico" (critical work), with emphasis on the change from noun to adjective. Criticism, for Jitrik, is a productive activity. Yet it is also an activity at the service of the text, a process of self-questioning that follows lines opened by the text. As such, it is necessarily open. One of the lessons of Jitrik's prolific reflections on literature is, in fact, the insistence with which he varies in approach, in analysis, even (or maybe especially) when he returns to the same texts. "Critical work" is unceasing. *Línea de flotación: ensayos sobre incesancia* (Flotation Lines: Essays on Incessance; 2002), published in Venezuela, is a collection of essays (edited by Roberto Ferro) on this "unceasing" quality of critical work. The difference is described well in his essay on Roa Bastos's great historical novel *Yo el Supremo* (1974), which I have included in this selection:

> In this sense this text is unusual, although a general law could be stated according to which there is not really a reading when the relationship with a text does not provoke a suspension of all guarantees of certainty, whether the text be obscure or transparent. Of course such guarantees affect a knowledge that in an inert way attempts to reaffirm itself or that can be submitted to the demands of difference. For me, only the activity that allows that second possibility, that vertigo, can really be called "reading." And in my opinion, by its very nature this book elicits it, foments it, and fosters it.

Already in the introduction to *El fuego de la especie* (1971), Jitrik outlines the difference between various schools of criticism that were significant at the time (stylistics, sociological criticism, and so forth) and what he calls criticism that is "a reading itself and, therefore, also a hypothesis about reading, a model of readings that are the most complete and profound ones possible" (10). And in this same introduction he argues (from his first exile, in France) that what makes the intellectual's work "dangerous" is that work's nature of "continuing, insisting, seeking, presenting hypotheses, without fear of exile or of marginalization" (12).

Gonzalo Aguilar and Gustavo Lespada, in their introduction to *Suspender toda certeza*, recall that Jitrik himself has written, recalling Coleridge's famous phrase, on the "willing suspension of disbelief," that "there is no real reading of a text that does not produce a suspension of the guarantees of certainty" (9).

Aguilar and Lespada observe that this radical questioning is what they term a condensation or crystallization of Jitrik's way of reading, which they see as constantly in debate with literary ideas of textual autonomy and immanence. They also relate this attitude of radical questioning to Jitrik's perceptive, often polemical, stances with regard to the relations between literature and politics (represented here by the essay on Argentine nationalism, a sharp critique of Peronism, which also contains a polemic with some of Jitrik's contemporaries, David Viñas most notably, for the cultural nationalism or "populism" of much of their critical production).

One of the difficulties we have come upon in translating and presenting the essays here is the variety of critical approaches that Jitrik has taken over the years, and the diversity of critical vocabularies he has used. While without doubt the major influence on his approach is French structuralist thought (and its background in linguistics), he has also used the vocabulary of psychoanalysis, of semiotics, of Marxism, and of various other critical discourses along the way. This is necessarily a small selection from a large body of work; even in Spanish, though, some of the essays included here are from books that are out of print, and Susan Benner has completed the bibliographical references in a way that is current now but may not have been so when the essays were originally written.

I will now briefly introduce the essays included in this selection, giving information on original publication and also on English translations that are available of the texts that Jitrik is analyzing. I have selected essays on Latin American works that are readily available.

"Complex Feelings about Borges" was first published in French in *Les Temps Modernes* in a special issue on Argentina under military dictatorship in 1981. It was also published in "Sábado," the Saturday edition of *Unomásuno*, May 23, 1981 (Mexico) and was included in *La vibración del preente* (Mexico City, 1987). Jitrik published several other essays on Borges, but this is the best known. Viking Penguin has published three volumes—Borges's complete fictions, selected nonfiction, and selected poetry—many in new translations.

"Between Being and Becoming: Identity, Latinity and Discourse," was originally presented as a conference paper at the symposium "La latinidad, su sentido en América Latina" in May 1984 at the Universidad Nacional Autónoma de México in Mexico City, and was published in *El balcón barroco* (Mexico City, 1988).

"Form and Signification in Esteban Echeverría's 'The Slaughter House'" is also from *El fuego de la especie*. It was republished in *Suspender toda certeza* in 1997. Echeverría's "The Slaughter House" (El matadero; 1871), translated by Angel Flores, is available in Roberto Gonález Echevarría's *The Oxford Book of Latin American Short Stories* (New York: Oxford, 1997).

"Canon and Margin" first appeared in the literary journal *Orbis Tertius* in La Plata, Argentina, in 1996, under the title "Canónica, regulatoria y transgresiva." It has also appeared in Italian translation in the *Rivista Trimestrale* (Rome, 1998).

"From History to Writing" was Jitrik's keynote address at a conference on the historical novel in Latin America held at Tulane University in 1985 (and published in 1986). In it he develops his ideas on the ways in which the literary and documentary facets of historical fiction interact, ideas developed later in the essay on Augusto Roa Bastos (included here) and in the book *Historia e imaginación literaria* (1995).

"Notes on the Latin American Avant-garde" is from *Las armas y las razones: ensayos sobre el peronismo, el exilio, la literatura* (1984), Jitrik's first publication in Argentina after the end of the military dictatorship. It was originally published as "Papeles de trabajo: Notas sobre la vanguardia lationoamericana" in the *Revista de Crítica Literaria Latinoamericana* 15.8 in 1982.

"Beneath the Sign of the Baroque" also comes from *Las armas y las razones*, having been presented first as an invited lecture in Berlin in 1982. In it Jitrik develops some general ideas about the relations between Latin American and European literature.

"The Rise and Fall of Argentine Nationalism" appeared for the first time in *El ejemplo de la familia* (1998). In this essay Jitrik provides an eloquent critique of Argentine nationalism, particularly Peronism (a subject he had already explored in a number of political essays, notably those in *Las armas y las razones*, 1984), and extends this to the cultural nationalism that is an important current in Argentine intellectual thought.

The essay on Domingo Faustino Sarmiento, "Autobiography, Biography, Narrative: Sarmiento and the Origins of Argentine Literature," is one of Jitrik's numerous essays on the Argentine "author of a nation," as he has been termed (see Halperín-Donghi, Jaksic, Masiello, and Kirkpatrick volume, which includes a translation of Jitrik's essay "El *Facundo:* la gran riqueza de la pobreza"). Two of Sarmiento's texts are now available in new translations: his *Facundo: Civilization and Barbarism,* translated by Kathleen Ross, was issued in 2003 by the University of California Press, and his *Recuerdos de provincia,* translated by Elizabeth Garrels as *Memories of Provincial Life,* is forthcoming shortly from Oxford University Press.

Another essay on autobiography, "Autobiography, Memoir, Diary," appeared in *El ejemplo de la familia* (Buenos Aires, 1998).

"Martí in the American Library" first appeared in the *Diario de Poesía,* a Buenos Aires periodical devoted to poetry, in issue 37 in 1996. It refers to an event held a year earlier at the University of Buenos Aires on the centenary of Martí's death. As stated earlier, Jitrik's first work on the Cuban poet José Martí dates from 1971. This essay from the mid-1990s is a reflection on the reception of Martí, focusing particularly on the ways in which critics (in Cuba and elsewhere) have used Martí to argue for the political commitments of poetry. At the same time, Jitrik uses some of these polemics to suggest that Martí's esthetics, his notions of beauty, exceed his political circumstance. In this essay Jitrik provides a further reflection on the functioning of literary canons, the subject of another essay in this collection.

"The Riches of Poverty Revisited" comes from *La selva luminosa.* The title of the essay refers to an earlier Jitrik essay on Sarmiento's *Facundo,* "El *Facundo,* la gran riqueza de la pobreza" (in *La memoria compartida,* 1982). Translations of the poetry of César Vallejo are widely available in English; perhaps the best known are those of Robert Bly and Clayton Eshleman; a good critical book on Vallejo is Jean Franco's *César Vallejo: The Dialectics of Poetry and Silence* (1976).

Jitrik's essay on José Bianco, "Lack and Excess in José Bianco's *Shadow Play,*" was published in *El ejemplo de la familia* in 1998. Bianco, best known as the editor of *Sur* from 1937 to 1961, was the author of splendid literary essays and of a few works of fiction; his novellas *Sombras suele vestir* (1941) and *Las ratas* (1943) are available in English translation as *Shadow Play; The Rats: Two Novellas,* translated by Daniel Balderston, Latin American Literary Review Press, 1983.

"The Suffering Narrator" comes from *Vertiginosas textualidades* (Mexico City, 1999). Onetti's *Los adioses* is available in two English versions: "Goodbyes," in *Goodbyes and Stories,* translated by Daniel Balderston (Austin, 1990), and

"Farewells," in *Farewells; and, A Grave with No Name,* translated by Peter Bush (London, 1992).

"Arguedas: Reflections and Approaches," first presented in France in a symposium on José María Arguedas, was originally published in *La vibración del presente* (Mexico City, 1987). Arguedas's novels *Yawar Fiesta* and *Deep Rivers* (*Los ríos profundos*) are available from the University of Texas Press in brilliant translations by Frances Barraclough.

"Notes on the 'Holy Place' and 'Otherness' in Cortázar's *Bestiary*" comes from *El fuego de la especie* (Buenos Aires, 1971). Cortázar's *Bestiaro* is available in English as *Bestiary* (London, 1998), in translations by Alberto Manguel, Paul Blackburn, Gregory Rabassa, Clementine Rabassa, and Suzanne Jill Levine.

"*I, the Supreme* as Historical Novel" is also from *Vertiginosas textualidades.* Jitrik's ideas on the historical novel are further developed in *Historia e imaginación literaria: las posibilidades de un género* (Buenos Aires, 1995). Roa Bastos's *I, the Supreme,* in a brilliant translation by Helen Lane, was published by Knopf in 1986.

"Thirty Years Later" was the prologue (under the title "Treinta años después") to a collection of interviews with Latin American writers that had appeared in the pages of the *Paris Review.* Jitrik edited this collection, titled *Confesiones de escritores. Los reportajes de* The Paris Review: *escritores latinoamericanos* (Writers' Confessions: Interviews from the *Paris Review* with Latin American Writers). In this essay Jitrik reflects thirty years later on the so-called boom in Latin American literature, taking the occasion of the publication of the interviews to provide a fascinating account of sharp changes in the institution of literature in Argentina, and more generally across Latin America, in the 1960s.

I would like to thank Susan Benner for the arduous task of translation, revision, and the checking of quotations for this edition. Susan and I would also like to acknowledge two superb graduate assistants, Alfredo Alonso Estenoz and Nicolás Lucero, who aided with aspects of this project, and Noé Jitrik for his help clarifying some details of the references.

Complex Feelings about Borges

For César Fernández Moreno

I have only met Borges personally a couple of times. I remember them clearly, though I'm sure he does not. The first one was in 1948, I believe; the student center I belonged to invited him to speak. It was in a house in the Belgrano neighborhood in the northern part of Buenos Aires. I have forgotten what he spoke about but clearly remember the way he stammered as he began, a timidity that, wrapped in good manners, created a certain distance. There was no choice but to feel oneself "young" when confronted with a totality in which the tremor in his voice, the lost look, the hesitant manner were a mask, a plate of armor, a way to protect himself. What united us was a complex process of bedazzlement (we had read his poems and the book *Ficciones* [1944] and knew him as the translator of Faulkner and Kafka) and a common hatred of Perón, which was neither explicit nor thought out but was there, nevertheless, an assumption

1

whose disclosure could have caused a scandal. The second time I saw him was in Córdoba, and there where he was watched over by Carlos Fernández Ordóñez, hounded by Emilio Sosa López, and celebrated by local personalities. I was vaguely introduced to him but could think of nothing to say. And that lack of words was mutual. I contented myself with watching him: he was almost blind, and his face had already begun to take on that marble-like look that can be seen in more recent photographs, that impenetrable air counterpoised against that air of helplessness, real or feigned, that he had back in 1948. This was in 1963.

I have been able to hear Borges speak on two occasions in all these years. The first one was, as I mentioned, in someone's home. I have forgotten what he talked about, but not the tone. The second time was in the auditorium of Radio Nacional in Córdoba, in 1963. The room seemed huge, and it was completely full. Borges talked about the book *Martín Fierro* [1872]; he stared straight ahead, his eyes half-closed or empty, and his phrases seemed to be pulled from deep within him, as if he were praying or as if he knew with absolute certainty what he wanted to say. He made his way up to the table accompanied by someone— perhaps all he could see were his own feet. He had no papers in hand. Listening to him was fascinating because of that complex elocution for which he was famous. Particularly impressive was the way he recited a certain stanza from the end of the first part, where Fierro and Cruz decide to go and live amongst the Indians—without a doubt, some of the most resounding verses of poetry in the Spanish language. Repudiation and fulfillment:

> Y cuando la habían pasao,
> una madrugada clara,
> le dijo Cruz que mirara
> las últimas poblaciones;
> y a Fierro dos lagrimones
> le rodaron por la cara.

> [And after they had passed it
> one clear early morning,
> Cruz told him to look back
> at the last of the settlements—
> and two big tears went rolling
> down Martín Fierro's face.][1]

His dense way of speaking took this piece we recognize as poetry and expanded it in the room. The culminating moment came when he spoke of a mastery, an intelligence, a certain plane where intellectual "things" slid into focus that could be received, admitted in. And yet everything else he said seemed familiar to me—it was the same thing he had written in his book *Discusión* [1932], in the thirties, and in his book about Martín Fierro,[2] and in the prologue to *Poesía gauchesca* [1955] that he wrote with Adolfo Bioy Casares. It was the same thing he would say about *gauchesca* poetry again and again ad infinitum in tiresome interviews, but that always sounded as if it were the first time he had said it, invoking those "big tears" as a way of getting inside the emotion of that other, as if he modestly wanted us to believe in his own theory of emotion, diminished, certainly, by reiteration.

I've written about Borges three times. The first was around 1951, in the journal *Centro*, of which I was a member of the editorial board. It was a two-page article on his book *Other Inquisitions, 1937–1952* [*Otras inquisiciones*; 1952].[3] I continued to be dazzled; I expressed my admiration for the mathematical precision of his thought and speculated that there could be such a thing as a purely intellectual passion—and it could be that Borges embodied this. The second time was around 1962, in regard to *Dreamtigers* [*El hacedor*; 1960]. There I insisted—anyone who is interested can find the article in the journal *Zona de la Poesía Americana*[4]—that César Fernández Moreno, Francisco Urondo, Alberto Vanasco, and I put together—that Borges was condemned to repeat himself, that there was nothing in the book that he had not already written or said, and that, to the disadvantage of that particular book, he had written it more clearly in the past. I indicated that with *Ficciones* he had come into his own, but at the same time, his repetition augured a success that even with *Ficciones* he had not yet enjoyed. And I was not wrong—it seems as if what we call "recognition," "fame," and so on, arrives just at the moment that a certain depletion appears, though it remains unnamed and unrecognized at the time.

Meanwhile, I referred to Borges in various texts that are not worth citing: but there they are, and he appears in almost all of them as someone who gave a solid form to the solitary and desperate message of Macedonio Fernández[5] and who could give that message a transmissibility that Macedonio himself not only was unable to do but scorned—Borges as a line of transmission that touches all

Latin American literature, and through that, Macedonio's revolution. Finally, I wrote a paper on *Ficciones* that I read in Cluny in 1968,[6] for an audience that without a doubt loved Borges, held him in reverence, and found his texts to be a source of self-confirmation. Considering the fact that Foucault had taken Borges as the point of departure for *The Order of Things* [*Les Mots et les choses*; 1966], and that the so-called nouveau roman had pronounced and proclaimed him as a source of inspiration, an attempt at criticism—even one using the weapons of those attending the conference—could only end in silence: if the French do us the favor of venerating a work of Latin American literature, it is not easy to accept criticism of that same work by Latin Americans, that is, a critique of that esteem.

There is no doubt that I was fascinated by Borges's intelligence and his economy, as well as his unity. And from that emerged an unformulated intuition about "what Borges saw" when he began to write poetry. He saw two things, I believe: first, how what we call "writing" emerges, that is, the functioning of an autonomous process, and second, certain ideological core beliefs that penetrate all of his subsequent work and refer to such concepts as origin (one's own), the nation, and society. On the one hand, we find a fertile productive system (of writing) set in motion; on the other, an obsessive, idealized restoration of substances that must have led him, obsessively, to a diffuse metaphysics that, as a side effect in his case, could have given rise to a conservative attitude, a fixed world, in which things (values) cannot be moved.

Are there contradictions between these two positions? Perhaps yes, if we see the one as radically generative and the other as negative from a certain human, revolutionary, and critical perspective. But perhaps we can look at it in a different way, one not so Manichean, since there are no guarantees when talking of points of view or beliefs, especially if they are not formulated from a position of power. At any rate, the contradiction could have another base, that is, if closedness is the predominant feature of a conservative political attitude, closedness in writing can be the code or key to richness. I suppose there is a tendency to consider generativity in writing to be based on its openness, its permeability, its capacity to manifest drives immediately, but I would suggest that perhaps it is equally true that a rigid writing, a closed one besieged by organization, still has the ability to illuminate a path. Perhaps that which represses, by the same token, penetrates—as the repressed often does—the surface of the perfect phrase, and perhaps this play between drives and repressions is the key to generativity, that which makes us think or desire. Looking at it from another angle, this would allow us to ward off the contradiction if we assume that the same schema could serve for the political arena as well, which could then be seen as a system of control of something that bursts its bounds. Correlatively, this does not preclude the possibility that, denying that writing has the capacity to transcend its external qualities, parallels can be established between the search for closure and perfection, and the requirements of fixity demanded by conservative political thought.

Of course there is a difference between one camp and the other: while, as I am attempting to propose, a writing can be fertile despite being closed because the struggle between drives and closedness or limits turns out to be illuminating, in political discourse, on the other hand, the repression of drives, or if this is too much, of desire or of the imaginary, exalts what is repressed, which, metonymically, defines the whole field and sanctions a blocking. What we experience as a contradiction in Borges, then, would take form in the opposition we are familiar with between the effects of his writing and the effects of his conservative thought. I reserve the right to not discount the possibility, on the other hand, that there actually is no contradiction, at least superficially, as far as the superficial is worth, between certain characteristics of his writing and of his conservative thought, although I am not fooling myself either about the risks of a mechanistic system that can arise in the pursuit of this analogy to the detriment of the analysis of the difference in scope of the two discourses. Could we not say the same thing about his admired Péguy and Bloy or Chesterton? Are they not, with their conflicts, a more disturbing example than many of the others that are invoked more often?

I have run across Borges various times in public places; the same day that I left for Europe for the first time, in March of 1953, he was heading west on Calle Florida and I was heading east. It is probably not necessary to mention that I noticed him, he did not notice me. I must confess that I felt as if I were bidding farewell to Buenos Aires, as unsteady in its unsettledness as Borges, who continued tirelessly, unsteadily wandering through the city. I returned from Europe in October of 1954, and the very next day I ran into Borges on Calle Florida—I was heading west, he in the opposite direction: was this the city welcoming me back? As quiet as the farewell had been, it was still somehow symbolic, as if Borges had something to do, if not with my destiny, at least with my most important uprootings. Since I decided not to return to Europe again, my encounters with Borges on Calle Florida became more frequent and less significant. All I had to do was allow myself to walk down Calle Florida, and after 1955, all I had to do was wander at times through the neighborhood south of the Plaza de Mayo. But despite my previous decision, my travels began again in 1958, and in 1967, impelled by the military coup of Onganía[7] three or four days after the death of Che Guevara, I left on another steamship. And as before, almost as a necessity, I saw Borges on the street the day of my departure, even more faltering, with someone accompanying him by the arm.

Recently I recounted these encounters (from which a reader of Henry James could extract a certain atmosphere or at least weave a kind of explanation) to Luis Dávila and Merle Simmons in a cafeteria on the campus in Bloomington, Indiana. I enjoyed pointing out that a writer can be physically present in our lives without there being any words exchanged whatsoever, which would have been useless in any case. We finished our coffee, took the elevator to leave, and when the doors opened to let us out, suddenly—there was Borges waiting to enter. Dávila and I looked at each other; I think he understood the significance of these encounters. And when I left that city that I never believed could be mine and where Hoagy Carmichael composed "Star Dust" one disillusioned night in a house that today is called García's Pizza, there was Borges, heading in the opposite direction, his face already petrified, his mouth full, leaning on his cane and on the arm of a young woman who appeared Japanese—they say her name is María Kodama. In the car as I was leaving I had my last glimpse of Borges, on a tree-lined avenue, walking away with his back still as straight as ever, as if defining for once and for all a system of relations, as if he were stubbornly pursuing the secret of those streets, which must have been hopelessly unknown except for the trees he could not see, chasing the secret of the spring sky, similar, perhaps to that of the pampas but put together in another way, and so different, after all.

In 1974, in September, I took a flight to Mexico, and since then I have not returned to Argentina. I knew this would happen. During the flight I read Roa Bastos's *I, the Supreme* [*Yo el Supremo*; 1974] and a long interview with Borges by Eduardo Gudiño Kieffer, published in *La Nación*. The book I found painful, the interview was entertaining: Borges shredded all of Gudiño's attempts to paint him as "good." Gudiño said, if I remember correctly, something about "Che Guevara, Latin American hero," and Borges remarked distractedly, "Guevara, Guevara: that's a surname from the area around Mendoza, isn't it?" Gudiño's line of questioning was designed to obstruct; Borges's answers underscored two things: that Gudiño wanted to obstruct Borges by using assumptions that were perhaps not shared, and that Gudiño himself did not really believe in what he took as a given but availed himself of it and was willing to use it for his own ends. Looked at in this way, Borges appeared more critical and more dynamic than Gudiño, who was revealed as someone who, claiming to examine a "truth" supported by many people, in reality, wanted to compel, force, dominate, and exorcise a celebrated agnosticism. Gudiño was left disconcerted once more, because for Borges, once again, there was nothing sacred.

Years later I experienced the same sensation reading several dialogues between Borges and Sabato that an Argentine publisher believed indispensable to put out. Sabato goes on about grand themes. Borges once in a while mutters a kind of "I guess that's the way it is" and does not even bother to attack Sabato's complicated and pretentious—philosophical—pronouncements, perhaps so as "not to appear impolite," as the *criollos*[8] would say, whose disdain Borges uses to nurture his well-known denigratory style. I am beginning to think that this is constant—people cannot accept that Gide's well-known comment is true: good intentions make for bad literature, although the contrary has not been shown to be exactly true either. Many people believe that because Borges writes well, without asking themselves particularly what it means to write well, he therefore must have good intentions, which they benevolently try to prove, and thus find themselves face to face with the obstacles Borges himself sets in their way. When this obsession of Borges's for not wanting to be "good" is linked to politics, it creates a scandal, outrage becomes widespread: how can he say that? Such a great writer and so reactionary—he must be under someone's evil influence. At one time it was a certain Di Giovanni, I believe, who became his López Rega[9] in a kind of parallel to the aged Perón that many found quite entertaining.

Naturally, besides those who wish him to appear "good," there are those who challenge Borges directly. I suspect that some do so not only out of a desire to destroy a pernicious myth, but also out of the seldom confessed intention of attaining some of that aloof glory that so surrounds Borges at this moment: nourished from the shadow cast by a giant tree, even as they deny it. In my anonymity, am I free of such a suspicion? Borges waits for the reproaches to arise and then, with one phrase, demolishes them. "Have you read the book *Borges político* [Borges, politician][10] that came out in Mexico?" he is asked. "Soon someone's going to write one called *Borges, Cyclist*," he murmurs as an aside, leaving the questioner, and above all, the book in question, with no response. Not only does he bring out the foolishness of those who see him as a "phenomenon of an era" without taking the trouble to examine the complexity of the term "phenomenon of an era," but he also shows, very simply—which gives it a devastating force—that he does not share certain assumptions, and even less, the critical systems that spring from such assumptions.

It seems to me in this respect, seeing Borges as a kind of disciple of Darwin and in addition, isolated, that no one gets it right, no one has been able to figure out what he thinks or what is going on with him, and he doesn't please anyone, unless from the outset he makes them happy. He lets his discourse flow without any obstructions, changes in focus, or destructive drives. In this respect he seems like a child; selfish and spoiled, he continues being the Georgie in whom a bad temper is cleverly replaced by an unfaltering intelligence.

Perhaps from this basis one can understand the often shocking things Borges says and then later retracts as if it were nothing, even the declarations he presents as absolutes without that fact preventing a subsequent relativization. I don't know what he said (or rather, I do know) about the inferiority of blacks and then later denied; I don't know what he stated about the "mere Spaniard" that he later denied, but I do know how he congratulated Pinochet and Videla[11] and how today he maintains that it is unacceptable that there are people murdered and disappeared in Argentina. At one time he said that Alfonso Reyes was the best prose writer in the Spanish language, and later he reduced him to "one of the best." And so it goes along this line ad infinitum, always disconcerting those who seek coherence and those who believe that the world will come to an end if someone is allowed to provoke or irritate others. In any case, what Borges wishes to do is to annoy his interlocutors, frustrate their expectations. It is as if, intellectually speaking, he retained a seminal fluid, as if he were rooted in a Bergsonian, or maybe Freudian theory of humor, or as if he considered himself to be, without stating or assuming so, a place where the Lacanian theory of desire is exemplified.

It could be asserted, then, that in reality he is not concerned with blacks or Indians or the disappeared or Alfonso Reyes,[12] or even the Peronists, around whom a wealth of comments has been generated, or soccer players. What he is

concerned about, in moderation, is or would be the way in which he can channel something, which in order to be brief, we could call his "cynicism." And he
does so at the cost of whomever or whatever, manipulating that "whomever or
whatever" but doing so in order to thwart his interlocutor at the same time that
his attitude, focus, or manner are affirmed, and not in order to thwart that
"whomever or whatever." In other words, taking advantage of the "subjectified
object" in order to destroy the "objectified subject." I am beginning to think
that if there is a truth about Borges, it is the truth of the cynic—and not even
that of cynicism, which would have a more general, systematic scope. Rather,
his truth, in the final instance, has the subjugating attention of his intuitive
character, capable of scorning all fundamental principles. But that is not all: like
all cynics, he has the ability to fragment or break the apparent totalization
presented by an obstacle, and from that, to present a model of the world that
has precisely that attraction.

Is this what Foucault saw in the bestiary Borges mentioned in his account of
a Chinese encyclopedia?[13] And if Borges's cynical tone is made manifest, for me,
in his form of refutation or his defensive system, in the realm of his ideological
movement, I believe it also penetrates his textuality and leads it to the world of
enumerations and superimpositions with which he has expressed his fictions
for some time. Let us take Foucault: it is possible that his acceptance of Borges's
fragmentary model does not imply a final concurrence insofar as Foucault's
interests configure a critical system of the process of production of the real or of
a discourse of the real. Then what and why? Perhaps, as Juan Carlos Marín
suggested to me, it is because Borges functions as an "operator"—he triggers a
process in the other, and when he is not suggesting necessary but fertile paths of
differentiation, he forces us to at least reexamine things. As I said, he annihilates
the foolish and leaves the prejudiced hanging, but he perhaps galvanizes the
philosopher just as he does the poet, without either the philosopher or the poet
having any reason to "Borges" themselves. Out of spite, out of sarcasm, Borges
forces them into motion.

Is the word "cynic" derogatory? It is, above all, useful, even if we do not display
all the elements of the paradigm. I use the term paradigmatically, and there is a
history of cynics that, as we know, has moments of great radicalism. Borges
would be central to all this. Certainly there are things that he believes in: the
rigor of a phrase, the desire to show the fragmentation of the real, family memo-

ries, and the history of the nation—the same as liberal convictions. All of which makes him an attenuated cynic, and for that reason, all the more triumphant; it is questionable to call him an ideologue, since in doing so we are only dealing with personal beliefs with which he may easily disagree. He utilizes cynicism as an instrument, and therein lies the key to his effectiveness, precisely because he imposes nothing personal at the same time that he destroys the personal beliefs of the other. From the history of cynics he has extracted one element that explains his triumph: have the last word, which implies having previously created the conditions such that you are asked for a word, and having astutely taken enough time that your word appears to be the final one. This device, as in the case of almost all cynics, reveals a brilliance and explains why, in general, except for Diogenes (and only up to a point), the cynics come out the winners.

But we should not reject the similarities completely: if Alexander blocked the light from shining on Diogenes, the Gudiños and Sabatos of the world and so many others try to block out Borges's sound and air. Yet they themselves are brushed aside by his sarcasm, disdain, and portrayals, or, to borrow from Quevedo, "a ship's compass for fools."[14] But the enigma of his effectiveness persists, in particular because it has lasted for so long and because somehow it continues in force even when he is silent, although he still continues to speak. There is a horde of people eager to disseminate his ironies, to reproduce his triumphant letters, who happily cite him, lured to his light, ready to add to his glory. I believe it is precisely his effectiveness that dazzles and seduces them, more than the verbal creation that that effectiveness is based on. What is surprising is that in a world that tends to make all expression uniform, Borges, a spontaneous *conceptista,* has managed to become almost a popular myth, at least for significant and growing factions: his effectiveness is the measure and the explanation, although we still do not know why he has achieved this so consistently, why he provokes jealousy, emulation, and the fantasy of identification.

And there is yet another tendency: he makes one feel as if "there is something important" beneath the surface that is the secret of his effectiveness and that one comes to savor. I suspect that if the structuralists in general held him in such high esteem that they almost revered him, it was due to such a hypothesis, although we cannot rule out the possibility that they find in him a superior flavor to the bland fare of stupefyingly comfortable French tradition: effectiveness in construction, for example, a structural and structuralizable object almost by its own epistemological right. Since structuralism is over (because it reached its limits and not necessarily because it was founded on absolute conceptual poverty), it is felt that if examining this effectiveness is worthwhile, in order to know something more about it, it would be necessary to take a more semiotic approach, destined, in the best of cases, to demonstrate the behavior of the signifier, which functions beyond effectiveness, constantly maintaining in us an active interest in his writing that he endeavors to cover up or erase by means of his cleverness. We could say, as Ricardo Piglia has said, that Borges's writing is "anticapitalist," which would allow us to understand his writing and how it operates on multiple levels. However, this would not be what Borges is arguing, whether that be a conformist procapitalism (somewhat innocuous) or a theory of perfection in which all value can be found.

There is no doubt, and in fact, it is a common assumption that Borges "knows" about literature. Perhaps the extent of his knowledge is apocryphal, but this does not in any way deny his wisdom, since the apocryphal is a construction whose stones exist—they are real and numerous. His handling of that knowledge is admirably natural, although it leaves out those who do not "know." Somehow it appears as a "wealth of knowledge," something like the quintessence of a treasure whose worth does not depend on being displayed; in this sense, Borges is the opposite of erudite. But he has something else still: he does not mind taking on this wealth, this abundance. He does not mind, nor does it make him uncomfortable, to present himself as a writer. He calls himself a poet and believes that in poetic discourse he can find themes on which to reflect publicly, or rather, in public, and without embarrassment. He pretends that everyone who listens to him or reads him is interested in the same things, and thanks to his persistence, those who read him and listen to him end up accepting that they are interested in the same things. In this sense, he opposes—or he highlights—the general guilty attitude of writers and poets who hide their identity as such, yet at the same time are continuously trying to apologize for writing, an ambiguous pleasure, a withdrawal from reality that to many is only acceptable if embraced as marginal. But not Borges—he does not "get involved" nor does he believe that Lugones[15] is a more trivial subject of discussion than Perón. In that unabashed undertaking, there is naturally a confrontation, possibly the most productive and the most easily shared.

There is also a temptation here: to consider this attitude to be anachronistic; it could be viewed as something that was current in the eighteenth century and in other places, not in Argentina and not in the twentieth century. On the other hand, I do not believe that Borges is unaware of the anachronism and its consequences: it seems to me that it is present in his "Poema conjetural" [Conjectural Poem][16] as an opposition between arms and letters, a formula that to a certain point, on one level, reiterates the tradition of Civilization and Barbarism. At least this is so to a certain point related to a prototechnical universe that would still continue to exist in the political realm, for example, but beyond that, the "defense of the craft" would imply the restoration of a system of production that the current "system of production" tends to make seem more and more insignificant. Nevertheless, his "literary knowledge," a core I will not elaborate on, has something monastic about it, something Borges himself is responsible for: he does everything possible in order to seem enclosed in his knowledge. It would seem that he does not care about learning, nor does he show any sign of questioning how this knowledge, both his own and that of others, can be organized beyond its pure affirmation, which, in its turn, is enhanced and disguised by his audacity. To put it another way, perhaps he is excluding something essential from his knowledge, a process that is expressed through a system of risks that threaten it and create it at the same time.

I have the impression that the characteristics noted in the preceding sections, his kind of "knowledge," his cynicism, the little boy that continues to exist in him, the seduction of his effectiveness, a "truth" that lies deeper down and that others must discover—all lead somewhere; they are translated into something that would arise as the cultivation of certain themes. I suspect that the place to which they all lead is the paternal library, the refuge of the little boy and of his knowledge, and, at the same time, the place of pride without equal and an affirmation without detractors. It is not that everything stems from there, but there he still remains, and everything else, including the imagination, is a reduced proliferation of substitutes that summon and conceal and materialize merely as favorite themes. Yet in reality, they are something more—they are obsessive internal figures, and, to the extent that insisting on them does not nullify them, they are exceedingly vexed figures, all of which, in turn, sketches out the scheme of a desire that the exactness of the form is unable to repress.

In mid-1974 I became indignant with Borges. Few knew about it since I did not feel it necessary to discuss the delicate details of my indignation. It was all because of Macedonio Fernández. Borges maintained that Macedonio had been an extraordinary speaker (who said one or two memorable phrases each night, nothing more), but not a good writer. An easy thing for him to say—he did not feel any need to reconsider it in an interview with my friend María Teresa Marzilla, published in Mexico in 1980—there are not many people who become passionate about the difference between speaking and writing. Then he provided examples that made me seriously question the solidity of his ideas about writing. According to Borges (and I am quoting from memory) "repetitions and abstract words *disfigured* his prose" [Jitrik's emphasis]. The powerful, unmistakable figure of Lugones emerged as an aloof, silent man, but one who "knew how to write." Two models, two paths, but in Borges—and this is what made me so indignant—one single lack of gratitude, a Stalinist correction of history, since one can clearly see that Macedonio opened the way for him not only to attack Lugones between 1920 and 1930 but also to write, because the revolutionary things this old man taught Borges—it was revolutionary to teach him about rupture, humor, the flash of the instantaneous, disbelief in the realistic—all this could be used to combat Lugones. Macedonio was the authorizing father figure, but in a destructuring sense, and that authorization would fulfill the most unconfessable but deepest desire of a talented young man, full of passion for things written. At the end of the road, he inverts the signs, dismisses that fertile presence, minimizing it, and restores the oppressive presence, magnifying it. A long process in which what he fought against as oppression has become incorporated within him, reshaping him in its turn?

This is surprising, because the Lugones paradigm has not managed to govern his writing completely, or rather, he, contradictorily, tries to make it govern his writing, but he has not achieved that end yet: his writing continues to be, both in the texts written years ago and in some of the current ones, a point of conflict, a battleground in which he uses Lugonian weapons in order to stifle the Macedonian libido that is then neutralized but not dead, managing, all the same, to generate its effects. Of course there are moments—not even Borges is completely homogeneous: his efforts and his respect, for example, turn more toward the harmony of a phrase than toward the bewilderment inspired by the convulsions of rupture (which he calls a process of *disfiguration*), to look at only outward manifestations. He chooses the solid weightiness of the signified to the extent that it refines precisely what he wants to say, only minimally free to be ambiguous, and he rejects the nervous, ungraspable, unpredictable freedom of the signifier. He has gone back to seeing the sense in conventions, and, using mere common sense arguments, he has discarded the perspective of verbal acts that come from and later produce transformations and the unpredictable. The unpredictable is becoming more and more unusual in his writing, something premeditated, and thus, put in the balance with the predictable, restoring its power. This way he reclaims measured verse and rhyme. His stories are articulated versions, as if it were a question of a whole whose parts were simply variations of the same themes. I'm bored as I read something about tigers, but suddenly run across a poem called "Soy" [I Am],[17] whose construction brings joy; it is free, revised with the help of a poet, Rodolfo Braceli, who helped type Borges's poems. Suddenly, when you least expect it, he drops his solemn tone, and he lets loose his love for words and his affection for images, which is converted into affection for his interlocutor, in the same way that he states that "the fact that there are disappeared in Argentina is unacceptable."

Until recently, Lugones was the one who triumphed in Borges: faced with the threat of another return to the despised Peronism, was this an attempt to defend himself from the outside world by invoking the strict and impervious father so as to be as invulnerable as he? Now, a shift: he laughs at Lugones again. Perhaps his world—beneath the firm hand of the generals—has once more become a secure and solid place, and now it is no longer necessary to be so rigid, which would have been something short-lived in any case. But something here remains permanent: Macedonio is defeated, but, as with the Roman triumph over the Greeks, what really matters in Borges is that which comes from the side of the defeated, not of the triumphant.

Perhaps this game of gratitude and ingratitude toward both figures will allow us to understand politics a little better: maybe the political options ("democracy, that superstition") of both men had a similar outline, and not because Macedonio was a democrat (actually, he was an anarchist), nor because Lugones ended up wrapping himself in a solitary fascism, uncompromising and bereft of hope. The existence of passion implies a parallel terror of passion, a fascination with going beyond limits brings a parallel terror of going beyond those limits, the spectacle of pain provokes a trite praise of happiness, and the dazzling image of the future (as Borges saw in Sarmiento) engenders the sad, difficult choice of the present.

Figurations, fantasies, perhaps an excessive faith in the possibilities of reality, an anarchist naïveté, because, when did he see that dazzling future? When has it not been possible to incorporate the pain of others with one's own eroticism? And now that Sarmiento's name has come up, perhaps this contest of strength that makes Borges authorize authoritarianism (but in whose manifestation there is always something of the other that disturbs us: "democracy, that superstition"—a phrase that scandalizes many leftists, yet, in another context, couldn't Trotsky have said the same thing?) is more an indication of patrician Argentine liberalism than of fascism, whether of the intellectual or of the *criollo* variety: to be tolerant of the future as long as it does not disturb the present, to be receptive to the movements of peoples as long as they do not disturb certain nuclei that took great effort to configure or that define the roots of the soul—this is perhaps the liberalism that I call patrician, because it is historic, a central element, what must be defended. And if that which can dissolve this, Macedonian anarchism, has lodged itself in you, then it must be eradicated. And thus, the downplaying of Macedonio and the exaltation of Lugones; thus the gradual renunciation of the concept of "writing" that Borges had been forging, one way or another, along the line of destruction-construction that Macedonio had brilliantly foreseen. Perhaps this fidelity—which without a doubt suffered serious attacks after 1945—can explain his obsession with correcting his oldest texts: the obsessive search for harmony between form and content, between signified and signifier, obsessive in that the disharmony that exists in those texts could make it appear that an intolerable disorder persists in us, could signal the establishment of the irrational that liberalism cannot tolerate because the destiny—of the class—becomes unintelligible in the dangerous book of history.

And, finally, since the list of his themes is short, in order to avoid the danger of disappearing altogether, his only option is to repeat himself, to insist: the origins of the family, the destiny of a class, the deep-rootedness of property—all would constitute, therefore, the backdrop for his insistence, tending to ward off the danger of any change. They would be the homologous list of a universe that always stays the same, is always set to support perfection, always secure, and, as can be expected, always threatened.

At this point in time, what has been written about Borges adds up to hundreds of works, articles, studies, notes, theses, books. A day does not go by in which some interview or commentary does not appear, at least in this part of the world—not to mention in Buenos Aires where, according to popular opinion, there is nothing else. Without looking beyond the past few days (May 5 to 12, 1980), I have read one interview with Borges and two (with Rodríguez Monegal and Ricardo Piglia) about Borges in *Sábado;* another one by Rodolfo Braceli, published in Mendoza, Argentina; a diatribe by Andrés Henestrosa in *Excélsior;* and a tidal wave of more and more interviews, references, attacks, possibilities, declarations (like the one he made about the disappeared, which, as to be expected, has in its turn been endlessly examined and analyzed: "How bad must it be if even Borges condemns it?").

A veritable tidal wave, but there is always something new, curious, strange. For example, Henestrosa points out that in the story "A Universal History of Infamy,"[18] Borges writes that Billy the Kid killed X number of people, "not counting Mexicans." Henestrosa considers this generalization offensive, and he transfers this *animus injuriandi* to Borges: a dizzying thought—it would never have occurred to us that Borges seriously meant this as an insult.

Be that as it may, it would be difficult these days to put together a truly "complete" bibliography on Borges. This profusion of works privileges older ones, which then, for this reason, should not be omitted from any list that aspires to be what we could picturesquely call a "bibliography," a word that implies the expectation of some sponsorship and of some responsibility. Let us remember Etiemble, Adolfo Prieto, Macherey, Sucre, Rodríguez Monegal, etc., etc. I could go on and on, but that would quickly get tiresome: they all have something to say, of course—there is a discourse about Borges superimposed over the discourse by Borges, endowed with historicity, sensitive, at moments, to supposed methodologies, passing through layers and layers of theoretical discussions. At times we find mimesis, as Yurkievich wished, at times we find distancing, as Viñas would like.[19] The only thing we can do with this mass is to classify it, in imitation of that moment in Borges that Foucault glossed [Foucault, *The Order of Things*] with the same metaphorical arbitrariness, but this time, emphasizing the significance of the works, aiming more for an axiological approach than for descriptive exactitude, even at the risk of being arbitrary.

a. In this category we can include all those writings that exalt the person of the author, Borges, and consider him to be a felicitous source of unquestionable work.

b. Here we can place pieces that exalt Borges's work and that devote themselves to discussing his most famous topics—labyrinths, tigers, circular time, courage—all generally thematic.

c. To a lesser degree there are those studies that avoid focusing on the person and even on the works in order to instead attempt a description of an esthetic that Borges outlines, in prologues, articles, statements, and indirectly, in stories.

d. To an even lesser degree, I understand that there are studies that seek to establish his implicit esthetic, or, in other words, that look for structures that underlie his texts and whose domination would imply the predominance of certain esthetic concepts, some in accordance with those he declares, and others discrepant.

e. Of course we must also realize there are studies that forego the obligation of discovering, recognizing, or describing a universe called "esthetic" and instead prefer to distinguish the structures that hold up the texts rather than the concepts that determine their scope, as well as meanings that go beyond the common and immediately visible ones.

f. There is a collection of studies that distinguish between the writer and the man, especially the political aspects of Borges the man; at the same time that they enthusiastically or soberly proclaim his merits as a writer, they either attack the debatable goodness of his political and human tendencies, or else choose to ignore the issue altogether.

g. As to be expected, there are those studies that rather than examine his merits as a writer, on the contrary attempt to show that the ideological contents of his writings are pernicious, in accordance with the perniciousness he never fails to exhibit in the political realm.

h. Correspondingly, there is no lack of works that directly attack the political significance of his declarations, his attitudes, and his loyalties, whether connecting these to his writings or not.

i. Not necessarily as a counterpart to the criticisms that critique him in one way or another, there are studies that, perhaps spontaneously, describe and glorify his evident philosophy, finding it valid, or else threatening, because Borges identifies with his sources, is an idealist, a follower of Berkeley, etc.

Perhaps because Borges is still alive and does not deny himself the pleasure when he wishes to undermine what others have so laboriously said about him, there is in all of this forced attempt at classification (covering a number of decades), something passionate and contingent, and thus, rectifiable, as if the attempt does not get very far in the delineation, not to mention the elucidation, of the enigma. Is he an enigma to the critics? Have we not, among us all, invented him as an enigma? Even if that is the case, it is now a fact that cannot be eliminated and, for the moment, cannot be resolved. What are the terms of Borges as enigma? To me it seems that fundamentally the enigma consists of the fact that a writer from a second-rate country who writes in a noncompetitive language has managed to transcend these limitations and become a point of reference, a myth, a sacred cow, on a worldwide scale, giving us the dizzying illusion that this is possible for everyone, as if, miraculously, enigmatically, we could overcome a slew of determinants that have programmed us in Latin America into localism, folklore, *costumbrismo,* a sensationalist approach to the avant-garde, self-congratulation, cliques, bureaucracies, and spectators—but not actors—in the dazzling spectacle of world literature.

What would happen, I wonder, if Borges were on our side? A mere daydream, an illusion: it would be next to impossible for him to be on our side, not only because he functions within different parameters, but also because of personal characteristics that would keep him from considering as something good a cause such as ours—to know a greater unity between words and life, between literature and culture, between culture and politics. Perhaps people like us do not do as much as we could for our cause, but we still make it—and its difficulties—a part of our daily preoccupations. I do not think Borges could understand this vagueness: on the one hand, social stratification creates no conflicts for him, although he admits it could be improved. On the other, utopia for him is invariably found in the terrain of the fantastic, not in taking sides about some current issue. With a difference like that, we would be gravely mistaken to imagine he could be on our side.

Yet despite all this, the case is not closed, and I realize that he does have something to do with us: at the least, he has been present in the adult lives of us all—in my case, almost thirty years, the same length of time that Perón has been present in my life. Both have invaded me, signifying to me the impossibility of my overcoming what they proposed and the ways in which they disagree. For this reason, I say that Borges has something to do with us, but what? There is one answer: literature, the love of literature, the possibility of a rewarding dedication, of a priesthood that resonates in each one of us who feel involved because of Borges's existence—as a hope, a provocation, a challenge to see if the word, constructed across a divide between itself and the object it designates, can give life back to us.

Thus, he does not have any problems with me, but I do with him. That is his advantage, my limitation. For that reason, he does not bother trying to understand himself; for that reason, I do try to understand him—a worthless endeavor while he is still alive. Later, when he can no longer talk back, perhaps we will be able to limit him, tame him, make him come to reason—and maybe we will be able to make sense of our own position, as has perhaps occurred to some extent with Perón.

In the United States in particular, but also in other countries—France, Spain, Mexico—Borges is the subject of numerous university theses and dissertations. I do not know if he enjoys absolute predominance over other literary figures— all I know is that his presence in this area is undeniable. I also do not know if the same phenomenon occurs in Argentina: is there an academic life in Argentina that would permit one to work academically, even about Borges?

Some of these studies manage to cross the tempestuous sea of indifference and become known. On the other hand, there is no reason to believe that all of them rest on the advantage provided by a renowned author who, in addition, has the added attraction of a widely celebrated exquisite difficulty. To the contrary, we could imagine that what motivates many of them is a fascination that is more than simply devout dedication to the "investigation of Latin American literature." I repeat, if it is a question of fascination, it is quite probable that it stems from the principal fact of a diction that, despite its extreme structuration, introduces "another" plane, or more likely, a plurality of planes that stretch out irresistibly before the reader. It is the same experience each time: all one must do is open one of his books and let the eyes land where they will— something will arise from those phrases that has materiality, carnality, and despite whatever one might think a priori, there is no way to escape a certain spell.

Very well, despite this first experience, the aforementioned theses look at something else, not that "other" plane nor what "rises" from the text; they note a kind of warping, because the point of departure should lead to a different place, one that affects approaches from the left as well as from the right. This warping, which reaffirms what has already been said, refuses to explain, and in the case of leftist approaches, is not able to neutralize supposedly pernicious effects that they wish to combat. A moment of confusion occurs, after which the signifier—which opened this particular process from the moment we allowed ourselves access to such complexity without surrendering ourselves, but rather exercising to the full a living, functioning perception—begins to be erased and opens the way for an attitude of enslavement to the Ambiguous, which is the fundamental and decisive signified. If the "value"—that is, what is released—was perceived through an inscription of a "how he writes" whose action is such that we can declare it to be the starting point, then an increasing attention to "what he writes" begins to manifest itself concretely, replacing a perhaps more desirable rigor. All of which shows to what degree we still have not been able to see what it is that moves us, although we feel that something moves us. And it furthermore shows to what degree a certain difficulty that might be that of the process of production itself ends up invariably appearing, wearily covered up by what is produced, at least to the extent we can discern on the horizon a certain intent to organize the initial perception. In this reduction—and perhaps it will be quite some time before a practice of the signifier will be not only legitimate, but also instrumental and ethically possible—"how" turns into "form," and "style" turns into "structure," thus becoming secondary or subordinate when in reality it is the object itself under consideration, enthroned from its materiality in our own materiality.

Borges's presence spreads across the most important period of Argentine literature. The most important not only because it covers sixty years, but above all, because it is the period during which the concept of a modern literature, of a modern country, began, problematically, to be established. It is not, certainly, that those sixty years have given us the "most important works," nor that they form a chronological unit similar to that of the 1890s, for example, and are thus comparable: rather, it covers various chronological units, diverse threads, an infinite number of conflicts, and unexpected effects, as much in the area of literature as in the social sphere. Above all, it was, it seems, the moment when it was time to leave *costumbrismo* behind and propose a more mature writing, one more connected to the sense of self held by a country and a city. Then came the irruption of the theoretical possibility of an avant-garde that opposes, mixes with, and integrates itself into an idea of the politicization of literature on a number of levels—politicization through representation, through belonging, through the elevation of a language, through an ideology of writing, and so on. Later came the social decline and economic depression, the widespread skepticism about a national literature, Eurocentrism, refocusing, refinement, mysticism, and the realist break. This was followed by the rise in Peronism and the parallel rise of populism in literature, another type of refocusing, an active one, and the expression of a crisis of power, during which another literature began to develop that could question. Or at least, this stage foresaw a number of scenarios for literature, just as we can foresee many scenarios of what the country itself could become: will we see existentialism next? Marxism?

We can imagine the possibility that literature is a system of objects in circulation, not only in preparation. What I mean is that if previously "literary life" was a conflict of writers, between writers—a kind of widespread conflict of self-affirmation—perhaps now there is a public to contend with, a public who must be given something, and that public becomes part of the phenomenon. When the euphoria was over, the return to Peronism and the military dictatorship that followed it (but that also had preceded it) established a more precise, almost mechanical modulation: social conflict predominated, and literature disappeared into the shadows, not only in search of what were probably not very fertile forms or ways to escape, but also because many paths became blocked. There was such a thing as "repression," and we cannot ignore its effects on writing, even on the writing of those who were happy with the repression. On the other hand, literature disappeared into the shadows because what mattered as never before was power and the maintenance of power that, created through expressions of frank brutality never seen before (disappearances, murders, torture, imprisonment), reduced horizons and forced a retreat, though certainly only momentarily, of the imagination.

And Borges passes through all of these moments unharmed—and somehow manages to express some of them. His writing is, in certain moments, that of the decade from 1920 to 1930, at other times, that of the decade from 1970 to 1980, an object that sociology could examine, not in the sense that he "tells what happens," but rather in the broader sense that he fulfills expectations connected to the deep structure of societal change. Of course he fulfills those expectations via obscure and indirect paths, but he fulfills them so concretely that today he is the alpha and the omega of Argentine literature. For those who have a historicist tendency, everything seems to begin and end in him, and for those without such a tendency, everything simply seems to end in him. Obscure paths, of course, because it would seem, apparently, that texts such as Borges's biography of Carriego [1930] have little to do with a still quite provincial culture with little capacity to formulate its own premises, and in recent times, texts such as *In Praise of Darkness* [*Elogio de la sombra*; 1969] seem to have little to do with a culture that appears to have lost its capacity to confront itself with its own dilemmas. Or they will have something to do with that culture; they will have to, even though, of course, entering into these relationships implies a previous responsibility, namely, to determine the structure or the needs or the drives of the culture, and analogously why Borges's work would correspond to these. This is shaky ground, more likely to lead to errors of analysis than to judicious explanations.

Nevertheless, there are some facts that we can indeed take note of: first, if Borges does indeed dominate the Argentine literary horizon these days, in reality he has managed to fill it so completely that apparently he is the only thing that exists, and correspondingly, what he dominates is a nonexistence that is loudly disguised by frequent actions that tend to glorify Borges. This does not mean that "there is no one else": what it does mean for one thing is that while Borges is alive, almost all of his competitors will languish. It also means that new writers have little chance to give free rein to their imaginations and to establish new links of meaning, ones as worthy of consideration as was believed or expected before the repressive system took hold. Let me also point out that many writers have disappeared and others are in exile, which, while it on the one hand obviously does not guarantee a new effectiveness, on the other hand, does imply new beginnings, reconsiderations, distancings, and convergences.

The second fact is that Borges is presented and experienced almost as an emanation of the military dictatorship, almost as if he were the "organic intellectual" of the dictatorship, one who, through his own significance, legitimizes the significance of the military dictatorship. But of course he is not an emanation of the dictatorship—he preceded it. Nor is he their servant—he is capable of suddenly rediscovering his old, original anarchism, the anarchism of his father, and of disagreeing with the dictatorship. Nor has he concerned himself with providing the dictatorship with an ideological or intellectual foundation; nor, similarly, does he adopt a political discourse that would mark him as an "adherent," militant or sectarian, of that ideological assemblage which, in order to simplify things, we call "dictatorship." He "is presented as," and frequently in recent years he has neither bothered to reject that manipulation nor to discuss it, nor has he tried to distance himself, but rather he has tended, through statements, jokes, or what have you, to emphasize a kind of "support" that ends up being a sort of legitimization we cannot consider involuntary.

Let us look at this question: why is it, if certain elements in his work will allow us to think it, that Borges, who also must have thought about it, has not as yet wanted to distance himself from the military dictatorship?[20] I am not suggesting that he lead an opposition movement similar to what seems necessary and adequate to me. I am only suggesting that he has never explained why he has not renounced the "support" that he has undoubtedly provided, when some of his work, even if it is only by the effect that it has, would seem to imply that such a renunciation is possible. At the least—and we are going in circles here—he has deceived us, and his work, for what it is and what we have not as yet been able to determine, establishes a bridge with the dictatorship, that is to say, it is one of its prefigurations. I do not believe very strongly in that statement: despite his opinions, Borges is not a Maurras or a D'Annunzio.[21] And that makes things more complicated, makes it difficult to understand. We need to go back resignedly to separating the pieces, leaving aside his work in its entirety (and leaving some of its characteristics aside); we must admit that he maintains a political perspective that years ago took a different direction from his texts, both in their form and their effects.

It could be; it could be that the military dictatorship restored his childhood enthusiasm for bugle calls and heroism, or better yet, that it restored a sense of security whose bogey man could have been Peronism. All of this is important in that there are responsibilities, silences, complicities, but it somehow continues to lead us down obscure paths. No one could say that Borges was an "accomplice" of the repressive machine, and even less that he was responsible for its terrible results. On the other hand, it is more clear that the growing brilliance of his prestige, in that it is uncontested, has been able to be used by the military dictatorship.

Of course, in this kind of utilization there is always a sort of spurious transference. The great name: if it holds no argument against me, it must be that it endorses me, and therefore something of its essence—and everything it has taken to create it—is transferred to me, becoming my own essence. The dictatorship was established in order to make "something else" out of the country using methods and projects created in the dark corners of the barracks or in financiers' offices, but suddenly, thanks to the "collaboration" or the "passivity" of men like Borges, it is as if these methods and projects had another origin, other roots, and thus, greater profundity. All to the extent, of course, that a great writer is still experienced as a concentrator and condenser of meanings, beyond what other social structures can say about oneself. Operation "validation" of the dictatorship has been a piece of luck for the regime, as it was also lucky for the dictatorship of 1930 to be able to count on Lugones, although of course the kind of support Lugones provided did not contain the slightest crack nor any humor or contradictions or contradictory claims. It is a piece of luck, as it was for the followers of Roca,[22] to be able to count on the acquiescence of José Hernández, or for Peronism to be able to rely on the approval of Leopoldo Marechal: was there something in Marechal's work that pushed him into the arms of Peronism?[23] At least we must admit that the issue is complicated, and similarly we must admit that the dictatorship benefits—not really directly, but rather by way of a cloud of self-conformity that the use of such prestige gives rise to. Dictatorships and authoritarian governments always look for legitimacy by aligning themselves with the "values" that characterize a society: if Fritz Lang had not said no to Goebbels, Nazism would have capitalized on him. What did Goebbels see in Lang's work that would make him invite Lang to collaborate, despite the fact that Lang was Jewish?

In this way the dictatorship takes advantage of Borges's existence. Since Borges dominates one area, it would seem that the dictatorship can then flatter itself with its own pretensions of dominating others. For his part, Borges takes advantage of the advantage that the dictatorship takes of him: they help turn him into a myth, they support him with such energy as has never been seen before, and he enjoys, thanks to this, a kind of coronation that perhaps has little or nothing to do with what occurs—really or very probably—in his texts. And that, what occurs in his texts, should be understood more in the sense of a process than as a desire for fame.

Perhaps things will not go beyond this level, or perhaps there will be new developments and broader analyses that will dismiss a focus such as mine, full of comings and goings, of vacillations and of fears of reducing, of mechanizing, or of impoverishing.

Why then, once again, has this been possible? Let us look at things from another angle—let us start over, more semiotically. As I believe I have already said, the important thing is the "how" and not the "what" in Borges's writing. Despite this opinion, almost everyone focuses, at least predominantly, on the what, perhaps because it is still not easy to think in terms of "production" and everything around us tends to value the "product" in which the substance, the "what," continues to catch our attention. If that is the case, it is appropriate to recognize that the scope of the what in Borges is limited, which has led some to a fascination with—contrary to Balzac—the energy of a certain steadfastness in Borges's work, its fidelity, in the end, to a world that seems all the more consistent for being reduced, the ideological phantom of specialization, synonymous in this world with seriousness. To put it another way, Borges always talks about the same things, and only a few things, a fact that, for its part, creates the illusion of "understanding" him through the elimination of a "how" that is infinitely more disturbing, since it is linked to the fantasy of "not understanding," of being overwhelmed.

It would appear to be an indisputable fact that these few things that Borges always refers to increase in value and give the impression of becoming multiplied with the "how" that in this case would be a variability, that is, a sense of novelty and a subtilization. Only a few things, and yet always new, always original—no two tigers are ever equal, although in his stories all the tigers are the same tiger, all the poets are Homer. I am beginning to believe that this relationship between a "what" that predominates in the incapacity of others and a "how" that, as long as its fundamental action is not noticed, nurtures a fantasy created by that what, supports a very immediate kind of reading, one of "interpretation," of "symbolism" that requires translations. As a consequence, it is easy for our interpretations, naturally, to impose something of our "content" on the reading, and for every phrase—maintained by the cultural compulsion that makes us attribute utter significance, real or possible, to every one of Borges's phrases—to be experienced as eminently significant for each person. In this way, Borges comes to function as a depository of what we place in him, implying—and thus compelling us to open ourselves to him—a fantastic confirmation of that little piece of ourselves that we have placed or are placing in him. What is more, it would seem that in general we all exalt Borges to such an extent precisely because we cannot abandon ourselves, we cannot renounce what we are in him.

Is this mechanism only inherent in Borges? Couldn't this be a principle of interpretation that is part of a much broader phenomenon? Be that as it may, from this assortment of multiple pieces of ourselves arises the "important," "invincible," "triumphant" figure, as he himself liked to say. And if this figure in which we have placed so much does not withdraw his political "support," a sense of deception arises in some of us, even a feeling of betrayal, as if the part of ourselves that has become Borges has been handed over to the enemy, who suppresses and attacks everything else we are made of. Of course, through this same mechanism others can find a comforting confirmation: having a piece of themselves fully identified with Borges restores a dictatorial totality. Perhaps for this reason those on the left and those on the right can still argue about the matter. All of which gives us some idea of what Borges means, of how he moves us, and of what he promises.

Between Being and Becoming

Identity, Latinity, and Discourse

Carlos Pellegrini, who was president of the Argentine Republic after the revolution of 1890, recounts that Valentín Alsina, the designated governor of Buenos Aires in 1852 and the first governor after the defeat of Rosas, would lunch at noon beneath the grape arbor in the patio of his house.[1] There he would eat a very basic meal—a simple stew with potatoes most likely, although I don't have any proof, a meal very similar to what Lucio Mansilla enjoyed, seated at the table of the *cacique* Baigorrita several years later.[2] Furthermore, according to Pellegrini, anyone could knock on Alsina's door and join him in the meal and talk with him while he ate. And of course he always came to lunch meticulously dressed in a frock coat as if following the fashion dictated by Sarmiento in the *Facundo,* which corresponded to Sarmiento's dichotomies: the frock coat versus the gaucho's trousers, over long hair next to a carefully shaved beard, and so on.

This scene presumes a particular way of life and immediately brings to mind a particular adjective, "patriarchal"—an adjective that, furthermore, Sarmiento himself in the *Facundo* links to exceedingly backward regions: to Palestine and to Afghanistan. What is missing here for this scene to be completely patriarchal, is, of course, offspring. But it still carries that feel and that security, a tone that I recognize in diverse Argentine voices of the nineteenth century.

The word "patriarchal," it seems to me, carries a strong connotation. Its semantic field is situational. It calls to mind bygone times, but also any time in which there was a recognizable division of familial roles. Personally, however, I prefer to find in the style of this scene a different quality that could be, and I believe is, much more productive. I would say that Alsina's posture and habits also carry a sense of the criollo tradition. This adjective, *criollo,* is one that has not only a history but also a specific social formation, for what does *criollo* mean? And what does *criollo* mean in Argentina?

I also wonder if this connotation might include the Caribbean concept of *criollo,* if this connotation occurs in other regions. I am a literary sort, my references are written ones, I read in order to know, and I don't know very much precisely because I read. In what is perhaps an arbitrary or forced manner, I seem to sense a similar tone in the clearly reminiscent early pages of Lezama Lima's *Paradiso.* This includes physical habits of the Cemí family, their table manners, the way they converse, and as with Alsina, a similar domestic, familial, and cultural linguistic horizon. I would even add that the evocations that Manuel Payno makes in *Los bandidos de Río Frío* [The Bandits of Río Frío; 1889—1891] during the era of Santa Anna carry this same coloring.[3] The sharpness of Colonel Baninelli's discourse, for example, the haughty familiarity with which he treats his soldiers, that wonderful autonomy of the referential horizon—it all makes me repeat the word *criollo* as a way of designating a form or system of behaviors that denote a common identity, perhaps in diverse regions of the continent.

But getting back to Alsina, that criollo tone, which one takes for granted and as a given, though naturally that is debatable—that criollo tone is not diametrically opposed to a firm cultural conviction that we could call "universalist." For Valentín Alsina was a Unitarian.[4] He was a man of the post-Rivadavia era,[5] and thus he was an heir to the French Enlightenment, though with logical and indirect ties to Locke and Adam Smith. His mentor, Rivadavia, was much more British. He had read Bentham and believed in the panopticon,[6] an institution remembered today in connection with the conversion of the Lecumberri prison into Mexico's General Archive of the Nation,[7] and also with George Orwell and his prison utopias. But in general France was the main inspiration, inspiring a love of philosophy and theater and shaping visions of utopias, though not ones modeled on Rousseau, since the individual had not yet come to the fore and written culture was considered primary. Valentín Alsina, like his friend Juan Cruz Varela, ignored neoclassical values, without meaning to denigrate them, and began to engage in literary criticism. Alsina's notes on the *Facundo* are prototypes of an incipient literary criticism, solid and profound. The criollo tradition, therefore, in this dimension, in this scene, in this staging, does not exclude the universal but involves a kind of faith in what we could call a historical residue that cannot be ignored by anyone who looks, who thinks, who eats and speaks. Alsina is not the only example nor the sole cultivator of this tone. From shortly before independence to the end of that century, it involved a kind of a key to understanding. First of all, the criollo tradition is a world of suppositions, and, in terms of politics, it is a complex and contradictory point of departure. I want to point out some Argentine examples: Beruti's *Memorias curiosas* [Curious Memories; 1942–1946] summarize the same information. Having witnessed more than fifty years of history, he views everything with a gaze that, not to get tedious here, I would call autonomous, a gaze that comes into full flower in the verses of Guido y Spano: "What do I care of life's vagaries / When Lady Luck's no friend! / For I'm Argentine to the end / Born in Buenos Aires."[8]

The same thing could be said about Lucio Mansilla's way of seeing and recounting, and even that of Victoria Ocampo, in that, as with Valentín Alsina, the criollo tradition does not oppose the European one, but instead attempts to adopt it and improve on it or propose itself as a superior model with respect to the European one in certain cases.

Of course, in the case of Argentina, the gaucho tradition or the popular tradition undoubtedly have something to do with this criollo character, and in that sense, they reveal with relative historical clarity the source and origin of that character. However, the gaucho and popular traditions could be seen not as the entire field, but as a partial expression of a feeling or a comprehensive mode of behavior that over time would become a characteristic of a local aristocracy. Precisely for that reason the aristocracy would be able to turn into an oligarchy around 1880, capable of establishing its project as a truly autonomous one without the drawback of having to be yoked (to use a metaphor recalling the Etruscans) to the cart of British imperialism.

What I would like to show is that this criollo way of life is so strong that it forces immigrants to adapt, even generating complementary and contrary responses such as, for example, such notorious xenophobic reactions as the massacre of Basques in Tandil.[9] Similar scenes or situations occurred in other parts of Latin America in the nineteenth century, and even into the twentieth. I do not mean to suggest that this was totally episodic; I am more interested in emphasizing the power of an idiosyncrasy that molded new arrivals to the region, and which, in its turn, underwent few modifications except those necessary in its permanent effort to maintain a voluntary link to European culture.

Of course, this has to do with nationalism, but also with the colonial situation in which the criollo tradition was formed. At the risk of simplifying, I would say that it results from an effect of distance, perhaps of abandonment, which at first involved the existence of a certain anachronism with respect to the process of central development, but in the long run produced the adoption of a distinct characteristic, one that was strengthened by what we know as the process of independence. This strengthening appears in all areas, from institutional frameworks to city planning, including questions of taste and language; studies and reflections on this subject are well known.

As sources of that criollo tone, these concepts—independence and a distinct characteristic—take me back a bit in time, evoking in my mind that radical moment extolled by the fiery young Juan María Gutiérrez in 1837. In meetings of the Salón Literario [Literary Salon],[10] Gutiérrez maintained that if we gained political independence from Spain, and if such political independence cannot exist without cultural independence, and if the main vehicle for culture is language, then in order to be truly independent we should, logically, abandon the Spanish language, the language of subjugation, and adopt a language of independence. The one that occurred to him was French, already tied to ideas of freedom and civility, which could steer the historic enthusiasm of the Generation of 37, of which Gutiérrez was a member and a founder. The idea of abandoning Spanish came up in discussions one afternoon, and while holding a certain logic, it obviously did not catch on. But there are two things we can say about this proposal: the first is that this reasoning had great appeal for those who thought about both the trivial and the treacherous secrets of ideology and who wanted to decipher the relationship between language and society. The second is that Gutiérrez squarely opposed the utopia proposed by the equally francophile Manuel Belgrano and José de San Martín (perhaps San Martín a bit less), who wanted to install a monarchy composed of descendants of the Incas. This idea also failed to survive, but somehow both options introduced a historical perplexity that reigned and continues to reign over the otherwise powerful sphere of the criollo tradition, in which, due to this perplexity, discourses arise that bit by bit turn metaphysical.

Let me put it this way: this issue of the criollo tradition and a distinct characteristic was the inspiration for a contemporary countryman of Gutiérrez, Juan Bautista Alberdi, and his notion of national consciousness: a nation is only a nation due to the deep reflective consciousness of the elements that compose it. This is Alberdi's idea of national consciousness, one that I find well formulated and difficult to surpass. Used as a lens to view the criollo tradition, it is an idea that implies an opening, the possibility of integration or innovation. For Argentina, this involved the stage of immigration, but that is another story. It is somewhere between a metaphysical essence, since it implies a preexisting and functioning "being," and a positive essence, since it allows for unforeseen changes whose evaluation must be carried out minute by minute.

I believe that here lie the roots of a continuing debate, one that at present has serious political overtones: a debate between those who think in terms of national essences and those who think in terms of constructions. For the latter, a "being" would not be a Hegelian point of departure to which one must inevitably return, but rather a kind of objective whose contours can only be defined from the projects dictated by necessity and history. While reflection about a "being"—whose relationship with the criollo tradition has been powerfully influential—cannot be dismissed, what matters for the others is a dynamic state of "becoming" that recognizes the form society itself takes in order to fulfill a destiny that can only be the result of struggle and social reconciliation.

Onto this struggle, the state of "becoming" imposes its perplexity, and its discourses can, therefore, be as indecisive as the discourse of Spanish American modernism seems from the point of view of a traditional writer, to use a literary example. For this dilemma or debate is not only a political one. This is especially the case for the Latin American avant-garde, both in the area of literature and also in the area of social creation: the working class in Latin America did not grow out of the Middle Ages but rather out of social changes (some of them produced from within capitalism itself) that modify appearances, practices of production, and language. Speaking of which, I wonder if the Mexican slang of Mexico City, used by prominent, joyous baroque poets such as Salvador "Chava" Flores, is not actually a new product that introduces models of identity as convincing as the criollo language that somehow springs from a dynamic state of "becoming," in an affiliation that begins with Sor Juana but proposes completely new challenges.

I believe, then, as much for Alberdi's Argentina as for Benito Juárez's and Ignacio Manuel Altamirano's Mexico, that French culture played a fundamental role in the tone of the criollo mode, both in its liberal manifestations and in its aristocratic and even reactionary ones. Of course the aforementioned anti-Spanish arguments now no longer resonate for me, although neither can one ignore the extent of the nostalgia for Spain of Manuel Gálvez (*El solar de la raza* [The Lineage of the Race; 1913]) or Enrique Larreta (*La gloria de don Ramiro* [The Glory of Don Ramiro; 1908]). For them, a Spanish "being" functions as a barrier against the grave danger of the frightening consequences of immigration, the "barbarians," or the genteel aristocratic dream of José Mariano de la Riva Agüero, or the strange nature of the mature thought of José Vasconcelos, for whom the Spanish Republic could always justify itself as long as its forebears assumed that Spain would recover the imperial mantle that should cover the incapacitated anarchies of our republics ambushed first by charismatic *caudillos*, and then by the indigenous or mestizo hordes who are always about to destroy "the race," that "being" so jealously revered and simultaneously threatened. This discourse was not innocuous, nor did it become reduced to a merely literary melancholy, but rather it created certain conditions such that the later political thought taken from Franco was conceived of as a venerable crystallization of a "being" that the aforementioned Vasconcelos began to dredge up from his disillusioned present to his most remote criollo past.

It is clear that acknowledging this discourse does not at the same time imply a rejection or a lack of recognition of the Spanish contributions to our dynamic state of "becoming." I want to point out, as proof of this assertion, what Spanish philology has meant for our own area of inquiry, not to mention the contributions of Spanish poetry or historiography. And this is due not only to the presence of exiled Spaniards but also, to return to the previous discussion, to the undeniable link to humanist and Latin roots, a search for origins and destiny. Of course it is also a fact that there was a violent break with Spain, and that French culture was a determining factor in the attempt to construct something out of that new, orphaned condition. The interesting thing is that it was complemented to some degree by the Anglo-Saxon influence, strongest in the area of technology and economics (there is, of course, a vast literature written on these relationships).

Perhaps at present the predominance of the Anglo-Saxon model is such that it has spread to areas where the French could allow the continuation of a residual vestige of Spanish influence. And in that concept, the identity of the state of "becoming" could operate, that identity to which I have referred here and with which I identify and which continues to hold a powerful attraction. This is a struggle, both economic and political, that we find in Central America, but also in other places where the struggle is constant and eternal, although it has not reached the level of violence that exists presently in Central America. For that reason, and insofar as these problematic and discursive lines of thought create an entity in which we think there are common traits and approaches, the expression "Latin America," which our friends from Spain are forever arguing over and refuting, seems convenient, although, of course, it is also limited, since, unsurprisingly, it ignores the fundamental phenomena inherent in both the originary identity and the desirable dynamic state of "becoming." I am referring to the phenomena that have to do with black and indigenous people and that, as we all realize, involve not only a racial slant on this problem but also a deeply cultural one. Clearly the expression is insufficient, but it has a superior inclusive capacity that involves the presence of the cultural sources of a process, sources that are not purely accumulative but that exist at indiscernible levels of integration such as the image of Valentín Alsina eating his stew beneath the grape arbor.

Furthermore, it occurs to me that this expression "Latin America" is supplementary since it is not merely by coincidence that a more adequate expression has not been found, but rather a function of our own historical process. Furthermore, I would say that while admitting its supplementary nature, the expression is still foundational, even originary. To begin with, I would say that Columbus's connections to Spanish culture were not only weak but also ambiguous. In this sense he could have represented Portuguese interests, though not in the sense we imply with the terms "Ibero-America" or "Spanish America," but rather in terms of an analysis that, taking liberties a bit with the expression, could have an imperialistic and Renaissance basis. To the contrary, in examining Columbus's prose, it appears to me that the interference of three languages—Italian, Portuguese, and Spanish—gives his language an elasticity that supposes or implies the recovery of a lost element that in a pre-Renaissance way we can understand as Roman or Latin.

A final issue could be whether this suggests a certain element of authority or is only a manifestation—which the expression "Latin America" would designate in a fractured and dramatic way—of our conflict between a static "being" and the dynamic state of "becoming." Because while Latinity may appear to us to be a revealing virtue and not only a point of departure for construction, it also involves an impasse, as foreseeable as that which gives rise to all metaphysics, whatever name it might be given.

Form and Signification in Esteban Echeverría's "The Slaughter House"

For Noël Salomon, whose kindness and friendship made it possible for me to experience an extraordinary French university in an extraordinary France.   —*June 1968*

The Specific "Form"

No matter how many times I read and reread it, from the outset, "The Slaughter House" [*El matadero*; 1871 (posthumous publication)] always leaves me feeling confused. It is true that the narration culminates in a dramatic concentration; it is true that everything converges on an *act* in which representative significations are deposited; nevertheless, there are reasons to question the rhetorical nature of this piece. We could say that it is a story, given that most of its intensity is built up around the dramatic core just mentioned, given that there is a solution and that all the elements in play, even the conceptual or descriptive ones, work together, and given that they fulfill the traditional requirements of narrative concentration. In any case, we could in the end say it is a story, having added up all the pieces, but also having lost track of the "narrative memory,"

35

that is, having lost that facility for accumulation that defines the existence of the reader and thanks to which what has already taken place does not disappear from the reader's consciousness but instead is integrated into what is presently taking place.[1] Thus we could say that "The Slaughter House" is a story if we omit the fact that it does not seem to be moving toward the presentation of a particular situation until close to the end of the piece. We get the impression that the author's formal proposal was not clear and that the "story" aspect occurred to him and inspired him quite late in the game. On the other hand, we can assert that he had an exemplary proposal—he wanted to write about the political situation of his time—but in the beginning he could not find the form with which to carry out that intention. He tried to feel his way along, letting himself wander through a world of images and words until he arrived at the particular instance, until he resolved, in one single situation, everything he had been trying to formulate. In this sense, "The Slaughter House" is not a story if we examine it from certain celebrated points of view such as those of Poe, Maupassant, and Horacio Quiroga, all of whom held that every word, from the first to the last, must function in support of, and thus must contain, the *act* that creates and gives unequivocal form to the story. And when I say "contain," I am not referring to a deductive logical-causal progression, as does indeed exist in "The Slaughter House," but rather a convergence and simultaneous interrelation of levels, functions, and elements.[2]

And yet, in the piece there is a moment in which the vacillation is interrupted, and the sense of "story" relentlessly extends over all the successive narrative stages. This moment emerges in the incident where the child is beheaded by the lasso. It would appear that the gravity of this event influences the language in one direction, but in another sense, one more closely linked to our examination, this gravity produces an evident change in the form of recounting. Yet in order for there to be a change, there must be something that is changeable. Let us suppose for a minute that it is the tone: the narrative wants to envelope us in a compelling tone, profoundly serious, involved in events that cry out their transcendent character, with respect to which one can do nothing but hand down a condemnatory judgment. And before this? Well, an ironic tone, a teasing, an ebb and flow, an almost entertaining change in planes, with only a few (secret) very generic elements that assume, anticipate, and provide the key to the drama that is going to occur and that will constitute the material of the story per se.

We can see, I believe, where in this case this rhetorical concern with defining the nature of the piece is leading us, a concern that we would not have in regard to other, more modern expressions. I say "in this case" because it seems clear that Echeverría held the notion that "genre" was something necessary for literary communicability. I can make this assertion based on inferences from at least three indications:[3] first, it is difficult to suppose that at that time and according to the tendencies of that time, anyone could question the viability of the idea of genres: the gains made by the romantics were reached by challenging the Aristotelian unities and the declaration of the need—satisfied, certainly—for a mixing of styles (see Victor Hugo, *Préface de Cromwell,* on the "sublime" and the "grotesque"). As a consequence, genres continue to be a mindset, a psychologically valid means for organizing expression. Second, in his poetic works, Echeverría is rigidly rhetorical—he accepts the romantic conquests but he knows how to distinguish between lyric poetry (*Los consuelos* [Consolation])[4] as the channel for the manifestation of individual sentiments and epic poetry (*Avellaneda*)[5] as the indispensable instrument for evoking objective events.[6] Third, Echeverría reflects on these expressive problems and generally translates "expression" as "form" in the sense of precepts.[7]

How then can we not assume that this question was important for him? How can we not notice, as a consequence, the vacillations he experiences, the lack of a sense of direction, something that he himself must have demanded? How can we not imagine that this lack of form has some significance? At any rate, Echeverría does not seem to follow his own premises, though this does not lead us to condemn him, as perhaps would have occurred in the previous century, and as he perhaps condemned himself, as he never published this excellent piece. We, in contrast, tend to alter values, and what might have seemed to be a deficiency becomes instead a kind of freedom, and what emerges from such vacillations becomes for us an organizing principle, like the trailing end of a tangled ball of yarn we wish to untangle. Consequently, let us get rid of the idea of genres—as the romantics were never able to do—and its anachronistic obligatory precepts, and look instead at the idea of "form," a route along which we will find an intention, and thus, an indication, as good as any, for determining the real structure that has been offered, the realized "form," and the instruments effectively put into use for the transmission.

But let us go back. "The Slaughter House" starts to become a story at a specific moment, and before that, it is not one. It is a story in its totality, but not in its parts, if we can imagine this sort of schism. What is it before it completes this totality? Echeverría himself explains this in a way: "Although the following narrative is historical, I shall not begin it with Noah's ark and the genealogy of his forebears" [59].[8] Let us ignore the double irony (with respect, on the one hand, to the traditional Spanish historians who used to go all the way back to the flood and, on the other hand, to the fact that he is going to write about a flood) and turn our attention to the conceptual attack of the phrase and his statement, which may very well not be attributable to humor: "the following narrative is historical." Thus it seems clear: what is not a story in this piece is reality. Perhaps it is fictional reality, but it is not certain that that is the sense in which Echeverría meant his statement. At any rate, I take it as a point of departure for reflection. Certainly the story—even where it clearly becomes fiction and does not make fiction out of reality—is reality insofar as it refers to a situation taken from reality; but it is also clear that it does not exactly become so real through the fact of being a story. Echeverría knows this; he knows that no matter how much compliance there is at the point of departure, there is always a distancing in the recreation, in the dramatization that springs from that point. And precisely because he knows this, he departs suddenly from what he himself calls "history" and adopts a different tone that is translated into a different verbal approach. On the other hand, history, even the most technical— and it is not necessary to assume that it will be faithfully reproduced—when it is put into words, is no longer history, but rather the words with which it is narrated. According to Maurice Blanchot, the word keeps reality at a distance while it tries to conserve it; it kills it in the very process of trying to animate it. Words contain the beginnings of "literariness," as Jakobson would have it, that which allows the "derealizing" passage. Thus history is also literature.

Looked at in this way there is no real difference between history and story; or at any rate, the contrast that can be made between these two categories should not be understood as a contrast between what is literary and what is not. However, there are subjective realms in both spheres, remnants of style, as Roland Barthes would say, that cannot be ignored, and that, this being "his story," as Echeverría says, require a special and different manipulation of the language, an expressive system that will no doubt contrast with what sets the story in motion. Very well, apart from these phenomenological considerations, Echeverría knows how far his objectivity and his rigor reach in this narration of "history." He knows this because he immediately modifies that superficially defining initial statement in such a way that it intensifies what was already there in its own right: its "historical" intention, upon receiving an extra dose of humor, of nuances, of winks to the intelligent reader, of carefully placed adjectives, is clearly defined, is vividly introduced into the literary sphere. The consequence is that from the verbal-literary approach with which it is transmitted, the invoked and manipulated reality begins a process of disintegration, as a result of which it will move, as just such a reality, to an allusive second plane, and it will remain only as a referential structure of what is being said about it itself.

But this does not exhaust all the ways that "history" can be used as a point of departure. Let us look at how he modifies that initial phrase: "Although the following narrative is historical, I shall not begin it with Noah's ark and the genealogy of his forebears as was wont once to be done by the ancient Spanish historians of America, who should be our models" [59]. Yes, there is indeed humor here, but nothing gratuitous. Instead it is so aggressive that it is impossible not to see an opposition in its substance. For this reason it is not arbitrary to surmise that a basic consequence arises from that statement: the "modern" historians (those steeped in historicism, no doubt) function in a very different way, if indeed the traditional historians did employ this particular method. One of those modern historians, to be more precise, is the one who is speaking, and in presenting this very concept he suggests at the least that modern historians allow themselves to speak about "history," that is, about "reality," and—why not say it—about "truth," with great confidence, very heterodoxically, to such an extent that they raise suspicions about their historical method and about whether they are really dealing with history. In effect, the ridiculing of the "ancient" historians with which we began is less of a criticism and more of a commentary. But nevertheless, this entertaining start of a polemic is framed at the same time in a very specific historical consciousness. The polemical at least suggests that there is an intention that, being correctional, is also systematic. The second consequence, then, is that it would appear there is a tendency to stay within the historical, but it is no less probable that the specific historical environment tends to become more diffuse as soon as the topic is raised through irony, whim, humor, or word play. Echeverría could not ignore the fact that this array of qualities should have led him to lessen the historical intention to the point of converting it into a mere point of departure from which a literary intention functions that becomes ever more clear to us. This game, this dialectic, was not invented by Echeverría; it had already appeared, as Noël

Salomon points out, in Cervantes, where it is even clearer, in my opinion, as a pretext rather than as a problem. In Echeverría the shift from the historical to the literary is embodied in a concrete and precise primary sign, a narrator who does not want to disappear, who wants to be present in the transmission that is now so specific to "history."

We should not let this element escape us. Certainly the narrator is one sign among many of the literary structure, but it is such a striking element that in and of itself it allows us to recognize the environment that is created from its presence. Having a narrator is sufficient for there to be a transformation of the real, and in this case, the narrator is someone who observes and recounts, someone whose point of view permeates the reality it transmits, a subjectivity that in this case wants to be reconciled with real information, with true information. The narrator reveals the existence of a tension, a balance between two forces in play, namely, the weight of reality and the tendency to present it as it is experienced—in other words, between history and literature.

What can we call this balance? What does it consist of in concrete terms? What is it made of? It is important to answer these questions because the answers will help us understand a part of the narrative, the part that preceded the "story" per se and which in the preparation becomes disjointed, leading us to think that there was a formal vacillation that would not allow Echeverría to satisfy his own compositional ideals.

Costumbrismo in "The Slaughter House"

Very well, let us call this balance *costumbrismo:* the transmission of a true history by means of a sensibility that the author wishes to preserve. Clearly this way of defining costumbrismo is very general, since, in the end, all literature is understood through this balance. But all literature develops from this balance; it confers a shape to literature such that it allows us to recognize literature to the extent that what has historically been known as costumbrismo remains the same without modifying the terms of the equation indicated, transmitting literature in its pure form. In this way, the novel and the story, as literary forms, are elevated above this balance by virtue of the fact that this sensibility, even more than transmitting "history," actually "realizes" it through invention and fiction, and—even though it more or less naively seeks verisimilitude, in that it tries to fasten or relate the fictional world to a history that is supposedly objective and irrefutable—it is governed through its own rules.[9] Costumbrismo, on the other hand, seems to reject the fictional leap. It is not interested in the conventions used to temper the disappearance of the real; it does not want to be verisimilar. It attempts to be true but always through a form of judging, through a personal point of view. It seems evident that this category is somewhat forced; there is a search for equilibrium that is not easy to maintain. It is also clear, on the other hand, that we tend to say "a costumbrista short story," "a costumbrista novel," as if that costumbrismo were simply a quality applicable to literature and not a literary-formal possibility in and of itself. I will insist: that balance in a state of permanent tension also configures a form; it is, if you wish, antispecific, but, insofar as that indefinition has meaning, it comes to be experienced as a form. This is how the "sketch" or "costumbrista article" grows and develops, which does not need to become a short story or a novel in order to exist. What is fundamental for costumbrismo, therefore, resides in the interweaving of "history" and "sensibility," but insofar as this interweaving creates a certain form that contrasts with others, its costumbrista nature will be filled out, will be perfected, thanks to various secondary features that will complete its physiognomy, its structure. We will try to recognize these features, responding in the process to the second issue, always of course in terms of this component of Echeverría's narration. Two categories of connections can be established at the time of the costumbrista act. The first is linked to literary history; the second is related to the critical intention that characterizes costumbrismo in terms of the semantic field. Of course these two levels are connected, but it is useful to look at them separately.

The costumbrismo Echeverría practices, which is the same as that of Alberdi or Juan María Gutiérrez, takes its inspiration mostly from the costumbrismo of Spain, and especially from the so-called descriptive articles that Mariano José de Larra (under the pseudonym Fígaro) used in order to carry out a ruthless examination of a less-than-perfect Spain. The acceptance of this influence implies a kind of cultural reconciliation whose source, I believe, can be found in the political sphere. In their turn the Echeverrías, Gutiérrezes, and Alberdis of the new world loathed traditional Spanish culture. They considered it to be anachronistic and artificial, and they extolled the freedom of the forms that they might have imposed and that they might have wished to continue to impose. However, they identify with Larra: Larra, after all, is a liberal, as are they, and fights against absolutism, backwardness, and the repudiated Spain—

and because he is willing to take on these confrontations, he becomes a model for this group of anti-Spanish Argentines. Consequently, his style of literature appears open, is susceptible to adaptation, is seen as suited to help in carrying out a similar program, one that embodies a process critical of reality, time, and institutions, carried out through sarcasm, sharpness, unconditional intelligence, and characteristics of costumbrismo that are seen as essential. From this we can draw one conclusion: historically, form is modified by virtue of the functions that it must fulfill. If, as we have seen, costumbrismo indeed *is* the result of a balance, a pure result, having been put in the service of criticism, criticism then begins to form part of its being, at least in a series of works that are modified from that point of criticism. There are, of course, costumbrista expressions that are not critical,[10] that in my opinion express the very beginning moment of the establishment of costumbrismo, the purely denotative moment. More important in relation to "The Slaughter House" and also in relation to the more mature form of costumbrismo, is the critical perspective that, like the structuring core of that moment, appears to us as an object to be delimited and that therefore configures the second approach that we need to determine.

But how is this criticism carried out? In "The Slaughter House," it is done concretely, on two levels that appear to be split. The first is through the elements that costumbrismo has provided and that Echeverría follows or inherits. The second level corresponds to declarations or quasi-declarations of the narrator who, in a rush to put forward a thought, leaps over those elements, the costumbrista structures. Let us continue with this same system. It behooves us, as a consequence, then, to discuss these elements, which are as follows:

First is a reference to real history as a delineation of the frame in which the objectives sought will be accomplished. Political, social, and even economic history is evoked through either local descriptions or the evident desire to provide new interpretations of a given moment in history. It is indisputable that he is talking about "Rosismo"[11] around 1838; he alludes to what made the man a historic phenomenon, and he suggests a well-formed interpretation of this phenomenon.

Second is the necessity of concrete facts that unequivocally specify the historical frame: "in the 1830's of our Christian era" [59]; "its white front pasted over with posters: 'Long live the Federation! Long live the Restorer and the Heroine Doña Encarnación Ezcurra!'" [63]. The necessity for facts is so overpowering that the narrator feels compelled to expound on them in detail when addressing distant readers: "But some readers may not know that the above-mentioned Heroine is the deceased wife of the Restorer" [64]. This type of information undoubtedly serves a clear political intention, but before that it is inscribed from a costumbrista impulse, namely, to provide the material for the brush strokes that will paint the scene: "The Convalecencia, or Alto Slaughter House, is located in the southern part of Buenos Aires, on a huge lot, rectangular in shape" [63]. These are indispensable outlines for providing information, without which the story would not be understood as such. The information could change or expand, but the effect would be the same. Its permutability indicates that its function is more of an integrative one; it has more to do with the composition of costumbrismo itself than with a perfecting of history.

Third is the presence of a verbal irony that the narrator is responsible for but that is not too conspicuous with respect to the level of objectivity. Verbal irony, that is to say, a phrase, a twist, an emphasis, an ability that appears as such precisely from the moment of a restraining movement—occurring there where everything was prepared to burst its bounds: "And since the Church has, *ab initio* and through God's direct dispensation, spiritual sway over consciences and stomachs" [60], or else, "The purveyors of meat, on the other hand, who are staunch Federalists and therefore devout Catholics" [60], or "the meat commandments of the Church" [60]. In these examples, we can distinguish the foundation of the expression, on the one hand, and the complexity of a super-imposed word that modifies, certainly but silently, almost as if it were only for select interpreters who from that small piece proposed, are able to sense a direction. I don't wish to push this too far, but to make sparks fly that, without damaging the objectivity, also illuminate other aspects of what is revealed. In any case, the reality being transmitted appears, and in that irony that is pre-sented as a necessary "seasoning," costumbrismo is recognized as such.

Fourth, one important variant of the verbal irony proposes a figure that can be called "opinion." It is not a question of a stronger or more biting irony, like those remarks that suddenly slip out uncontrollably and that serve to express the indignation of one's conscience ("What nobility of soul! What bravery, that of the Federalists! Always ganging together and falling like vultures upon the helpless victim!" [69]), but rather the result of an ironic form of narration that tends to indicate a distance between the narrator and what he recounts: "This war manifested itself in sighs and strident shrieks during the sermons as well as noises and sudden explosions issuing from the houses and the streets of the city or wherever people congregated" [62]. The desire for observation and clarity, which is quite marked, displaces the attention to the role being played by the one who observes: the clarity occurs through a gesture of distancing and consequently implies a beginning examination that is translated in this case by a rough outline of judgment. This is not the only form this subtle "opinion" takes. If we analyze the passage with the sermon, we will see it reappear using a privileged technique: "This is the day of judgment, they proclaimed, the end of the world is approaching!" [60]. The irony lies in the words "they proclaimed," which combines all the priests into one single voice. Furthermore, since they are so generic and correct, we come to see they are hypothetical priests, that is, they are invented, naturally, by Echeverría: he places a discourse in their mouths that the reader can judge on conceptual grounds, and the concept is so repugnant that those who express it are questioned and condemned. But the author has limited himself to nothing more than transcribing: he is not the one who condemns the priests or makes them look ridiculous—they do this to themselves. In this distancing created by the act of transcription, the author slips in his own unformulated judgment—as merely an "opinion."

Fifth is the use of *pintoresco* or picturesque resources that run the gamut from the choice of a strange and unusual setting, one out of the ordinary, to the presentation of the most explosive details: "From a distance the view of the slaughter house was now grotesque, full of animation. Forty-nine steers were stretched out upon their skins. . . . Hovering around each steer stood a group of people of different skin colors. Most prominent among them was the butcher. . . . At his back, following his every movement, romped a gang of children, Negro and mulatto women, offal collectors . . . and huge mastiffs. . . . Forty or more carts covered with awnings of blackened hides" [64]. Without a doubt the picturesque as a system of descriptive resources can be linked to the idea of "local color," typical of romanticism. To the extent that it surpasses the merely descriptive role and functions to serve a social criticism, we can by all rights group it together with the rest of the elements that make up costumbrismo, which in its origin and its diverse forms is also perhaps a romantic invention. Of course the picturesque—the word says it all—is created from the pictorial, and in some way, therefore, it demands or presupposes the famous transcriptions of art that would become so popular later, but in their early form were also discovered by romanticism.[12] From a literary perspective, all attempts to find a language suitable for communicating the expressiveness, color, and movement of certain aspects of reality are a picturesque gesture. In itself it is a productive attempt; through it there is a broadening of the world, an opening with respect to the themes through which the costumbrista intention will take form. We can see then that the costumbrismo in this piece of Echeverría's is sustained by the pintoresco, which is clearly the channel that collects and transmits the material from which the story is created. By virtue of this hierarchy, the picturesque component is the one that offers the clearest and most significant lessons, some of which we will look at again later. As is natural and predictable in all pintoresco perspectives, reality imposes itself on this word that wishes to flee from itself in its attempt to express vividness. The limits of the picturesque can be found in its very aim—words are not able in the end to transmit the pictorial, and thus they give up their pretensions and their power and, in order to complete the transcendence of descriptiveness, seek the help of a different device, one more capable of seeing and giving form to its material: "In short, the scene at the slaughter house was one that must be viewed, not one that could be described in writing,"[13] the narrator admits, as he reaches the limits of his possibilities for continuing.[14]

We indicated earlier that the vocation for all-embracing criticism in this text and in its costumbrista component is also carried out at a more suppressed level through declarative comments by the narrator. These are slight excesses, offshoots that do not germinate, flashes of thought that come mixed with verbal irony and that stand out when placed on a different stylistic level. These phrases, which contrast with the humor—or the irony—that accompanies the desire not to forfeit history, break the spell that can emanate from the coherent concurrence of costumbrista elements. Their importance resides in the fact that the change in levels does not refer to anything indirect nor to any kind of elaboration, but rather to a thought—it alludes to a complete system clearly situated beyond the narration, in the realm of the author, who enters the story in this way, revealing bit by bit the entire thought that is going to arise from the narration as a whole.

"Numerous reasons I might adduce for not pursuing their example, but I shall pass them over in order to avoid prolixity" [59], the author tells us at the very beginning of the narration, after having discussed how the "ancient Spanish historians" worked. Echeverría has in fact mentioned these "numerous reasons" in other places (in concrete form in the gatherings of the Salón Literario" [Literary Salon]), and they are linked to all the reasons for opposing the older Spanish culture, an attitude well known to be held by our author.[15] This mechanism occurs frequently; in order not to overload this essay, I will give only two examples of its application. The first: "Perhaps the day will come when it will be prohibited to breathe, to take walks, and even to chat with a friend without previous permission from competent authorities. Thus it was, more or less, in the happy days of our pious grandparents, unfortunately since ended by the May revolution" [62]. As we can see, of the two parts of this quote, the first one can be placed in the category of costumbrista irony, but the second, the one that refers to the May revolution, synthesizes the thesis favored by Echeverría and his friends by virtue of which May should be converted into an objective, a historical—and thus sacred—banner of the struggle. The allusion is completed through the interpretation of Rosismo carried out by the romantics—namely, that that system degraded the country and the colony, and thus destroyed the spirit of the May revolution. The second example: "All a representation in miniature of the savage ways in which individual and social conflicts are thrashed out in our country" [65]. It is almost redundant to state that this idea is practically a compendium of what Echeverría's *Dogma socialista* [Socialist Dogma (1846)] seeks to remedy. It is a synthesis, the result of a careful observation of reality that produces not only the denunciatory movement but also the meticulous preparation for an appropriate ideology to exterminate its causes and put an end to its consequences.

Organization: Thematic Substrate, Narrator, Fluctuating Inflection

Once the features of the costumbrista aspects of this piece have been enumerated, we need to look at its organization. We have already noted the presence of a narrator who fulfills an active role in the presentation and development of the costumbrista material. But this is not his only function. In truth he is the heart of the organization of the piece; he is the organizing axis. Here I will examine in more depth this role played by the narrator from the pintoresco perspective.

The pintoresco movement originated, as we said, from a genre-related need to create a theatrical set, but the result goes beyond the merely decorative. Furthermore, in order to create this, certain things are selected, and this selection, like the secondary characteristics that help form it (color, more or less; movement, more or less; typical characterizations, more or less; extravagance, more or less), is the point of departure or the basis on which an expressive intention operates that can also be considered apart from the picturesque. From this perspective, we can note that "The Slaughter House," as a human and social aggregate, is presented in its animation above all as a setting that would function something like a center where the expressive intention is concentrated and through which that intention is formulated. Yes, we do of course find in this piece a study that we could call photographic, one of light and movement but that freely gives way to the idea of a place in which extraordinary events occur ("From a distance the view of the Slaughter House was now grotesque, full of animation" [64]). These events—which are framed within a striking description[16]—are judged by the person situated within that "perspective," that is, the narrator, and they undoubtedly create a sense of confusion for him, of chaos and a formless jumble ("a group of people of different skin colors. . . . At his back, following his every movement, romped a gang of children, Negro and mulatto women, offal collectors . . . and huge mastiffs" [64]). From here, the idea of a jumble, which sustains the image he tries to create, has an undeniable connotation. Simply recognizing its existence qualifies both what seems jumbled and what seems recognizable and by that act actualizes or puts in motion a philosophically valuable cultural thought whose core is an appreciation for the results of the application of reason to reality. In this way, everything that springs from that jumble is irrationality in and of itself, a world of unleashed force, a demonic world.[17] But the presentation of this setting has another sense as well: this is also where a more transcendent action will develop that will shed light on a significant event: the sacrifice and the death of the Unitarian.[18] In this way, what is presented as the setting from a pintoresco perspective becomes imbued with a content that converts it into an environment that produces criminal acts, or at least dramatic ones, and finally, into a symbol that unites all levels of a reprehensible reality. Thus, it will become the thematic substrate, an element that from its level gives structure to the tale. As we will soon see, the narrator will also act as a structuring element, as a complement to the thematic substrate.

The chaos we are speaking of is seen by a gaze and transmitted by mouth. And if, varying the sign, the chaos turns successively into setting—surroundings—symbol, it is because someone is creating the passage, someone organizes it, and in order to do so, they must have previously understood it: to understand is to organize, and to organize is perhaps to perceive a meaning, but even more clearly, it is to bestow a meaning. "But as the activities progressed, the pictures kept changing. While some groups dissolved as if some stray bullet had fallen nearby or an enraged dog had charged them, new groups constantly formed" [64]. The gaze is that of the narrator, and his organizing behavior proceeds from and mixes with the "perspective" from which he acts. Thus the one who is doing the seeing is the narrator, who condenses it and combines it. It is he who measures out the materials and presents them in this particular "order," without which we would not be able to understand, an order that for him is so very intimate. In this function, the narrator is complemented by the material, what we have called the thematic substrate. The order he imposes, at the same time also organizes the narration, gives it its form. Hence we can say that between the two, thematic substrate and narrator, the structure of the story takes shape.

But the gaze of the narrator does not stay fixed on the chaos, waiting for that chaos to transcend itself on its own and start the process. It is a restless gaze that seeks to discover reality, that seeks "from a distance, the view of the Slaughter House" [64]. "But as the activities progressed" [64], a line is drawn that is composed of all the moments of a keen, shrewd convergence that moves from the primary and broadest view to the narrowest. From the most generic, even in the historical sense ("stating merely that the events here narrated occurred in the 1830's of our Christian era" [59]) it moves down to the smallest details, in a movement that, upon ending in an action overflowing with meaning, bestows all of the significations on the narration. It is worth pointing out the successive moments of this movement; thanks to the narrator's organizing gaze upon the material, certain topics begin to appear, something like a synthesis that organizes the direction of the narration. The order is as follows:

1. The historical realm (the broadest one)
2. Lent
3. The abstinence from meat
4. The church and its dictates
5. The rain
6. The consternation of the faithful
7. The Unitarians as those responsible for the disaster
8. The lack of meat and its consequences
9. The empty slaughter house, symbol of the scarcity
10. The government decrees
11. The massacre
12. The slaughter house and the description of its surroundings

13. The gift to the Restorer of the first steer
14. Typical characters and characteristic actions
15. The animal that fights back
16. The severed head of the child
17. The Englishman who falls off his horse
18. The sacrifice of the bull
19. The arrival and depiction of the Unitarian (the most detailed)

With this last topic, the circuit is complete and we find ourselves in the middle of the story; we have arrived at the place—here and now the principal scene is going to develop, here the significant contents are going to be revealed, now the story will take on flesh and physical form and acquire the total critical tendency that it has been preparing.

So there is a movement in the piece toward the particular and the brutal. As we said earlier, the episode in which the bull cuts off the head of the child shatters the costumbrista humor and indicates a change in the narration. The death of the bull and the castration scene can also be viewed as one option the butchers could carry out against human beings and that they will carry out with the Unitarian. In that movement toward the particular and the brutal, themes appear, as if formed from the topics, themes that are like those of a symphonic poem, that other romantic creation. The themes are created from the topics, and the topics are harmonic motifs that represent a primary level of elaboration, while the themes—more extensive harmonies—are on a secondary level. The themes cover various topics that they dismantle and then organize in significant functions that outline a beginning structure. In this way, we can see that there are themes that begin to be deepened but do not complete the process and suddenly disappear, leaving room for others: emergence, growth, decline, reappearance, disappearance, all intertwine, providing a musical effect that reaches its height with the death of the Unitarian. First we find the theme of the church (C) as an object of criticism or satire, above all due to its ties to federalism (a connection that is presented as aberrant or debased). Then there is the rain (R), like an unwavering obsession that carries a considerable amount of description, and after that, the meat (M), or lack of meat, and its amusing or ridiculous consequences, without taking into consideration the most important philosophical-economic meaning with which it is imbued. Next is the slaughter house (S) from whose description we can begin to discern the symbolic transcendence (the country is an immense slaughter house), and finally, the Federalists (F) as the perfect creators, supporters, and representatives of this medium. Rising above all of these is the Restorer of the Laws (L), heralded by a brief drum roll, a governing presence, the principle animator of these "savage ways in which individual and social conflicts are thrashed out in our country" [65]. At this point, the barriers of costumbrismo are crossed and new themes appear in the realm of the story, themes that specify what was mentioned earlier, that is, barbarism, and Rosas as the principle person responsible, not to mention the Unitarian (U), a theme in which all the others become refracted.

We have talked about the organization of the themes. Going further, a scheme such as the following can be developed from the system of accentuations and combinations (capital letters indicate major emphasis, small letters indicate minor emphasis):

C	Rc	MRC	Mrc		Srm
FSM	Lfs	and finally	L	FU	FUl

This diagram indicates certain regularities in the frame of the story, but as with all descriptive pictures, by itself it does not provide reasons for the appearance of each of the new themes: why these and not others?

Perhaps because we are still within the costumbrista component, which in its realist aspect, presumes an accumulation of facts, while a technique of possible logical operations in order to understand the way themes are linked proves not to be viable.[19] The appearance of a theme, on the other hand, could perhaps be explained from within the system of the author's ideas or obsessions, or rather, of his deepest objectives, or, what is really the same thing, of those elements or facts from reality that attract his notice and that are inscribed in his critical consciousness, reemerging when that consciousness must be put in motion. Why is he attracted to these elements and not others is the next obvious question. Without looking for an answer that would demand a psychoanalytic foundation, I can say very generally that they attract him either because, looking at them from the outside, he sees in them a considerable symbolic force— they are themes that represent complicated historical situations that are important to elaborate on—or because they have become engraved on his psyche and he cannot help but to express himself through them. It must be seen if they reappear in the rest of his works and if this reappearance is sufficiently obsessive to confirm this psychological source.[20]

Be that as it may, determining the origin of the themes would help us considerably in understanding the kind of action the poet undertakes, including his way of relating to the world. Without going farther afield, if we examine the elements we have at our disposal, taking into account the culmination of the story in its entirety, we can see that this way of bringing up themes, of projecting them and either obscuring them or illuminating them, indicates a fluctuation, a search for an object that seems to be related to the aforementioned movement of topics in terms of the general-historical starting point and the successive stops along the way that become progressively more specific. Can we consider this parallelism significant? If the topics constitute the harmonic motifs that give rise to the themes, it seems natural that both levels have essential characteristics in common and that they are shifted from one to the other. At any rate, this searching movement, inherent in both, also expresses the search for a form, and its discoveries are also discoveries of form. As a consequence, it is necessary to add that fluctuating inflection (without which, as without the others as well, this tale would never have been created) to the organizing role that the thematic substrate and the narrator play. But this formalizing character of the search, naturally, has significance: the leaps, the fluctuations, the passages and the variations, crescendos and diminuendos, appearances and disappearances, demonstrate, above all, the irruption of a material whose emergence can perhaps be gauged—as the thematic scheme demonstrates—but not constrained. Lack of control? Incapacity for elaboration? Rather than all that, perhaps a whole system in which the fluctuation, the thematic substrate, and the narrator's organizing gaze are fused to such a point that, as we have said, they maintain the structure, but it is a structure in which nothing can be constrained, and in which what originates from the philosophical-political choices of the author, or what is manifested in his deepest psychic needs, is not able to achieve a univocal direction, free of vacillations. Carrying this line of thought to the historical level (Echeverría was surely somewhat in hiding when he wrote this piece, helpless in the face of Rosismo's ever hardening position, without any hopes of playing a positive role in the immediate political process, and with his friends scattered), we can conclude that Echeverría no doubt knew what he wanted to say and whom he wanted to condemn, but the way to do so only came to him along the way, with all of its essential lack of coherence, at the margin of what Echeverría himself could have required for a narrative. To conjecture, this might explain, at least partly, why he never published this very powerful narration.

Two Languages: From "Realist" Style to Romantic Conception

I said before that at these junctures we had arrived at the story component of the piece, just at the moment in which the form is discovered. The fluctuations and the search for atmosphere come to an end, the setting is fixed, the characters are detached from the medium to which they were originally affixed and begin to revolve around the unique drama that also has a dramatic solution: a young Unitarian is murdered in the slaughter house. Everything is clear; the pintoresco practice, or pintoresquismo, is diluted, and in its place we can discern an indignant condemnation. Furthermore, in order that the dramatic solution can take place, the themes all converge at one point: church, meat, slaughter house, federalism, Rosas, are like the successive layers that configure a singular environment that is the crime. With this conclusion, we could consider our task finished. We would have come very close to an understanding of this narrative and its significance. But one might suppose that the difficulty in finding the form of the piece suggests something more, that this arduous way of assembling the two components of the narrative can surpass the fundamentally naive stage of condemnation in order to propose other levels that carry more signification.

Thus, just as we previously started from pintoresquismo, now let us use as our point of departure the verbal irony, which is another one of the principal categories that link this narrative to costumbrismo. Now we can say that the verbal irony ends when the taut lasso severs the neck of the child sitting on the fence, that is, as I indicated at the beginning, when this anecdote appears that functions as the dividing line between costumbrismo and story. The irony comes to an end, and a serious tone appears that slowly begins to dominate. But let us be more specific: the irony has not really disappeared yet, and it reappears later, in the same way that before this transitional moment, there were also other serious moments. I am not referring to what I described above as indications of a way of thinking, but rather to the expressions that indicate a certain respect, or at least a certain circumspection in what he says ("In mid-air a flock of bluewhite gulls . . . fluttered about, drowning with strident cries all the noises and voices of the Slaughter House, and casting clear-cut shadows over that confused field of horrible butchery" [64]), a circumspection marked by an ordinary and somber construction and by a descriptive neutrality. In terms of the irony that reappears after the episode with the lasso, it could be a good example of those kinds of etchings in the style of Goya: "It is said that one of the women voided her self on the spot, that another prayed ten Hail Mary's in a few seconds, and that two others promised San Benito never to return to those damned corrals and to quit offal-collecting forever and anon. However, it is not known whether they kept their promises" [67]. The lasso that severed the child's neck evokes such an unbearable image that the author must abandon it, for immediately afterward he makes his mocking comment, which, above all, expresses his sense of discomfort, a tension that disguises itself as irony. We could refer to this obscuring motion as the "modesty" effect: he does not know what to do with an overly powerful scene and so he distracts us from it, he surrounds it with another event. Be that as it may, the fundamental thing is that the costumbrista realm finds itself covered with expressive threads that come and go and intertwine, forming a web similar to that woven by the themes we discussed earlier. And what threads are those? The verbal irony, the serious tone, the "opinion"—all of these are found in the first component of the piece, and between them all, the costumbrista expression is carried out, but they would not explain the full stylistic effect if we did not also keep in mind the typical speech patterns among the characters from the slaughter house. Thus we have four threads that comprise a somewhat disintegrated, and thus easily disrupted piece of writing. Let us work with this material in order to get closer to the area we have been seeking that is richest in significations.

In the first place, the language that signals the costumbrista component as a whole contrasts with the language of the story component. While the critics may have already examined this contrast, it is worth our while to look at it again. We can note the fundamental difference starting with the presence and the speech of the principal character of the story, the handsome and valiant Unitarian. At the least, he expresses himself from a particular and unmistakable cultural register: "You, slaves, were the ones to order it so as to flatter your master and pay infamous homage to him" [71]. It is clear that this differs from the butcher's expression, fully expressive in its vulgarity and carelessness: "Hey there, black witch, get out of there before I cut you open" [65]. One could argue that there is not much of a conceptual difference here—each person speaks in his or her own typical language, and those languages differ. However, since the characters are very powerful, and their respective languages, each one in turn, influence that of the narrator, the contrast takes on meaning and provides significations. How is this influence, this contamination, produced? When the narrator, perhaps motivated by the concept of local color, makes the butcher speak, he creates a linguistic environment that he himself cannot or does not wish to escape. In this way, his own way of narrating becomes permeated with this essence, not because he as the narrator begins to use the same words, but rather because he appropriates one among the gamut of elements that surrounds the butcher's language and that characterizes costumbrismo. I use the term "butcher" to refer, naturally, to the whole group, and in terms of the narrator, this permeation consists of the fact that he accentuates a directness in his language and he modifies the pintoresquismo in terms of its precision and sharpness, stylistically speaking: "Nearby two Negro women were dragging along the entrails of an animal. A mulatto woman carrying a heap of entrails slipped in a pool of blood and fell lengthwise under her coveted booty" [65]. And since directness, precision, and sharpness, which are characteristic of the speech of common people, are positive qualities, the results, as they concern the narrator, are also positive.

Similarly, when he has the Unitarian speak, the narrator also becomes permeated with *his* inflections, but in this case, the results cannot be placed on a par with the previous example because the rhetorical point of departure here is a cultured and inflated language, and the result can only be an increase in this negative quality. As in other examples, this transference of features is manifested in descriptions, and those connected with the Unitarian are indirect, paraphrasal, almost mimetic. Rather than transference, we could speak here of an identification, because it is as if the character has awakened in the narrator a language and a set of values he had ceased to engage with and that now he resumes with great vehemence: "His muscles assumed now the flexibility of rushes, now the hardness of iron, and he squirmed like a snake in his enemy's grasp. Drops of sweat, large as pearls streamed down his cheeks, his pupils flamed, his mouth foamed, and the veins on his neck and forehead jutted out black from his pale skin as if congested with blood" [72]. If this form of description is constituted in a very general sense on the loss of irony and humor, it somehow reclaims the sign of seriousness. But if we look at this closely, although it is no longer in the adjectival realm, we will see that the seriousness is really solemnity, a verbal hedge placed in front of a cherished reality, and the embellished style is the vehicle for a linguistic devotion. What the Unitarian says is pronounced in such an abundance of devotion that it is necessarily presented to us as something worthy of esteem, the most lofty, the respectable. In contrast, the costumbrista realm comes back to us: despicable, repulsive, that which does not need any transformation or enriching by the artist and that can be described as directly as the speech of the people who comprise it. In order not to leave this conclusion dangling, let us combine it with one that has already been reached: the world of the slaughter house, the federal world, a world that we already know is condemned, at the same time is the one that asks to be expressed directly, the one that is either not highlighted through the use of words, with all the trappings of that most noble of crafts, or, if it is highlighted, it happens despite the action of words.

Secondly, certain scenes of utter crudity arise from the costumbrista language, scenes that for comparison, we could call realist. This is a very delicate point, full of nuances. At any rate, it is possible that Echeverría found the unpleasant, the horrible, the base, the vicious and the brutal to be realist, and this reality comes to form the material from which he creates the scenes of crudity. But immediately a language appears that attempts to present certain things and that, as we have seen, is shaped by them. This language—the narrator's—reproduces these things, and this reproduction takes place through an organizing process characterized by rigor, precision, and suggestion. But the organization is not neutral: because of the sense that it holds and the load of intention that it carries, the things presented by the narrator have such force that what is indicative becomes evaluative, and therefore, everything that appears, appears as a fusion of the thing and of the organizing consciousness. In this sense, we can say that the dialogues are realist, since they have a certain elaboration, that is, through them, not only is a peculiarity transmitted, but a way of being is interpreted. By extension, we can say the same thing with respect to certain descriptions or scenes.[21]

On the other hand, there is a shift from the picturesque to realism, and there is an identification insofar as the same elements that helped us recognize the pintoresco nature, that is, characters, dialogues, and descriptions, constitute the material base that allows us to define realism. And since the picturesque, as we have indicated, springs from "local color," an essentially romantic concept, the realism of Echeverría's story retraces the genesis of all realism, but revealing in one single text both the beginning point and the end point. The origin, then, gets lost, and various sections of the story seem autonomous; they seem to be suggesting a new perspective, and in the end, we experience the entire story as a realist one.

However, the realist esthetic did not exist when Echeverría wrote this piece.[22]

That is to say, it had not been formulated, although after the romantic blood-letting it might seem that it was necessary, or, more concretely, that it was a path writers were searching for. Echeverría had discovered it from premises which, if not the same, were at least very similar: political and social criticism and the intention to use literature in the service of an extraliterary cause. Perhaps he thought that even with these premises in mind, the consequences of their application could signify having gone too far, that they could lead to such an abrupt break with an esthetic conception that he could not assume such conse-quences with the same clear vehemence with which he did for his long poem *El ángel caido* [The Fallen Angel; 1846],[23] the manuscript of which crossed the border clandestinely and was eventually published, despite the difficulties en-tailed. Perhaps for that reason, that is, perhaps because he felt that he was profaning something sacred more than he wished to do, he chose instead, if I can say it this way, a vacillation that caused the narrative to be divided into two sections. But there is another consequence that is more transcendent: after all his complicated configuring, Echeverría's realism ends up reduced to a mere collection of realist elements serving a solidly romantic scheme, firmly installed in the author's consciousness. I find this to be particularly noticeable toward the end of the narrative: if a realist esthetic somehow also implies a certain system of knowledge, opting for romanticism implies abandoning that system and everything that that action signifies esthetically. In this sense, the final apotheosis is clear. There is a qualifying mass, a condemnation in the name of a particular value or a system of abstract values that, naturally, springs from the spirit of the narrator, who is unable to combine it with what reality may be demanding.

Schisms in Romanticism: From Hell to Heaven

Let us move on, then, to another area of analysis since we have found that a romantic criterion has prevailed. But what do we mean by this in a concrete sense? It is quite clear: a dualistic image of reality.

To begin with, if it is influenced by a certain abject reality, language becomes sharper, more precise, more rigorous and objective; the depiction is more finished, more verisimilar.[24] From the point of view of our present area of interest (understanding of an era, vividness, communicability), this is a more artistic depiction, that is, it would be fulfilling its own esthetic aims. On the other hand, when influenced by a different reality, which he appreciated on an ideological basis and which theoretically should be able to be expressed as effectively as the first, Echeverría produces a rhetorical and inflated language, solemn and formulaic. Faced with this primary schism into two opposing poles, one could ask oneself why this criterion of mixed styles—which could be explained by the simple fact of two levels of language, one more elevated, one more common, living side by side—has not worked in this case. In my opinion, the realist component, esthetically concrete, has been sacrificed to the other, more highly valorized and favored more among the two "mixed" styles. For those aspects that depended on Echeverría's creative intentions, he seems to have preferred the "elevated" language, although theoretically it should be as rich in possibilities as the "ordinary" language. We can note, then, a second level of schism: a romantic has a certain idea of the world, an image of something perhaps nonexistent, but imaginable, which in this case is the reign of culture. He also has a language, in this case a mixed one, with one component that corresponds to a newly developing world and another that it is opposed to—the anticulture. The mixture is dehierarchized because it threatens the image of the world. As a consequence, the elevated language is favored and one possibility is stymied. This is the sense that comes from the rhetorical under-current that accompanies the arrival of the Unitarian. Thus, Echeverría prefers a verbal environment that he considers coherent with his image of the world—and therefore secure—over a new relationship with his own language and, we could say, with himself as well. As a consequence, the world of the Unitarian, thanks to the adjectival and metaphorical richness, is exalted to the point of idealization, while the Federalist world, via an unadorned language, is exasperatingly condemned.

He chooses. He prefers. Surely this does not mean a crude deliberation. The choices, the preferences, are generated in the very center of his artistic project, which, as we know, was supported on an elaborate theory that attempted to understand not only literature, but also the country as a whole in all of its structures—a true ideology that took into account the national history, the position of the country in the world, its social class organization, its cultural possibilities, and its destiny. An ideology articulated out of frustration, the fall of Rivadavia and the emergence of Rosismo, phenomena that instigated another line of thought, one that took its focuses from another, already formed ideology, one that was a mix of utopian socialism and eclecticism. This thinking becomes a manifesto that allows a reconsideration of all reality subjected to a thorough analysis, after which it is clear what needs to be done. That manifesto is called *Dogma socialista*, and its "symbolic words" are precisely the reduction to a formula of a thinking that presupposes a process of formation. Literature is implicitly part of this "catechism," and in fact, was explicitly part of it in the documents of the Salón Literario, in the works of Alberdi, in Echeverría's letters, subsequently in Sarmiento, and within the ideology in its entirety. And that is what must be done: avoid plagiary, paint a picture of the autochthonous natural world and social customs, follow the French example, show the way for national progress.

Thus, the tug-of-war that occurs in "The Slaughter House" reveals both that manifesto and the results of its application in the literary sphere, where the preeminence of ethical objectives becomes linked to a reduction of realism and conditions the entire structure of the expression, all to the detriment of the censured component of reality. Since everything in the narrative converges on the exaltation of the hero, who embodies the ethical manifesto, and since the language, functioning as a powerful transmitter of pressures, yields, the thinking is finally superimposed on reality, breaks into it, and covers it up. It seeks to diminish that reality or annihilate it. What needs to be done, what needs to be defended in order to change the world, struggles violently against how it really is and tries to deny it: all value is piled up on one side, and the other side is denigrated, repressed, annulled in an act of censorship that, covering all levels from the linguistic to the ethical, becomes a formal structure.

But another question arises: where is Echeverría in all of this? That is, to what degree are these elements incorporated in him? To what degree do these tensions run through him and what form does he give them? The answer will perhaps be paradoxical: Echeverría will appear to value what he actually despises and to scorn what he cherishes.

Let us recapitulate: the Federalist world is the reviled realm, while the character of the Unitarian (and therefore the world he comes from) is glorified. This is clear. But also, there is one language for the Federalist world and another for the Unitarian one. This means that the writer has fused with the narrative at every moment, always: his emotions, his intelligence, his sensibility, in short, his totality, converge and provide a kind of expression. And in conveying the barbarous Federalist world, as we have seen, he obtains a different expressive result than that which he conveys about the Unitarian world. What are these two different worlds like? The former is rigorous, precise, lively, vigorous, vivid; the latter is lifeless, rhetorical, emphatic, and solemn. Is each of these respective worlds really this way? One would have to assume that this is how it was for Echeverría, who, loyal scribe that he was, was unable to give force to what conceptually should have had force for him within his well-defined ideology: theoretically the Unitarian world, without departing from its peculiar linguistic styles, should have been exalted in its expression, while what has actually been exalted is the Federalist world. But the Unitarian world for Echeverría was not false, empty, solemn, and emphatic, at least not ideologically. Could it have been that way for him emotionally?[25] Could it have been from the point of view of an excessively divided relationship with reality? Echeverría managed to become a writer, that is, he managed to concretize an artistic proposal around material originating in a reality that politically he hated. He failed, however, to give form to a material that he admired. But we already know that human feelings are radically ambiguous, although this does not mean that we have to invert the terms from this new perspective and declare that at heart Echeverría loved Rosas and hated himself. But it does suggest that certain aspects of the hated reality fascinated him, while some aspects of a reality he cherished provoked nothing more in him than an intellectual loyalty, not very deeply conceptual. He was fascinated by violence, by elementality, by action. He was fascinated with that American[26] landscape that he saw springing up all around him and that he so determinedly wanted to understand—when all he could manage was to sense it surreptitiously, like a part of oneself that must be repressed and hidden.

Romanticism, then: a tortured conscience drawn toward evil and adoring it while inflicting on itself the persecution of goodness in accordance with a political and social duty and a thinking that is not well fused with the reality to which it is supposed to be applied. Here, then, the superimposition becomes violent; the compulsive legitimacy and the rejection of the Federalist world is all the more dramatic because deep down Echeverría has not finished working it out, because it continues to reverberate with a force that comes from the very essence of what he is fighting against. And are these not the terms from which the vacillations of the entire group arise in the face of Rosas? Isn't this perhaps the implication of Alberdi's musings, from which Echeverría seems distant, but also indulgent? Was there not perhaps a moment when Rosas became appealing because he represented a reality whose signs Echeverría was trying to decipher?[27] But this whole conflict was soon resolved—the possibility of the concept of federalism died away, the new slogan "Neither Federalists nor Unitarians" disappeared, and painful choices had to be made, leaving so many points of conflict unresolved deep inside. There was nothing left but to grab on to fragmented models, purely intellectual ones, and create for oneself a verbal sensibility, to cut off part of oneself and voluntarily give up an integration in order to create a different ideal, a belabored, perfect, and abstract one—that was the only route left.

Returning once again to "The Slaughter House," the conflict is between a factual world, one of action, that provokes a renounced fascination, and a cultural world that the story attempts unsuccessfully to establish. And, since this factual environment facilitates a rich, nuanced, and real transmission where esthetic creation can be erected, a relationship between this environment and the poet who expresses it can be predicted: the poet emerges with all of the conditions, elements, and guarantees such that we can assume he experiences this as real life, that this world appears directly, a world that incites and inflames, a world that by arousing indignation also influences the most transcendent answers. The cultural world, on the other hand, is a reflection, it has no vigor on its own, it is mediatized as it mediatizes, it becomes pale, it is connected more to an intention than to a totalizing synthesis. Thus it is a semblance of life, although that has not been the case for Echeverría at the declarative, public, and conscious level.[28] But we must understand that culture is not a mere semblance nor is action alone real life. A romantic spirit could suffer from the limitations of its own view of culture as an absolute impotence, and from that point, it could idealize what it sees as immanent, as self-sufficient, as capable of dispensing with an objective understanding but all the while hating it, and at the same time, not being able to separate itself from that impotence. In itself, valuable; for itself, untenable. A very romantic schism, it left its traces in Echeverría's work and that of his generation and became a constant dramatic actor in Argentine literature and thought: the unrenounceable but false culture, and thus the perfect picture of compulsion; action as valued but unrecoverable, and thus the object of compulsion. Do we need anything more in order to understand the life and actions of a Sarmiento? To predict the ponderings of a Güiraldes? Do we need anything more in order to bring to mind the anti-Peronism of our greatest writers, the hatred that is fascinated with force? As we can see, the conflict turns into a school of thought and becomes national in scope. After Echeverría, and not just because "The Slaughter House" professes it, these became to a large extent the terms in which our literature has been formulated.

However, for "The Slaughter House," the possibilities for showing the consequences of this schism and of the romantic preeminence that in and of itself promotes a divided reality, do not end there. Let us look at the culminating scene of the whole narrative, the death of the handsome young man. They wanted to humiliate him, to strip off his clothes. It is quite clear: they wanted to rape him. The narrator censures the sexual perspective; he does not want to subject his character to that kind of suffering, and he keeps the indignity imprecise, that of a humiliating struggle—that *those* hands should touch him. The character's heart bursts—better dead than have his clothing stripped from him. But the sexual overtones do not disappear despite this censuring. To the contrary, his attempts to gloss over the sexual nature of the affront only serve to make it stronger and more complex: the indignity is worse because it is sexual. The thugs from the slaughter house, and thus, the Federalists and federalism, are all the more brutal because they are manifested through sexual sacrifices presented as barbarous and loathsome rituals. Furthermore, the fact that Echeverría has repressed or hidden or shifted away from the sexual nature of this last scene is less important than the fact that he has arranged things such that in the end he was put into that position. If he had to avoid it, it was because he had gotten to that point in the first place, and if he had gotten to that point, it was because he had spontaneously linked this sexual aspect to the viciousness of those for whom it would be inherent. And also linked it to real life? The Unitarian, on the other hand, seems above everything; he represents passivity, measured language, the handsome figure, the victim of sexual assault. Does it not follow, then, due to successive attributions, and due to an analogy that becomes impossible to halt, that sexuality and viciousness go together? Does it also not follow that this analogy suggests its counterpart? If viciousness is the opposite of culture, if the Federalists, who embody that viciousness, oppose the Unitarians, what is sex opposed to? Well, according to the system of romantic options, sex is opposed to love—no doubt that pure love that Echeverría exalted in his poems. But we must also think in terms of polemical effectiveness: Echeverría acts on certain options but he avoids employing black and white ones. Sex is not a black-and-white issue, but more of an insinuation, an elaboration that makes the political attack a complicated proposal since human shame has more space to make distinctions among acts. On the other hand, it is inconceivable that Echeverría should admit that his dignified character was the object of sexual degradation. That idea is excluded from his esthetic schema, based on a mechanism of identifications. It is appropriate in this case, because the vagueness of the situation and the interpretations that are triggered, or the ever increasing connotations of baseness, allow us to recognize that the political has invaded all areas of humanity; human beings are in danger.

And the humiliation of the flesh of the man is preceded by a long analogy that paints a picture of the appropriate setting: the slaughter and the meat as an expression of bestiality, as the ambiguous human need to feed itself, to glut its cruelty, in order to understand itself. This is important for the romantic because in his quest for the absolute, he must believe in a point where all beings of creation come together and illuminate each other. Clearly the only one that has a spirit is the human being, but do not humans also form part of the secret of nature just the same as the animals? Thus the sacrificing of animals in order to eat them cannot be ignored. The sardonic tone at the beginning is also the start of a protest, an initial disapproving and disgusted approach to this betrayal of the spirit: the dead animal is like a spirit interrupted, and its bloody, tormented meat is pure material that falls like guilt, like a stain, on those who consume that interruption. This ritual of death is not where human beings will find the secret of their existence, the secret of their origin, nor even the indicated path. Given this evidence and using these methods, meat, then is material itself, the materiality that denounces some people who thus become accomplices in this crime against the spirit. Perhaps it is not even necessary to point out that sex, understood as pure biology, and meat, understood as pure material, represent a union, a partnership, that tries to attack a superior ideal, that of an elevated human life that Rosas's vicious assassins are preventing from taking form and leading a people to civilization.

A final clarification: why choose the slaughter house as the physical space that ties together all these significations? The choice is surely related to the idea that within a system or a country, there are places or centers that illuminate the totality: "and from the foregoing episode it can be clearly seen that the headquarters of the Federation were located in the Slaughter House" [72]. That center, "located in the southern part of Buenos Aires" [63], that is, in the outlying area, constitutes an urban outcropping and serves the part of the city closest to the countryside. The tasks carried out there are cultural in a sense, because there is a certain organization that produces a consumer product for the city, but the people charged with doing this are marginal and participate in the project as rural beings. It is a hybrid character that is reflected in the facilities of the slaughter house and in the characters' psychologies. It is not surprising that the Federation is situated in this very prominent, hybrid spot ("Long live the Federation! Long live the Restorer and the Heroine Doña Encarnación Ezcurra!'" [63]), because the Rosista federation is equally hybrid. As a political system, it represents the triumph of the cattle lands over the city. And the terrible crime cannot help but result from this monstrosity, Echeverría seems to be saying. And since this is what he believes, this is what he shows in its originary and symbolic site. It seems clear that in this sense he anticipated Sarmiento's famous dichotomy "civilization and barbarism." This proves, at the least, that there was a generalized way of judging sociocultural-political phenomena, and that the organic thinking that emerged afterward has its roots in a complex reaction to reality, a reaction that involves everything down to the most intimate levels of existence. We can see this clearly in Echeverría: all the accusations of the story are concentrated, the sense of humiliation and everything it implies about the attack on purity and culture, the viciousness, the meat, the slaughter house, the federation, Rosas—the whole circuit from its most tragic individual consequence to its earliest traces, it all springs from the predominance of one terrible group, that of the cattlemen, over all other groups. Echeverría, in contrast, proposes a uniting of groups and classes, a new bourgeoisie that would not exclude anyone, a union where a certain attitude would predominate, a certain rationality for which the group of intellectuals he led would be the spokespeople. But he would have to wait for that fantasy to occur—an unfortunate delay, especially for Echeverría and his friends.

Canon and Margin in Latin American Literature

There is no doubt that the mere mention of the word "canon" immediately calls to mind another word, "marginality," which appears to be not only complementary but also subordinate; in this sense, the one cannot be fully understood except in relation to the other. The canon, the canonical, would be the normal, the established, that which is allowed admittance as a guarantee of the system, while marginality is that which voluntarily pulls away or that which, it turns out, has been pushed away precisely because it does not accept or does not recognize the canonical requirements.

The foregoing implies that in order to reflect on this pair of terms, it is first necessary to keep in mind the semantic scope of the canon, a notion or concept that in its literary sense is derived, since, as we know, it is borrowed metaphorically from its liturgical or musical sense. One could even say that while in music the concept is well defined, because it is technical and formal, and in liturgy it is employed with a regulatory, interpretive, and sanctifying significance, the shift to literature has been ideological. By that I mean that certain components of the notion of a canon are "applied" to literature either because of interdiscursive pressure or because the word is essential in the world of those who are able to read phenomena in one field using concepts employed in another, even though the subject matter is different from the musical (a specific arrangement) or from the religious (a type of conduct that endeavors to foresee and guarantee).

Perhaps, like the derivation of a mathematical principle, the idea first entered the musical world as a kind of noun: little by little it came to designate a structure based on a specific melody that is repeated, in regularly differing tempos, by different voices. Popular canons appeared at the beginning of the first millennium, and their maximum perfection was of course reached in the baroque era. Additionally, these regularities form a model that spread from religious music to liturgical-legal discourse: here it became equivalent to a norm that must be followed, implying a certain rigor, and from the point of view of the one who enacts it, it is essential and controllable. But when this is applied to literature, or more specifically, to the process of literary construction, it appears more diffuse, although derived more from the liturgical-legal adjectival quality than from the musical noun. Metaphorical or not, what it means is generally understood when it is seen, assumed or applied, even if it is extremely problematic to try to define it.

In the literary field, however, this understanding cannot last for long without inviting complications. In fact, it is difficult to recognize the application of previously established norms such as these in the midst of ongoing processes. Most frequently it is only recognized a posteriori that norms have been followed, indicating that something is "canonical," although even then I believe that the canonical is more of an attitude, since the norms are either not formulated—they are "ethics" or are part of "common sense"—or they tend to contain, contrary to what happens in the area of liturgy, important contradictions.

Be that as it may, from the point at which a clear sense of "the norm" is established, it can be said that the notion of the canon is concretized in rhetoric, above all because all rhetoric that is imposed in a specific place is canonical. But it could also be said that because "rhetoric" exists in every verbal act—and, as a consequence, every literary act—not all rhetoric is imposed. As a consequence, a primary distinction can be established in the sense that the canon, strictly speaking, has the connotative character of certain rhetorics: in actuality it originates from a preliminary decision, in itself not rhetorical, that determines a rhetoric to employ and all that one can do with it—a kind of control, in order to impart what is believed to be an appropriate, established, and stable direction.

If, therefore, the canon amounts to a system of norms connected to a rhetoric, we must begin by recognizing first that there is no one single canon and that during many stretches of literary history the canons that were being followed were not even written, as well as the fact that many of them have changed over the course of history. Second, written or not, canons spring from a source that emits them and that watches over their fulfillment. But it must also be admitted that such sources have shifted, and those who took on the responsibility of declaring canons, applying them, and proceeding later to the consecration—the canonization—of those who could follow them successfully, have changed over time.

Having established these general principles regarding the canon, we can say that by the term "marginal" we mean a manifestation that, deliberately or not, is situated outside of the canonical order. On the one hand, this could occur because of a deliberate and determined rejection of the canon in force at a particular moment, carried out in full knowledge of what this implies; on the other hand, it could occur because of ignorance of the existence of the canons or because of finding oneself spontaneously outside of the official universe of artistic production, beyond all knowledge of the canons.

In terms of the first situation, the rejection is at times justified and active, as happens with the manifestos of avant-garde groups. At other times it resides in practices that simply stray from systems of production that are coherent with the logic of a global system. In some instances, of course, such rejections become apparent, and the respective gestures end up in reconciliation or clearly reveal the true intention they have pursued—that is, to enter the canonical universe: can one really say that Dalí's work is marginal? And could one define as marginal—even though produced in seclusion and silence—Antonio Porchia's curious experiments?[1]

In one form or another, the dominant canon establishes and controls, as can be clearly seen in the aforementioned manifestos, which never fail to include an explanation of why they are opposed to the canon. At times, the projects that develop from a sought-after and cultivated marginality prosper, sooner or later, and their success knocks the canons off balance. At other times, certainly more often, marginality is the consequence of failed attempts to temper the authority or the pretentious omnipresence of the canon. It could be said in this respect that the history of literature, and of art in general, is full of dark episodes, of grand threats that failed and ended up confirming the marginality from which they attempted to combat the canon, just as Manuel Gálvez pointed out in *El mal metafísico* [The Metaphysical Problem] (undoubtedly following the model put forth by Zola in *The Masterpiece*) in a narrative comment on certain omnipotent errors by the modernist or symbolist poets.

By the same token, one cannot deny that there are constant attempts that, formulated from a reasoned, ethical, and resolute marginality and undertaken with critical clarity, have on occasion succeeded in tempering the rigidity of the canonical system and forcing it to modify itself, partially or completely, both in turbulent times, as occurred with modernism, or in quieter times, as happened with the filtration of the avant-garde into the general process of discursive change that has occurred in contemporary literature.

Ignoring the spontaneous and unbridled marginality that proposes nothing in relation to the canon, and taking into consideration only that which has been calculated, a political dimension could be attributed to such marginalizing projects in that they constitute an option with respect to the literary system, conceived of as a system in relation to the global system and its strategies for enduring. For this reason, one starting point for thinking about the canon is that it is the foundation of an "official" art, with all of the ambiguity that implies, that is to say, an art whose generative principles are congruent with those of the system in power.

For that reason, marginalizing projects sometimes affect the immediate political character of literature but do not necessarily imply a separation or a deviation from the canonical literary axis: thus, the aims of naturalism, majestically executed by someone like Federico Gamboa,[2] while marginal in respect to the canons of what literature "should say," are not marginal in relation to the "how to say," that is, to the enunciative principles of the narrative. While different from the official conformist literature in theme, content, or message, because of the crude social criticism that they carry out, they not only do not differ from it in terms of narrative rules but also end up renewing and consolidating those rules. So, if in the beginning the situation of marginality appeared to be defined by contrast, now one can observe that there are diverse and complex spheres and grounds in which it operates that must be studied in each case or situation. Let us examine one such situation, to a certain extent contrary to that of naturalism, that never fails to create problems: it is commonly accepted in literary circles that a writer such as José Lezama Lima is marginal, especially in his major novels. This, in fact, would be one of his most interesting characteristics, and in it lies an unusual capacity for provocation—a feature that, on the other hand, all marginalism is accustomed to claiming. Nevertheless, one can say that he is not really marginal at all because of the nature and substance of his utterances, which are, wherever one looks, a reaffirmation of a classic knowledge left unrevised and unaltered—in sum, a canonical knowledge. Perhaps, if calling something marginal is not merely an indirect elegy, the product of a custom that makes the irregular its highest proclamation, then *Paradiso* [1966] and *Oppiano Licario* [1977] are marginal texts because the "pulling away" that they propose—and that functions as a reading that makes strange—is immune to all attempts to rechannel it; these texts "resist," just as Vallejo's *Trilce* [1922] resists, no matter how much *The Black Heralds* [*Los heraldos negros*; 1918] and *Human Poems* [*Poemas Humanos*; 1939] have influenced so much poetry that followed. Just as the fragments of Macedonio Fernández resist—and this is what their radiance consists of, which contrasts with the tranquillity proposed by other texts that only appear to be semantically transgressive, as is the case with certain texts by García Márquez—and even structurally transgressive, as can be seen in a contemporary reading of Julio Cortázar's *Hopscotch* [*Rayuela*; 1963].

Taking these preliminaries into account, there are, at least in relation to the idea of a canon, these aspects to consider: what person or persons produce canons or what, in a particular moment, produces a canon; how are canons applied, or who follows them, and, correspondingly, what is implied by not following them; in what way canons persist or die out; and, finally, what relationship can be established between obedience to a canon and full literary realization in a particular place. The first three are perhaps more theoretical issues; the fourth is historical in nature. In terms of marginality, we will ignore for now that which is marginal simply because it was unable to enter the canon— something like a waste basket of failures—and systematize the positive attempts or projects, that is, those actions deliberately and consciously undertaken against the canon. Of course we must also consider the ambiguous or speculative marginalities, and even those attempts that merely appear marginal, those that soon made it clear they were not trying to pull away from the canon or splinter it or modify it, but rather to reenter it through another door.

Production of the Canon/Production of Marginality

Tradition, "officialdom"

If the canon is the result of a cross between different codes previously authorized at various levels—rhetorical, grammatical, preceptive, and so on—it is evident that its components originate, above all, from a cultural memory. This fact raises the subject of tradition, which, while it may at first glance appear connected to the idea of the canon, also covers, under certain conditions, the idea of marginality, although, of course, the notion of tradition overruns both concepts insofar as diverse traditions exist that compete with each other or articulate each other or, at the least, converge in order to explain a literary peculiarity, including a certain identity, as Carlos Fuentes explains in his investigations of Latin American narrative.[3]

Furthermore, the idea of tradition, which involves the image of an expanse of time, does not necessarily cover that of "officialdom," which is more contingent and exhibits a type of homogenizing response to the necessity for structural order. Vasconcelos resorted to a direct classical tradition in order to establish one official art over another one equally based in an indirect classical tradition—the post-Napoleonic French model. And one can say that, effectively, he achieved this with muralism, which for its part, with respect to the classical tradition of easel painting, involved an inversion insofar as he brought about the marginalization of this tradition for a time. With the Mexican "Contemporáneos," opponents of his project, the paradox is even greater: in the midst of Vasconcelos's classicist project, they recover certain elements of that same tradition—the equilibrium, the rigor, the objectivity—but do so in order to oppose all officialdom.

But it is also important to remember that in all of Latin America there are many traditions arising from popular origins. Due to their conditions of production, some of them are marginal; what happens, then, when the state—as has occurred in various countries—takes charge and supports them, even adopting some of their forms?

The canon, therefore, is both something more and something less than tradition, and that tradition subordinates it in its organizing aspect, like channeled knowledge. In terms of marginality, tradition is more a construct of behavior that reappears under certain conditions: the young, for example, are almost inevitably initiated in marginality, and that is a tradition. In Cuba, the poetry of the *décimas* [a type of Cuban country ballad] is part of a popular— and marginal—tradition, as are the Mexican *corridos* [a type of Mexican folksong] and numerous types of sung poetry that, from time to time, are the objects of revival. Political denunciation in literature, which would certainly appear marginal, similarly forms a tradition that operates in certain social conditions and literary crises.

Thus it can be understood that, composed or produced by cultural memory, the canon possesses possibilities for spontaneous persistence, limited only by, at times, a critical gesture that constricts its impositional power. Likewise, in terms of a direct confrontation, marginality may be a question of outbursts that, despite being constantly produced, last only a short time, although given the nature of certain practices, marginality itself is also a constant. In other words, the canon is interwoven with and sustains tradition, while marginality actually makes up part of tradition in that marginal endeavors never cease to arise; however, their intention, when they become programmatic, is to weaken tradition's hold.

Furthermore, since in their primary initial moment the codes that compose the canon are rational forms of social articulation, their generation and control are in the hands of the enunciators of power. In modern times, the mere name "academy" is synonymous with the idea of the source of production of the canon, just as before it was the church or individuals or institutions who were recognized as the authority. Suffice it to remember, as a form of metaphor, how and why Johann Sebastian Bach composed his Royal Canon. In another field, the concept, without saying so, runs through all lexicographic reflection: the dictionary is an essentially canonical entity—not only does it state which words exist, but also how to use them and how not, and in so doing, invokes certain authorized and authorizing uses.

In short, up to a certain moment, perhaps up to the romantic revolution, the idea of the canon occupied all of the imaginary universe of "high culture," but bit by bit, it was cut away by a new type of discourse, "criticism," which moved from its role of overseeing adherence to the canon to that of being itself the producer of the canon, whether occupying social spaces of production (the university) or competing with previous canons and creating new ones (journalism). In the modern era, that is, from the middle of the nineteenth century up to now, other shifts have occurred; by interpreting the state of the economic circuit, the editor, who theoretically is only a momentary link in the chain of production, actually produces the canon, and perhaps with more force than ever, either directly—in the mythical personal editors, now on the verge of disappearing,[4] or indirectly—through experts, whether called "agents," "readers," "editors," literary journalists, and so on. And finally, the "marketers" themselves produce the canon, in that from the point of view of the "public," they are the mechanism for suggesting, through the technique of rejection, what "should" be written.

At the same time, one cannot speak of "the production of marginality" except via metaphor; first of all, everything that is not canonical is not necessarily marginal, but rather is marginalized insofar as it simply does not correspond to the canon to which it wishes to correspond. Second, the quality of "marginality" should be seen in a positive light, that is, everything that lies outside of the canons, rarely due to rejection but rather to a conscious decision, should—and in fact does—create some kind of effect on the global corpus of a literature and even causes the canonical to falter. The classic polemic between "classicists" and "modernists," as a moment of confrontation between canonical and marginal, would have little consequence if the triumph of the modernists did not imply a modification in the rules of the literary power in force.

Application: Reproduction and Cooptation

The application of the canon corresponds in the first instance to an act of inertia that constitutes a tradition (if that is what we can designate as "reproduction"), a foundation, as we know, of the educational system. So powerful is its force that what we know as literary education is, above all, the transmission of a "how it is" that "should be," similar to the projection of the imaginary. All the same, by virtue of the force with which the canonical universe is inscribed on a cultural community, for many the canon was and continues to be a cause and a goal: inert reproduction turns active. On the basis of a similar principle, certain literary criticism is carried out that "knows" with certainty how to distinguish between what is poorly or well done, what is pertinent or not in regard to criteria for specific genres, what generates value in texts, and what causes value to degenerate.[5] The same thing occurs with those who award and justify prizes, and, of course, with those who support the dissemination of a work or maneuver to suppress it precisely because it does not correspond to canons that should have oriented it.

On certain occasions, however, there is a reversal in favor of a marginality that all the same responds to canonical circumstances: in the decade of the twenties, General Heriberto Jara, governor of the state of Veracruz, granted an official space to the project of the estridentistas,[6] who, as we know, proposed and practiced a radically antiofficial art. The operation could have been coopting, but it seems to have recognized that which moves from the semantic to the semiotic: artistic antiofficialism "interprets" the new political officialism in such a way that, if before the triumph of the Mexican Revolution politics and art were marginal, the new politics, no longer marginal, recognize that art, which continues to be marginal, can be used as a means for combating an ongoing canonicity. Under the first Peronist government in Argentina, populism was a politically "official" artistic doctrine, but everyone knew that the truly official art, in the long-term scheme of things, was that embodied in forums such as *Sur* or *La Nación*—marginalized by that government.

But it is possible that when a contracanonical formulation makes itself heard, supported or not by some power—say a government (the first Cuban government in connection with an avant-garde art or popular art), an academy, a university, a newspaper (*El Diario* from Buenos Aires, in connection with modernism), or an authority (Secretary Estrada[7] supporting the Contemporáneos), attempts are made to domesticate its effects and to reinforce an order, albeit a renewing one. This occurred of course with the modernists, but also with the so-called Boom, which arrived to challenge the traditional Latin American narrative and which then, after its great victory, turned into the canon, in the sense of how one should continue creating an acceptable narrative. At any rate, this literary experience revealed not only new producers of the canon—publishing companies, journals,[8] and newspapers, but also revealed how the "material" of the canon can be reconstituted to include positions of marginality. One can suppose that the same phenomenon occurred with avant-garde painting, which, from a position of formal opposition in both the semantic and canonical domains, created an audience of collectors and restored a function to museums—a place, apparently, to house the canonical.[9]

Canon and the "Art of Poetry": Identity

Canons, as we have said, are not generally written down, and yet, they possess the necessary force to ensure that they are followed. This force springs from a type of cultural conscience, maintained by an implicit recognition connected, surely, to traditions, but most of all, to identities that guarantee continuity. On occasion, however, in obedience to the rules of their semantic fields, canons are formed into propositions, called, for example, "poetics," which, availing themselves of rhetoric, are able to cover at least part of a broader canonicity. Perhaps Latin American literature arrived belatedly to this strategy in terms of the decision and the capacity to formulate "poetic arts," but at certain moments, the need for doing so became almost absolute. This has indeed occurred, one clear example being the case of romanticism, which whether or not presented as marginal, was at least seen as a renewing influence on the classical canon, and which allowed canonical reformulations in the famous polemic between Bello and Sarmiento. The work of Sarmiento itself implies a possible canonicity, being formulated as a "how it should be," and the same could be said of the work of Vasconcelos, although in neither of these cases has it developed into a program that is, at least in one aspect, a "poetic art."

Be that as it may, written or not, the life of canons can be limited, and their expiration, when it occurs, follows from the fact that new social relations engender new canons, which, like these, tend to conserve traces of the ones displaced. At the risk of being repetitious, we can say that these new canons are fed by manifestations originating from a marginality that has managed to impose its objectives and has opened the airways of suffocating bodies of doctrine.

The Latin American Situation

The question of "place" predominates in the focus of this reflection on the Latin American situation, a situation where the canon occupies a well-defined space of production, either as a tendency toward the norm or as the capacity to clarify and promote it. In order to discuss this issue, we should start by pointing out that one way to begin constructing an idea about the literature from the first few centuries of the continent must consist of understanding it simultaneously both as the continuation of a European process and, at the same time, as marginal.

Certainly the latter is true inasmuch as the first texts written, whether during what has come to be called the Discovery and Conquest or immediately after that period, have the impressionistic quality of epistolary testimony—only indirectly canonical or, at least, heeding a loose conventionality that tolerates spontaneity[10]—or they have the quality of a chronicle of recent events. This suggests that, as the organizing principle of genres of written production, rhetoric, like the grammar of the canon, not only was not in operation, but above all, lacked any sense. For some, this results from the allure created with unequaled force by a peculiar, new, and enigmatic reality whose presence shattered all the grammars operational at the time and created relatively unforeseeable behavior. Without resorting to such generalities, however, one could say that in their urgency, the events of the time at first impeded the educated and learned from any concern for forms—understood as codified structures, regular and canonical—and simultaneously, created conditions under which the uneducated and unlearned, on the margin of anything canonical, began to write.

Thus a parallelism appears here between the confusion of those first perceptions and the turbulent style of writing, as if in its own space, freed to follow its own forces, writing had had to respond to what was happening and had lacked both the distance necessary for appreciating linguistic signifiers as well as the formal instruments available to do so, and as a consequence, could set aside the investigations that syntactic edicts demand.

But, as the early furor calmed down and a regular or regularized existence was initiated, complete with institutions and social relations (that is, what we call "the colony"), writing recovered from its early fever (how else could one characterize the writings of Columbus, of Cortés, of Sahagún[11] himself, of Bernal?). An orderly existence began in which the idea of the continuation of European literature was not only useful, but also ambiguous: Bernardo de Balbuena's ambitious poem,[12] written in accordance with the canons and anachronisms of chivalry, ignores such initial turbulence, and its rebellion against the formal and moral canon is null. At the most, it establishes certain interesting referential chords with this reality, which writers such as Sor Juana, Sigüenza y Góngora, and others explored more deeply. The important thing, above all else, is the idea of "ambiguous relations." On the one hand, due to literary debate and rigor, including that of the formal work of writers such as those mentioned above, colonial texts were in tune with the demands of Peninsular literature.[13] On the other hand, however, one can see in certain cases—some more public, such as that of Sor Juana, some more in secret, such as various parodical or humorous tendencies—a certain modifying inflection that neither seeks nor reaches marginality, nor even so much as insinuates it, although this gap in marginality could be an embryonic indication of an identity.

Thus, combining the two arguments, one could say either that the canon was absent, without which marginality was not a deliberate reaction, or that there were faint traces that the present-day reader can note of certain modifications in obedience to canons that the culture endeavored to follow with the same rigor that governed institutional life. The degree of such modification was variable, but that does not discount the concept. Simultaneously, if one believes that this game of adherence to and variation from has something to do with production, one could conclude that obedience is relatively fruitful, and modifications produce results only when there is a syncretism that goes beyond intentions—in architecture, in painting, in esthetic taste, in language, and to a lesser degree, in literature.

The easiest way to understand the beginnings of Latin American literature is to assert that the Spanish and Portuguese introduced the concept of literature together with everything else they introduced: institutions, structures, mores, and of course, language. This means, above all, that nothing existed before their arrival; this belief is indisputable if one is speaking only in European terms, that is, in terms of the consequences of a process of formation of literary structures, and not in the foundational terms of the process itself. In other words, it is of course clear that even in Tenochtitlán, much less in the Orinoco region, there were no lyric poems or epic poems or *autos sacramentales* [allegorical or religious plays] or short stories or novels. There were no verses in hendecasyllables, monorhymed alexandrine quatrains, eight-lined stanzas, or epigrams, but it is also clear that there were other narrative modes, lyrical modes, dramatic modes, and certainly other kinds of modes. Mentioning the well-known work of Nezahualcóyotl[14] will suffice to illustrate this point.

In order to be clear, we will point out here that such modes are essentially discursive, and as a consequence, they maintain certain relationships with words. We perhaps recognize now that words are not simply instruments of such relationships, but in Europe, as in this barely discovered continent, that is how things were viewed after this world became a part of the World, even if they did not think of it in such terms. However, while the Europeans believed that words were instrumental in and indispensable for realizing the discursiveness we call literary, in these lands, images could serve the same purpose, since in some cases, the very idea of graphemes did not exist or differed markedly from that of Europe. There is a world of codices—I will resist the temptation to exalt these documents here—that not only narrate or explain or examine but that also indicate that there was indeed a definite consciousness of literariness, to use a word that exhibits a rich semantic field. When such codices are translated into our language, they reveal discursive structures that were, in general, also part of European culture or that European culture was beginning to claim as its highest glory. There is also another point to consider here: hieroglyphs or petroglyphs suggest, perhaps, a more primitive state if considered from the perspective of phonetic writing, but that does not mean that they would not have provided support or foundation for a literary dimension that could have developed further and encountered the other, including possibly dominating it and infusing it with a texture and a density it lacked.

But we aren't here to prophesy "in reverse," nor to lament once again what, historically, did not occur; to make such judgments only serves to recognize that the reading of these strange manifestations by the Europeans was a case of "text under erasure," which led them to imagine they were dealing with a literary no-man's-land in which, as in other areas, they tried to introduce implantations.

Such implantations were carried out even to the point of implanting, with the Bourbons, academies, which were founded after the universities. From this moment on, syncretic spontaneity was limited, and the canon began to reign, with respect to which, the only imaginable marginality is geographical: what is written here, no matter how much it might attempt to "belong" to a certain order, is not taken into consideration by that order. It suffers from isolation. It is not enough to try to belong—a separation always exists. Converting text to metaphor, I believe that this is what that beautiful novel *Zama,* by Antonio Di Benedetto, describes and illustrates: no matter how much one might wish it so, this world is not the same as that other one, which, in the imagination, is where a sought-for truth lies—but a truth that cannot be found from here.

Nevertheless, at that same moment, there was another kind of marginality, one we could call "second degree": by this I refer to the use of Latin, for example, or languages other than Spanish, by various religious orders including the Jesuits. The encapsulated character of these languages with respect to Spanish did not keep people from producing texts in them that followed canons found in other places—the discourse of the religious order or of their respective languages. Be that as it may, the effect of that marginality, as Mariano Picón Salas has pointed out, was very important in the development of proindependence thinking, nurtured, as it was, by marginalities of all types.[15]

Independence revealed these conflicts: the desire for political autonomy (such autonomy assuming that the marginalized—Creoles or blacks or priests— would begin to have a voice in formulating the rules—laws, constitutions, institutions, and so on—and, therefore, to convert into canon, in the best of cases, the substance of what defined the marginal act—freedom of commerce before monopolies, freedom of the womb before slavery, freedom of the individual before despotism, and so on) sees the preexisting canonical form as the only possible channel for its expression: the Bourbon neoclassicism in all of its facets. Carpentier satirizes this crisis beautifully in *The Kingdom of this World* [*El reino de este mundo*; 1949]: the black monarch dresses himself like a French king, and in his court they sing languid arias by Lully.

Nevertheless, in that expression itself, marginality bubbles up and escapes to the surface: it is the gauchesque poetry of the Río de la Plata region or a work of localist observation like that of Fernández de Lizardi in Mexico, and, in general, this creates tradition or describes the aspirations of Latin American popular art. These are good examples of a marginality existing before a canonical reformation. They often triumphed in obtaining recognition of their marginal situation, though not the defeat of the canonical, which, with respect to these types of manifestations, would only accept their utterance or their substance, as occurred in this century with Puerto Rican or Cuban *negrista* poetry, but would never accept a challenge to poetic form. However, the canonical, in its aspect as "high art," cuts off processes begun at the margins, or else it absorbs them in their thematic aspects, as occurred, most notably, with Argentine theater. If, as it appears from what little is still extant, there was a certain local production (*El amor de la estanciera*)[16] toward the end of the eighteenth century, though crude in its language in both senses (and this, in some way attests to how the universe of the rustic was preparing itself for gauchesque poetry), around 1870 the so-called Theatrical Society explicitly defined the national theater as being subject to rules, Creole in theme but European in form.

It is also a matter of debate between form and substance, at least as it appears in the Bello-Sarmiento polemic; the former firmly believed in fidelity to the most elevated rhetoric known, the latter believed that there was an American temperament that should generate a congruent expression. This is what Sarmiento attempted in *Facundo* [1845], which, in challenging genres, implied the proposition of creating a literature all Latin America's own. I believe that Latin America has never let go of this idea, which in fact revives what occurred with the writings of the chroniclers from the discovery: this is the sense of Hostos's invocations, or, subsequently, of Vasconcelos, or before, of Juan Montalvo[17]; the autochthonous, repressed, would be the marginal, and the program would be the way to bring it into the hierarchy of the canon. In Sarmiento, however, there is not an idealization of substance: the barbarous world, which is the autochthonous, can and should generate a literature, though not a barbarous one, but rather an elevated one growing out of a critical stance formulated in turn from the most elevated elements of European thought and with a tendency to find a place in the most elevated European universe.

That the formulation continues is indicated by much later movements even more radical in relation to a repressed subject matter. One example is negrista art, the Puerto Rican even more than the Cuban, which in the work of Guillén, via an apologetic representation, appears mediatized to a great degree by the language. This can be seen in the work of Palés Matos in Puerto Rico: he begins by trying to reproduce the natural sounds of his country in an elemental onomatopoeic proposal, and later moves to a sort of classical folkloric sensibility; it is as if he first sought to forge a language that springs from the autochthonous but later reconciled with at least one aspect of the canon—language. As a consequence, the American substance doubles back on itself, fixed by history, and the interplay between marginality and canon is established in a different mode, in the order of words, within the established rhetoric, as would be the case with Lezama Lima's intents or, more clearly still, with those of Borges, who, after a decisive experience of incorporating the quotidian, returned gradually to "literature" in the most Western sense of the word. But in this area, it appears he wished to destroy certain canons or extract from them a richness that, in and of themselves, faced with the turbulence of marginality, the reigning, postmodern canons could not exhibit.

From History to Writing

Symmetrical and Asymmetrical Tendencies

in the Latin American Historical Novel

It is a well-known and frequently mentioned fact that the historical novel is a product of romanticism, or more precisely, that it enjoyed its greatest brilliance and the height of its popularity during the romantic period. However, as has occurred with many aspects of romanticism, it had actually begun to develop as a form before that, in particular from the historical visions of the encyclopedists, although certainly its major force and legitimacy came from the more remote Shakespearean historical theater and even from its French neoclassical offshoots. And could we also mention here the historical inclination of Spanish conceptist poetry as part of this process? Perhaps, although in this case, as well as the others, it is important to point out that a number of conceptual and historical transformations were necessary in order for what we intuitively recognize as the "historical novel" to be able to achieve its shape and its identity.

In effect, the historical Elizabethan theater, which in its turn has a long tradition of a thematic search, shows romanticism that verbal imagination can be used to shape a history that is fundamentally a history of a power that seems consubstantial to the existence—problematic, to be sure—of the state. But the predominant feature of Elizabethan theater is that it emphasizes the didactic character of the tragic element that this history experiences. For its part, and this is certainly where Shakespeare's historical work serves as a model, the tragic element grows out of what is invariable in history from the moment in which the imagination acts on the known facts. In this nexus, then, it is not surprising that all the protagonists of historical novels are tragic characters, since they narrate what by definition has occurred, and, on the other hand, it is also natural that all historical novels are developmental in the sense that they should explain the process that culminates in what is already known. Later historical novels, ones more defined in their scope, support that knowledge with documents that, although they also must have played a part in Shakespeare's work, surely have a more genre-bound scope in his case.

In terms of the encyclopedists, if I can include the work of Voltaire and Marmontel in this category, the historical vision that achieves narrative status results from a kind of intellectual curiosity about the "other," supported in part by an epistemological faith, and in part by an irruption of exotic realities that, in a rationalist way, cannot be understood except as metaphors of classical history. For that reason, I believe, the historical novel in that case is not an interpretive instrument, as it was after the Hegelian rupture, when the very concept of history became essentialized and overshadowed the concepts of nature and society and even that of the individual itself. We can note, in this respect, that the "documentary" nature of the encyclopedist historical novel has its parallel, if not its very source, in the testimonies or tales of travelers (especially in the case of America) that later became documents, not because they propose a formal historical discourse but rather due to their inaugural fervor supported by direct observations, very much tainted, of course, by the gaze, by "what one wishes to see."[1] Be that as it may, something of the encyclopedist rationalism was, according to Lukács, transmitted to the "realist" expressions of the historical novel, and because of this feature they can be differentiated from the romantic novels, which that author defines as "reactionary."

In terms of Spanish poetry and theater from the Golden Age, it is not easy to establish their relationship to the historical novel in general, nor even to the

Spanish historical novel. While for Góngora, historical material is interesting because of its mythological condensations, and Quevedo uses it to make certain allusions mediated by philosophy, in the case of Cervantes and Lope de Vega, historical material functions to support an idea of national political destiny on which a troubled present places its diminishing hopes. At the same time, we must consider this historical inclination in light of the corresponding ignorance found in the chronicles, which were surreptitiously modifying not only history itself but also documentality, and even, in the most hidden and remote way, the very sense of telling [*referir*], which as we know, is etymologically linked to "relating" [*relatar*]. Precisely because this whole process was encapsulated, it is not easy to establish the link between the way that history was converted to literature during the Golden Age and the sharp profile that the historical novel developed in the nineteenth century.

In any case, it is now quite clear that besides the philosophical factors, powerful social factors (namely, economic and political), such as the violent experience of rapid global changes in the structures of life in general, were necessary for romanticism to take form in Europe, and with that, what we have called the "historical novel" began to appear. The least we can say about that in this preliminary investigation is that it accompanied the process of development of the nineteenth-century European novel and even expresses the most developed form of that category. This statement makes sense if by the term "novel" in general we mean a search for balance or compromise between two drives—that of "knowing that one wants to tell" and that of "fiction," which permits the telling of a knowledge in a more specific way, increasing the communicability of that telling via mechanisms that take into account the productivity of the reading. To put it another way, this concept of the novel supposes the appearance of a democratic and literate society in which the imaginary possibility of "identification" with idealized expressions or with possible social ideals is a supreme unifier.

Of course the great attraction in producing historical novels persisted after romanticism and continues up to the present time, although perhaps Europe is no longer the exclusive scene where this occurs. Be that as it may, the complete history of the historical novel is organized as an array of displacements by virtue of criteria, concepts, or functions that substantially modify its form. In this way, if *Ivanhoe* [1791] is a historical novel, and also *The Bridge of San Luis Rey* [1927] or *I, the Supreme* [*Yo el Supremo*; 1974], it is clear that we should try to understand the modifications that occur from one to the others, and that we should ask a number of questions, as much about the structural tensions of all historical novels as about the external, extratextual factors that might have created the conditions for such modifications to take place.

In this sense, and in connection with an examination of what occurred with the historical novel in Latin America, we should note that, above all, the development of romanticism traveled almost simultaneously to the American continent, either because the European novel was read in the Americas, or because what was being written on this continent was considered to be an adapted, formal model, syntactical and ideological. However, there are differences in sense and usage that are barely noted in the relationship that Latin American literature had with Europe, especially after independence. In this way, the historical novel of the romantic era, from Walter Scott to Michel de Zévaco, including Dumas, Gogol, Manzoni, Vigny, Pushkin, Suè, Hugo, Merimée, and others along the way, linked to the explanatory system we call "historicism" (Herderian in origin but ideologically dependent on the need to affirm bourgeois dominance), always has to do with the search for an identity that would find its source and its origin in the most ancient depths of a people and a community: the typical historical situations that appeal to it would be dialectical condensations of the establishment of that identity, and in that sense, they are representative. To develop them through fiction is to question them while at the same time integrating them into the imagination as a power that allows us to approach these objectives and that also provides the formal route to reach them. Be that as it may, because of what is incorporated in it, the historical novel of the romantic era is a typical product of a generalized anxiety about the present. In the structures that satisfy it, it reveals the insecurity of the Hegelian spirit that is always beyond reach, shifting from certainty to improbability in the same way that the internal tension of the romantic historical novel exhibits a growing shift from historical fact to the vicissitudes of the protagonist, a hero of a necessarily progressive nature, and at the same time, a tragic one. Nothing else, I believe, explains the conversion to novel form of "cloak and dagger" material with the ensuing literary fortunes of certain protagonists.

In Latin America, this implantation met the general fate of a literature conceived of less as a qualitative development of a continuity than as the necessary initiation of an essential practice. To paraphrase Ricardo Rojas, we did not really have literature, and then finally we managed to develop it—a perspective that recognizes that a very important concrete lack has gradually been replaced by a desire for construction.[2] However, it is necessary to emphasize that the historical novel that began to be conceived and realized in Latin America was not merely a crude copy, but that it produced, in the adaptation, essential differences. The first one has to do with the very nature of the historical novel. It is about a search, like the European model, but not for a social and class identity; rather it is about a search for a national identity, a search for legitimacy. Through its mechanisms it seeks to discover not from whence it comes, but rather what it is in relation to other identities, since its identity is problematic, hazy, stigmatized, or at least, composed of intermittencies. When this problem is linked to the idea of political independence, the criollo being something not clearly defined, an almost generalized stigma is spread over everything connected to the indigenous world, that is, over a considerable part of the past, since it must be rejected in favor of the other experience, the colonial one, against which the idea of the nation "in progress" emerges.

The second differentiating trait, in relation to these stigmatized elements, resides in the historiographical perception itself, which is quite weak since history was barely beginning to be constructed. This idea of the freshness of the past perhaps explains why *Amalia* [1855], by José Mármol, is considered to be a historical novel, and why we would have to wait a while for colonial history to become the "novalizable" one, in works such as those by Riva Palacio or Sierra O'Reilly. Of course when taking inventory of this type of novel, one finds important exceptions, such as that of the Venezuelan/Cuban José Antonio Echeverría, who with his *Antonelli* [1839][3] situated the action at the height of the colonial era. Furthermore, the Argentine Vicente Fidel López, with *La novia del hereje* [The Heretic's Bride; 1846], along with the Cuban Gertrudis Gómez de Avellaneda with her *Guatemocín* from the same year, manage to break the historiographical inertia and recover the indigenous dimension as something novelizable, suitable for creating this kind of product.

Finally, another noticeable difference lies in the characters, which are not historically secondary, as they were in the European model, but instead are principle actors, as is proven by the fascination elicited by Juan Manuel de Rosas, Henri Christophe, Pancho Villa, or Dr. Francia, though this did not mean a renunciation of realism nor an attempt to convert it to romanticism. Lukács, as you will remember, establishes this distinction: the true historical novel for him, in the tradition of Walter Scott, is constructed from heroes who historically are of "middling" importance, while the romantics, such as Vigny with *Cinq Mars* [1826], for example, or Tieck, deposit a heavy dose of fictional heroism in the "great men" of history.

But in all these examples the history is read or is assumed, and it takes its material from second-hand sources, conventional and genre-bound. In this respect, it is worthwhile to point out that Vicente Riva Palacio was, if not the first, at least one of the first, to explore little-known documents in order to imagine his novels: he investigated the original documents of the Inquisition, and his fictional inspiration, which is only superficially a reproduction, stems from those readings. What makes his novelistic work so important is precisely the documentary investigation, which on the one hand reflected, as a gesture, the modernizing impulse of Mexican liberalism, while on the other, it postulated a historical continuity that is easily verifiable in circumstances and places that are still there and that resound with conflicts that, stemming from the colonial period, constitute the imaginable core of a nationality.

There is much that could be said about the "function" of the historical novel in relation to the process of construction on a national, institutional, social, and cultural level in our countries during the nineteenth century. All of this has been mentioned before, including the fact that, although the novels referred to as historical have a critical character with respect to the course of such a process, they themselves express that process—it being understood that there are conceptual doubts about its meaning. The scope of the search, therefore, is different from that which characterizes the European historical novel, in the same way that their respective concepts of nationalism are different, as are of course the class conflicts, although the conceptual instruments we use to understand them may be similar or spring from common paradigms.

As we know, the year 1832 was at the same time both the triumph of romanticism, with Victor Hugo's *Hernani* [1830], and the beginning of its decline, with his *Les orientales* [1829].[4] However, this did not affect the vigor of the historical novel, which, inasmuch as it was converted into a sociological phenomenon, has tended to disseminate and consolidate ideology. It was so strong that it remained largely untouched by the positivist attack, which as we also know, changed not only the social function of literature but also its foundation. Furthermore, if the historical novel managed to resist the positivist attack, it is because it exemplifies better than other forms of literary discourse that capacity for searching, for investigation, for experimentation that naturalist positivism promotes and requires. We could even say that historical fiction was the only path left, given the impossibility of denying the imaginary aspect in the more general struggle to deny spiritualism, the sign beneath which romanticism developed its discursive process.[5] Perhaps, however, in this understanding, the classical historical novel must reach a compromise with the novelized biography, which is a kind of reduced but illustrative history, similarly subordinate to the document, but whose global justification in terms of bourgeois power is realized in the idea of the "representative man," rather than that of the situation or the objective conflict.

This "scientific" attitude of positivism, then, when it arrived in Latin America, did not create a kind of paralysis, as might be expected due to its reductionism, but instead created a genuine blossoming, especially of the historical novel: beneath its banner, writers from all the Latin American countries, wishing to be linked to the spirit of social and political affirmation taking form in the last quarter of the century, reorganized their strategy and broadened the historical dimension that could function as a referent for them. With the republics established once and for all, with the anguish of the civil war behind them, and with the state organizing powerful and relatively stable classes everywhere, writers rediscovered the colony as a source of local history, as well as discovering what we could call criollo identity, and, though to a lesser degree, the indigenous world. Citing the titles of the various respective works would not perhaps be very uplifting to the audience, but one cannot avoid mentioning two titles by Eligio Ancona, *La cruz y la espada* [The Cross and the Sword; 1864] and *Los mártires de Anáhuac* [The Martyrs of Anáhuac; 1870], as well as *Enriquillo* by Manuel de Jesús Galván [1882],[6] considered the most interesting of the lot; *El inquisidor mayor* [The Head Inquisitor; 1871] by Manuel Bilbao; *Monja y casada, virgen y mártir* [Nun and Wife, Virgin and Martyr; 1868] by Vicente Riva Palacio; *Los bandidos de Río Frío* [The Bandits of Río Frío; 1889–1891] by Manuel Payno; *Ismael* [1888] by Eduardo Acevedo Díaz, *Tomóchic* [1893–1895] by Heriberto Frías; and so many others in various countries across America. Not only the novel, clear and simple, was flourishing then, but also the historical novel, which in its documentary record confirmed without a doubt that founding gesture of sociological investigation that positivism spread throughout a recently organized society.

Somehow this inquiring gesture also dominated the endeavors of the Spaniard Benito Pérez Galdós, whose patriotic conception of the historical realm would have an influence on Latin America somewhat later, in relation to the belated expansion of classical realism, particularly conspicuous in the work of the Argentine Manuel Gálvez.

Of course, the history of the historical novel in Latin America does not stop there. Notice, furthermore, that its course is relatively simple, as indeed the concept itself appears to be. But surely neither one is as simple as that, and before beginning a journey through the most recent period of the historical novel, which continues up to the present time, it is worth our while to examine more closely what has up to this point appeared to be an acquired and obvious knowledge. As if, if we could start all over again, we could ask, classically speaking, but what is the historical novel?

In accordance with a certain epistemological move, in order to begin to respond to this question, we would first have to detail all the texts that in one way or another are designated as historical novels, from Félix Varela's version of *Jicoténcal* [*Xicoténcatl*], which ushered in the tradition in Latin America in 1826, through *Trafalgar* [1873] by Benito Pérez Galdós, all the way up to *La llegada* [The Arrival; 1980] by José Luis González. Later, via successive abstractions, we would have to establish principal characteristics for formulating a definition at last. This route is not only impossible but also methodologically weak—on the one hand, because we do not have a very clear idea of what the criteria for this designation have been during various periods and, on the other, because although the majority of historical novels consider themselves to be following the rules of the novelistic genre, we come at this from a perspective not bound by genres in order to understand that vast manifestation. Consequently, let us choose a different path, probably the only one left—namely, to propose certain hypotheses, taking into account specific authorities, especially those who claim the concept of the historical novel as their method. I hope that these hypotheses can perhaps find their embodiment or exemplification in particular expressions, although none of them in one single text, in the supposition that there is a wellspring, even if only subterranean, of reflection accumulated over the course of a life of reading, whose elements could be susceptible to a certain organization.

If we start from the simple statement that the historical novel proposes to represent social conflicts and that its specific form is a detail, a particularity, within a larger narrative horizon, we could say that that detail is produced by virtue of a double mechanism: on the one hand, an accentuation of the collective aspect of the social conflicts mentioned above along with a parallel subordination of the individual aspects, and on the other, the choice of material socially representative of the individuals who, in this role, relegate the social and contextual to details of a panorama. Both situations attempt to understand the notion of the "historical novel," but they also open up a broad area where various manifestations can enter, including those of costumbrista movements, social criticism, political manifestations, or even those of social psychology, as could be the case with Carlos Fuentes's *The Death of Artemio Cruz* [*La muerte de Artemio Cruz*; 1962]. In such an expanse, one unavoidable constant would be the reference to historical events, either well known or relatively unknown, but at any rate, inscribed in a body of knowledge.

With respect to this expanse, which has given rise to diverse commentary such as that of Julio Leguizamón who discusses the novel of "historical topics,"[7] or that of Alberto Zum Felde, who in some cases talks about the novel with a "historical setting,"[8] or that of José Luis González, who maintains that his text, *La llegada*, is simply about a historical "theme," I would like to delve into this issue from the negative side, that is, by indicating what we can say for certain the historical novel is *not*, although, of course with many qualms. The clear and decidedly introspective novel, such as *A Grave with No Name* [*Para una tumba sin nombre*; 1959] by Juan Carlos Onetti, is not a historical novel, nor are the ones referred to as "language novels," such as the texts by Julieta Campos, nor are science fiction novels, such as *The Invention of Morel* [*La invención de Morel*; 1940] by Adolfo Bioy Casares, nor parodic novels such as *Galaor* [1972] by Hugo Hiriart, nor "atmospheric" novels, such as *Nobody Nothing Never* [*Nadie nada nunca*; 1980] by Juan José Saer, nor detective novels, such as *Chronicle of a Death Foretold* [*Crónica de una muerte anunciada*; 1981] by Gabriel García Márquez, nor "stylistic" novels, such as *Salamandra* [Salamander; 1919] by Efrén Rebolledo, and not even the novels that make political denunciations, such as *A Funny Dirty Little War* [*No habrá más penas ni olvido*; 1980] by Osvaldo Soriano.

It is quite likely that we could all agree that all of these options indicate numerous possibilities of "non"-historical novels, but it also seems clear that in all of them there is some element that is related, and sometimes in a very fundamental way, to history, and not only because it is impossible to write something that is ahistorical, but also because the historical can be generative, whether because it offers an understanding of the relationship between the individual and his or her milieu, or because of the historicity of the narrative or the writing process, or because of the intervention of ideology in the configuration of the narrative, which always has a historical base. This is so strongly the case that a text can suddenly turn into a clearly historical novel without any doubt as to that classification—a text, that is, that like José Mármol's *Amalia,* in reality only examines abstract-concrete elements (motivated perhaps by a distant and indirect Hegelianism), which turn out to be, as in the case of the dichotomy "civilization and barbarism," the true actors of history, not the economy or politics, and not even the concrete historical subjects. Hence, we have the justifiable accusation that their characters are not convincing, as well as the hazy historical juncture, but on the other hand, quasi-symbolic aspects are made to stand out that result from conceptual comparisons.[9]

In short, starting from what it is *not,* what sets the historical novel apart is the reference to a moment "considered to be historical and commonly accepted as such," as well as certain documentary support conducted by whomever proposes this representation.

In effect, documentation is fundamental in order to recognize a historical novel, and in fact, the major cultivators of the genre, from Pérez Galdós to Roa Bastos, including Carpentier and Manuel Gálvez, invoke that documentation to support the objective they seek—in the first case, a moralizing objective; in the second, epistemological, as Jacques Leenhardt indicated; in the third, mythical; and finally, political.[10] And, with respect to documentation, these words by Pedro Díaz Seijas are a good example and could be applied to all those who have produced historical novels: "Carpentier's investigative capability is amazing. For more than two decades he accumulated information that would serve as the backdrop for the novels he has written in recent years."[11]

But surely this documentary "action" should be coupled with other actions because the limits of a document are bound by its "transcription," and, as we know, what matters is something else, even when, as Maurice Blanchot maintains, the "derealizing" act of writing, of all writing, modifies the nature of all discourses, even those that, like the discourse of history, wish to be *only* transcriptive.[12] That "something else" is achieved by establishing a very close and concrete relationship with another element, that of fiction (not necessarily narrative, since almost all historical discourse is narrative), which has, or to which are attributed, other capabilities. In this way, the document is stripped of its narrativity, and what is then applied to it or imposed on it is characteristic of fiction, at least as it is conceived of since the major development of the novel. We could say, then, that historical novels result from an equation, considered well balanced, between two qualities that are assumed to be incontrovertible: the authenticity of a document and the reinterpretation of a rhetoric or of particular rules of a praxis. Apparently, the act of relating and interweaving these two planes, which reflects a philosophical ideal originating with Hegel, is ethically justified in the sense of an ethic that can take on a social function in a given society and that should have some coherence with the most widely held values of that society according to the predominance of history, or, what is the same thing, in service to a certain "value" that history possesses for society as a whole: the value of elucidation, of exemplification, education, spiritual confirmation.

Fiction, on the other hand, has an instrumental scope, one of didactic effectiveness, a transmitting element. In this relation, therefore, we could say that the literary expression that is known as the "historical novel" is something like the "form" that has created the conditions for the absolute triumph of the "theme" over the "structure." And with this kind of conclusion, we now have something more, I believe, in terms of the definition we have been seeking. And, fittingly, it is worth remembering what, according to Emilio Carilla, Heredia had already observed in his *Ensayo sobre la novela* with respect to the historical novel—a struggle, for him, between history and fiction, between information and creation,[13] in order to show that this idea has already existed for some time.

I said "apparently" a moment ago because with regards to historical events and since the very beginning, since Walter Scott, as Lukács said,[14] the second element, the one that should be useful, that of fiction, has always ended up winning the struggle. This is perhaps because its effectiveness, before it could yield to a body of knowledge and adapt to it, veered off onto the uncertain but seductive path of the Aristotelian "possibles," inverting the ideological terms and subordinating history until it achieved the miracle of making us forget it. We can see this in the novels by Dumas, and, even more so, in texts such as Alejo Carpentier's *Explosion in a Cathedral* [*El siglo de las luces*; 1962], Augusto Roa Bastos's *I, the Supreme* [*Yo el Supremo*; 1974], or Juan José Saer's *The Witness* [*El entenado*; 1983].

On the one hand, a possible consequence of this imbalance in favor of art and to the detriment of a historical reading could have been the persistence of this post-Hegelian occurrence, which is constantly renewed and continues to have an enormous attractive force. On the other hand, the most elemental ideas about the mechanisms of writing explain it, since all writing that tends to produce a text is established from a genotext, and no doubt, any document, no matter how historical it might be, will also belong to a genotextual class. If any poem or novel is established on the basis of experiences, extended readings, and imagination, then a historical novel, using similar mechanisms, is established on the basis of a document, but it does the same thing as the primary sources, and it can end up, as indeed it does, becoming independent of the facts, rediscovering its own dimension. What at any rate must be considered is the turn or direction taken at a given moment by the writings, and the reasons why a decision of this type can continue to seduce us. Following from this, with the exclusive objective of providing an example, I would propose the following as possible alternatives to those reasons: Is this type of writing chosen out of a social necessity? Is it chosen due to having exhausted the criteria of fantasy? Is it chosen because of a determinism that fulfills some function beyond all rationality? Is it chosen because it turns out to be very difficult to spatialize space in the imagination, but it is possible to spatialize time?

Naturally, I am not going to answer these questions here—I realize that Lukács has taken it upon himself to do so. I would simply like to add, in order to provide evidence of the autonomy that the historical novel has achieved with respect to history, that what remains of that history are a few of its characters, who, in my opinion, are the clearest things to emerge from the force of fiction's triumph. Indeed, Lukács discusses the "heroes" and the characters and finds that converting men of middling importance and a common sensibility into heroes is not simply the genius of Walter Scott but a specific site of the transformation that the historical novel assumes or implies.

However, I would like to consider this point using other devices, also literary. Leaving aside the form and the intention of the preromantic historical novels, we could say that starting with the romantic historical novels, what predominates in them is a *realist* perspective, in the sense that from their imaginary origin par excellence, they are articulated from a "representation." As we have already indicated, this is the representation of an era, of a period, of a historical situation, in accordance with the descriptive demands of verisimilitude that characterize so-called realism. But realism does not exclude the imagination, and through it one can, as the romantic Vicente Fidel López maintains, reconstruct the "lost piece" of history[15] in such a way that in the endeavor, certain elements take on more force and escape from the fundamental proposition. What in particular escapes, again, are the characters, who suddenly betray the originating information, or rather are invented in order to explain what happened with another character, who is the truly real one. In both instances this character accumulates so much narrative libido and becomes such a "hero," that his exploits take him out of the realm of verisimilitude and realism. And this occurs to such an extent that he could rate either the Lukacsian definition of a character from a bourgeois novel, or that of the degraded hero who wanders through an equally degraded world in search of pure values, or that of Freud, of a location and expression of the indefinite persistence of the "I," unharmed until death, postponing it with the same skill with which the final threat of history is postponed. And this is as much the case for Michel de Zevaco's character Pardaillan as for Vicente Riva Palacio's Martín de Garatuza, or, using a different technique, for Alejo Carpentier's Mackandal. And in this double dimension, many historical novels end up becoming so deeply fantastic that they establish another value that has "greater historical evocation than does the patient accumulation of archeological fragments," as Antonio Castro Leal put it.[16]

But as we know, the "realism" of a text lies not so much in its representational intention, which is manifested in description and in the construction of the characters, as in the action of the narrator, whom we could superficially define as the organizer, from inside the text, of the narration. For in realist narration, the narrator suffers from a conflict between omnipotence and objectivity: when he allows himself the satisfaction of the former, the ideology takes on a crude aspect, it becomes immediate, projected—a "way of seeing" pervades everything before he can organize it. When, on the other hand, he attempts objectivity, his ideology becomes that of a truth that imposes itself. Furthermore, one or the other possibility is translated in particular terms in such a way that the narrators can be seen as wanting to be closer or farther away from what they narrate. I do not want to get involved in discussing theories of the narrator, but I will say that these brief thoughts can be incorporated into the material for observation provided by the mass of historical novels in order to understand, from their realist position, essential slippages, or displacements. So, for example, a narrator who is too close to the historical aspect of what he tries to present ends up moving toward the side of the chronicle, which is precisely what the most classic historical novels have tried to avoid. On the other hand, the narrator who is too distant can and indeed does fall into a kind of archeology (as occurs in *Salammbô* [1862] by Flaubert or in *La gloria de don Ramiro* [The Glory of Don Ramiro] by Larreta; 1908), which would be the culmination of the genre, something that other authors have avoided no matter how much knowledge they have possessed, and also no matter how much they have turned documents into material that is then incorporated into the narrative structure, as is the case with *Ides of March* [1948] by Thornton Wilder or *I, the Supreme* by Augusto Roa Bastos.

In certain attributive attempts to find local and autochthonous antecedents to the Latin American historical novel, the chronicles of the discovery and conquest are generally invoked: there is no doubt that, despite their at times notorious partiality, they are indeed historical documents, nor can we deny the fact that they are full of situations that in and of themselves are novelesque and that subsequently could be reworked in a literary way. But precisely because their narrative lacks distance, the reconstruction of a possible historical plot gives way to a vindication that is considered necessary, or to the defense of a cause or of a prestige. In that case, history predominates completely, and, as a consequence, we are no longer talking about a novel.

Nevertheless, there are certain problematic cases, such as that of Bernal Díaz del Castillo who, because he was writing many years after the fact, achieves the distance but not the narrative objectivity, or that of José Oviedo y Baños who seems to have broken this barrier, not only because he does not offer any testimony, but also because, beginning from documents, he reconstructs a movement so complicated that, perhaps involuntarily, it becomes fictionalized. While Bernal, despite everything, continues to be a chronicler, Oviedo y Baños *appears* to be a chronicler, which allows us to suppose that he mystified history *avant la lettre* and introduced a formula in America that needed European romanticism in order to be aware of its power. I will say, in order to finish off this issue somewhat sketchily, that the lack of distance in the chronicle gives rise to other manifestations that similarly touch upon the historical, renouncing the novel without at the same time renouncing narration—namely the "memoirs" and the "autobiographies" that are so abundant and rich in the history of our culture.

Of course all of these clarifications and limitations adopt categories and concepts that could have justified a practice in its own context, as well as involving a particular intellectual exercise that attempts new readings of what are in a certain way old texts (because they are produced in relation to other modes of production), without abruptly breaking with the old readings. From a present-day position that does not pay such close attention to genre-related distinctions and that, instead, extracts from them elements that as they develop, give rise to other things, one could say that the "historical novel" is also a way of reading. Our way of reading, for example, tends to convert texts and see in them not only what they "say," but also, beneath what they say, what it is that initiates multiple discourses with reality. So, for example, certain chronicles seem interesting to us for their narrativity, which is constantly discovered in documents such as those from the Inquisition or literary journals: the act of reading novelizes them, valuing their narrativity. But reading also rearranges them, and when presenting them with the necessary intention, it emphasizes a value that genre-related demands keep from being elucidated. And this occurs in particular in the modern novel that either wants to be or disguises itself as a historical novel. *Zama* [1956], by Antonio di Benedetto, reconstructs, as Vicente Fidel López wished to do, the colonial existence that had been lost, yet all the while actually parodying the chronicles and literary attempts to reconstruct historic scenes. It is an absolutely modern text that asks questions of itself in its intimate identity as text. *I, the Supreme,* which seems to be an almost orthodox historical novel in the sense of a notable documentary quality linked to a desire to restore a sense of nationality of a country, can also be seen as a reflection on power, or as an extremely refined narrative elaboration on the relationships between writing and orality, one that puts diverse contemporary theoretical instances into play.

It is evident that the emergence of new ways of reading has influenced the evolution of the historical novel from its initial realist orthodoxy and its idea of service. The act of reading, that great modifier, has pushed down to second place not only the strategy of the historical novel, but also its functionality; today, Manuel Gálvez's cycle about the Rosas era or the latest war with Paraguay seems as encapsulated in its circumstances as *La gloria de don Ramiro* while, in contrast, texts such as Carpentier's *Explosion in a Cathedral* or Ricardo Piglia's *Artificial Respiration* [*Respiración artificial*; 1980] resonate with a contemporary reverberation, as do José Luis González's *La llegada* or Juan José Saer's *The Witness* or Rosario Castellanos's *The Book of Lamentations* [*Oficio de Tinieblas*; 1962] or Carlos Fuentes's *The Death of Artemio Cruz.* In all of these the historical aspect is no longer used simply to support a cause or imply a well-founded choice of a time period, and instead moves to a genotextual level, an opportunity for a literary transformation that is more and more demanding and bold.

A novel in which the historical aspect (conceived of as a significant condensation of collective events) plays a role, maintains its attraction and its validity, but not with the same impetus or certainty that we have tried to delineate and that seems to be part of the designation of a historical novel. In the past thirty years, more or less, the old concept shattered, giving rise to manifestations that have to do with the history of literature and, to an even greater extent, the history of writing, more than with history in the strict sense of the term. This is most likely due to the general process of modification of literary concepts, or rather, to a certain expansion of capabilities or qualities inherent in writing, when given their own freedom. In its turn, this process of modification (which in order to explain we would have to invoke social, political, and philosophical reasons, just as in the case of the appearance of the historical novel on the romantic horizon) is manifested in certain intraliterary practices, which, even if only briefly, I would like to highlight.

The first of these, it seems to me, resides in the extraordinary proliferation of narrative possibilities that, despite their diversity, all claim to be novelistic. Another element that has had some effect, I believe, is the interrelationship of literary discourses, not only as a possibility, but also as a necessary response. We can find this most conspicuously in the penetration of poetic language into narrative, which as a consequence has displaced and at times eliminated even the discipline of the referent in general and the historical referent in particular. Third, I would like to mention the force of the theoretical attacks against what would appear to be major pillars of all novels, past and future: verisimilitude and linearity. I would like to say a few words about this precisely because what is happening in this issue is somewhat similar to the epistemological rupture that opens the door to new perspectives, or at least authorizes new attempts at freedom. In terms of verisimilitude, we can begin to see not only that the concept was difficult to maintain but also that the most interesting things happened when the rules of verisimilitude were broken, even when one believed one was following them. Furthermore, attempts at total rupture, such as those by Macedonio Fernández, cleared a path for an opposing construction, the inverisimilization that by synecdoche appears to define all narration, and not only that which intellectually evades verisimilitude, appealing to fantasy or excess.

In terms of linearity, the objection to its conventional character, which in its turn rests on the idea of continuous temporality, allows the articulation of a rational response to its worn-out coherence via a fragmentariness that opens up an immense and sweeping possibility: it is not that the fragmentariness wants to contradict temporal logic, but rather that it wants to tie it to more profound paths, distancing itself with respect to the causality in which linearity seems to be protected and authorized. In terms of the historical novel of this century, while on the one hand it proposes the inverisimilitude of magical realism, on the other it functions either to disrupt a previous historical line, destroying its apparent discursive armor, or to create, through reading, an existing history, discursively and in fragments, in a discontinuity perhaps irritating and unintelligible to historians.

I have been asked not to focus too much on particular texts in presenting this talk in order to deal with critical problems of genre. I have tried to honor that request; however, I can say that, as in other literary terrains, the concrete approach to each text raises issues in such a way that hypotheses could continue being formulated indefinitely, not in the sense that each text is an immanently self-codifiable universe, but rather that each text provokes new themes that are added to those that have emerged from other readings and that weave, along with others, a complicated web that is much more interesting, certainly, than what has been presented here. And now that I have said that, and in conclusion, it occurs to me that my approach has ignored historical-epistemological aspects that should be taken into consideration, such as, for example, what kind of history is the history that the historical novel in general and in particular takes on as material. But that history is another story, and for now, I will leave it be.

Notes on the Latin American Avant-garde

Working Papers

For José Pascual Buxó

In an article entitled "Nota sobre la otra vanguardia" [Note on the Other Avant-garde], José Emilio Pacheco points out that we can speak of two avant-gardes: one inherited from the European tradition, and the other Latin American with a certain relationship to the United States, embodied in what would later come to be called "antipoetry" and, secondarily, "conversational poetry." Pacheco ignores the first and makes several observations about the second; the first issue he deals with has to do with North American poetry, with the so-called New Poetry of 1922. Salvador Novo's *Antología de la poesía norteamericana moderna,* published in 1924, is a milestone work and a confirmation of this connection. Novo, Henríquez Ureña, and Salomón de la Selva[1] were the pioneers and innovators of this spirit, which would later have other manifestations, such as *Trilce* by César Vallejo, the journal *Proa* in Buenos Aires, "La semana de arte moderna" in São

Paulo,[2] and the Estridentismo movement in Mexico and the journal initiated by that movement, *Actual, hoja de vanguardia.* Then in 1927 José Coronel Urtecho founded the group Vanguardia in Managua. The idea that conversational poetry and the avant-garde are one and the same has also been proposed by Roberto Fernández Retamar (*Panorama de la actual literatura latinoamericana*). At any rate, the designation "avant-garde" is somewhat belated.

According to Pacheco, the introduction of North American poetry in Mexico was facilitated, in particular due to the influence of the three names previously mentioned [Novo, Henríquez Ureña, de la Selva], by the spirit of "nationalism without xenophobia" that flourished during the Obregón era and which, bearing out Vasconcelos's prophesies, promoted a kind of cultural "renaissance."

In Argentina and Chile, where the avant-garde movement that developed carried a clearly European stamp, the presence or influence of North American poetry came considerably later, and if there was conversational poetry, it was connected more to Europe, leaving aside the "sencillismo" that in truth has little to do with the avant-garde. If we think of Alberti Girri, very "North-Americanized"—although belatedly—and difficult to incorporate into the avant-garde, we can see that conversational poetry was excluded from his literary expression. It is more likely, instead, that Nicanor Parra's colloquialism stems from that source.

The interesting aspect of this line of inquiry is the relationship that is established between "nationalism" and "avant-garde," although what the nexus of the two terms consists of might be debatable, however infrequent such debate might be.

One important question to consider is this: in the case of avant-garde movements, what sense or emphasis does the old relationship of cultural dependence between Europe and America take on? Is it the same as in the case of romanticism or modernism or naturalism?

First, we must approach the topic admitting that it is a constant and a depository of grave ideological questions, such as the tension between diachrony and synchrony.

Looking at it diachronically, the relationship of dependence has not always been manifested in the same way; the adherence to European models has varied, and with that variation, we can say that the ideologization of the models has also changed.

The fact that there exists a Latin American avant-garde that stems from a process specific to Latin America (Vallejo, Macedonio Fernández, de Rokha) and that at the same time serves as a guide or model for Latin American avant-garde movements—Eurocentric, it is true—modifies somewhat the terms of the present scheme of "dependence" and forces us to reconsider its scope once again.

In this respect, Héctor Libertella points out that "the American avant-garde movements have managed to just barely connect with other avant-garde movements in an extreme point of contact; they have all drawn closer to an investigative and critical atmosphere that demands the repositioning of traditionally accepted limits and functions: the attack on literary forms 'naturalized' by social convention, the uncovering of that local materiality as a way to defend a text-object that avoids the given custom of exchange and destroys that materiality."[3]

Reconsideration of the American approach is valuable in this response, which does not eliminate the current way of looking at the phenomenon, according to which the "circumstance" (which, if it does not define "the national," at least integrates it) forces us to see as aberrant a language that wants to "free" itself from that circumstance. In this struggle, an analogy is established: "avant-garde equals cosmopolitanism"—which, when it is proposed as an explanation, hampers the ability to see a more complex order of productive relations between the avant-garde and nationalism, as the first paragraphs of this work claims might exist.

At any rate, insofar as economic underdevelopment continues to exist, all problematization of objectives from a "productive" perspective, that is, all avant-garde movements, will be conflictive—either because they reach beyond the limitations that the medium imposes, or because they endeavor to guide or lead what cannot be—and therefore does not want to be—avant-garde, or because they become isolated in what at first glance appears to be technological pretension. But the same thing could be said about modernism, also a kind of avant-gardism in its own way.

It is not necessary to view the array of avant-garde experiences as if history were linear, made up of perfect links in a chain: "after" cubism "comes" dadaism and "then" ultraism. There is, certainly, a chronology, but that does not necessarily assume a clear historical articulation, and even less, a causality from experience to experience. In order to historicize, it is necessary to try to understand not only the programs of each avant-garde experience but also the elements that are effectively put into play, and similarly, the significance of their appearance.

This last seems particularly clear if, for one thing, we think of Latin American "nationalism" as being situated in the appropriate climate for the emergence of forms of expression, and for another, of its receptivity to external influences— or finally, if we take into account Spanish *ultraísmo,* generally considered to be an attempt to fit the Hispanic rhythm to the rhythm of modern art (which would not be anything new for Spain, either).

In this regard, one cannot stop thinking of Gaudí or Lezama Lima: avant-garde, naturally, but avant-garde through a kind of representation—or imagination of what is represented—that seems to deny modernity. This would show that besides the general frameworks for understanding the avant-garde, there are concrete concepts that go so far as to establish avant-garde movements by denying the contributions of other avant-garde groups.[4] In this respect, Julio Ortega points out that "that is the peculiarity of avant-garde writing in our language. In opposition to the dadaist and surrealist models of writing, its texts and its practices raise their own model, a paradigm formulated from the tensions and promises of our own culture."[5]

From which comes, once again, the idea that we must consider the phenomenon in a dialectical manner and let go of the prejudice that the Latin American avant-garde is pure Europeanism, a thesis that, deep-down, is populist.

The presence (in some cases thematic, in others structural) of the referential elements "modern" and "mechanical" in almost all avant-garde movements can make one think that the avant-garde is a phenomenon of civilization, impossible to conceive of in previous eras—a direction that Ortega y Gasset's reflections take (*The Dehumanization of Art*). Contrary to this, one could think that the attitude of rupture, which would be a constant and a prerequisite for all avant-gardes, and which would also be present in previous literary moments (Lautréamont, according to Kristeva, is an example of the poetry of rupture),[6] would no longer be the defining element of the avant-garde.

This conclusion would shift the axis from the semiotic to the semantic, since the "rupture" would be seen as an "element" and not as a "condition" of production. If, on the other hand, we are to salvage this concept, we must broaden that of the avant-garde, going beyond what seems like a characteristic of a particular era (ours), since there have always been "conditions of production"; the noun "avant-garde" could give rise to an adjective, "avant-gardist," applicable to all experience that tends to alter certain codes.

On the other hand, according to Huidobro, "the modern" is only a prolongation of "the natural": from the eye to the photograph, from the ear to the telephone, from vocal cords to the gramophone, there is an artificial series that parallels the natural one. If we add to this relationship something that Huidobro did not mention, namely, the role that space plays and that marks the fundamental differences of the era (in architecture and in urban planning, but also in a new sociability of public places that is essentially spatial in nature), we confirm its existence. What is more, we could say not only that modernity is a moment in which multiple artificial prolongations of nature exist, but also that this transformation is guarded and protected by a clear consciousness of its existence, simultaneously upheld by all sorts of spatial redistributions.

And another thing: the avant-garde, as a phenomenon of an era, would also become a manifestation of the conscience of that era—or of some of those who endeavored to be its spokespeople—in terms of the parallelism (sought for centuries) that developed between nature and human invention. However, as a concrete realization or as a formal proposal, a considerable number of avant-garde expressions (futurism and its sequels, all of the constructivisms in general, etc.) seem to have distanced themselves considerably from the natural. Did these avant-garde movements, either because they wished to do so or proclaimed that they were doing so, eliminate these remnants of nature from their articulation?

If we think about the relationship established between Cézanne and cubism, or about Gaudí, or even about Apollinaire's *Calligrammes,* this idea of Huidobro's about prolongation is evidently confirmed, especially since the *Calligrammes* (and their *ultraísta* manifestations in Argentina) suggest an even more profound relationship between nature and construction: they attempt to show how the physical form of a poem not only reproduces a natural or cultural form, a mountain or an airplane, but also that by making an opening for the unconscious to act, they should produce a natural, or at least significant form at the juncture between nature and production. It is clear that we could ask ourselves, leaving Lacan aside for the moment, to which sphere does the unconscious belong—the natural or the cultural?

Jaime Concha has observed that "the case of futurism in Leninist Russia and in prefascist Italy is one of the most famous for its ties to the political options of those societies."[7]

Playing with this assertion, we can show that on the one hand, Russian futurism preceded Leninism without really becoming entangled with it, and, on the other hand, while Italian futurism was perhaps originally equally prefascist, later it was indeed fascist. Furthermore, in reality the only thing the two movements had in common was the name, although due to the respective relationships that they developed with the aforementioned structures, the following question arises: historically, what is the relationship that existed and that exists now between the avant-garde—in all its manifestations—and politics?

The nature of the problem is this: the desire for change that characterizes the avant-garde not only seems to be in homologous relation with political projects that also seek change, but is also destined to become enmeshed with them. It is not surprising then that the majority of avant-garde manifestations have declared themselves to be "leftist," that their members have indeed been involved in leftist politics, and that their literary manifestations have almost always introduced a political dimension into the final interpretation of the implications of their project.

But they have also been connected to the "right" as well, primarily through the decisions or evolution of some of their adherents (Marinetti, Dalí, and others), not to the original programs of the avant-garde strictly speaking. But this is less important than determining whether or not the original project of the avant-garde movements in general and in particular, once implemented, necessarily implies an obligatory relationship with the political left, or if it is possible or conceivable to have an ideological neutrality that can move to either side depending on the circumstances or the evolution of adherents after the conception of the avant-garde idea or the development of programs that work with that idea. In fact, it is more likely that certain non-avant-garde endeavors, such as costumbrismo, are actually much more suitable for political uses, whether on the left or the right.

We must make it clear, therefore, that what a work claims to do is one thing, while the utilization to which it might be put later is another. In terms of the avant-garde, certain conditions must exist in order for it to be utilized. The first is that in some way the avant-garde must have triumphed; the second is that the state must carry out certain activities or actions that tend to incorporate triumphant movements with the aim of using them as a tool to augment, or in contrary cases, to reduce, their scope. This was the case with expressionism in Nazi Germany, suggesting the productivity of the avant-garde as an image in that country after the First World War.

It would be most prudent to say that an avant-garde gesture that wishes to be founded on an analysis of the culture will attempt to be coherent with a political logic of change, although at times the political expression will not be understood this way, creating a rift, as occurred during the Stalinist era in the USSR. It also depends on the structural crisis whose nature may or may not support questioning, as well, of course, as any attempts to bring the two series of changes or the two logics closer together. This last point introduces the Latin American question: what is it that, during a crisis, favors the emergence of avant-garde movements, and what relation might these movements have to any political modifications taken in response to the crisis?

In truth, in almost all avant-garde movements there is an ideological element that tends toward anarchy, which explains up to a point the suspicion these movements tend to generate both in the left and the right, as well as in people's "common sense" in general. In this respect, we can consider the curious relationships that developed between Trotsky and Breton,[8] and Diego Rivera's on again–off again relationship with the Communist Party and Trotskyism, as well as the evolution of Communist Party attitudes toward avant-garde movements in general, such as the rejection of such movements manifested by hard-line political regimes, except, of course, the possibility previously discussed that such regimes might appropriate something from these movements, as might have occurred, for example, with futurist architecture. As a contrast, we can think of the Bauhaus school as a form of avant-garde, and note the reception given to its masters in the United States, taking advantage of everything the Germans had sacrificed.

Renato Poggioli has observed that the avant-garde tends to flourish in a climate of political *agitation*, although this is not necessarily valid in the case of Latin America, as proven by Argentine ultraísmo, which grew out of a period of prosperity. Nevertheless, the idea of a political context that favors the emergence of such movements suggests a new kind of problem: that of the autonomy of art and the relation that is established between the two planes. In one of them, the plane of art, things can be achieved that for the other, the political plane, while it certainly seeks the same finality for itself and for the whole, are simply a dream or mere proclamation or postulation.[9]

The word "avant-garde" comes from a military metaphor. It can be analyzed according to its origin: "to go before." But to go before with respect to what? To a column, to a body that, by a similar metaphor we can call "tradition" or "establishment." But that going before is not merely, as it is in an army, to set a course; rather, it establishes a "break" with respect to what remains behind: the avant-garde form is adopted in order to break with what remains behind and even to shatter what preceded it.

Actually, this attempt to "go before" is almost always translated into a kind of renovation, and the rupture is generally temporary; there is usually reconciliation with the avant-garde, as perhaps can be seen in the history of the relationship between ultraísmo (Borges) and modernism (Lugones). According to Héctor Libertella this idea redistributes the avant-garde movements into "two coexisting *avant-gardes:* one, which rests on a certain theoretical device, encourages the fantasy of a critical 'evolution' (the avant-garde as a series of consecutive steps); on the other hand, its shadow restores the Greek myth of the ruse, pretending to function in the body of society as if hidden in a Trojan horse, and, while awaiting the moment of deception when it will break loose, comes to understand its disguise."[10] Very well, leaving aside this bifurcation, what do we mean by "evolution" here? For Tynianov, literary evolution revolves around the creation of new functions for the formal elements of a text.[11] Is there "evolution," historically speaking, after the practice of the avant-garde? In what sense can it be said, and it is indeed said, that it is impossible to return to the point where Vallejo or Borges began? Are there new functions that are definitively incorporated into the corpus of literary discourse?

But if subjectively the intention of rupture, of "beginning from zero" (which if it does not absolutely negate the past, at least questions and attacks it) predominates, we understand, then, that all avant-garde movements propose a strategy—a word that, in order to return to a previous point, not only implies a disruption but also indicates that it is preparing a plan with a final goal in mind, with an arrangement of tactics, with a marshaling of resources and a time line. In one sense, everything that characterizes this strategy agrees with the idea of a rupture that comes only with a struggle, without polemics, in order to unite semantic fields and allow characterizations of behavior.[12]

It is understood, therefore, that there are common and recurring characteristics in the behavior of all avant-garde movements that stem not so much from similar designs but from a shared strategic position. These characteristics could be

- a proclivity to form solidarity groups, almost clans, with fights over leadership positions and the distribution of women and/or men
- a radical critical position that apparently is irreconcilable and destructive
- the production of manifestos and the emergence of proposals that parody and replace the previous precepts
- participation in extraliterary actions, gestures, or riots as moral expressions of a superior ethic
- the creation of journals that harness the nervous energy of the struggle, in addition to the production of books.

Admitting that reality, as a contest of strength or as a system that resists alteration, imposes or has imposed limits on basic proposals and corresponding compromises, strategy tends to adjust itself until it admits that "mere" innovation in the "merely" literary can be or is an end in itself. It is a question of compromises, which can also be seen as "betrayals," because that first moment of establishment of a strategy generally implies the postulation of a "new world," articulated from the literary word.

In this new, almost fatal, perspective of literary "innovation" (almost fatal, but not submissive—it is as if there were slight lapses in the strategy), precisely because it is not foreseen, language undergoes two types of operations:

a. *des*-truction—prosodic, syntactic, and semantic
b. *dis*-covery of what is covered up and adulterated by the culture against which innovation struggles.

A primary and very generalized aim of verbal "creation" can be linked to the first of these strategic aspects in an implicit dialectic, since all destruction includes its opposite. And for its part, within strategy itself the compromise that will alter that strategy may be hidden.

Concrete verbal action guides the two principal perspectives of the avant-garde strategy—innovation and a new world—but the paths that it takes are in turn also double: (1) intuition and (2) analysis and the establishment of procedures.

Most likely, these two operations (destruction and discovery) and these two paths differentiate all of the various approaches of avant-garde art, including the creationists. In terms of the two paths, the intuitive one is translated by the scream, the choice of unintelligibility, the opportune place for the appearance of drives, the affirmation of the health that exists in sickness, and so on, while the analytical path is translated by a restoration of syntax, planning, the manifestation of intentions that have to do with society and politics, and respect for the instance of power.

Getting back to a point discussed earlier, it seems that the idea of rupture is a decisive trait of the avant-garde. All avant-gardism, of course, is a kind of rupture, although not all rupture is avant-garde. Stating this implies a critical act of distancing with respect to a common truism or an assumption generally accepted as necessary. On the other hand, the rupture that defines the avant-garde, or avant-gardes, is never, or almost never, simply the rupture of a poetic system. Furthermore, perhaps not even those who propose such a thing are able to effectively create a rupture in the political system against which they struggle, but the decision of rupture, which they never cease to formulate, goes beyond this and reaches the culture itself (only literary culture?), whose economy may be altered (in the case of success) or may remain untouched.

It must be seen how the culture (in general) is affected by the avant-garde intention of rupture, and which aspects of the culture would feel the most impact. One possible answer might be those aspects most weakened by the crisis. Correspondingly, what would the terms of the semiological conflict be if this does indeed occur? For a "semiological-transcendental" aspect, such as the one proposed by Juan Larrea, the work *Ecuatorial* by Vicente Huidobro can be compared to the Apocalypse.[13] As evidence, he mentions various indications of the "end of the world" (or of culture) in the works of different poets.

Considering the avant-garde in this double direction of rupture, either of the poetic system or of the culture, and taking it as a given that it is this way, perhaps the philosophy behind the powerful avant-garde impulse of this century is not so much Nietzscheian as a generic neo-Hegelianism that illuminates the semiotic avant-garde gesture: attack and destruction (negation) in order to make space for a new creation.

This last objective—adopted and proclaimed by a few critics—might be the ultimate objective desired, even though its expression is suppressed in almost all cases. Why suppressed? Because once it is established that words, due to their implacable semantic energy, influence and fix meaning (thereby impeding the dialectical moment of pure creation, since pure creation should be done with new words but has to be done with existing, familiar ones), the avant-garde adopts the following options:

    a. Re-dis-cover original semantic nuclei, or meanings, concealed, blocked, or closed off by the culture against which they struggle (this was the route adopted by Gaudí and surrealism, and in part would also become the focus of the search by the *ultraístas* and even by César Vallejo).

    b. Parody the usual structures in an attempt to create an empty zone in which there is no affirmation (Lezama Lima).

    c. Invent words for one's poems (Huidobro, Girondo) or extend their functions (as Vallejo did at times when he would make verbs out of nouns or conjunctions).

Looking at things from a different perspective, if the avant-garde project rests on—or rises from—a desire for "rupture" that is never satisfied, perhaps because the semantic and syntactic instances remain standing, and if syntax is what configures the plane of "articulation" par excellence, the principal problem of the avant-garde becomes the appropriate "articulation of desire," which, in turn, cannot be seen as such but rather as a metaphor, while the expression "articulation of desire" itself is projected in another direction, without taking into account that, as an expression, it itself is metaphorical. It is not surprising, then, that "metaphor," speaking rhetorically, appears as the concretized but also idealized vehicle (idealized in that it is experienced as what gives form and explains). And from there, a shower of metaphors is produced, an accumulation, one on top of the other, in some avant-garde expressions. That is, it appears as a kind of "abundance" that of course conceals a radical lack: the unsatisfied presence of desire, the lack of fulfillment of its demands. Perhaps this is where the isolation of the avant-garde resides, or the generalized feeling, in this respect, of unintelligibility, of incompleteness.

As for the aspect of avant-garde "criticism," we must make a preliminary clarification that goes beyond the conventional sense of the word. The adjectival sense of the word—"criticism" in the romantic tradition—is one thing, and a critical capacity as a "bringing into crisis"—in the Socratic tradition—is another. This second variety is what the avant-garde tries to examine and elaborate, as idea and as operation.

And how does one bring about this bringing into crisis in literature? Precisely by criticizing, in concrete textuality, the neutralizing pretension of universality that literature generally establishes for itself—in short, a certain ideology in which literature takes refuge, inexorably granting itself this in certain moments. This critique comes into play via two ideas:

- the denunciation of the clear, declaratively restrictive character of the code used, for example a certain rhetoric or certain formal demands or a certain imagined universe
- the act of emphasizing the "legal act" of writing, uncovering its procedures and making its operation material.

The value and attraction of this focus lies in that it allows the examination not only of that which the avant-garde struggles against but also of the avant-garde itself, in that the avant-garde can also come to essentialize its criticism (and indeed it has done so), naturalize its program, and transfer its results (whose success can come from circumstances that are diverse but not necessary) to its proposals, which in this way, would come to appear universalized in their products.

But it is also a fact that the mere appearance of the avant-garde implies the manifestation and development of a criticism—of which the avant-garde itself will then become a victim after a certain length of time. It forces us to consider the concept of the "old," but at the same time, its own inevitable aging draws the gaze of its criticism back to itself. The current "revivals," of expressionism, for example, would be nothing more than the opportunity to view, with a critical but calm—not agitated—eye, movements that implied the staging of a critique with the aim of observing it beyond its moment. An ambiguous gesture, and perhaps a slightly perverse one, since it would be a homage to what is perhaps still living, within what is surely dead.

Within avant-garde movements, internally, there is a kind of struggle between concepts that are sometimes antagonistic but that suggest a transition between conflicting terms, such as, for example, between verbal automatism (free) and verbal control (restricted). If dadaism almost completely embodies the first term, and expressionism the second (to the extent that a program models an esthetic), then surrealism would be a synthesis of the two, presenting itself as "controlled automatism," even in the case of Oliverio Girondo's work.

All the same, these conflicting concepts encompass other conflicting pairs: irrationality and rationality would be one of the most notorious. Here again surrealism synthesizes the two insofar as there exists in that movement a clear consciousness of the existence of the unconscious (which would reproduce the fundamental gesture of psychoanalysis and explain the historic connections between both states), whose manifestations it attempts to understand and explain, and to convert into esthetic material and truth.

Similarly, but on another plane, we can note in the preceding two sections a process of differentiation in another relationship: that between "I" and "not-I," which in turn gives rise to a new differentiation between the "lyrical" and the "geometrical."

Of course most likely there is no pure "lyric" or "geometric" expression, but rather an intermingling of both registers beyond their intentions: in America, ultraísmo would be this unintentional point of encounter.

This intermingling is precisely the interesting part insofar as it puts into play a concept inherent in literature, beyond the scope of avant-garde or realist "intention." This allows us to escape from the narrow sense of the term (which would be something like a chapter in the history of literature) in order to try to understand what a particular experience means from the point of view of the development of writing understood as a broader area of concern.

Can we generalize about the *language* of the avant-garde? First of all, as with other terms and aspects, we need to pluralize: *languages*. Then, we must come to some agreement about the meaning of this word: closer to "parole" than to "langue," language would be the idiomatic realization, but restricted to an experience or a social sphere in which the stylistic element is a decisive one. Or perhaps it would after all be more convenient to call this language "discourse"; this concept encompasses more instances related to a specific and precise production. Thus, we would say "avant-garde discourse," or in plural, "avant-garde discourses."

Second, there are those who differentiate between "poetry" and "poetic discourse." Tristan Tzara conceives of poetry as a spiritual *activity* and not as a *means* of expression.[14] This phrase raises a number of issues: first of all, the notion of the philosophical background, like the idea of an essence—poetry—as something active in the Hegelian sense; second, there is the problem of expression as imperative but incidental; and third, there is the question of what is missing, the affective content attributed to poetry. Most likely, the reaction against this way of thinking and the rejection of this spiritual "activity" was at the root of the cubist rupture, and it continued, at least partially, into ultraísmo.

But even if one professes the preeminence of "poetry" over "discourse," as a question of one being more important than the other (which would, furthermore, suppose a very special and hierarchized process, although that would raise the question of the basis of such a hierarchy: would it be through philosophical recognition? or psychological identification? or via the manipulation of a system for hierarchizing values?), poetry could not dispense with "discourse," which should always be the object of a description that should always, of course, make its starting point clear.

We can find a description of avant-garde "discourse" in the aforementioned work by Julio Ortega, "La escritura de la vanguardia." According to Ortega, in the avant-garde articulation, we can find a fluctuation between harmony and schism as an all-encompassing characteristic of diverse experiences in which first one concept predominates, and then the other.

It would seem that on this point we must work with very general categories. For example, from the perspective of a theory of enunciation, there would be a search for the conflict with the utterance from the moment in which an absolute agreement would mean the elimination of all metalanguage. In this sense, we can recall belletrism, a later, radical experience, in whose texts the enunciation, even though it seems almost like a pure signifier without a signified, still includes a certain implicit declaration of its intention, and for its part, the utterance seems like a battleground of opposites: survival of expression or of emotionality, survival of the subjectivism of the anecdote and of description—a conflictive relationship at times between the kind of images used, as constructed objects, and the referent.

This returns us to the possibility of studying "discourses," examining, for example, the question of whether there is a predominance of certain types of images, what the component elements are of metaphor, and so on.[15] All the same, this perspective is limited if we assume that "writing" is a confluence of diverse instances and not only a realization. Let us examine other aspects.

With respect to "new meanings," the creation of words, which we discussed earlier, would be a primary and visible instrument, as, for example, distorted or destroyed words (dadaism), "portmanteau" words (Huidobro), or entirely new words (Huidobro or Girondo). And yet all the same, there are avant-garde movements that leave words be, neither attacking nor manipulating them.

Let us examine the first case: such innovative operations tend to recreate familiar linguistic or grammatical functions—the formation of nouns and verbs, and even poetic and discursive functions, such as rhyme (the effect of the aforementioned belletrism is based as much on the accumulation of senseless syllables as on the combining of this accumulation with an ironclad respect for "rich" rhyme).

But if "new meanings" arise from this, they cannot be understood except in relation to the old ones, that is, through general linguistic competency. From the most radical position, insofar as the writer postulates that he is producing a new world, one can think, at least partially, of totally new meanings, arising from an almost mechanical relationship (due to its directness and lineal nature) between reality and sign.

One theoretical approach that can be inferred from this scheme tends toward the prophetic, reclaiming an older function of poetry. We can find this in Juan Larrea's discussions of Vallejo: according to him, the avant-garde is, or would be, a mystic "revelation" that, through Vallejo, poets undertake in order to counter not so much a language in crisis but a culture in crisis.[16] We can say the same, more cautiously, about Martí. The point of departure for this prophetic attitude would be symbolism and the destruction of the past as a necessary act of purification.

The "creationism" practiced by Vallejo (*Trilce*) or Huidobro introduces the idea that an attempt at destruction such as this could perhaps take another direction: such a possibility would follow a reformulation of the signifier by a process of pulverization, and following that act (which runs the gamut from the simple construction of a word to a complex superimposition of the existing linguistic order), the installation of a graphic or sonic materiality that challenges the dominant logos—hence the compulsive or violently unintelligible, the antirational or antirationalist.

From a semantic point of view, however, avant-garde poetics could be defined as the relationship between what remains of tradition on the one hand and elements of social modernity on the other, all of which does not provide more than an external image of the phenomenon. We would have to find a productive code in such poetics, that is, we would need to see what is new on the level of semantic relationships, either through the way new syntactic relations are established, or, more specifically, through the system of the construction of images or of confrontations between current ideas on poetic articulation: sonority, rhythm, rhyme, metrics, and so on.

In his first *Manifesto of Surrealism*, originally written in 1924, André Breton wrote:

> SURREALISM, noun. Psychic automatism in its pure state, by which one proposes to express—verbally, by means of the written word, or in any other manner—the actual functioning of thought. Dictated by thought, in the absence of any control exercised by reason, exempt from any aesthetic or moral concern. [26]

Translating and clarifying these terms, we can say:

- Noun: Surrealism is a thing (implicitly material, not simply a literary approach)
- Psychic automatism in its pure state: an activity of the subconscious, without interference from the conscious
- Breton is trying to express something real
- Writing is not the only medium
- Thought is not the only activity of reason
- An esthetic or a moral are not the objectives or the limits of surrealism

This definition, more than any descriptions, underscores or suggests the contribution this avant-garde expression has made to a modern (transgressive) theory of writing.

Psychic automatism is a correlative of the irrationalism of the conscious, not the unconscious; insofar as thought seeks to express itself directly, it assumes one or several possible forms.

In a broad sense of avant-garde writing, considered such for its accumulation of characteristics and experiences, and thus using the term with all due caution, we could employ two organizing or classifying ideas:

- One, originating from an aspect of avant-garde theater—from Pirandello to Artaud and including Brecht—is that of "the theater within the theater." This formula, which is essentially modern even though it already appears in Shakespeare and which is to theatrical action what psychodrama is to "information" in psychoanalytic therapy, involves an important concept from the point of view of a theory of writing: the development outward of a movement that includes its own materiality. If this is indeed true, that is, if such development is a generalizable feature of avant-garde writing, we could try to examine what happens in other kinds of discourses, that is, investigate how the material structure of the discourse is included in the representation— or, to put it another way, how each discourse represents itself as well as representing whatever it is that provides it with an aspect of its identity as such. This way of thinking also appears in cubism via the device of illustrating the theme of the text with the arrangement of the physical words on the page. In this case, it is a question of a materialized "figuration," but only of a thematic universe. It is more difficult to conceive of "self-representation," except in suggestive theatrical discovery or in the more trivial area of ars poetica, in which it "says" what it believes the discourse is and also what it does.
- The other idea comes from a philosophy of "progress," conceived of as an active will that is manifested in one direction as "deconstruction" of the natural language, generally through an attack on naturalist-representative discourse, and in another direction, as the creation of new verbal structures, at times, as mentioned previously,

by creating new words, at times, as was also mentioned, by attempting to produce new meanings, and at times by defining verbal activity as the creation of objects.

But it is also possible to look at issues of avant-garde writing from another angle, one that is perhaps a variation of that just discussed, by asking a question, for example, about whether an exercising of self-consciousness in writing began with the avant-garde and whether, correspondingly, the avant-garde as such embodies that intention to make that self-consciousness explicit and productive.

One fact that would undoubtedly support this is poetic experimentation. In order to understand its importance—as part of the avant-garde and significant in that sense—it would be necessary to make use of a theory of poetic language. Such theories do exist; what we must see is if they help to understand an avant-garde project—that is, a furthering of the experimentation that they can describe or help to describe.

A second fact has to do with the reordering of syntax, for example, the predominance of metaphor over metonymy. This equation can perhaps explain the avant-garde "rupture" we spoke of earlier. From the moment in which metonymy yields and continuity is undermined, an experience of emptiness occurs without any apparent hope of recovering wholeness. A complimentary fact, in another syntactical sense, is that this rupture implies a fragmentation whose coherence is salvaged by an attempt at juxtaposition, and in particular, an attempt at montage, a concept that is linked, on the other hand, to technoartistic "modernity" as this concept is used in film.[17] Here a connection is established with narrative: an articulated object that structuralism reconstructs as articulated, recovering—or superimposing—apparent unities arrayed on multiple planes, the fragmentation of linearity, the absence of connections, and the montage of structures.

Finally, if writing is established as specialization, its trace, its outline, can be an act of signification when, as was mentioned earlier in this section, we speak of "self-representation." That writing may be either deliberate or involuntary, but when it is the latter, a problem of interpretation arises.

Beneath the Sign of the Baroque

It is a well-known fact, clearly established by literary historians, that narrative writing developed belatedly in Latin America—not so belatedly, however, that the development of the European bourgeois novel and short story were not noticed, at least from a distance. The delay, or nonexistence, of a narrative tradition should be considered in relation to the narrative development of the Spanish Golden Age or narrative development in Europe in general during the eighteenth century. In the nineteenth century, Latin America developed various responses to Europe, characterized, it is true, by a certain chronological disjunction. In effect, the fact that there was no narrative tradition during the colonial era eliminates the idea of a process of narrative development at that time, but concurrently, it creates more and better conditions for an adherence to models. If indeed it is true that the earliest appearances of an embryonic narrative (*The Itching Parrot* [*El periquillo sarniento*; 1816–1830]) by José Joaquín Fernández de Lizardi, for example, or the basically unedited novels of education by the priest Rodríguez from Córdoba)[1] possess an interesting inflection of "newness" overcoming a secular inertia, the common feature that runs through them is a certain distant neoclassicism that quickly becomes antiquated without any productive possibilities. The novel or the short story started to develop its own truly American characteristics during the romantic period, and at that point, the real process of narrative was initiated and began to evolve.

Furthermore, some of the issues or problems that appear in texts such as *Amalia* [1855] by José Mármol, for example, do not disappear or, if that is too strong a statement, take a long time to disappear, and instead, they confer a certain continuity of various profound notarial and philosophical concerns of the continent, such as, for example, the dichotomies "rural versus urban" or "dialect versus linguistic universality." But neither does this mean that the continent was relegated to the margins as concerns writing during the preceding centuries: the colonial era is rich in testimonies to the contrary. And these in turn, as in the case of Sor Juana Inés de la Cruz, established another class of approaches, perhaps just as profound and suggestive as the others, or at least infused with renewing reflections such as, in particular, that approach linked to the concept of the baroque. To put it briefly before moving on, colonial literature, as a particularly baroque one, tends to be viewed as the source and the origin of what would be more properly American, while those aspects that developed from the narrative writing of the nineteenth century would have more to do with a modern, constituent, almost capitalist and practical schema, contrary to the "necessity" that pervades baroque expression.

Now since the lack of a process would determine this condition, from its initial manifestations up to the present day, Latin American narrative has above all been sensitive to a model that we could call "realist" and that links together a vast and varied series of narratives. The model that predominates to the point of being considered the "very nature of narration," it constructs another story, that of narrative itself, and allows us to see the chronological disjunction with what occurs in the productive center. For example, realism developed as a reaction to romantic expression, but when realism appeared in Latin America, romanticism had already evolved at its original source almost as much as had what we technically refer to as "realism," strictly speaking, and even naturalism. Yet the chronological disjunction is not so absolute, and there are moments of a contemporaneity so marked that one cannot help reflecting on the intuition of Latin American writers who were able to capture immediately the contemporary form of the model. However, this is not as important as the fact that this permanent realism stems from a model, and furthermore, that the model has such a powerful draw that for many it has become synonymous with a "how it should be" in Latin American narrative. I would like to emphasize here an aspect of this issue that would tend to explain its enduring organizing force: realism supposes, in terms of a narrative attitude—that is, in terms of the preeminence of point of view over other elements of narration—a fascination with the "other," with studied and deciphered "alterity," the enigma one believes in and feels can be reached through a self-confident gaze. From this point of view, the gaze, the point of view, what technically is referred to as the "narrator," appears to harbor no doubts about its identity and instead allows one to be dazzled by a natural world, by a society, and by a culture that has not yet taken form and to whose morphology the narrator will contribute. A number of well-known ethical considerations spring from this, which have provided narrative with an extraordinarily dense presence and weight in the cultural life of our societies that perhaps does not exist in other places. Be that as it may, if the other exists, uncontrolled, then narration, through knowledge of that other (via description, diverse actions, typical or representative characters, defining themes), attempts a socializing appropriation established from the outset through a direct appeal to the members of the community—that is, the readers. As a consequence, we could say that the realist attitude, in its exultant discovery of the other, seeks its effects from a first reading, a basic condition of a broadening of its sphere of action in which the cognizant motor of desire communicates and concentrates its power.

However, what we are designating as the other here cannot be reduced to a world that claims or demands an identity under construction, a world that in daily life only shows the incomprehensibly disordered aspect—chaotic and dramatic (for the narrators)—of such claims and demands. This can also be applied to the possibilities inherent in writing (fervently believed in), conceived of as the capacity to transform visible wretchedness (which must be explored through "description") into imaginary glory, a project that allows us to understand not only Sarmiento's *Facundo* [*Facundo, o civilización y barbarie* (*Facundo: Civilization and Barbarism*; 1845)], but also *The Eagle and the Serpent* [*El águila y la serpiente*; 1928] by Martín Luis Guzmán or *Doña Barbara* [1929] by

Rómulo Gallegos, as well as Arguedas's *Deep Rivers* [*Los ríos profundos*; 1958] or *The Seven Madmen* [*Los siete locos*; 1929] by Roberto Arlt. It is a question of obtaining, through writing, great riches out of poverty as a way to resolve the constantly renewed enigma of social or national identity.

Here it is important to keep in mind that while the realist perspective may predominate, it is not the only element in the mosaic that is, and has been for many years, Latin American narrative. I am looking for a way to understand the diversifications in a more general and essential sense, rather than in terms of such obvious aspects as the historical tale, *costumbrismo, indigenismo,* the political or protest novel, or the social novel. In this sense, if this continuing realism stems from a foreign model, this diversity could perhaps be understood through the application of a model that in its place of origin was antithetical or incompatible. And, if we are talking of realism, we can also legitimately think of "idealism" as well, of which European literature, certainly, and literature in general provide very powerful and visible evidence. It could undoubtedly be confirmed that this tendency, whose definition would stem from a philosophical metaphor, infuses the corpus of western literature with the same energy as its antagonist and complement, although the designations could be rather confusing if we consider that the corresponding philosophical concepts have their mechanical development in those texts that we designate with one or the other of these terms. It seems to me that one way to avoid becoming entangled in this overpowering web would be to state what in the narrative is understood by one or another designation. Or better yet, to define what is essential in their respective articulations, remembering that in concrete texts, at times, powerful contradictions exist between the narrative gesture and the philosophical support such that a realist text, because of the particular relationship between point of view and description, would be perfectly capable of postulating an idealist world, something that frequently occurs in romantic and even naturalist expression. Conversely, a text designated as idealist may not be so in the philosophical sense, in that it may postulate, as is the case with Joyce's *Ulysses,* a predominance of the signifier.

Be that as it may, we could also say that if the force of the other extended throughout realism, then idealism may have as its axis the drive of the "one," that is, a kind of narrative in which the fundamental aspect of writing occurs in the field of the "I" that narrates and not in the object narrated, a perspective that places all of its focus on the narcissism of narration. This may imply at times passing through uncertainty and doubt, and at times the manifestation, via diverse forms and subtle means, of a consciousness that must recognize itself, affirm itself, and search for itself in the execution of the narrative. To put it in more or less psychoanalytic terms, in this category of narrative account, drives are situated in a "here and now" of "what should be narrated"—as much Eros as Thanatos—while in realism, it would seem that everything is further away in a "hereafter," a spectacle with no return, permanent departure, a designation.

The curious thing is that this second model never took root in Latin America, or at least it never overshadowed the first one, and it never really became an option, although in one case it was proposed as an almost absolute opposition—I am referring to Macedonio Fernández, the beginning and end of this possibility. Modernism, on the other hand, which is frequently placed in a similar category, or certain moments of the avant-garde, do not fit within this other possibility and are not good examples, since from a historical perspective they actually embody a search for writing rather than for the consciousness of the *subject* of the writing, whose identity, in idealism, is or would be, if not unstable, at least problematic in the very realm of narrative economy.

But this absence does not mean that we cannot think of an effective alternative that would organize an assortment of differential or differentiating sensations. In my opinion, a large number of texts that do not fit on the realist axis could be grouped beneath another concept, that of the baroque, which, more than any other, is aware of what unites such texts and gives them their local feel—namely, responding in a unique way to human and social needs of different but clearly deeply rooted sorts.

I am aware of the difficulties that the use of such a word involves. For the moment, and by virtue of an enormous concentration of critical energy produced in recent years, it seems to define several very particular works, such as those of José Lezama Lima. Furthermore, the term "baroque" is related to a glorious—and orthodox—antecedent, that of Sor Juana Inés de la Cruz, an example that would form a very substantive arc between both names in relation to a Latin American capacity that is very deeply rooted, not only in certain narrative processes, but also in permanent, constant, and initial geographic, geologic, and spiritual conditions. Appearing during the era of Sor Juana (who was almost miraculous in her genius) but very much linked to a Spanish notarial system, the baroque sensibility would reappear later in the works of others, almost intact, in "what is" and in absence. I would prefer, however, to leave this focus behind, above all so as not to get caught up in the objections that can undoubtedly arise from the use of such a specific term—easy objections to raise, since clearly not everything that is not orthodox realism is Lezama Lima or Sarduy or Carpentier or Asturias or Guimarães Rosa or Arturo Cerretani.

In order to focus on the term, let me begin by saying that if in realism the other, as an enigma to be deciphered, determines the structure and the writing separately, what I am going to call baroque establishes a lively dialectic between the *desire of writing*, the *pursuit of the other*, and the problematic of structure, as if what is emphasized in realism will find a place to interweave itself and textualize itself. To this assembly, which to me seems very present and active in a text such as Lezama Lima's *Paradiso* [1966] (in which the theory of the image does not exclude a problematic of narration nor an investigation into what is Cuban), we can add what would be a contribution to the idealist argument, namely, the examination of the "one" as the consciousness of the narrator (as can be found in texts such as *El perro de la escribana* [The Scribe's Dog; 1980] by María Luisa Mendoza, an excellent example of its application: not to narrate a "way" but rather to narrate in an eternally fragmented point of view). These four planes establish a complex articulation that in its turn demands an adequate linguistic actualization. It is not a question, when looking at the texts in which we can find such an articulation, of reducing it or restraining it, but of admitting it as a whole, situated before the gaze of the reader, demanding, fundamentally, a deciphering that we could call a "rereading," referring not to the difficulty of the text but to the possibility of textual action whose presence can be sensed in the first reading, and which plays out its effects in an "afterward," namely, in the second reading, to which one must incessantly return.

It is in this sense that the term "baroque" becomes useful, because the reciprocal action of the four planes is generally resolved by such typical baroque procedures as the effect of mass over that of the line, the effect of the spiral, the curve, the pictorial, parodical intertextuality, ellipsis, disguise, and chiaroscuro. But if, as it seems, the classic baroque also includes a conceptista[2] facet (since not all baroque is Góngora, although it is not all Gracián either), another element is introduced into this widely employed concept, a rational element, one of balance, that gives rise to the appearance of or concern for structures, despite all the linguistic explosivity found in the term. And this double facet (which is present even in Lezama Lima's *Oppiano Licario* [1977] and in a more watered-down form in María Luisa Mendoza, in whose work the phrase predominates over the story) allows the inclusion of works as apparently dissimilar or that have such apparently different aims as Roa Bastos's *I, the Supreme* [*Yo el supremo*; 1974], Borges's *Ficciones* [1944], Juan José Saer's *Nobody Nothing Never* [*Nadie nada nunca*; 1980], Hugo Hiriart's *Galaor* [1972], Arturo Cerretani's *Matar a Titilo* [Kill Titilo], José Emilio Pacheco's *You Will Die in a Distant Land* [*Morirás lejos*; 1978] and Juan Carlos Onetti's *Body Snatcher* [*Juntacadáveres*; 1964].

These works are too dissimilar, one might say, and thus the label I have tried to put them all under appears too vague, forced, imprecise. But of all the objections, the one I consider most important is this: that too many categories converge to be able to create a schema that most likely is not even necessary. Too many categories and too few, since if we accept for the moment that there is some systematic relationship between, at the very least, the texts mentioned, we would then have to establish a whole system of secret connections and dissimilarities that would still not destroy the whole arrangement, and I have not really done that. All the same, I keep feeling that the condition I have described of a "rereading" being indispensable and also inherent in many texts that are not realist, or that challenge realism, repositions many things and constitutes the basis of many fractures, confrontations, and readjustments that make up the most interesting and lively part of modern Latin American narrative. For example, we could say that if a text limits itself—or rather, is limited—to only one reading, then reading, as an activity, ceases and, concomitantly, the writing that generates and provokes reading also ceases, creating a serious problem for our culture. A rereading, and the texts that demand it, open the way to a decentering of all configurations—of the subject with respect to itself and of the object in all its possibilities. For this reason, it is only from a perspective that takes *this* idea of the baroque into account that we can think on the one hand of a relationship of writing to reading that transcends the excess with which it occurs, the sickly proliferation of the word that startles, and on the other hand, of new forms of narration through which the very notion of the short story or the novel, common and conventional, can give way to "narration" in the strict sense of the word, the "narrative gesture" that emerges from words and is embodied in totalities, before which "representation" and "reflection" appear to be little more than pale inventions of some intellectual laboratory.

Similarly, if realism was the preferred site in which to house more or less vague concepts connected with ideology, I would dare to assert that a grouping like the one proposed could come to see more clearly an "ideological action" that determines and gives form to writing, but which goes unnoticed in a first reading because attention is devoted to other things. But this is not because by rereading one can see the ideology better, but rather because a rereading, under the conditions in which it becomes just that, is also the location or the object of the ideological action in such a way that the texts that demand a rereading ask to be revealed and thus have the opportunity to show what they are composed of and formed from. From this exposition and because of its existence, the ideological action begins to be neutralized, the phantom of facility is cleared away, and the type of meaning begins to emerge that can start building a culture through its literature insofar as it manages to see the shape of the determining "ideological action." Somehow Lezama Lima tells us this in *Oppiano Licario,* in the midst of his verbal jungle:

> Only the difficult is stimulating; only the resistance that challenges us is capable of confronting, provoking, and maintaining our potential for understanding, but in reality, what is that which is difficult? Only what is submerged in the maternal waters of darkness? That which gives origin without causality, antithesis, or logos? It is the form that occurs in which a scene moves toward a meaning, an interpretation, or a simple hermeneutic, in order to then move toward its reconstruction, which is what definitely marks its usefulness or its obsolescence, its powerful strength or its pale echo, which is its historic vision. Here then is where we find the difficulty of meaning and historic vision. Meaning, or the discovery of a causality regulated by historicist values. Historic vision, which is the counterpoint or tapestry provided by the image, by the image that participates in history.[3]

In other words, texts arranged along the four dimensions and articulated in order to make us work.

It is of course obvious that realist texts can be read a second time. But that does not depend on them, but on the external intention of the reader, which in this way can indeed discover many things. What I want to emphasize here, however, is that in the texts I consider to be "baroque," the rereading is inherent in the text; at the point that rereading is undertaken, its fundamental necessity, essential and basic, is revealed and interpreted, with all of its consequences.

The Rise and Fall of Argentine Nationalism

The Dazzling Splendor of an Era

Let us begin talking about nationalism by exploring a certain aural experience. Let's start with music, avoiding Russian influences (Balakirev, Glinka, Glazunov), or those of Finland (Sibelius), Hungary (Bartok), or even Argentina (Aguirre, de Rogatis, Guastavino) that are linked to a predominantly rural, folkloric tradition. Instead let's consider the tango, an urban phenomenon, during one of its transitions, embodied in the work of a famous trio, Irusta, Fugazot, and Demare.[1] The version I have is from the forties and contains two parts; in one, Lucio Demare plays the piano solo; in the other, the trio fills the entire space.

My first impression is that one can note a curious difference between the two. When the trio plays, their interpretations—which at this point in time carry the appeal of something from the past kept safe in the dark corners of memory—seem to lack sparkle. They represent a peaceful and even a tranquil form of the tango, a sense of playing it safe, as if something held them back; perhaps, just to conjecture, the bandoneon and the piano refuse to stand out, out of courtesy, perhaps, and the voice, at the same time, still carries strong criollo overtones (the tango sung with attention to style) that hold it back. We could say that the music wants to remain in the same place, to resist time, which keeps pressuring and pushing it. In terms of the voice, Agustín Irusta's that is, one must note, in homage, that he does not allow himself to be carried away by the influences of Gardel,[2] influences that in his time reigned supreme. He remains true to a more introverted, subdued mode that suppresses resonances, and he renounces any new language of the time.

In contrast, when Lucio Demare plays by himself, the least one can say is that he is absolutely brilliant, perfect, and at the same time, emotive. He "belongs" to what the tango has created of itself over the course of its long history. The clarity of the phrasing and of the contours of the story narrated seem incredible. Furthermore, that brilliance (which is not merely an effect of the historical association) is what gives character to the story—a narration that, being musical, has nothing to narrate—and demonstrates a quality that we can approach only with discernment: it is exceptionally mature.

But there is something here that grabs our attention: some of the pieces he interprets (as if he were in a concert hall, like Arrau, totally absorbed and in complete control of his instrument) have titles that in one way or another refer to the French: "Mañanitas de Montmartre," "Grisel," "Dandy." Without meaning to infer that "everything" in the tango is linked to the French, I want to examine this detail. Is there some relationship between what this means from the perspective of his preferred repertoire and his performance of the work? Or if that seems excessive, with the range of his playing, a kind of temptation of grandeur?

Remember that, as tradition has it, "the tango triumphed in Paris," and that that triumph revived and then consolidated old fantasies that had their first and clearest embodiments in people such as Lucio Mansilla and Ricardo Güiraldes, and even, though less well known, in Gabriel Iturri from Tucumán, who was secretary (and lover?) of Count Robert de Montesquieu, who in turn was friends with Marcel Proust. In *El juguete rabioso* [The Mad Toy; 1927],[3] Roberto Arlt, who perhaps not entirely by chance named one of his characters Lucio, writes the phrase "bailar el tango en París" ["dance the tango in Paris"].[4] But getting back to the issue, in this selection by Demare the French element, both as goal and guarantee (to put it in a somewhat schematic way), appears to be the universal to which something as particular as the tango has conformed— the tango, with such dubious origins and still so linked, in Irusta's wavering voice and Fugazot's laments, to an elemental clay. But we cannot forget that all this would not be possible without Demare's interpretation, which clearly meets all the requirements of a major art form.

Certain consequences or at least questions or tangents arise from all this. The first is an idea, or, more precisely, an image, of "the construction of figures," that is, the process of constructing a sequence of steps in dancing the tango: Demare shines when he plays alone, while in the group he is overshadowed. All the same, however, given the genre in which he works and whose recently established rules he respects, not only does he not lose anything by playing alone, but he also gains representativeness: the figure that is created is representative. In other words, we can confirm that his manner, brilliance, and certainty herald a great Argentine moment, and all the more so because it involves a universal or universalizing pretension—the French connection.

The next tangent has to do with the chains or series of signification that this figure establishes; the first, rudimentary one is that of the cult of the caudillo— Demare holding himself back—with all that that entails in the stormy relationship between the individual and the group, as if there were a history penetrating the relationship among musicians. Remember that right-wing nationalisms cultivated the memory of the caudillos—Facundo in de Paoli's works, Rosas in those of José María Rosa, and Peñaloza in Fermín Chávez's. The left, perhaps not to such a degree—though not to emphasize this too much—had leaders such as Hipólito Yrigoyen and Perón, who were in some way evocative of the historical caudillos.

The second series is connected to the flowering of so-called stars of the popular art world that took place between 1920 and 1940, years in which what occurred with Argentine culture could be viewed along at least three lines of analysis:

  a. Argentina, in the continuation of its liberal founding ideology, lived as if it had realized its western, European, and culturally French dream of being a "Nation" with capital *N*. This experience continued to elicit what we could call "nationalistic" reactions.

b. There was a true flowering of symbolic-artistic endeavors (theater, music, painting, literature) that seemed to confirm the conviction that there is a here and now, the indubitable foundation of all national projections, as well as an inherent and unique national talent—in short, a value.

c. A theory, and a practice, of nationalism as theory, began to spread, which proposed the veneration of this value as if it emanated from an essence—proclaimed, affirmed, and more rancorous than happy. In trying to shape it to fit a grandiose project, it was diminished; it became political ideology, something that is never absent from any program we could call progressive. It is as if it could no longer renounce its state of being. And if for the right wing that being is static and immutable, for progressives or leftists or populists, it is always a dynamic state of "becoming."

In short, any manifestation, and in this case the example was Lucio Demare, radiating a sense of maturity (we could also include Emilio Pettorutti or Jorge Luis Borges or Alberto Ginastera), leads us to a point of affirmations, of continuations that evoke a sense of security and an unmistakable semiosis, now undeniable—that of a defined culture, the closest one can imagine to the idea of "national identity."

Wealth and Security

(A parenthetical aside on point b. It would be good to consider particular, limited aspects of this flowering in order to include a history of the culture based on the recognition of an exceptional, localized creativity. If we were to do so, we would see that between 1920 and 1940 there was significant and lasting production in all areas of existence, at a similar level in all of their respective spheres. As I indicated in an earlier article,[5] if in 1926 there appeared around a dozen books [Güiraldes, Arlt, Borges, Rossi, Fijman, Larreta, etc.] as lasting as they were indicative of a decisive move away from what had been rural toward what was thematically and syntactically urban, and if the Argentine sainete[6] became the typical and unmistakable manifestation of a profound historical process, if the literary journals and serials distributed inordinate numbers of copies compared to the timid numbers of previous editions, if there was a more than promissory beginning of philosophical speculation and scientific investigation, if movie and radio personalities, especially comedians, emerged everywhere, and if sports took off with a legendary strength, we must also say that a particular form of creativity appeared in the use of a metonymy, with local roots, through which the name of a particular brand of a product came to stand for the product itself—all brands of it. Thus, people began to freely use the term "Geniol" for any kind of aspirin, "Perramus" for any kind of raincoat, "Gomina" for any kind of hair gel, "Toscano" for any kind of tobacco, "Singer" for any kind of sewing machine, "Gilé" [Gilette] for any kind of razor blade, "Frigider" [Frigidaire] for any kind of refrigerator, "Puloil" for any kind of cleaner, "Brasso" for any kind of metal polish, "Kolynos" for any kind of toothpaste, "Quaker" for any kind of oats, "Buda"—which perhaps came a little later—for any kind of insecticide, and similarly, "Curitas" for any kind of adhesive bandage. And certainly there are more examples. The important thing is the rootedness and the universalizing tendency that these uses reveal. As well as the sense of security: Borges's *El idioma de los argentinos* [The Language of the Argentines; 1928] —which was not reprinted for good reason—and Borges's disputes with Américo Castro[7] would be an almost impeccable declaration of linguistic pride. And this, of course, becomes integrated into an idea of nationality, revealing secret mechanisms of an inherent genius, of an identity, whatever the area might be.[8] Nothing could be more auspicious for closing this parenthesis, however, than to attribute to this sense of self-sufficiency auspicious conditions for what we call "nationalism" to prosper.)

The Nationalist Idea in Argentina

Let us look in particular at this generative aspect that, without yet defining it, we have been calling "nationalism." For the moment let us leave aside the certainty of the here and now and the contours of its manifestations. Let us also ignore the issue of the material structure that sustains the aforementioned productivity, or against which such symbolic-artistic productivity develops, and whether there is or is not yet a national bourgeoisie that ties its destiny to this country (a question, however, that we will need to consider at some point)—by which I mean the play of the symbolic economy in relation to economic wealth. Let us turn instead to the formation of the nationalist idea in Argentina.

One could say, in the then recent tradition of Rousseau, that this idea began to take shape as pure desire with the coming of the revolution and independence; this is obvious and recognized now, though not so much so in its time except by visionaries such as Moreno and perhaps Monteagudo or Castelli,[9] for whom the nation as it was being established was a dream, or a goal, or in the best of cases, a task, a work in progress, interrupted by reactionary rage before it began. At the outset of these ideas, other elements emerged that had been in existence but with little force and that, when the idea of the nation was born, began to exert pressure, to demand, and to proclaim: these were the regions, what would later become the provinces, the groups from the interior who perhaps knew little about ideas but who acted through their caudillos, miraculously sprung from the war. And these ideas included the possibility of autonomous structures, confirmed in a certain idiosyncrasy, not in a project. Yet if "nation" is a totalizing concept, the regionalist triumph over the Unitarianism[10] from Buenos Aires should not have allowed a nationalist ideology to develop. But that was not how it was—in fact, quite the opposite: the caudillos were the origin of nationalist practices, and, on occasion, the climate was favorable for the development, albeit embryonic, of this concept, such as, for example, when Rosas confronted the English and the French at the Paraná River. The element that emerged was that of a rejection of foreigners and a determined defense of the territory—notions that, when nationalist principles developed, became inherent to them. However, Rosas's behavior was not so coherent in the case of the Malvinas Islands. His laissez faire stance meant the loss of that territory, yet, on the other hand, gave rise to a vindicatory invective that also appears to have been incorporated into the nationalist discourse and ideology—so much so that with this idea we could say that nationalism was universalized in Argentina, as could be verified when the government of General Galtieri decided to invade the Malvinas in 1982.

Alberdi was among the first to take up this idea, mixing Saint Simon's philosophy and a diluted Hegelianism, and certainly with two directions in mind: on the one hand, he wanted to give Rousseau's ideas a more appropriate form for the time—it was a period dominated by Rosas, not by the revolution. On the other, he wanted to generate a conceptual tool useful for facing a necessary future for a workable country. The formula he developed, "A nation is only a nation due to the reflexive and profound consciousness of the elements that compose it," has a sufficiently open character to allow consideration of not only what the nation was at the time and the resources to support it, but also its future possibilities.[11] I believe that that thinking is at the heart of the major historical formation that positivist liberalism carried out, starting from the beliefs of Mitre[12]. This formation, we should say in passing, reclaimed for itself, from what it inherited from Alberdi, the adjective "nationalist," which in this case indicated a political unity as its objective, not an affirmative ideology. At any rate, the only affirmation was that of the program designed to achieve it (and in that sense, "progressive"), a demographic program in one direction (eliminate the Indians and import immigrants), and a military project of political cooptation in the other; in short, a program encompassing the integration of opposite centers (which its adherents referred to at the time as autonomistas), a limited concept at that time, despite the fact that it would later form a part of the ideology most characteristic of Argentine nationalism.[13]

Perhaps due to early Catholic reactions against a liberalism that altered powerful cultural conditions, a reformulation of political terms began to develop that, after the revolution of 1890, included the element of the masses as an inalienable component of the idea of the nation.[14] It is embodied in radicalism,[15] and its beginnings have a strong moral content; there are values inherent in this human formation called "Argentina" that the "regime," "deceitful and false," according to Alem[16] and Yrigoyen, had trampled on, and it is a question of reclaiming them. The "regime" is happy to adopt foreign customs; it does not believe in traditions; it exploits the wealth of the country to benefit only its own members; it drives the country into debt, corrupts it, and alienates it. It is there that the principal themes are born that could be called "popular nationalism," and that popular nationalism has continued up to the present after undergoing various vicissitudes.[17] But it is still a reaction, a feeling, in a certain sense, a spiritual movement.[18]

The crisis of liberalism, spurred by the populist and leftist movements—socialism and anarchism—along with the results of the disintegrated integration of various generations of foreigners, gave rise to a reflection with apparently spiritual scope. With its origins in Spain, this reflection began—in the discourse of intellectuals such as Rojas, Gálvez, Larreta, Ibarguren, and later, Lugones—to provide some answers to questions of national identity. Hispanism, centered on Spain, had, once again, a dual path: one was aristocratic, Catholic, purist, and chauvinist, the other, popular or populist. In Lugones we find both, although in succession; first, with the rediscovery of the gaucho tradition, he reclaims a mixed origin, with a remote, telluric foundation. Later, seduced by the power of the gun, his rhetoric takes on a defensive tone with respect to the foreign immigrant "invasion."[19] This characteristic, which had already been manifest since 1890, would become inherent to a nationalism we could call "fear-driven" that had begun to organize and function around 1919 after the "tragic week,"[20] and that gave rise to the Liga Patriótica Argentina [the Argentine Patriotic League], whose organic intellectual was a forgettable figure: Manuel Carlés.[21] His approach was composed of all of the themes of the already consolidated nationalism of the European right, one of whose early manifestations in Argentina was Julián Martel's famous novel *La bolsa* [The Stock Market; 1891], in which he sums up arguments from Edouard Drummont's *La France juive* [Jewish France], a popular book in 1886.

The league was the precursor of the later Alianza Libertadora Nacionalista [Nationalist Liberating Alliance], a *grupo de choque* [a kind of shock troop] that defined its program more clearly: antiliberal and revisionist (celebrating Rosas) in terms of history, xenophobic and anti-Semitic, pro-Nazi and anti-British, in favor of "order" and a firm hand against communists and Jews, and fond of grandiloquent patriotic symbols; the nation existed beneath the nationalist sign of the Alianza, to paraphrase the title of the book *Bajo el signo nacionalista* by Bonifacio Lastra. Since the latter part of 1930, heartened by the fall of the populist—we would now say "democratic"—Yrigoyen, the members of the Alianza became more and more integrated into government structures. During the decade of the 1930s, they supported the decidedly fascist governor of the province of Buenos Aires, Manuel Fresco, but it made them very uncomfortable that the fraudulent governments carried out pro-British policies. It was as if they could not resolve the paradox of political control by an oligarchy that sympathized with the nationalist ideology—a source of ideas that were useful for affirming their own position—but whose economic interests, meat and wheat, which they had handed over to Great Britain, proved stronger than their protective ideological impulses.[22]

The persecution of radicals, communists, socialists, and anarchists, not only at the hands of what had become the shock troops but also the state itself, whose actions leaned toward fascism—a leaning from which it has not cured itself yet—generated a nationalist response from the left, which tried to recover the popular origin of radicalism that had been lost after their defeat in 1930. This was a group known as FORJA (Fuerza Orientación Radical Joven Argentina [Argentine Radical Youth Force]), whose intellectual interests shifted from the essentialism of identity that was so in fashion in the decade from 1930 to 1940, that of "being Argentine," to economic issues. They discovered imperialism (especially that of the British), recognized the role petroleum played in a dependent economy, anticipated what would later be called "national liberation," integrated the intellectual and scientific factor into any program for a future Argentina, and in general, prepared the way—with little success at the time—for a nonoligarchic and nonfascist national politics, the only option left for the oligarchy and the military after 1919.[23] The latter, after the events of the "tragic week," began to claim—and practice—an autonomous role, not determined by civil powers. To hell with the constitution and the slow, painful process of constructing democracy. They were the ones who toppled Yrigoyen and initiated the long military cycle, always with programs in which the thinking, consistently right-wing nationalist—if there was any thinking at all—formed an indiscernible part of the very thing they proposed to correct.[24]

The emergence of FORJA (Dellepiane, Raúl Scalabrini Ortiz, Marcelo Del Mazo, Cuzzani, Arturo Jauretche, Hasperué Becerra, Manzi, Gutiérrez Díaz, Molina Massei, and others) was justified by its promoters at the time as a response to the disintegration of radicalism; Marcelo Alvear's followers had taken over the organization after the fall of the old mystic Yrigoyen, but then began to negotiate with the opposition and to give ground, and people began to leave its ranks to join the conservative program, the so-called concordance. The members of FORJA believed in that radicalism and wanted to revive its reason for being, its self-confidence, and the strength to regain power.[25] This coincided with the beginnings of a growing industrialization that would give rise to a so-called national bourgeoisie, or perhaps it would consolidate that bourgeoisie, which had only hazy ideas and few ideological prejudices. But in any case, that bourgeoisie functioned as an indirect support for what could be an anti-imperialist, autonomizing popular nationalism that had a national project and thought not about national essences as a requirement but about national will, and which, powerful and vigorous, could attempt to take control of the shape of the country and of power.[26]

We need to take into account the climate in which these events occurred and for which the process narrated is a backdrop and in a certain sense, a condition. There are texts that serve as "witnesses" to that climate that we should be sure to consider, such as, in the literary sphere, the newspaper column *Aguafuertes* [Sketches][27] by Roberto Arlt and *History of an Argentine Passion* [*Historia de una pasión argentina*; 1937] by Eduardo Mallea or *El hombre que está solo y espera* [The Man Who Is Alone and Waiting; 1931] by Scalabrini Ortiz, and the appearance in 1927 of the political journal known as "the voice of Argentine nationalism," *La Nueva República* (Ernesto Palacio, Rodolfo and Julio Irazusta). And like a project inherited from Hispanist and Catholic pretensions, there was the appearance of the journal *Cruz y Raya,* in which former ultraístas such as Leopoldo Marechal figure heavily, as well as those nostalgic for the viceroyalty, such as Goyeneche, and nationalists such as Amadeo—in contrast to the journal *Sur,* which was internationalist, democratic, liberal, skeptical, and ambiguously official. Also forming part of this climate, although generally considered an expression of the so-called infamous decade, were the oft-mentioned tangos by Enrique Santos Discépolo, whose constant theme, blurred by nostalgia and a powerful dislike of change, was, in reality, a nationalist reflection of the "It's not what it could have been" sort. We should also include Vacarezza's sainetes, with their restrained rage over the result of that "mix" of peoples and races that created the Argentine common people, as well as the intense theatrical production, from González Castillo to Armando Discépolo to Eichelbaum, that dramatized the most intense problematic of national formation.[28]

Perhaps we can conclude that this complicated, contradictory, and always poorly understood process produced results that, like unquestioned ideologies, filtered into the thinking of this country, not perhaps as a belief that everyone wanted to restore the condition of "nationalism," but rather as an interpretant that allows the description or definition of everything that occurs. Thus, for example, the drama of Lisandro de la Torre's death could be interpreted in a nationalist manner: he is attacked in order to defend national interests and resources. But the fascist government of Fresco was also considered, correctly, to be nationalist, as were the industrial politics of the conservative Castillo, censured by the nationalists because he continued to align himself with the Nazis during the war. And so, whether on the right or on the left, it seemed difficult to construct discourses that did not embody this ideology. For better or for worse, left or right, nationalism arrived in Argentina to stay, although these days, especially in right-wing practices, it has not developed political programs that attract followers and instead repeats the old programs—chauvinism, authoritarianism, anti-Semitism, Catholic dogmatism, and so on. These programs seem to take root only in lost souls, like the melancholy Biondini, the unidentified profaners of Jewish tombs, or the more tenacious but more tempered Aldo Rico: in resentful people who hope for some redemption through the magic of old exorcisms.

The Country's Hour of Redemption

Let us examine another aspect of this topic. On June 4, 1943, a military coup took place; it had probably been incubating ever since the previous one in 1930. In fact, some of the protagonists were a part of both, so there is a congruence of characters and certainly of sentiment between the two. In the beginning, the coup was able to succeed because of an agreement between diverse sectors, politically speaking, in particular, that between a liberal group on the one hand, upset with Castillo for not aligning himself clearly with that traditional partner, England, and on the other, the so-called GOU [Grupo Obra de Unificación, or Group Working for Unification], which had a nationalistic bent and was in reality profascist in its political and economic analyses of the country. As soon as the coup triumphed, the liberal sector was quickly eliminated and all power was concentrated in the hands of the nationalistic military sector.[29]

This gave rise to the possibility of realizing the long-standing nationalist dream: if the state, in accordance with the most widely accepted philosophy of its role, embodied the most tangible form of the national idea, now the government also did so, and, therefore, it acquired a unity that had never before existed (which in particular is why Yrigoyen was overthrown), except in the fragmentary and isolated experiences of strong provincial governments such as that of Fresco in Buenos Aires, on the right, and Amadeo Sabattini in Córdoba, on the left—using those terms with some trepidation.[30]

In principle, the triumph of the GOU was that of the ideological and conceptual apparatus fabricated from European fascism, adapted and translated by local interpreters of various kinds, from the military lodges to the Alianza Libertadora Nacionalista [Nationalist Liberating Alliance], whose members were pro-Nazi, coup-supporting followers of Rosas. It also drew on leaders of the Juventudes Obreras Nacionales Católicas [Young Catholic National Workers], the Hispanist intellectuals (who took their inspiration from Spain), and those from the political journal *La Nueva República*, reinvigorated some time before by the Spanish Falangist party of Primo de Rivera, and later, the triumphant reign of Franco. It also included the sinister creators of the slogan "Dios, Patria, Hogar" ["God, Fatherland, and Home"], alternating from time to time with another, "Tradición, Familia, y Propiedad" ["Tradition, Family, and Property"], which attracted small groups of well-off youth, well dressed but very adept with the cudgel, custodians of churches in which violent priests, such as the notorious Virgilio Filippo, railed from the pulpit in Belgrano on the coming of the communist, atheist anti-Christ.[31]

This was not a mere whim. For the nationalists, correcting the culture's straying was, until recently, an obsession, from the dictatorship of purity to the cult of tradition and the exaggerated respect for phrases from the Catechism. Thus it was not a coincidence that one of the most notable actions of this military government was to impose religious education in the primary schools, expel secular and leftist educators, persecute leftist labor leaders, and control the practical aspects of the symbolic, from the university to the use of language. Of similar importance was the attempt to redefine politics; not only were the traditional parties dissolved and any activities prohibited that could lead to more or less collective, cooperative, or labor-related social formations, but also there was an attempt to impose a kind of apolitical language, controlled by the military government, as if that lack of politics were an ideal to strive for, and, manipulated by the media, it was presented as inherent to the now recovered nation itself. Without a doubt, it was in this context and this spirit that the curious prohibition against the use of Lunfardo[32] in public media was established. Given that the concept of "linguistic politics" is better understood nowadays, we can now recognize in that purism not only a kind of yearning for Hispanism, a bridge of sympathy toward Franco that began to weave its "national" nets through, precisely, linguistic initiatives, but also a repudiation of the results of immigration politics, of which Lunfardo is an ordinary, common, and crude manifestation.[33]

But we must also consider the economic aspect: the military government began to encourage a certain industrial development, perhaps having learned from what the previous conservative regime had observed and experienced, thanks to the historic opportunity provided by the First World War. But this was less an encouragement of the national bourgeoisie than a task for the state. It should be enough to recall the "stimulating" figure of General Edelmiro J. Farrell, who baptized one of the vehicles produced by the early military factories as "Déle-déle" ["Onward!"]. The revolutionary measure the government took of changing the side of the road one drives on can be understood in a similar sense; up until June of 1943, vehicles were driven on the left side of the road in the British fashion. Did the military think that soon the Volkswagens that Hitler was promising his German workers—and which were driven on the right side of the road—were going to start pouring into the country? Or were they dreaming of fabricating vehicles in Argentina that would radically differentiate themselves from British automobiles? That first thought, perhaps premature, quickly lost any basis in reality, but in contrast, the other dream was not so naive: not many years would pass before it began to come true.[34]

We should not forget the role the war played in the organization of all the signifiers that we have been accumulating. On the one hand, Europe's need for raw materials did not alleviate the agrarian crisis that had existed since the middle of the 1930s. At the most it allowed the accumulation of large quantities of gold in English banks, thanks to the continued exportation of meat in accordance with previously signed agreements. On the other, that demand for raw materials did stimulate the aforementioned industrial development. The two factors together produced the incessant migration of rural workers, now unemployed, looking for the resources that, in principle, the cities had to offer. This phenomenon had enormous consequences for Argentina; besides creating those structures known as *villas miseria* [shantytowns around the outskirts of the city] that seemed to become a permanent fixture, it "nationalized" the urban working class, introducing ways of doing things that came from the interior, which then gave rise to new and increasingly crude political languages that neither the old nationalism nor the old liberalism nor the old political left would manage to interpret.

The military carried out a program we could call "nationalist," and which they had been conspiring to prepare for many years. But its ferocity did not last long, and the illusion of its applicability and efficacy slowly began to lose possible international support. The advances of the Nazis and the modifications to the map of Europe seemed to provide assurances to the regime, but soon that began to fade, all of which had its consequences in Argentina. One question we might well ask is whether the historical intuition that created Perón's political fortune from the new social protagonists—rural and urban workers and a middle class dependent on the state and on industry—did not draw its substance, though not necessarily its model, from the failure of the Germans and the defection of the Italians. In other words, we can ask if these were not the catastrophes that made him "see" those who would later be called the *descamisados* [or "shirtless"] populace—that is, the mass of workers who had not become radicalized—as the starting point for a new political formulation.[35]

Be that as it may, the general use of nationalist slogans began to reveal their insufficiencies, their schematic quality, and a rigidity that Argentine society, to which we are attributing a certain maturity, would come to feel as unbearable, not only because fascism had begun its downward spiral and no longer provided the contextual support necessary to confront a deeply rooted liberal mentality enjoying a resurgence thanks to the resistance to fascism, but also due to a reemergence of the left in general, nurtured by the growing Soviet success. This reasoning can be attributed, obviously, to the final experience of the coup of 1943, and provides us with some elements for understanding what came later. But this is less important, for the present essay, than considering what the coup was attempting, and the opportunity that it had to achieve a dream that earlier had been condemned to dissatisfaction and frustration, resentfully confined to military barracks or to pseudo-study groups that were really only concerned with learning to use weapons.

General Rawson had originally justified the coup by arguing that Robustiano Patrón Costa, one of the candidates for the presidency, was planning fraud. Patrón Costa, a sugar baron from Salta, was one of the most exalted products of the country's "infamous decade" (a very apt expression, by the way, which was coined by José Luis Torres, a nationalist intellectual). He was a large landowner without scruples of any sort who exploited peasants, and a model example of conservative politicians. Once Rawson was thrown out, Pedro Pablo Ramírez took over the seat of power and installed in the various offices a group of men who felt their positions were authorized by blood, faith, and patriotic sentiment—and because they had organized themselves patiently and discretely in the shadows of the barracks or the sacristies (Hugo Wast, Olmedo, etc.) in order to create medieval heroes like the Cid in twentieth-century guise. The invaders, those who must be expelled, were in this case representatives of an invisible, though no less dangerous, utterly contemptible empire, made up of Jews, communists, atheists, liberals, Masons, and so on.

As history has taught us (and the lesson has been repeated every so often), while the installation of these types of national redeemers are accepted in the beginning, Argentine society quickly tires of their excesses and tends at a later, perhaps more analytical, time to reject or isolate them. What Argentine society does not seem to manage very well are those disingenuous votes of confidence;

Argentines do not seem to recognize in the beginning who and what their "saviors" really are, and when they grow tired of the messianic language or excesses of social control, or simply when they realize that their hopes have once again been in vain, it is already too late—too many compromises have already been made, and they find it extremely difficult to develop some kind of action out of their growing desire to rid themselves of the guardians of nationality. Their hesitation multiplies, and the preludes to the end of the governments are, de facto, always dramatic.

In the case of 1943 through the end of 1944, having noticed the rejection mentioned above, the group in power still could not and would not retreat. On the contrary, some of their most prominent members thought of making some concessions to the left and thus, without losing legality, they were able to inject some legitimacy into their government. That insight can perhaps be attributed to the defense of Stalingrad and the reconquest of Paris: what was now seen as the beginning of the end for Nazi power aroused unmistakable manifestations of enthusiasm by large sectors of Argentine society. This apparently indicated not only that proalliance and prodemocratic sentiment had not been stamped out by the authoritarian measures of the government, but also indicated a growing ungovernability, since it involved not only foreign policy, but also innumerable conflicts of every type (with labor unions, students, etc.) for which the strictly nationalist program had in no way found a solution or been able to contain. A rapid analysis of this situation suggested that they make such a change, one of the most conspicuous manifestations of which was to abandon the doctrine of neutrality and declare war on the Axis powers almost at war's end. And the formula that adept politicians such as Perón found was to move as quickly as possible from an authoritarian nationalism to a populist one, choosing what was for them, in my judgment, a lesser evil as they determined how little and how much could be saved of the nationalist utopia so recently established.

The protagonist of this transition, the pivot point of the change, the sibylline and convincing voice that previously had inspired many of the initiatives already discussed and that now began to indicate that it was necessary to adapt to the new situation in order not to lose everything in the face of the bleak perspectives of the Nazi defeat and the rise of liberalism and communism, was, as I have said and as we know very well, the then colonel Juan Domingo Perón. It was he who changed the emphasis and made the discourse more flexible so that it ceased to be crudely ideological and domineering and became more pragmatic and dialogic; he began to talk with those who had been silenced, with politicians he brought around to his point of view (it is known that he spoke with Amadeo Sabattini and Ramón J. Cárcano), with union leaders, even prisoners (to all of whom he promised comfortable jobs and social progress designated as "conquests"), as well as with leaders of public opinion who, from within the state power structure, gave him the answers required by a developing society. His discursive mode was that of a shovel: scoop up everything that is lying around loose, be it unsatisfied needs such as legitimate rights that have always been postponed, or political and personal frustrations, or ambitions routinely reined-in by the powerful. And with all of this, he put together an ideology that, without betraying its origin (namely, the nationalism of the right), corresponded to what popular nationalism was always seeking. His genius consisted of giving that old, traditional aspiration a new form, bringing together old rivals according to models no longer limited to European forms, including fascism, and instead looking to successful initiatives such as those of Vargas in Brazil or Cárdenas in Mexico, which from the earlier fascination with corporativism retained only the organizing scheme and, in contrast, allowed elements of the democratic tradition to enter the picture, especially in Cárdenas's case, as well as those of others from socialist backgrounds. Was it due to this inspiration that a year after coming to power Perón developed his program for the country beneath the title or slogan of a "five-year plan," an expression that came directly from Stalinism, and that indicates the reach of the powers of the state in terms of its proposals and responsibilities?

The First Worker

On June 4, 1946, a new stage began, this time one of popular nationalism, if only because "the people" were present in the official discourse; with the momentum provided by a majority vote and the postwar reconstructive fervor, the by then president Perón developed a program of action that had various ingredients whose conceptual or ideological origins are not difficult to discern. At any rate, after having announced a theory of "leading," he was named, or named himself, "leader" [*conductor*] (as well as "The First Worker," a syntagma created by the ineffable author of "los muchachos peronistas" ["the Peronist boys"]), reminiscent of terms such as "duce," "Führer," or "caudillo," though

without the authoritarian and vicious connotations that those terms had previously carried. What this title suggested, in contrast, was the idea of an authority that entails, as a corollary, the correction of a recent anarchical past.

Immediately it became a question of organization: labor unions, rural workers, business people, together with other political "branches"—women, youth,
the armed forces—all formed blocs in which the groups that originally gave
birth to the "national movement" were subsumed and diluted. The term "national movement" in turn referred to an organizing paradigm; as we can see, it
was not a question of "classes" or of parties but of convergent structures. The
parties or groups that had allowed the government access to power (laborismo,
Unión Cívica Radical Junta Renovadora [the new, reform wing of the Radical
Civic Union], etc.) disappeared, or if they did not accept the new forms, were
made to disappear. This was the case with Cipriano Reyes, the organizer of the
historic events of October 17, during which, as a declarative application of an
anti-imperialist principle that was dear to FORJA's nationalism, the phrase "Up
with maté, down with whiskey"[36] was heard, together with another emotive,
populist, and anti-intellectual one, tied to the ideology of the Nationalist Liberating Alliance, that came from the voluntarist arsenal: "Up with *alpargatas,*
down with books."[37]

Thus, it became an issue of an economic development based on the so-called
social conquests, state and regional planning as a panacea, state recuperation of
foreign commerce, state control of the banks, institutions for centralizing foreign businesses seized from the "enemy" (which became the Germans in the
final days of the war), nationalization of public services, and, finally, a cultural
plan aimed at affirming "national values," including the mandatory promotion
of folkloric music, an intent to make the university over in the image of the
Falangists, nationalization of the radio stations, all combined with old nationalist ideological sources, such as scholasticism, Christian existentialism,
tellurism, criollismo, and so on.

However, as in other similar historical moments, it was on the international
plane that the modulations began that would pragmatically alter the orthodoxy
and necessitate a nuancing of language, with the consequences this brings. Let
me point out one incident: the Argentine delegate to the Conference of San
Francisco, the first constitutive assembly of the United Nations, was not a
fervent fan of the Axis powers but favored rather the pro-British Miguel Angel
Cárcano, heir of a noble liberal and progressive tradition with conservative

roots. It is true that at the same time, Argentina became a kind of second home for a number of Nazis who had been able to escape from their defeat, a topic that has given rise to considerable conjecture and suppressed findings up to and including the present time.[38] But just as important is the fact that bit by bit Argentina under Perón began to enter the international milieu imposed by the United States and came to accept the instruments that "imperialism" created, for example, adhering to the Chapultepec Accords.[39] This generated a real crisis of conscience for nationalists on the right who were members of the government. One example is that of the chief of police, General Filomeno Velazco, a renowned nationalist put in charge for that very reason and for other specific merits, who took on the role of repressing those militant nationalists who considered the signing of the accords to be treasonous and manifested their outrage.

We could say that the Peronist leadership never completely lost the characteristics it inherited from authoritarian nationalism, but it is also important to note that during its development, and perhaps due to the actions of Eva Duarte de Perón, it underwent changes that we can recognize as coming from a sensitivity to real social problems and evident national idiosyncrasies: words such as *trabajadores* [laborers], *cabecitas negras* [mestizo migrants to the city], *el pueblo* [the people], and so on, were terms that, on the one hand, displaced others from the canon, such as *obreros* [workers], *lumpen* [proletariat], bourgeoisie, classes, and so on. On the other hand, these were terms that were able to interpret real processes that took place in Argentine society and that were led by the popular nationalist conception—for example, the idea of an all-protecting action by the state, a declared confidence in the here and now, the messianic image of a grandiose future, and a sense of identity.

However, traces of a fascism that was impossible to eradicate continued; we can quickly mention social control and control of people's movements (the spread of espionage and accusation, the creation of secret services, glorification of the police and military—members of these institutions enjoyed economic privileges that everyone was aware of), a certain xenophobia (foreigners were expelled under the anachronistic Residency Law that before this had been sleeping the sleep of the just for decades), glorification of the leaders (streets, cities, and even whole provinces were rebaptized in their names), a propensity for spectacle and pomp, modifications to the electoral codes and schemas and even to the constitution, an increase in the repressive system, and so on. It is impossible to forget that the intellectual formation of members of the newly created Secretariat of Aeronautics, that is, airmen, was entrusted to people long familiar with nationalism. I should point out the example, because he deserves it, of Giordano Bruno Genta, who can perhaps be criticized for his fascist ideas but not for the tenacious way he sustained them all of his life.

To close this chapter, it could be said that by the end of its first period, Perón's government abandoned an originally close tie with the church, a natural supporter of all Argentine nationalism, and became so antagonistic as to incite the burning of various churches and the labeling of clergy as "internationalists"—that is, people without a country. Of course this episode kindled the enthusiasm of many anti-Catholics and led them to believe that Peronism was falling into a kind of Sovietization, but that is not how it appears to me. On the contrary, due certainly to insufficient answers to economic problems that made it harder and harder to sustain a populist policy of inventing make-work jobs, as well as due to the European recovery, a rupture was produced with what was left of the nationalist right, and a required definition of popular nationalism began to develop, similar to what had occurred in Mexico with the Cristero crisis.[40] Perhaps it was too late for Peronism; the liberals, who had not forgiven him, and the Catholic nationalists, who were now up in arms, united once again as they had in 1943 in order to put an end to the endeavor, except this time their alliance had a different conclusion. The Catholic nationalists, with the pious General Lonardi at the helm, were neutralized by liberals, such as Aramburu and Rojas,[41] that no one knew existed in the armed forces, and who, once in power, took on the delicate task of dismantling the entire Peronist apparatus, without, of course, touching anything involved with state power, as if they, too, had accepted something about nationalism that Perón's team had wanted to impose, as if it were inherent in the existence of the country itself.

Obviously, it is not the goal of this essay to examine the benefits that Peronism brought the country, nor to counterbalance them with the frames that it imposed and that no doubt continue to exist in the political and mental habits of Argentines. Nor is it my intent to recount, no matter how succinctly, the story of Peronism, which here I am treating as merely one chapter in the history of nationalism, itself an inexhaustible topic still subject to all kinds of interpretations.[42] Thus, for example, it is not a question of continuing to show how Peronism's basic principles and behaviors evolved over the years and how power was manipulated (from Perón's exile and the so-called resistance to his return and the emergence of a leftist current, the "socialist nation," which fought against the dinosaurs left in the "Peronist nation") in order to arrive at the present where we find people who have fought Peronism all their lives being more "Peronist" than many card-carrying Peronists, tied to ultraliberal slogans and doctrines created, uttered, and imposed from the very centers of world power.

The Unlimited Textual Universe

It is almost inevitable in any consideration of the topic of nationalism to repeat citations and end up in shared textual spaces: the corpus is very well established. Perhaps it would be more exciting to uncover the misdeeds or the misfortunes or the misadventures of the diverse types of Argentine nationalism, each one according to its particular orientation, a job that would require an extremely tenacious and detailed investigation, for which I declare myself incompetent. Therefore, in the previous pages I have instead resorted to my memory in examining this topic, and in terms of the various texts of the various nationalisms, I can only refer to the most well known, those that in essays, fiction, or poetry adopt some facet of that ideology. Presumably there are also texts that indirectly carry this ideology, but that raises a question about historiographic criteria, something that Ricardo Rojas resolved in his *Historia de la literatura argentina* [History of Argentine Literature; 1924–1925] when he defined as "Argentine" almost every text that had ever been recorded (without them having to satisfy any requirements in order to enter that temple) that had been written by Argentine authors or that referred to Argentine affairs.

Perhaps we need to look at Sarmiento, always so denigrated by the nationalists, for the first organic texts of what would later constitute this tendency: *Condición del extranjero en América* [The Foreigner's Condition in America] and *Conflicto y armonía de las razas en América* [Conflict and Harmony among the Races in America; 1883]. The affiliation is reasonable, but it is only partial in relation to the whole range of topics that, strictly speaking, make up what can be called "nationalist." Those texts were the first to sound a chauvinist alarm based on racial criteria that quickly turned racist in a tradition that held dear to positivism. But it was not seen this way; nationalism at that time was only a political concept and an organizational project, not a doctrine. One way or another, it called attention to the question of identity, to which the antigaucho and anti-Indian emphasis on progress that emerged after Caseros (1852) offered no resistance. There was such a sense of security in the ruling classes that Sarmiento's warnings had no effect on immigration policy, and immigration continued to increase. In other words, for leaders such as General Roca and his team, the criollo foundation of national identity was solid, and it could only be strengthened by the influx of European immigrants. Bit by bit, however, the foreign presence, now well established, began to generate an uneasiness and sense of anxiety in the same people who had promoted it.

In order to analyze these sentiments, one text that will serve us well and that was very much in vogue in Europe is *La France juive* by Edouard Drummont, and another, *The Dialogue in Hell between Machiavelli and Montesquieu* [*Dialogue aux enfers entre Machiavel et Montesquieu*; 1864] by Maurice Joly, as well as the insidious appearance of the fraudulent "Protocols of the Elders of Zion." Each of these, if taken seriously, explained the dangers posed by foreigners.[43] As has been pointed out before, this formed the basis of the book *La bolsa* by Julián Martel, as well as helping create the mental climate that produced *En la sangre* [In the Blood; 1887] by Eugenio Cambaceres. Jews in the one case and Italians in the other constituted the "foreigners," a term that immediately calls up its opposite, "Argentines," who seemed to have no doubts or hesitations but plenty of arrogance (only a short time before, Guido y Spano had composed the lines "What do I care of life's vagaries / When Lady Luck's no friend! / For I'm Argentine to the end / Born in Buenos Aires"),[44] and in that atmosphere, foreignness began to be seen as anomalous, almost a disease. It is clear that in this implicit interplay of opposites there is a summons, a call to action that would take form a decade later with the promulgation of the Residency Law (1904), and, much later (although there was a tragic precursor in 1872 with the massacre of Basques in Tandil,[45] led by a fanatic who thus started a tradition), with the first roundups by the *grupos de tareas* [task forces] of the death squads, who persecuted bearded men in 1919 and subversives starting in 1974, with similar episodes in between. And this comparison is not without merit.

Of course there was not a unanimously enthusiastic reception to these kinds of proposals, which in other texts came disguised as scientific seriousness, with descriptions of causes and consequences, with realistic and objective observations of what was happening in Argentine society. The authors of these texts (Drago, Ramos Mejía, Ingenieros) in truth limited themselves to prolonging the positivist system in order to get closer to the fascinating enigma of a society that was rapidly taking shape, and to that extent, what we are calling "nationalism" had still not acquired its final form—only a few bricks had been set in its construction. Those who rejected these proposals were socialist or anarchist writers; however, we still find even in them an acceptance of a positive pronationalism. For example, in Alberto Gerchunoff's *The Jewish Gauchos of the Pampas* [*Los gauchos judíos*; 1910], his idea of integration presumes identities—some dominant, whose tolerance he appeals to, and some dominated, for whom he begs understanding. In Florencio Sánchez's *La gringa* [The Italian Girl; 1904], in turn, there is a similar proposal. These formulas would come to summarize the foundational proposals and to usher in the notion that "Argentines" include "immigrants." This was not, however, as a humiliated acceptance of an indisputable law, but rather as a philosophical program: racial mixing as the condition of a new nationality that neither shuns the previous dominant population nor bars the way for the developing nationalities of the coming flood of immigrants.

Around the centennial, several intellectuals took the bull by the horns. As I have already indicated, Manuel Gálvez (*El diario de Gabriel Quiroga* [Gabriel Quiroga's Diary; 1910] and *El solar de la raza* [The Lineage of the Races; 1913]), Ricardo Rojas (*La restauración nacionalista* [National Restoration; 1909]), Enrique Larreta (*La gloria de don Ramiro* [The Glory of Don Ramiro; 1908]), and Leopoldo Lugones (*El payador* [The Folksinger; 1916]), were the principal exponents of a dual concern, Hispanist in the first three, criollist in the last. According to some, national identity, which is the point of the debate, resides in the Spain of their origin, and, more concretely, in its most classical values (not, of course, in the stereotypes satirized by Antonio Machado). For others, the key to nationality must be sought and discovered in the gaucho, the compendium of Argentina's own history, the racial consecration that also involves an epic element, the most appropriate for defining the sought-after, and verified, identity. As can be shown, the nationalist quests grew out of these books. It is there that the elements reside that will help form later definitions, at least in part, of course, and perhaps to be used for other purposes. But here what we might call a spiritual quest, later, as it alters, modifies, and reinterprets these elements, becomes ideology, hard and defensive, violent in one direction, which is the most frequent though most often frustrated one, and prospective and programmatic in the other direction, more positive and slow to develop, more capable of giving rise to government programs and global assertions of a community in the world.[46]

The Hispanist sketches, which celebrate the Spanish tradition, take their theoretical support from French legitimism, inherited on the one hand from a monarchist and institutional tradition, and on the other, from Catholic thought, which, if it did not include a racial ingredient in its initial postulates, it was probably due to the fact that its principal enemies were secularism and free thought. Action Française, a right-wing nationalist group in France established by Charles Maurras before the First World War, served as a support for those Argentines who quickly left behind speculations about their origins, Hispanic or gaucho, and began a crusade with a more political scope, but that all the same preserved from its source the idea of an unbearable national decadence. This is the Lugones of "La hora de la espada" [The Hour of the Sword];[47] and it is the monastic style and mood of intellectuals such as Carlos Ibarguren and others, whose doctrines illuminated the task that the Liga Patriótica [Patriotic League] proposed, in which civilians and the military would combine their utopias. The most important of these doctrines is certainly *La grande Argentina* [Greater Argentina; 1930], the title for which is taken from Lugones's inspired phrase.[48]

This literature created the conditions for a thriving development in diverse fields; in history, for example, it was integrated into the traditional revisionist line begun during the previous century by Adolfo Saldías, but connections were made to the autonomist, regionalist, federalist, and caudillo-connected past. Nevertheless, Rosismo would be a constant that would be forever integrated into the catalogue of nationalist topics.[49] During the period under discussion it would become the basis for a later revisionism that would try to link the figure of Perón to that past. I am referring to the contributions from a leftist populism, such as that of Jorge Abelardo Ramos or J. J. Hernández Arregui, who aspired to explain all of national history from the perspective of a popular nationalism that would culminate in the new caudillo. But prolongations occurred in other fields as well; these include the leanings of those from FORJA, who, as previously mentioned, managed to emphasize anti-imperialism. José Luis Torres's book, which I cited earlier, *La década infame,* would perhaps be a good synthesis of these proposals, as would be Raúl Scalabrini Ortíz's subsequent writings on petroleum.[50] Not to mention the nationalist readings from the revolution of 1930 or those that followed the resurgence of radicalism, such as that of Gabriel del Mazo or, more clearly, that of Arturo Frondizi during the 1950s. I am speaking of *Petróleo y política* [Petroleum and Politics], in which the economism of FORJA converges with the intransigent redefinition (Declaración de Avellaneda)[51] that attempted to go beyond Peronism in terms of state obligations, antioligarchic sentiments and anti-imperialism, and social justice—all banners that Peronism was assumed to be abandoning.

In short, this chapter could continue indefinitely. The issue is complicated because no text that came after these goes beyond the dimension of affirmation and pragmatics. In the area of the former all the well-known topics are reiterated—racism, anti-Semitism, authoritarianism, order, corporativism, religion, family, and so on. In the latter, we find new alternatives—"national liberation," "popular government," the "third world movement," "urban guerrilla wars," the "socialist nation"—each of which discovers its limits according to the opportunity provided it by history.

A Farewell to Arms . . . but Not Completely

One of the most spectacular actions of the so-called Liberating Revolution that took place in September 1955 was the bombing of the building occupied by the Alianza Libertadora Nacionalista [Nationalist Liberating Alliance], vacant at the time, on the corner of Corrientes Street and San Martín. Many people experienced the collapse of its walls as a powerful symbolic act, as if it removed a tumor in the "national movement" that even offended fervent populist Peronists. Although this entity had become simply an armed, criminal group, leading to the flight of the intellectuals who had joined its ranks, its destruction began a dispersive cycle of right-wing nationalism. Dispersion, unraveling, but not disappearance.

That unraveling would reappear in various moments, from political cells such as the Tacuara movement, some of whose members joined the Montonero guerrillas (Rodolfo Galimberti) or the proto-Trotskyite ERP [Ejercito Revolucionario del Pobre, or Revolutionary Army of the Poor] (Joe Baxter), to members of the Triple A [Alianza Anti-Comunista Argentina, or Argentine Anticommunist Alliance],[52] recruited by López Rega's death squads, and task forces from the organization for the "Process of National Reorganization" [the "Proceso"][53] as well as members of the country's secret service or agents of fundamentalist terrorism. It could probably be verified that it was a question of an unstoppable process of political depravity, whose seeds could be found, in my opinion, in its very conceptions. It is not a coincidence that numerous torture chambers of "the process," according to accounts by survivors, were decorated with a portrait of Hitler, and that the interrogations of the detained had a strong Nazi flavor to them.[54]

That disintegration favored the other tendency, what we have been calling "popular nationalism." Immediately after the collapse of Peronism, some intellectuals regained their enthusiasm and returned to the arena. Those on the Catholic side had supported the coup against Perón and now tried to rally around the ephemeral general Lonardi, but once he was destroyed, they renewed their efforts at an ideological campaign that proved effective. The newspaper *Azul y Blanco* and the journal *Mayoría* served to demonstrate to what point, as a kind of fascination, the principal slogans of national populism would be prolonged during the transition period, no longer carrying the ideological emphasis on vindication and without the calls to xenophobic violence, but rather as a tool to denounce what, in general terms, could be called the "surrender" that was attributed to the liberalism in power. It was as much a question of natural resources as of the lack of protection of national industries and the castration of the labor movement.

It seemed that the Peronist alternative, as a concrete interpretation of nationalism, with all of its imprecisions and contradictory stakes, was becoming the only way to think about reality; it was not only a matter of the equation Peronism/working class/the masses/votes, without which no political program would have been able to maintain its course (and which the followers of Arturo Frondizi believed and carried out), but also of an ideological fascination, as if it were not possible to imagine the country using other categories, categories that had to be purged of authoritarian elements, of course, and that had to be redefined, but there could be no other categories but these. I am referring to the direction taken by the thinking of people like Arturo Frondizi, people who, despite having formed the most direct opposition to Perón, bit by bit seemed to be seduced by Peronist followers and concepts, although giving them other names, following the suggestions of mentors or ideologues such as Rogelio Frigerio.

In effect, it was he who invented the term "development policy" [*desarrollismo*], later adopted by Frondizi in opposition to the radical terminology of radicalismo inspired by the historical Declaración de Avellaneda. Frigerio did not waver in breaking with the party, and eventually, with those that accompanied it, in recognizing that the old radical language was lacking and that his was much more adequate for the times. The term "development policy," as one can read in the journal *Qué* run by Frigerio and Machinandiarena, had the following scope: it was the tactical aspect of a "national" strategy that tended to create its own economic force, guided and supported by the state, but not statist. The state, from that perspective, should not lose any of its powers but should be at the service of "development," such that the political policies carried out tend to diminish class conflict, support the sectors of society that contribute the most, and guarantee social peace. Welfare, a social democratic ingredient already incorporated into the political thinking, would have to wait, as would the anti-imperialist formulations subjected to the examination of economic independence that was to be achieved by the exploitation of resources (petroleum, minerals, marine resources, and communications) with the support of either foreign or national capital, without which such resources would have remained buried in the earth, generating poverty instead of a promised ultimate wealth.

This thinking allowed at least two things to occur: for one, the political pact with Perón, and for another, the incorporation of development policy by traditional theoreticians, that is, nationalist ones, such as Mario Amadeo, Pedro de Pablo Pardo, and others along that line. And, as was necessary in order to guarantee the success of that movement, the development project sought the protection of military power, whose glories it proclaimed, as well as the blessing of the church—to whom it promised and then fulfilled aspirations long postponed—private universities and an unhoped-for respect on the part of well-known secular leaders who had achieved a certain mass following by their manipulation of symbols, such as university reform, the acceptance of divorce, liberal attitudes toward cohabitation, and civil liberties.

And if in all of this we find traces of nationalism, it was, of course, of another kind. No longer a question of anti-Semitic or corporativist *ultrismo* [extremism], it was about achieving what Peronism had never accomplished, because it put its accent on other syllables, because it never redefined what it could be, remaining still tied to what it had been: a popular nationalism attempting to base itself on an identity and a goal.

Meanwhile, the military, independently of whether or not they understood development policy, continued to cultivate what we could call "their" mentality; they were suspicious, closing themselves up in a conspiratorial silence, and their ideological mentors owed little to the theoreticians of popular nationalism. The Scalabrinis, Jauretches, and Hernández Arreguis were all steeped in the same ideas, and nothing military could change their stubborn belief that what was needed was order and discipline, patriotic parades, and new weapons in order to keep away all danger of communism or subversion.

Between 1960 and 1962, the fickle but persistent Frondizi swore by the military and their very existence on a daily basis. He recognized their legitimacy as if it were a creed, forgetting the entire civil and democratic discursive legacy with which he had reached political maturity. But it did him no good; the military did not believe in conversions, and in 1962 they overthrew him without ever having received from him the slightest reproach or censure, so convinced was he that they would carry out, better even than he, a national destiny that he and of course his inseparable Frigerio had reformulated. With him, the nationalists who had converted to development policy disappeared again, and in the army, the orthodox ones reappeared, for whom new possibilities would present themselves in 1966. They defined their "Argentine Revolution" with less precision than the nationalists of 1930 or 1943; it was enough for them, for the time being, to concern themselves with the university and science (they were the authors of the "noche de bastones largos" ["night of big sticks"]),[55] which they damaged so irreparably that hundreds of researchers who had managed to create a first-rate network were forced to emigrate.

The language of the "Argentine Revolution," however, was not so extreme: they contented themselves with promoting a distillation of Peronism that backed those addicted to various neo-Peronist movements from across the country. Union leaders who were so inclined managed to get what appeared to be conspiratorial winks from Perón, who, from exile, seemed to have moved to the left, speaking in terms of the Cuban and Maoist revolutions, and attentive to new mass movements, negotiating through some of his faithful followers, known as his "delegates." The dictatorship began to grow shaky, and in one of their permutations, they called on Aldo Ferrer to manage the economy. Ferrer, with radical roots in Frondizi's movement, then reintroduced "national" slogans that seemed like they might be viable: "Buy Argentine," he proclaimed, and converted the state into a consumer sensitive to the origin of the products it buys. The national bourgeoisie and nationalism were reinvigorated in actions, though not in declarations; there was hope: people believed that there could still be formulas that would lead to "Argentina as a world power," a synonym for Lugones's "Greater Argentina"—and just as empty.

The enthusiasm was ephemeral, as were the results, but the experience also reinterpreted the country's situation without proposing a single change, as if to say that leaving things just the way they were, the country could still revitalize itself—and yet almost everyone knew that this was not the case. And so began the conflicts, in step with the popular reactions that occurred all over (Córdoba, Rosario), and this encouraged the guerrilla movement in all its facets. One of those guerrilla groups, the Montoneros, reclaimed their place as the vanguard of the "national movement." They began as a group of Catholic youth who had only partly learned the lessons of the Cuban experience and of what the third world perspective had to offer. It was a mix of people who wanted to win the recognition of Peronism, and eventually they achieved this: they became involved with one of the branches of the Peronist movement, the Peronist Youth, obtained Perón's blessing ("those marvelous young people"), bit by bit gave his slogans a leftist slant (such that many people of that ilk became integrated into their ranks), and finally, threw themselves into the "radical armed critique." During Cámpora's brief moment—from June to August of 1973—the Montoneros sought to save the nation through economic measures, but at the same time they borrowed authoritarian and hierarchical structures from the by then firmly rooted nationalist tradition.

And we all know what happened after that. The military intervened once again. Repression is their only solution, but this time, following in the footsteps of the Nazis, they rejected all legal contrivances. Thus began a long night wrapped in a dense fog—kidnappings, disappeared persons, prison camps, torture chambers, and extermination camps in places that at times, as has already been mentioned, were watched over by the august figure of Hitler—an expert in this type of affairs. All as if to demonstrate that certain nationalist dreams, this time the elimination of those who put the sacrosanct nation in danger, still persist in the Argentine imagination, and how invulnerable they are—are they?—to criticism and all human understanding. And also to show how they could reconcile themselves with neoliberal economic policies (Martínez de Hoz) through which they destroyed what little national industry remained and provided illusory comfort, based on financial games, to middle classes willing to turn a blind eye to the whole situation as long as they were paid with access to abundant consumer goods and guaranteed a strong currency. This was completely the opposite of the old austerity envisioned by the criollist and ascetic nationalism dreamed of by the Gálvezes and Lugoneses.

For this direction of nationalism, the final moment of this moment was the war for the Malvinas Islands, an episode in which there was an organic fusion of signifiers once again, and perhaps for the last time: the grand acclamation "Las Malvinas son argentinas"—"The Malvinas are Argentine"—united everyone in Argentina under the leadership of the military, and there was the possibility of humiliating British imperialism at last; the uproar of the war would make the world forget about Argentina's economic crisis, and Argentina would be able to present itself to the world as a world power capable of confronting another world power. We all know the end result. Those nationalistic impulses were revealed as ridiculous, and their protagonists were forced to flee the political scene and almost even had to face punishment. But that does not mean that they have not left encysted remains, secret service agents, bands of kidnappers, grotesque neo-Nazis who dream of a terrible army of hook-nosed Jews, of Masons wrapped in ankle-length robes, of terrifying communists, and of sighing homosexuals—all about to swallow the country. And, when they wake, there are other nightmares—crimes to forget, robberies to be committed, weapons to be gathered up, or services to be offered to others just as delirious about identity, who wander through the world plotting assaults against the government and blowing up buildings full of people, intoxicated with obsolete rhetorics that once upon a time had a more or less noble aim.

In terms of the other direction, that of popular nationalism, the least one can say is that, because it creates new political structures that try to respond to the neoliberal attack so in vogue, it is emerging as an alternative once again. I worry that its language has remained the same, although the intention has been purified. Thus I worry that in the clash, if there is such an opportunity, lacking primitive drive, that popular nationalism will return to the alliances that have characterized its history. And that once again it will obfuscate the legitimate desire to fully develop an identity, and for its own ends, will sow a convulsive ideology of an assertion that is more ostentatious than functional.[56]

Like Something in a Museum

One could say, then, that at present, nationalism in all of its manifestations is on the decline. One proof of this is that it no longer has theoreticians, only those who study it, as if it were something in a museum. And not just one, but all brands of nationalism: that which seems most characteristic, the arrogant, self-sufficient, and aggressive version on the right, as well as the persuasive, rational version tied to and expropriated from the left—all appear to be something from the past. There is nothing left of their din, just as it seems that no one is going to risk their life again for Argentine petroleum, austerely reclaimed in what seem like long-ago times by Enrique Mosconi's sober discourse. It is true, however, that grotesque and shadowy, almost sorrowful figures appear, distributing poorly written pamphlets aimed at saving the country, just as there are political groups who critique neoliberal "proposals" and advocate once again the nationalization of the country's wealth as a prolongation of the Peronist programs that seemed feasible in 1973. But none of this changes the general mood of the country.

The situation in the rest of the world is much the same; in a similarly anachronistic way, nationalism exhibits some signs of life or prolongations of its old manifestations: on the right, there are the neo-Nazis without hair on, or anything else inside, their heads. In one aspect, they once again propose a vague national greatness to be gained if they can manage to exterminate Turks, Armenians, or Moroccans, while at the same time, a group of Algerians without the slightest doubt about their brilliant although long-suffering destiny purge their beloved territory of women who work and French Catholic nuns and priests. On the left, even if their statements are not leftist, countries and regions reappear that fight for their autonomy in the Balkans and struggle to recover identities submerged by political groupings that have been imposed on them, while in other places, new voices reiterate an old confidence in their own resources, in the right to specific idiosyncrasies and to exist without losing their own character rather than be washed away in a huge, spiritless and leveling wave as despotic as was the old imperialism. I am referring to the Zapatista National Liberation Army, as well as the Irish movement and certain reformisms tied to a third world movement whose political and religious discourse still survives.

Nationalism seems to have lost all sense due to wide-spread globalization and the seemingly limitless triumph of capitalism. According to some, and the prodigies of communication technologies most of all, with the fall of the Berlin Wall, all countries are now interconnected and it is difficult to think in terms of true autonomy. To which we must of course add the foreign debt: nothing links countries more than does indebtedness. Some are thrilled by this while others lament it. One cannot say, however, that these are the only causes. Perhaps there is something anachronistic they feel in their gut, although for me there is nothing anachronistic about a community formed by culture, language, and territory trying to attain its own realization according to its own model.

What no longer seems to function is their formulation, their rationalizations, or more specifically, it is nationalist discourse that is in decline. It seems to have lost validity, although what sustained it has not completely disappeared and has resurgences, as we have indicated. One could say that this discourse has lost much of a precise referent, and that its teleology is so utopian that it has little chance of recovering.

However, paradoxically, both discursive aspects remain in use, as residues or resonances. We hear these discourses, we endure them, we pay them little heed, and yet their legitimacy cannot be denied, perhaps because no new discourse has decisively and clearly emerged, and this perhaps because the internationalist discourse that at one time opposed it has also collapsed and suffers from the same disease.

It is precisely this that we talk about when we talk about nationalism: the limits and the origin of its erosion reside in the question of legitimacy, which is present in all forms of nationalism. That legitimacy resides in a supposed—but unimagined—being that is to be converted into an actual being who, through his actions, would define a "not-being" that is excluded and banished to other vague and generally enemy regions. In the best of cases, these would be other nationalisms, which are thus obstacles to its consolidation, and in the worst, a stateless zone in which illegitimacy, the lack of belonging, the lack of roots, the lack of tradition, and nothingness, reign.

Examining these particular terms, one could say that legitimacy, once it is confirmed, cannot be argued with; it exists and accompanies whomever claims it, and it is defined as an innate possession and property in which one takes part and which no legal structure can modify. That is why the idea of foreignness is so strong; in the most traditional type of nationalism, it means rejection of any equality under the law and of any mix that would threaten to alter the inherited terms. And in terms of "being," what the various forms of nationalism presume is that, simply by "being," nationalism possesses attributes that are easy to demonstrate. For these nationalists, to claim to be "Argentine" is to say everything; nothing more needs to be added. To be described as such is a summary of essence and existence—the adjective synthesizes certainty and the past, guarantees ties, defends them from uncertainty, and thus limits the field. In turn, the "not being," defined through exclusion, is threatening and must be restrained if not directly eliminated.

Autobiography, Biography, Narrative

Sarmiento and the Origins of Argentine Literature

I do not believe that any of the critics or scholars of Sarmiento, both as a public man and as a writer, have failed to notice the relationship that exists between *Mi defensa* [My Defense; 1843] and *Recuerdos de provincia* [*Provincial Recollections*; 1850].[1] That relationship is, above all, ideological: the evident justificatory movement (redundant in the former) is common to both texts. But it is also developmental: *Mi defensa* could be seen as an embryonic form of *Recuerdos de provincia*: the central idea of the latter also appears in the former, and though only roughly in the earlier work, it is full of indications of the style that would later stand out in *Recuerdos*.

In terms of the ideological relationship, despite the lineage of the two texts, distinctions can be made between them in terms of their "intention," or in protoreception theory, in terms of the intended audience: while *Mi defensa* was written to restore Sarmiento's image in the eyes of the Chilean people as a kind of vindication, as well as lending a hand to his political supporters, who were perhaps at a disadvantage as they attempted to protect someone who made himself an easy target for attack, *Recuerdos,* above all, takes into account a certain Argentine public ("To my compatriots only," is the title/dedication of his introduction). That public at the time was perhaps reconsidering human values within the political arena, an area in flux because of impending changes in the national scene, with the predictable appearance of new actors who had been readying themselves anonymously or hidden in the shadows, biding their time until their moment came to play some role. Unknown, or almost so, despite the repercussions of *Facundo*[2] and his public involvement in Chile, Sarmiento wanted to say, through a synthesis that would highlight his ability to synthesize, that is to say, via his condition as a writer, "Here I am; this is who I am."

It seems to me that this relationship and/or distinction between the two texts is clearly worthy of consideration, although at this point I am not interested in the psychological reasons that could be invoked to explain it. I am not saying, however, that there is no reason to consider them—it simply is not my intention to examine that here. What I will say about the relationship between the two texts is that it clearly gives rise to an observation about writing or what we could understand as such, even though it could be said that I somewhat imprecisely include notions of style. Be that as it may, the circumstances of his presence in Chile in the first piece would have favored an incontinent prose that overflows in torrents, almost violently, so that the effect would appear to be the totality of allegiance (allegiance to the figure who is the object of such energetic unfolding) or the nothingness of rejection, as a declaration of the inability to understand or of a routine adherence to an insulting and/or slanderous argumentation.

However, in the general expository system, we should not rule out from this confusion the action of discursive mechanisms or of reasoned arguments—theme by theme, piece by piece, comments against, clarifications in favor—that appear to be filled with an emphasis we cannot really separate from a search for empathy.

The second circumstance, characterized by a radical notion of distance (inasmuch as we do not know precisely what the intended audience of the locutionary system is like, and, therefore do not have much chance of predicting the concrete perlocutionality, even though, certainly, the perlocutionality may tend, with all the associated risks, to create such an intended audience in this way as do all literary intents), perhaps gives rise to a more organizing point of view, with a certain amount of calculation, but that paradoxically gives less attention and even less value to the general expository structure.

Briefly, and looking at both texts from their respective and different contexts, we could say that they move from indignant spontaneity on the expressive plane, though with an eye on its effectiveness before a hypothetical tribunal, to a completed self-portrait, but one cast into a no-man's-land of a little-known discourse with respect to which it would not be easy to say, from a discursive point of view, where it is going. This idea is seductive because it takes into account the romantic impulse to mix everything, and it will certainly reappear in another section of this discussion, in relation to *Recuerdos de provincia*.

Looking at things then from the developmental side, we could also say—and it has been said frequently—that *Mi defensa* is not only the embryonic form of *Recuerdos de provincia*, but also its protonarrative and, even, its concrete geno-text. There are differences between these things. Thus, the image of the embryonic form seems convincing and reasonable because, while both texts have the same creator and also the same subject of the enunciation and of the utterance, one seems to be a further development of the other as well as containing the other, despite or because of the fact that in *Recuerdos*, the exhibitory strategy encompasses regions of memory that either do not exist in *Mi defensa*, or are very sketchy or serve other purposes. However, and because this way of looking at things allows for unforeseen development when examining the embryonic hypothesis (which inevitably leads to the image of a "creative center" that is difficult to establish), it is more productive perhaps to consider *Mi defensa* as a *protonarrative*, which although it seemed to have exhausted its original function (though not its reverberation) when it was produced, its effects were left suspended along with certain approaches and themes waiting for new narrative conditions. But considering the one as a *genotext* of the other, the idea is even more concrete in that it was sufficient, perhaps, to go back again to the first text and rewrite it—or at least believe that that was all that was happening—in order to produce the second.

Furthermore, I think there is another factor that must be considered, namely, that the time period between one text and the other was filled with two notarial structures (as well as with very entertaining and intense activities of the sort that a certain kind of imagination can generate and give itself over to after much reflection), one called a "travel chronicle," and the other a "biography," and that, more or less between these two texts, a transcendent possibility is revealed, a divergence, a narrative project or program.

I can say the same thing in two ways. First, perhaps *Recuerdos* takes its principal scheme from *Mi defensa*—to focus attention on material from one's own life—and then develops the cause that that implies. But in any case, it is *Facundo,* as the prominent biography (although we know it is more than just that), that opens the dizzying philosophical possibility of contrasting two kinds of perfection—that of evil, mentioned earlier, and that of good, and further-more, all in a dimension that has long been sought by good romantics (to unite literature and philosophy). The progression that occurs then between *Facundo* and *Recuerdos,* from biography to autobiography, also supposes an access to literature, understood as a dimension in which the enunciative circuit tends to become objectified in a complex model, something like a superior projection or synthesis of numerous planes, observable from the not-so-distant time of the Enlightenment in terms both of concepts put into play and of the romantic analytical capacity being configured as well as of *acting,* even in literature.

Second, let me mention Sarmiento's idea of the social role that biography plays, and in that regard, it would behoove us to look again at his essay "De las biografías" [About Biographies], published in 1842 ("the biography of a man who has played an important role in a given era and a given country is a compendium of contemporary history, illuminated with the vivid colors that reflect national customs and habits, the dominant ideas, the tendencies of a civilization, and the special direction that the genius of great men can leave on a society").[3] I would say that these objectives were indisputable for Sarmiento with respect to Quiroga, and before that, perhaps with respect to Aldao,[4] as great men of the act of negation, but if the model of affirmation that he admired was Franklin, it seems unlikely to me that he would have taken on the role for himself of being an example of that category well before the full development of his talent and during a period when he suffered from psycho-logical depression. It is difficult to believe he would have been able to think that he had—I stress the past tense—played "an important role . . . a compendium of contemporary history." But on the other hand it is quite probable that he thought of himself as someone who could "see" and recount what he saw, from unheard-of novelties to myths—and what lay in his memory. Looking at that improbability and this probability and eliminating most of the justificatory compulsion, I suspect it is more a question of a predictable displacement of the moral objectives of a literary genre toward one of the angles—the formal accident of narration that, from a perspective in which the point of view is that of the one who controls it, could not help but see autobiography as an opportunity. The narrator discussing himself, the smallest distance imaginable between experience, memory, and writing—that is narration.

In an extrinsic approach to both texts, and despite all the relationships presently established (the preceding ones already discussed and others that one could establish from a comparatist perspective), we can note differences in structure, or rather, in construction if we think from within a constructivist mentality, in dynamic terms. *Mi defensa* is articulated, predictably, by virtue not of a respect for the rules in a strict sense, the definite judicial-justificatory discourse, but rather in a sequence of aspects or moments of an object or theme central to the dissertation occurring as connected items or chapters: "Introduction," "My Childhood," "The Military Man and the Man of the Party," "The Son, the Brother, and the Friend." Each of these chapters examines, as would a lawyer, different themes that are raised by the accusation, injury, or slander that has occurred relative to diverse facets of the personality in question and which, grouped together, could be responded to or thwarted by virtue of the clarity provided by each grouping. Let me mention in passing that I find it suggestive that the chapter entitled "The Military Man and the Man of the Party" is the longest: I suppose that therein lies a key for understanding the scope of his "mission" and of the "Republican sacrifice" that will later recur throughout the myth of Sarmiento. In addition, perhaps that chapter is the most stylistically tormented of the work, in the romantic Promethean sense of the soul imprisoned by its destiny, and indicative, therefore, of a centrality, a centrality that could also be clearly noted in *Recuerdos de provincia,* insofar as the life depicted is in essence a public life, cast together, as has been pointed out many times before, with the very life of the country in—as has also been noted—a prospective and visionary homology.

However, getting back to the point, while indignation about his mistreatment, as a typical reaction of an exile hurt by misreadings of his actions, was the impetus for writing the text and therefore a powerful factor in the subjectivization of the writing (one indication of which would be the frequent use of augmentatives, modals, and adverbs of quantity), the structure, on the other hand, has a certain harmony, that of a "presentable" piece of writing; this structure, as a consequence, *should be* discursively effective in terms of his aims and objectives. Thus there is a gradual argumentative development through which runs a gestaltic rationality in the sense of completing a depiction in an organic manner. And if, as I believe, everything in this organizational dynamic with double planes (subjectivization and discursivization) tends to configure that depiction, we could say that that constructive spirit owes a debt to painting, which would be its authorizing and legitimizing force, as can be observed in the costumbrista writings of his contemporaries, from Larra to Echeverría, understanding that costumbrismo as a clear romantic feature. This makes the small initial apologue that evokes, or appeals to, Apeles and his painting *La calumnia* [*Slander*] seem less fortuitous and more simply illustrative.

For its part, *Recuerdos de provincia* follows a very different structure. Of course the notion of structure that I am using is not that of structuralism, but rather a very general notion, descriptive in scope: it alludes, above all, to the form assumed by the articulation of the totality. To that aim I would say first of all that it would be impossible to assimilate Sarmiento's discursive schema into any discourse type in particular. He rejects the juridical, and the sentence he wrote in the chapter entitled "Juan Eugenio de Mallea" ("Leaving aside the annoying courtroom style and phraseology, I will give a brief narration of the events")[5] could be a conscious expression or even a thematization of this. Furthermore, he manipulates the historical aspect as soon as he mentions "investigation." Because of this, *Recuerdos* has much more to do with *Facundo*, as a mosaic not so much of genres but of genre-related approaches or outlines or even modifications of genres, than it does with *Mi defensa*. In the comparative vein, it does not seem as if the "argumentation," understood as structural support of the totality, is the central element that articulates, connects, or confers rationality to the different moments of the whole in its interaction, as the expository-juridical might have been able to do in *Mi defensa*. Furthermore, it does not seem to me that an argumentation of this type—which, functioning in the totality, can go back over the various parts of the writing—could sustain his writing in the same way that one could think that a logic of actions, as a particular "mode" of argumentation, was what sustained the novels by his contemporary Balzac—and by this I mean the principle instances of their development, including the metaphorical horizon of their descriptive aspects. In *Recuerdos de provincia*, on the other hand, one can see that there is a predominance of emotionality, which is translated into an abundance of emphatic elements, destined, predictably, to produce conviction.

But I am talking about the whole, not each section; in each of these sections—which are types of illustrations that among themselves retain a relationship of very vague parentage in terms of the objects described—there is, in effect, because it is not a question of descriptive chaos, a certain argumentation that is inherent and characteristic and that supports the central aims or motives of each one. So, for example, the chapter dedicated to Domingo de Oro follows the model of "life stories," that is, a predominance of narration with a bit of "fiction" included above and beyond the historical information, while in the chapter on Brother Justo Santa María de Oro, what predominates is what we could call the contextual aspect, in the sense of a "residue" of historical discourse. Furthermore, though at the risk of acting only on the surface, we could say that the chapters or sections ensue without the aim of contributing to the development of a depiction, which in the end is the main objective of the autobiographical gesture. In that sense, if each chapter is warranted, that is, its presence is not arbitrary or capricious, it is because the central nucleus, the autobiographical figure, has something to do with the motives for the chapter, a tangent that was enough to spark a development that seems almost autonomous in the telling. But such an association is not insubstantial or purely coincidental: it is produced from a diverse backdrop of memory and experience. So, for example, in terms of the second illustration, the one about the Huarpe Indians, which carries an unexplained sense of a "return to the archaic," this chapter may have been the fruit of some precise imaginary residue, the affectionate figure of Calíbar the tracker, whom Sarmiento raised to a mythological dimension in *Facundo*, a dimension that could synecdochally persist as a creative presence, something like "Calíbar, c'est moi," for its imaginer. Sarmiento becomes a kind of tracker as well, a sociologist and man of letters, one who reads the destiny of a lost country. And while the genesis of the chapters, in their autonomy, can perhaps be explained this way, what in reality they produce is, I believe, another effect, based in my opinion on a displacement. I will talk more about this later on.

However—and because one cannot ignore a subject such as that of argumentation, perhaps because we are dealing with a text by a man who spent his whole life arguing—one could say that maybe a different type of argumentation governs this collection, or at the least, that there may be a certain intention of expository logic that does not depend on a more precise discursive model, as was the case with *Mi defensa*. One element that supports this idea is revealed in this declaration typical of Sarmiento: "Here ends the colonial history, as I call the history of my family. What follows is the slow and painful transition from one way of life to another, the life of the nascent Republic, the struggle between political parties, the civil war, banishment, and exile."[6] Presented as a historical premise, I would say that it *only* indicates a desire, of a historicist nature in this case, to provide rationality to a discourse, since the divide between the colonial experience and the republican one never really existed: the pictures that make up what he calls "colonial history" not only are seen from and with a republican gaze, but the bits and pieces that might be inherently or intrinsically colonial are constantly interlaced with others linked to a historical present or to ways of seeing the present. Note this historicist interference in the description of the Huarpe Indians: "Alas for the peoples who do not progress! If only they merely survived!"[7] Furthermore, what he presents as "colonial" does not have, in light of the fact that this is after all an autobiography, a personal character, one of intrauterine history. And yet, the colonial element could be the preparatory one, the previous antecedents of someone who, born in 1811, always defined himself as having been born and bred in the revolution.

It is necessary, then, to look for what could be his own argumentative key, his particular expository logic.

There has been a tendency on the part of critics to want to see *Recuerdos de provincia* as a moment of calm in Sarmiento's generally energetic and spirited, even complex, writing. Those who have done so have been compelled by two central but superficial motives. The first is that, in relation to *Mi Defensa*, *Recuerdos* is a kind of expansion characterized not so much by the potentiation of polemic energy—the man who defends himself tooth and nail as he recounts his actions—but rather by an introspective reconcentration that, perforce, gives rise to a tranquilizing calm: Sarmiento also as an affectionate son and loving brother, as the poet who comes from quiet, rural beginnings, as a man who appreciates the little things that give life meaning and on which transcendent values are based—love, religiosity, respect, the gentle tinkling of cow bells reminiscent of one of Leopardi's idylls. The second motive is that, both in perspective and in retrospective, *Recuerdos de provincia* seems to dampen somewhat the stridency found in *Facundo*—in a backward movement, by the tone with which it evokes, and in a forward movement by the perplexities that are raised by that interdiscursive monster, that phenomenon set in the very center of political and literary backwardness.

Digressing for a moment, I believe that the tradition of Argentine letters has needed the arrangement in which *Facundo* is the price paid to concern and worry, and *Recuerdos* is the poetic counterweight—the responsibility and social commitment of *Facundo* balanced by evocation. Be that as it may, before reviewing the position of *Recuerdos* in this scheme, it is important to recognize that these two texts constitute two permanent temptations for Argentine writers because they appear in national literary history as almost ethical options, forgetting that in reality it is a question of the double satisfaction of a need for romantic dialectic and its constant search for answers to a singular enigma. I would say, however, that in truth both books are nothing more than two chapters of one single text, linked to a single explanatory gesture, but also in another way that seems fundamental to me: what Sarmiento wants to insinuate and even propose in *Facundo* as the inevitable path for a particular literature, in *Recuerdos* functions as if that literature were already constituted and producing, quite naturally, its texts: reviewing the use of fiction in *Recuerdos de provincia*—in the movement from the anecdote to the inserted story—actualizing and concentrating the enunciative mechanisms, reformulating the role of the narrator (in the future and in the past), resolving, through an "actanciality" that creates a "story" out of that which explanation, in the end, cannot grasp. What I mean by the term "displacement" is becoming clearer, I believe: it is displacement toward the narration.

Very well, getting back to the text, one could say that the title, because of the word *recuerdos* ["memories"], refers to an important genre-related expression, the autobiography. This seems clear and obvious. All the same, the title has another implication; it alludes, perhaps, to a specific content because of the word *provincia* ["province"], deeply rooted as a seme of a culture whose values are distributed and located—Sarmiento himself is one of the most evident priests of that distribution—in precise places, a context that understands the terms "capital" and "province" appropriately. The capital is tumultuous, as Baudelaire proclaimed; the province is profound and painful, as López Velarde came to announce in this century with his metaphor of the "suave patria" or "sweet homeland." But province is also "village," which leaves another mark on the cultural consciousness: "Describe your village and you will describe the world," Tolstoy noted. Perhaps in a Tolstoy-like manner *avant la lettre*, Sarmiento also foresaw this, discovering in Argentina's impoverished reality a dimension that would only seem to be possible in other spheres of writing, not in one so rudimentary and initial as this.

But furthermore, we must consider another factor. One would think that in order to come up with such an apt title, he must have engaged in certain comprehensible political speculation: in mentioning the word "province" he restores an equilibrium in terms of oppositions in Argentine culture (both oppositions contemporary to Sarmiento and those previous to him) in that he postulates not only that the provincial universe (whose proximity to untamed nature, as he had stated in *Facundo*, is the origin of barbarism) is not the exclusive property of the Federalists, but also of the Unitarians. And it is the Unitarians in particular, the group to which he belongs as we all know, though also including a few educated and cultured Federalists such as his kinsman Oro, who truly understand the essence of this entity, its meaning—and yet of which they are dispossessed since they are all exiled. They have lost authority over and use of the word in the place where they should be able to speak. Sarmiento fights then for the symbolic, which, as we know, constitutes a site of "reparation" of a truth. It is in that same restorative direction, it seems to me, that he refers in passing to the Unitarian Valentín Alsina (an attentive reader of his *Facundo*), who in the face of Rosas's silence on such a delicate issue, reclaimed the Malvinas Islands, a subject that seems unquestionably linked to the Federalist tradition: who are the true keepers of nationality? he seems to ask.

Furthermore, we must remember that the word "province," which has a more Bourbon origin than the word "region," historically was the one that won acceptance, and that there was agreement about its semantic field, which was why it was a term that spawned conflict between *porteños* [people from the port city and capital, Buenos Aires] and *provincianos* [those from the provinces]. And it continues to spark dispute, though perhaps more tenuously, as a conflict of interests, certainly, but also as a clash of values: commotion and rest, manipulation and reflection, news media and poetry, violence and coexistence, deception and simplicity.

Thus, considering all of these interpretations as what sustains this text, I would say that what Sarmiento evokes is only a small part of what we could consider, even for him, the provincial "being" to be. In reality, he does not entertain this possibility and creates a synecdoche: when he writes of certain people, including those of his own genealogical tree, by virtue of recreating them, he is stating what the provincial virtues are, in an act that supposes a certain empiricist dominance in the philosophical undercurrent that organizes his vision of things. To put it another way, the majesty of human beings clarifies the enigma of nature. This synecdoche, although it continues to view the evocative aspect as a condition of autobiography and to consider both dimensions to be located in the production of an image, is one of the most fruitful because it leads to the sketching of partial biographies, and it permits, by attenuating the explanatory movement, the expansion of narration. As a consequence, *Recuerdos de provincia* is in reality a collection of numerous stories that, as I indicated before, try to reduce the fictional element, contrary to what at that time Bartolomé Mitre with *Soledad* or José Mármol with *Amalia* were more or less attempting to do, and that also emphasize a privileged enunciation, as a system, by virtue of the interplay of pronominal signs.

But there is something else we might highlight here. In truth, while the scene of the actions narrated is the province, the spirit in which they are narrated is far from provincial: it is emphatically national. But this is not because of interpretations that consider the experience of the province that is evoked as being "representative" of the nation, but rather because of the emphasis that is placed on the events recounted—the battles, characters, incidents, the entire mass of multiple threads that are interwoven in the narrator's space; the "first citizen of his school" is a proud designation whose origin and ideological scope is clearly national.

The elements that I have used to help elaborate on my preceding notes should make it clear—because they are among the most common aspects of literary criticism on Sarmiento—that it would be imperative to turn to a technique of forgetfulness in order to have a fresh reading of a text that we could readily admit is vibrant and alive. Forget all the accumulated readings, forget the seemingly inevitable obligation of pigeonholing one's conclusions into one of a set of preexisting categories. To put it simply, it could be said even today, whether as mere commentary or through very sophisticated "methodologies," that one has only three options in analyzing Sarmiento: that he was a good man, with everything that implies, or that he did more harm than good to the country (as shown by the general feeling at the end of an era that included the major teachers' strike in 1988), or that he was neither a genius nor a victim, but merely was representative of an emerging social class. To end up in one of these pigeon holes is, I believe, completely contrary to what a fresh reading should be, although perhaps the means to free ourselves from that fatalism do not exist, nor is it perhaps philosophically viable to do so. I suppose that the possibility of other options depends on a teleology of leaping into the void, outside of the ethical or political or esthetic compulsions that have guided traditional readings.

In my particular case, I do not believe that the readings carried out from those types of libido have been useless or absurd or invalid, no matter how contradictory they might be. My possible difference in this respect is due to the fact that I try to situate myself in a different teleology, according to which the literary aspect of Sarmiento is not merely a general quality but rather an entire dimension. And that dimension is what I try to capture and the place in which I want to locate myself.

Facundo, as many have noted, myself included (which only goes to show once again that the memory of past readings is persistent and even insidious and harmful when it is a question of one's own texts), is a mosaic of genres. Perhaps, apart from any other more refined consideration, this is due to the contradictory characteristics of the material being dealt with, the transitory features, the transferred images, the explosions of rage, the demands of the time, and so on. In *Viajes* [*Viajes por Europa, África y América, 1845–1847*],[8] the extrinsic world demands an immediate and attentive gaze that allows concentration, and if there are any deviations, they are a sort of illustration, a sort of commentary; the divergence in relation to the observable has a capacity for creating sparks. All of this gives the text of *Viajes* an evident enunciative unity. I believe that in *Recuerdos de provincia* there is something of both of these writing experiences, not as an "averaging" or a synthesis, but rather as a third possibility in the arduous foundational ground of a literature in which Sarmiento situated himself— deliberately, I would say. To put it another way, while the autobiographical aspect of the text acts as a concept in discursive harmony with *Facundo* (since, being a *mode* of biography, it contrasts, as I indicated, two ideas, that of an evil genius and that of a good genius, an integration that would explain the evolution of history), in *Viajes*, the itinerant digression and the visual path that runs across the surface of experience turned to memory are pared down as a gesture.

However, the tribute owed to both previous texts is never directly paid, and a new organizational proposal persists, that of the genealogical tree already established, and from which Sarmiento chooses only some of the fruits—those he feels contribute to his central objective, such as, for example, the figure of Juan Eugenio de Mallea, the sons of Jofré, or the Albarracín family.

For now, let us leave behind the relationships between these texts and turn to look more closely at *Recuerdos.* Could it be that that particular organizational proposal is the system of argumentation that, opposite from or different than that of *Mi defensa,* I said we needed to discover as the inherent and inescapable proposal of *Recuerdos*? I understand that this is nothing more than an organizational point of departure, not a system that determines writing. Is this what one should try to grasp, as if to show that such a dimension exists, and are Borges's words in his prologue to *Recuerdos* about the value of the whole of the text (once again the memory of previous readings rears its head), a suggestive corroboration?[9]

Turning at last to writing, then, I believe it is dominated or guided by two fundamental impulses—impulses in the sense that a natural phenomenon, the pulse, can, after being exposed to a notion of the unconscious, acquire there a certain directionality that transforms it into a cultural phenomenon. One of these impulses can be placed in the category of the utterance, and the other, correspondingly, in that of the enunciation. I should make it clear, however, that in turning to these two categories I am not surrendering to the magic of dualism. I suppose that their merit lies in the fact that, as categories, they are all-inclusive and go beyond the recurrent, seductive dualisms such as "form" and "content."

As for the category of the utterance, it is a question, I believe, as an impulse, of an obsession that we could call "concentrating," and that I would like to define as a constant return to a peripheral frame of reference—writing colonial history, for example, or describing the customs of the Huarpe Indians or domestic practices beneath the shade of the grape arbor. It is a return to a particular center, a powerful magnet, and we do not know if it comes before writing, something that exists in the mind and from which we cannot escape, or if it comes after, as an effect of the writing. I am referring to the politics that would be contemporary to that writing. It is worth our while to look at an example of this mode of concentrating, which, since it occurs quite often, cannot go unnoticed. It is found in the chapter entitled "El historiador Funes" [Funes the

Historian]: "The learned city [Córdoba] has not been so contrite in recent times when its ancient doctors were succeeded in their rule by the sons, fresh from working in the countryside."[10]

Whether this center comes before or after the writing, writing cannot help but have a relationship to it. It yields to it in the sense that its contours become spiral in nature, allowing it to avoid the referential divisions, those belonging to the utterance, such as the "colonial period" and the "republican period." From the point at which that spiral develops, it becomes exclusively a question of the present. It is for that reason that I asserted the existence of a unity of objectives between *Recuerdos* and *Facundo*. But at the same time, since this writing is the result of an intercrossing, I would say that the spiral form, motivated by politics as an impulse to return obsessively to a particular issue, emanates from a gaze situated in a high observation point, a figure that may explain the intertextual relationship with *Viajes,* as a textuality constituted in its totality on the gaze from on high, the gaze of the chronicler or the traveler.

For its part, the impulse that dominates the enunciation is configured as an eccentricity with respect to a central nucleus of a thematic nature. It is as if it moves, without any way to restrain it, from one expository category or sphere, to another category, another sphere. So, for example, when he turns to a circumstantial description, both in the case of circumstances that he knows from his own experience and those he reconstructs from other references, he falls back on an anecdote or situation that illustrates it, including economic and productive, cultural, or anthropological aspects. Look at this paragraph, full of wit: "A long procession of mourning neighbors accompanied the funeral carriage to the mausoleum, when the wheels creaked, the carriage broke, and they struggled to lower the coffin at the very door of the unfortunate Mallea, who at that moment was hurriedly trying to figure that fatal sum that had him so confused."[11] But the illustration continues to develop, and it acquires—the example gives some idea of the possibilities—the character of an independent story that changes the descriptive atmosphere. That move is never carried out in a lethargic manner. It is precisely at this point of articulation that the spiritedness of his prose is applied, and even, although this is another point of reflection, is born.

It is by virtue of this very mechanism, this derailment, that his prose avoids the risks of conventionality, and perhaps this explains its vitality in the sense not only of the fate that so many of his "stories" have had, if we can call such expansions that, and the "figures" that they metonymically embody, but also in the sense of the multiple readings that the concentrated and decentered whole supports, outside of a discursive typology or in accordance with types of discourse, but within a "Latin American" logic that requires a narration of self in order to explain or understand itself, whether or not this narration of self is the result of a displacement.

Earlier I called attention to the relationship that Sarmiento establishes between the referent—poor and lean, certainly—that brings him to report and the telling that results, "the great riches of poverty."[12] I believe that the displacement observable in *Recuerdos de provincia* abounds in this quality and demonstrates, once again, the model that can be developed from a perspective of "the riches of poverty."

Autobiography, Memoir, Diary

According to one version, put forth by, among others, Raúl Ortíz, Eduardo Mallea, and, in an even more labyrinthine sense, Roberto Arlt (or perhaps merely as the result of a poor reading of their texts), Argentines are silent, introverted, aloof, and inclined to hide their feelings and not allow anyone to get close. As maintained by these authors and those who follow this tradition, it is difficult for an Argentine to acknowledge any weakness, any damage to his ego, or merely any surrender to his feelings. Argentines could be described as being in a prepsychoanalytic state; they suffer from a "language" problem; they do not know how to "disclose." This seems to be the case if one agrees with these and many other authors, particularly those who write for the theater: pride, ambiguity, difficulty in relating to others, a sometimes tragic silence, a feeling of being misunderstood, and all the aftermath necessary to create interesting dramatic or narrative scenarios.

Of course, Argentine *women* would be excluded from this reasoning, perhaps because when this philosophy was established they could not vote, and surely because by being the unspeakable object of all that men should but do not confess, women were placed outside of such notions of "national character." And as you may recall of this "national character," according to the intellectual demands of the time, between 1910 and 1960 it was vitally important to define what it meant to be Argentine. Ever since the disturbing visits by Ortega de Gasset, the Count of Keyserling, or Waldo Frank, few have not felt that compulsion for defining national character. Martínez Estrada himself was not able to resist its pull, nor could H. A. Murena, even as he attacked Martínez Estrada.

Of course, such national traits, so intimate and yet so generic, should have been conspicuous in all communicative endeavors, and the necessity of verifying them was so great, at least in texts and discussions, that they were seen everywhere, even though the facts denied this with their characteristic stubbornness, as Leopoldo Marechal did not fail to observe with evident sarcasm in *Adán Buenosayres* [1948] or Juan Filloy in *Op Oloop* [1934], to name only two clear though indirect critiques of the subject. For my part, and I am not being sarcastic here, I would like to contrast these characteristics with the tone found on national television these days, and, although the comparison might be surprising for evident reasons, to contrast it with the irrepressible inclination of politicians, from the president on down, to say whatever occurs to them, even when it is personal, ridiculous, or full of rage or tears. Not to mention the incorporation into normal language of expressions once considered embarrassing, very personal or even vulgar, and used only by men, which are now regularly used in advertising and by everyone in general, including women, once so circumspect, and most certainly by academics, who want to keep up to date on barroom speech or that from the soccer fields.

The world has changed, no one could deny such a powerful truth, and the same has occurred with language—perhaps the one can be inferred from the other, if language, as it seems, translates the changes in the world: we have gone from extreme modesty to shamelessness, perhaps, and no one much cares. Such modesty would have existed when a town was still young, a mere village, and such shamelessness would exist in its maturity—a strict dichotomy that is only acceptable, of course, if one ignores the falsity of both assertions: modesty does not characterize underdevelopment, nor shamelessness adulthood.

The argument of modesty, behind which were hidden numerous other mechanisms such as fear, censorship, insecurity, or immaturity (I cite the expression as a recollection of the argument insistently repeated by Gombrowicz),[1] has been used to interpret Argentine literature, and particularly, to enter the universe of those who have created it and compose it. The period covering most of the nineteenth century and more than half of the twentieth, has been understood as the provisional stage of one particular strategy of concealment, or more specifically, an elusive constant, as if, upon saying what they said, writers were avoiding saying what they should have said, and what they should have said was (and for that reason they did not say it) an unspeakable truth, contrary to their stated and perhaps deeply held personal convictions. According to some critics, this truth was a carefully hidden homosexuality; for others, a secret complicity with reprehensible political interests or structures. We might note that in the game of truth and evasion, censured writers appear, voluntarily or involuntarily, defending the worst causes, the most spurious interests of the class they belong to, the most irrational privileges. As a consequence, according to this argument, Argentine literature was formed by something contrary and even antagonistic to what can be implied in the generous act of writing, which, as everyone knows, is the height of the relationship between a human being and his consciousness, and of the collective consciousness with itself.

A subject for debate, clearly; in my opinion, this perspective is reductive and stifles the realization of something greater: where and how did literariness, strictly speaking, arise, in spite of the authors themselves and all that they are and think and feel and hide? How is literature produced in texts by someone who, like Sarmiento, could be accused of such terrible things, as has occurred since before Alberdi up to our own times? What is the nature of the change that makes certain texts indispensable on one level, while on a different level, they attempt to silence aspects of themselves?

From the argument about Argentine modesty, let us move to what writers cover up and critics denounce—it can be said that the modesty argument does not stand up to the quantitative test. The fact that the number of memoirs, autobiographies, and diaries published or unpublished up to the end of the nineteenth century clearly exceeds the number of novels (the largest group) and poems (where the naturally confessional tone makes them less common) belies the strength, if not the existence itself, of such modesty. And even the fact that in this century drawing to a close these proportions have become inverted—that is, there are now more novels and poems than memoirs—does not mean that this self-referential gesture has disappeared. One could say, in summary, that for the nineteenth century, what we refer to as "Argentine literature" was composed of memoirs, such as those of General Paz;[2] autobiographies, such as those of Sarmiento;[3] or diaries, such as Mansilla's[4]—to give some definitive examples. Such an overwhelming profusion, which continues into the twentieth century, indicates not only the force of one means of expression considered to be legitimate or authorized by a cultural form, but also the persistence of a desire to place material in the public sphere that could have been silenced if, indeed, the Argentine temperament really were characterized by modesty, or at least by silence and aloofness. Is it not the case that Argentines like to write about what they see, feel, and do even more than they like to see, feel, and do? Is it not the case that Argentines, more than any other group, felt and feel an irrepressible desire to move the private into the public, the personal into the social sphere?

This could be true, but it is also necessary to ask what type of Argentines we are dealing with. If one considers social interaction in general, it is quite likely that certain oral idiosyncrasies constitute the only vehicle for such desire: think of a café, friends, conversation, murmurs, gossip, "frankness," all traces that indicate an urgent need to not hold back anything; a generosity of feeling that does not hoard events or experiences but instead shares them in the hope that there will be more, that something will always happen that will give rise to a confidence or a confession, innocent intrigues, in short, blocked only by political or ethical disagreements, always already limiting a relationship. Similarly, if the confession is not expressed via concealment, if it is not a trick, it must be seen how far that contradictory, unarmed defenselessness will go in the most canonical situations—the psychiatrist's couch or the church's confessional—no matter how adulterated this canon might be.

But while such reflections might be applied to Argentines in general (if such a thing exists), or more specifically, to the "oral Argentine," something very different occurs with Argentines who hold what we could call "civil or symbolic responsibilities," that is, those who do not limit themselves to simply watching the world pass by, but rather do or want to do or try to do something transcendent with their lives in the social realm—in short, the politicians, the military, the intellectuals, the writers, or the leaders of any sort of prestigious or consequential activity for society. Those Argentines, and perhaps that sort of people in general, Argentine or not, sooner or later end up writing their memoirs. If what they have experienced gives their lives an exceptional character, they consider it imperative to write their autobiographies. And if what they have experienced, by virtue of the fact that they have experienced it, seems remarkable to them, they keep a diary. And if they feel that what they have seen should not be lost, they write their memoirs. It is clear that the quality of the results varies and depends less on what they have experienced than on the talent for writing each possesses, but what is most important is that many members of this group have felt compelled to carry out one of these three gestures—from the supreme director Gervasio Posadas to María Rosa Oliver—or two of the three—from Lucio Mansilla to Victoria Ocampo.[5]

For some, this compulsion was gratuitous: they simply wished to leave a testimony; others wrote in a more literary spirit—in order to establish a literature, as Sarmiento did, or in a paraliterary spirit—in order to explain a literature, as was the case with Enrique García Velloso or Manuel Gálvez. Of course this option creates a problem: at first, all pieces of writing, as has been said, comprised a national literature, perhaps because up to a point, there was nothing else. But their place in that literature was diminished or changed character when Argentine literature became more established and began to develop an order distinguished by genres. Thus writers of autobiographies, memoirs, and diaries began to carefully choose the purview of what they wrote, shifting their attention from events to the act of writing, endeavoring to enter the literature as full members (as can be seen in Victoria Ocampo's *Autobiografía* [Autobiography; 1979]), and not simply to be lodged there because there was nothing else, as was the usual case before Sarmiento's *Mi Defensa* [My Defense; 1843]. That work could well be considered the moment of transition from prehistory, when actions were spontaneous and their purpose purely referential, to history, where literature had to be established because it formed a part of a greater entity, a culture, which, in its turn, regulated, expressed, and guided the development of a nation.

The desire to write memoirs is strong in this class of Argentines. According to Adolfo Prieto in his indispensable *La literatura autobiográfica argentina* [The

Autobiographical Literature of Argentina; 1966], what was recounted in texts from the early part of the nineteenth century up to well into the twentieth tended to protect or restore or glorify the values of an elite, and even more, of a class—the oligarchy. Their analyses, which above all heed the assertions authors make of themselves, emphasize the classist, and therefore tendentious, character of the respective authors, whose evocations were strongly historicized, although seldom escaping the familiar focuses: revolutions (of May, of 90),[6] civil wars and wars of independence, the political periods dominated by Rosas and Mitre, the political compromise of 1880, immigration, and the organization of the modern state—all constituted the crux of the stories, in which the subjective inflections were like tenuous stitches, faded traumas, convolutions of the individual in homage to transcendence. However, there are temperaments like that of Manuel Belgrano[7] in whose pages there are romantic forerunners, a way to endure the war that surpasses, on the sentimental side, what would become Mansilla's self-consciousness or that which is implied in the title of Narciso S. Mallea's book, *Mi vida, mis fobias* [My Life, My Phobias], clearly indicative of a fundamental change in tone.

When Argentina was at last a modern country, after the presidency of Hipólito Yrigoyen, the memoirs and autobiographies that were published pursued different objectives, antagonistic to those of their predecessors, which, except in the case of the intellectuals, always maintained as their horizon the particular relationship between private and public that was typical of the old oligarchy. This can be clearly observed in the memoirs of the socialists Enrique Dickman or Nicolás Repetto,[8] testimonies to a new style of political struggle, witnesses to the rise of a new culture. This is also true of the anarchists (for example, the work of Eduardo G. Gilimón, *Un anarquista en Buenos Aires, 1890–1910* [An Anarchist in Buenos Aires, 1890–1910]), who were more mystical, preferring action to recollection, and as a consequence, they developed the genre to a lesser extent. This change in tone also occurs between generations: the memoirs of Gregorio Aráoz Alfaro, a national hero to this day, still carry the old stamp, while those of his son Rodolfo, several decades later, take stock of the social struggle and ridicule what for his father would have been sacred, including the familial tradition.[9] Ramón J. Cárcano (*Mis primeros 80 años* [My First 80 Years]) describes the change from a provincial country to a cosmopolitan one and takes stock of the country's protagonist-founders, while his son, Miguel Angel (*La fortaleza de Europa* [The Strength of Europe]) recalls the diplomats and aristocrats, not the fighters. The diaries of Eduardo Mallea relate the exploits of a tormented "I," locked in the verification of his struggle against the world. We have come a long way from the "exemplary I" of his perhaps relative Sarmiento, who believed that biographies, and with even more reason, autobiographies, were a mirror in which others should see themselves in order to sense, in a post-Hegelian way, the breath of the Spirit.

The compulsion to write memoirs, therefore, exists in the Argentine tradition, and encompasses, in a spectacular parenthesis, the apparent dimension of national modesty and reserve—and to such an extent that one must ask why the genre flourishes here perhaps more than in other places. It is possible that it is a belated, local, and anachronistic manifestation of the renaissance "eulogy," which apparently drove human beings to engage in exploits in order to obtain such glory, since not doing so meant living in limbo, outside of reality. If we replace "eulogy" with "national destiny" or "God is Argentine," terms adopted by one social group, perhaps we have an answer, though always provisional and insufficient. On the other hand, it is easier to recognize the apparent functions that the memoiristic or autobiographical act satisfies and that serve as an explanation if we ask of these writers why they wrote this kind of text. Sarmiento—to cite him is unavoidable—did it to combat slander; others in order to correct a misconception; others in order to avoid forgetting and to extract lessons from the past; still others to honor a lineage, and finally, steeped in sincerity, to uncover a despicable lie.

These are the stated intentions; what makes them attainable, that is, what makes it natural for one to set out to write, is not the existence of a rhetoric, which is more the case with poetry, but rather a new historical relationship between subjectivity and public space, which, in its turn, acquires a value—a democratic value—greater than that of private space. Changing relationships occur, then, when the public becomes consolidated and its structures are believed to be definitive, when the private and the subjective regain ground and the contents of memory is shifted. The one who narrates is no longer like Juan Manuel Beruti—who in his *Memorias curiosas* [Curious Memories; published between 1942 and 1946] reported for five decades what he observed around him—but like Gálvez, who recounts his participation in a restricted sphere— that of literature.[10] In this century, those who insist on chronicling their actions, such as Agustín Lanusse,[11] are not respected as writers; they are limited to continuing the nineteenth-century gesture, and they work with the same categories: exposition of a historical circumstance, justification of certain conduct, rectification of errors, and exoneration of responsibility.

This indicates that the times being evoked are convulsive times that, in addition, produce notable personalities capable of acting and of looking sagely around themselves, besieged at the same time by a neurosis of destiny. I have already defined these times; I could add that in these personalities, from Ignacio Núñez at the dawn of nationhood to Cárcano at the pinnacle of its pride, there was an equation in play whose terms were a sense of liberty, intoxication of decision, a clear desire for success, and, in decompensation, anguish in every one of these stages. On the one hand these terms have been exalted by romanticism, which, ever since Rousseau, places in the subject all hopes of understanding its own enigma and the enigma of the world. On the other hand, these same terms are quite appropriate for transferring experience—both the collective experience of great deeds and the individual experience of great passions—to literature as a possible way to renew it and find in it the path that dusty neoclassical rhetoric had kept blocked.

But the recent times of repression have also been convulsive and yet have not produced memoirist writings (General Camps's book is merely a detective-novel prolongation of his participation in "the process");[12] neither will they, I believe, give rise to autobiographies, although I have heard that Admiral Massera is organizing his papers. I suspect that the executants or executioners, in a manner inherent to the function they fulfilled, must be trying to forget as quickly as possible, while the victims, the other side, channel their memories, when they can, toward action through testimonies, which is not the same thing: they are attempting to denounce a crime, not defend their prestige or glorify their deeds.

This web, as we can see, is complicated, moving from a glance to a grand spectacle, and in the process, passing through protagonism and a capacity to interpret via a writing seen as imperative to create, and which, at some moment, is transformed into literature, into a country's own literature, as one of its most enduring forms. And if this assertion is pertinent to the past, that is, to the time of the formation of Argentine culture, in the present, it would all stop there if interested—as they could only be—points of view and information were all that could be found in texts. But if, on the other hand, we look at this breadth of material with a literary eye—which is not the same as judging its quality—we can see that there is an interplay between these three structures, autobiography, memoir, and diary. All three are very different, certainly, but cited or referred to as if they were one and the same, as if the common element in all of them, a gaze that accumulates observations, played the same role in all three. But it does not, and this is worth pointing out.

For we can say that autobiographies and memoirs are spread over the past; diaries, on the other hand, presume or pretend to enclose a present, or, at least, its sense. Furthermore, although the speaker—or narrator since come what may, it is always a question of narration—is always an "I," barely disguised at times as a discreet "we," he nevertheless is different in each case and adopts specific tactics, and this has its consequences.

Thus, in autobiography, the narrator is the principal actor but narrates from a distance, parsimoniously choosing the relatable points in order to reach a finality. For that reason, he naturally censors himself, if not falsifying outright, for which reason the testimonial value of what he says of himself and of the objects of his drama is dubious or cannot be trusted. But because there is contrivance in this arrangement in order to create an effect that does not rest on the truth but rather in the ambiguous shadow of the truth, autobiography approaches literature, borders on fiction, and in a way, surpasses it, because it deconventionalizes it. The fiction in autobiography is very different from that in force in the novel, at least in the more traditional model: it narrates by molding and not just reproducing, veils without obscuring, emphasizes without overwhelming, it eats away at fiction without weakening the illusions that fiction engenders, and above all, it reveals the enunciative operation of the narrator insofar as it makes this happen at the smallest distance possible from its referent. If narrating consists of overseeing the point of view of that being narrated, and, in order to do so, it is necessary to possess information for which the position of enunciation is determinant, then autobiography, in which the narrating "I" merges with the narrated "I," would be the point of narration par excellence.

In memoirs, on the other hand, the narrator makes us believe that he disappears. In this illusion of emptiness, he takes on the quality of a witness; he shifts toward the events recounted, whose condition is, then, their prestige or importance, and he feigns objectivity in his descriptions and judgments. If these are extreme or turbulent, it is because of their gravity and not because of the passions of the narrator. This shift benefits his memoirs and makes it possible to hear them—it is not the same thing to remember the plague, as does

Carlos Guido y Spano,[13] as to recall one's pleasant student days, as does Miguel Cané,[14] who was thus relegated by the spareness of events to the novel or to autobiography. What the narrator of a memoir recalls and writes is useful for history and not for providing an example for people, which is the proper aim of biography.

Finally, in diaries, the subject reveals himself to be something like a space where events occur and whose value is found in his participation in those events, whether they be major or minor in historical terms. His account records how within him, from a proximity that does not necessarily imply being an actor, everything reverberates that enters a gaze whose appropriateness for classifying needs no justification. Thus anyone can keep a diary, although of course the more important ones are those kept by subjects found interesting for other reasons: famous writers, warriors, saints, brilliant scientists, adventurers—these interest us more than those sentimental accountings or touristic notes that, at the most, are like photographs that evoke a moment only when they are shown.

Not that I am against diaries; indeed, I endorse them, for they have disciplinary value. I can be quite enthusiastic about some, and I am pleasantly surprised when I find that someone close to me keeps one in secret. As far as memoirs are concerned, I cannot imagine who would undertake this enterprise these days: the media and professional chroniclers now provide the information that before gave memoirs their meaning, besides which there are no longer great spectators or great actors, or even great discoveries. Autobiographies, on the other hand, or an element of them, "the autobiographical" (which for its part appears in various ways in all genres of literature—novels, poems, short stories, or theater), offer an outlet for narration that is becoming more and more interesting. It is interesting for psychological reasons, for one thing: in truth, everyone wishes to write, if not about themselves, perhaps from themselves. And for another, because it controls and regulates the interplay of fiction that seems to be depleting itself in a smothering of stereotypes only redeemable by a return to sincerity in whose unfolding the notion of proximity to what one narrates (nothing is closer to narration than one's own imagination) appears to be the only true exit.

Perhaps this reasoning explains the proliferation of autobiographies that we have seen in recent decades, not only here, but also in the rest of Latin America: it could be a response to the worn-out state of the mechanics of fiction and a

others are not? That question is essential, so much so that finding the answer constitutes the object of one important part of the study of literature.

But books and authors are not the only thing that the histories of literature contain, confine, or examine. Without a doubt, there is another system, implied by the first, but which can be differentiated from it, one that the first system takes part in: it is the system of the literary processes themselves that, on a different level, constantly in motion, nourish the aforementioned histories so they are no longer static but instead begin to stir. For they are, seen in this light, scenes of a struggle that diverse opponents maintain in order to sustain and renew them. Some of those competitors have already been established there on the inside, while others are still outside. The former fight to defend their place, while the latter attempt to conquer a place of their own, which, if they were to accomplish their goal, would always mean displacing those already installed, triumphing over someone. To put it another way, certain books and certain authors cling to the spot where they have been placed, and others try to take their spot, try to displace them.

In this way, one could understand the construction and reconstruction of literatures from the perspective of their histories; however, on a perhaps superficial level, what we refer to as "histories of literature" are always trying to be obstructionist, an objective they seem to achieve when we come to think of these libraries as definitive and unquestioningly consider the names that comprise them to be authorized, sacrosanct, fixed. Nevertheless, this process of struggle continues, even when it adopts that compact and homogenous shape of being finished.

José Martí has formed part of the Latin American library for several decades now, or at least one would think so, considering everything that has been written about him. Literary criticism, especially that of the 1920s and 1930s, wanted to hold him tightly, nailed down and stapled in place. His work, however, deserved a different kind of treatment. It took many historical upheavals, not only literary ones, to knock him out of that position and to make it clear that beneath that immobility there was a continuous movement. Once it had been stirred up, it was possible to ask questions of his work, questions that should be asked of all works included in the literary histories situated in those libraries: Why this author or this book? Why do they belong in the library?

There were of course external factors in this necessary dislocation, especially the Cuban Revolution and what it did with the figure of Martí, from his mythification to the creation of critical works. The result was that Martí was brought out of obscurity and was rediscovered by an anxious criticism of a different nature, which omitted or overcame or ignored the fact that previously Martí would have formed part of that predictable, immobile library that imprisoned on its shelves a long list of untouchables. The questions (Cartesian ones, to be sure, since they instill a doubt) that we should all ask, especially literary scholars (generally subservient to the literary institution) would take this form: Why Martí? Why do we need to worry about his work? Why is it important in his case to try to discover a secret that, furthermore, has been unveiled many times? Why does he continue to be important to us? Why do we try to see him in a new light?

I would like to respond to this in a roundabout way here. I will begin by recalling something that took place in this very room here at the University of Buenos Aires, about a year and a half ago [in 1993]. On that occasion, Roberto Fernández Retamar received an award: he was named professor honoris causa. His acceptance speech discussed Martí and Martí's journalistic experience in Argentina.

I am not going to summarize what he said. I merely want to recall a moment during his speech that I remember very well because "something happened" in that moment. It was when he indicated that the first reader Martí had in Buenos Aires, when he published his first article, was none other than Sarmiento. Fernández Retamar read a fragment of the letter from the illustrious writer to the young poet, with its exaggerated expression and high praise, as if impressed by the images and perhaps, I think, by the prose. If I remember correctly, Fernández Retamar emphasized Martí's assertions, resplendent truths that had given rise to Sarmiento's commentaries, also resplendent. But the situation was reversed a few years later, Fernández Retamar recounts, when Sarmiento made some vehement negative commentary about another article of Martí's on women in the United States.

So, there was a positive commentary and a negative one. Fernández Retamar, a defender of Martí, agrees with Sarmiento in the first case and disagrees with him in the second because, according to him, what Martí "said" was justified by certain reasons or explanations that, according to him, Sarmiento did not understand. In my opinion, he fell into the trap of truth.

But that is not "what happened" that day. What happened was that when he read the two initial fragments, the one from Martí's article and the one from Sarmiento's letter, a current ran through the auditorium—I could see it happen from the stage, and I can tell you that we all felt a reverberation, something that happens very rarely. We all looked at one another when we heard those phrases, from one to the other, as if saying: "This is literature. It has lingered here a moment, in this privileged place, that ever-so-ephemeral thing we call literature."

But this did not happen because the phrases confirmed blinding truths about something important, long sought as a revelation. They introduced truths, perhaps—we won't debate now, if it's been debated before, just what those truths might be—but what we felt was a power, a force so overwhelming that no one who heard those phrases was unaffected. But let me explain; it was not something mystical, but rather something else that I insist on calling "conditions of reading," a concept according to which there is no true reading if there is not a suspension of knowledge. And what permeated that scene was nothing less than "the letter," in the material sense of the word: the letter as the foundation of the linguistic—and thus, social—mortar, the letter as an element in whose work human beings are entirely situated.

Sarmiento, as convincing as ever, noticed this in Martí, and he remarked on the vitality, the confidence, the power, but what he later criticized was an idea, a conception. According to him, Martí did not understand very well the process of the liberation of women in the United States; Fernández Retamar, in turn, perhaps looking at it from a perception of how Sarmiento is experienced critically in our present intellectual and political climate, attempts to rebut Sarmiento's critiques and defend Martí, or explain his position on this point, excusing the influence of Spain on his language, as if that were a reasonable excuse.

Who is right is not the important thing here. What is important is the reverberation of the word, and any value of this brief story stems from the consequences of Martí's situation and what his textuality implies for literature—that is, the starting point by which he is recognized and which would be the center point from which his figure emerges. As for the consequences, I would say that various critical approaches to his work spring from all of this.

At any rate, to synthesize what I have just indicated, there are those who want to see in Martí a "summary" of the truth, everywhere and in all respects. On the other side are those who are prepared to recognize the vibration of the word, which would not be the mere mechanical presence of beauty; to speak in those terms would of course create a third position, an archeologizing one, it seems to me, in that Martí himself spoke in those terms—beauty as an ideal.

In terms of the antagonism between the first two positions, we should keep in mind that the image "Martí = truths" tends to prevail, even though it does not have as much force as its supporters attribute to it: there will always be someone who contradicts it, there will always be a political context that will allow reinterpretations. The form of such truths can change depending, in turn, on the form of the social conflict or the possibilities for using his texts; in fact, in the past (I am referring more or less to the period from 1960 to 1985), the result has been an idolization that allows us to explain other factors, though not necessarily Martí's significance.

With respect to the second position, it has been said, and continues to be said in a preliminary approach, that Martí's language is deeply rooted in the language of Spain, with archaisms and expressions that could have no other source. My lack of background in stylistics keeps me from being able to describe the other mechanisms that characterize his language (but that without a doubt are there): that language has a connection, it rests on tradition and on a certain history. But what I can say is that his language, just as it appeared that afternoon in this very place, is above all "substantive," and by that I mean "materializable," that is, it is felt and worked like material.

This seems simple, and its results are, but (and it could be no other way) it is the fruit of a long historical process that has given rise to powerful displacements and to a tremendous dynamism. What I mean is this: romantic prose or poetry gives the impression that the language is not all that important, that in a certain sense it is transparent with respect to the uses for which it is employed—sentiments, ideas, or ideologies. But in modernity, to the contrary, including the experience of the Latin American avant-garde, the language is seen and felt to be opaque, like material to be worked rather than a mere vehicle. This displacement is immediately noticeable in Rubén Darío; it is part of the basis for what is called, erroneously, "Darío's obscurity," but it is also noticeable in Martí with a different kind of radiance, with a different kind of quest.

Given this assertion, we can turn to Martí's *Simple Verses* [*Versos sencillos*; 1891], whose force resides in the incessant cascade of images; seen as a whole, the book is a kaleidoscope of great imaginative wealth. So much so that we could link it to his essays in terms of their use of the gaze, although of course in this part of his work the gaze is turned outward, while in *Simple Verses*, though continuing to nourish itself from the outside, the gaze seems to be turned inward on an interior of great depth, reflection, and anguish. In both cases it is a question of a gaze that collects, and in that collecting nothing is lost and what is gathered serves to stimulate it, to go on making and producing images that are organized in a succession or in a series. In this way, the images come one after the other, and what is common to all of them is that there is an "I" that binds them together and that constitutes the space of the imaginative experience that allows them to emerge.

This observation gives rise to a number of questions concerning the aforementioned displacements: this cascade, which is of course implicit, establishes an idea of narrative as shrouded and interrupted, not a referential or narrative narration in a traditional sense. The narration of which I'm speaking has its starting point and its articulation, and perhaps its endpoint as well, in the "I," which, if confirmed, would reveal a kind of recursiveness, a figure that I believe corresponds to narration.

I would say that this kind of articulation and this function of the "I" are traits of a Latin American modernism that placed the key to poetic freedom in a productive subjectivity; I indicated this already with respect to Darío in whom it would function, to paraphrase Deleuze and Guattari, like a desiring machine and a very condition of his poetics. A similar "I" can also be noted in Martí: hence the affinity and the correspondences between the two poets, which explain why one can be evoked by the other as mentor and why one can recognize the other as a son. These relationships would not be born of simple affection but must come from some kind of more profound communication or a common understanding of a discursive operation that is in the midst of changing.

In these discourses, the "I" does not have a confessional character, although at times it does not renounce that entirely, but rather is an articulator and, at the same time, a key, a condition, and a guarantee of narrativity. Here the issue of separation by genres is called into question. And while in Martí's case the "I" has a good deal of the lyric romantic "I" (which is also true of Darío), I do not believe this is a ruse or disguise or concealment, but a vestige that does not impede us from recognizing its essentially discursive character, that is, its function to support narrativity like that which pushes poetry to escape from its isolation.

To put it another way, there is something very powerful and very secret in Martí, a displacement that operates as a condition of the reading still possible for his work, and that a present-day reading seeks beyond the consecrations—in the texts themselves and not in the position they occupy in the libraries.

In connection with this issue, there is another theme I would like to raise. It is in regards to Ottmar Ette's article on Martí's reception.[1] He points out something that we all recognize and that we all continue to suffer from: Martí has tended to be viewed (especially during the decade of the thirties, when Cuba was less a republic and more a culture dissolving) as divided—one minute he is seen as a politician, the next as a literary figure. In the former case, his work can be appropriated by certain causes or used for certain ends, and on the other side are those who approach the poet or the writer in order to encapsulate him or isolate him from any possible contamination.

Ette wisely asserts that we should go beyond this division and see Martí holistically. But how can we go about this? The method Ette proposes is reception theory, which in turn also involves a decentering without taking into account the inflationary character it possesses; it would no longer be a question of what occurs in the texts but rather of what goes on in the readers, who thus by their own volition would adopt a new perspective.

And thus a new problem: when we read a poet or a writer, can we maintain an innocence, allowing us to see beyond the inflated criticism imposed on them and that makes each one a victim of what occurs outside of them? At one time this led us to see Martí either as only political or as only literary; today it could lead us to see him as the "product" of a struggle in which he would be merely one cog among many.

It occurs to me that we could examine this question in light of the three critical possibilities that are more or less operative presently. First, there is a group of studies, which we could consider to be above all Cuban, that are sensitive to what we could call Martí's "truths." It surprises me that Roberto Fernández Retamar felt the need to assert that Martí had anticipated Lenin in more than one theoretical aspect. Martí, by this account, can be seen not only as someone who gave his life for a cause but also as a perceptive prophet of the present, like a Text in which we can find everything we need.

Second is what we could modestly call the "Argentine school": dispense with these issues and return to the texts themselves so we can once again focus on the material they are made of, so that reading them is not reduced only to the perception of values, but that also the reader can understand what could be termed their productivity.

While the first two are pitted against each other, there is yet a third possibility: the "European school." Its spokespeople show up like spectators of a very Latin American combat, adopting the discourse of one side one minute, and that of the other side the next minute, tensely awaiting the shape the dispute will take.

We can assume, obviously, that the adherents of each possibility have already staked out their position, and thus there is no use on insisting. Instead, and in order to conclude, I would like to share an observation having to do with this proposal to return to the texts. It grew out of a reading not of the *Simple Verses* nor the *Versos libres* [Free Verses; posthumously published in 1913] nor the *Crónicas* [Newspaper Articles], but of the *Declaración de Montecristi* [Declaration of Montecristi; 1895],[2] a text that could easily be considered the foundation of a mode of discourse. Reading it was an experience of rupture for me: to think that someone in an extreme political situation, confronting or initiating the process that will lead to his own death, which he could perhaps foresee, could write a text so absolutely poetic and at the same time political. But it is not poetic in and of itself for rhetorical reasons; rather it proposes another idea, that of a discourse permeated by a verbal dimension that the norm excluded and still excludes.

And if this reading has some consistency, it is because in recent years one of the recurrent and dramatic themes of political analysis in Latin America has been the obsolescence of political language. Critics abound, but rarely do they tell us what elements or what perspectives we could use to renew or replace the old, worn-out language. The usual reaction is to admit that the providentialist languages of leaders who arise from nowhere are new, in the same way that people believed that Hitler's discourse was new. And the extraordinary thing is to consider the subject in terms of linguistic codes, that is, as a question of an interaction according to which all language turns political when (refusing to renounce its own circumstances, its own experiences and knowledge) it is used to serve political ends.

To put it another way, why exclude poetry? Why should we assume that poetic language cannot be the basis of a new political language? This, I believe, is what Martí dared to do in the *Declaración de Montecristi*. And that daring or that vision is not limited to this document: it infuses all of his work. And if we consider that this could be the key to his effectiveness and dynamism, we will also have an explanation for why he remains staunchly in the library, where he confronts other texts and responds to the secret motion that is always rearranging that library in never ending crisis.

The Riches of Poverty Revisited

Early in 1984, the Universidad Nacional Autónoma de México [National Autonomous University of Mexico] published two large volumes containing all the "chronicles" or newspaper articles of César Vallejo, including those he wrote in Europe between 1924 and 1938, published originally in *Mundial, Variedades, Favorables Paris Poemas,* and other journals, mostly Peruvian.[1] The first volume also contains Vallejo's university thesis from Trujillo, which dealt with Spanish American modernism, and a prologue by Enrique Ballón Aguirre, who conducted the research and prepared the annotations. Ballón Aguirre is also Peruvian and an ardent high priest of both the highly visible and the obscure works of one of the greatest modern poets. He also edited, in Peru, Vallejo's plays, which are not very well known, and it was he who wrote the prologue to the Biblioteca Ayacucho edition of Vallejo's poems. His competence, dedication, and results in this far-reaching project enrich our understanding of a complex and at times contradictory body of work, which in many aspects continues to present us with the enigma of its singularity.

Thus, in terms of his "works," I suppose that everything that Vallejo wrote has now been published and is available to whomever wishes to engage in that passion. The only thing missing when I first started writing about this, and now it has been accomplished, was for the National Autonomous University of Mexico to publish Ballón Aguirre's study of Vallejo's articles, which formed the central part of his doctoral dissertation, researched from primary sources in accordance with semiotic theories from the school of Greimas.

An entire world is brought to life in these at times hastily written but always fevered and intelligent pages. The world is that of Europe between the two world wars—a particularly complicated time, as we well know. We can imagine Vallejo at the juncture between his poetry and that world, and we can question the various fundamental points: his intellectual and dynamic unity, his relationship with Latin America, or, rather, the relationship of his work with Latin America, and his ideological trajectory. We can even sense or intuit why he did not return to Peru, what kept him there in Paris, despite his poverty and suffering.

When I first began writing these notes, I was not aware of Ballón Aguirre's earlier thesis. That ignorance allowed me, illustrating a general principle in reading, to approach the "articles" without any mediation. These articles span, as already suggested, a turbulent historical period, of which the least one could say is that it was filled, just as now, with an unprecedented proliferation of artistic avant-garde movements and by organic authoritarian political undertakings, as well as by an enthusiasm for technological and social innovations along with their problematic counterparts of underemployment, violence, hunger, and serious misgivings about human life and labor. Vallejo speaks to us of all this. He narrates that tormented multiplicity also portrayed in the caustic French cinema of the period between the wars—gray, critical, shadowy, and despairing.

As was Vallejo himself? Of course the most important thing, from the perspective of Latin American literary history and even of literary history in general, is César Vallejo the poet. But Vallejo the man, due to his strange charm, makes one uneasy, with his hat, his rumpled suit, his way of descending hotel staircases, his reserve, and above all, the way he stayed tied to a compelling but cold city, resolutely trying to differentiate himself while at the same time mingling with those crude, common citizens, grumbling and practical. One of them, Georgette Philippart, became his wife and later his literary executor, to the horror of all those followers of Vallejo who, beginning with Juan Larrea, proliferated after his via crucis came to an end. But before then, she shared with Vallejo that vast suffering that he never ceased to express, with her typical manners of a "middle-class" French woman, as far away from César's Andean dreams as she was also close, protecting him from the tropical viruses that sapped his strength and finally killed him.

These articles, covering all imaginable topics, were written—one guesses, one knows—out of an urgent need for money, money that nonetheless arrived too little, too late, or not at all: an elementary exchange—news or opinions for money, an exchange that in Vallejo's difficult life was always thwarted, as it is today for others in Paris, in Lima, in Mexico, and across the whole world. That thwarting, which contributed to Vallejo's wrapping himself in silence, was the cause of his major despair, which in turn, augmented the hermeticism of his poetry and gave rise to a teleological or symbolic-transcendent approach, such as that formulated by Juan Larrea in his book *Vallejo, o Hispanoamérica en la cruz de su razón* [Vallejo, or Spanish America on the Cross of Reason]. Despite the mystical sense he saw in and attributed to Vallejo, Larrea never forgot the chronic lack of money that hounded the poet, nor the financial support Larrea himself provided him, a disinterested support, it is true, but nevertheless, always insufficient, hampered by a sense of decorum. Without stereotyping, we can say that Larrea appears as the well-fed rich man who does the interpreting, modeling what we call "interpretation," and Vallejo as the poor man who produces the raw materials for that interpretation. Are we not still perhaps "raw material," theoretical and practical, from which others construct an image of Latin America, raw material for their discussions at conferences and for their publication of impassioned research in expensive volumes that will never become a part of our miserable libraries?

Be that as it may, and curbing these dangerous analogies, we should say that despite financial assistance or fellowships or subsidies or payments,[2] the lack of money was constant throughout Vallejo's life; he always lacked the basics, always lacked money, and there was always deprivation and an obligatory asceticism, the severity imposed by poverty. But out of that poverty and deprivation also came the lush and resplendent imaginative transformation, the so-called human poems,[3] as others called them, since Vallejo could not even give a name to his "products."

Poverty then, as the point of departure for writing, as a fundamental theme that becomes concretized in multiple negative images, like a reverse inventory: "O, bottle without wine!,"[4] "From this bench I'm off, from my breeches,"[5] "No. Its guffaw has no plural";[6] it is the "now famed centavo" (famous, most certainly, for its lack) that he exalts in the poem "Today a splinter has entered her,"[7] a synthesis not only of what Vallejo wanted to say or express or in fact did say, but also of where he said and to whom he said "how much suffering," "human men."[8]

An equation comes to the fore here: poor conditions, rich results. How are we to understand this? Vallejo wrote many articles and poems, some plays, a few short stories, and a novel. Certainly what has most deeply affected Latin America are his poems (his plays are weak and thematically wedded to a knee-jerk communism, his novel *Tungsten* [1931] follows the same path, his articles are incidental), poems illuminated by everything else, at least to the point that we can see the concrete, material base from which they are forged, especially those he wrote during those terrible years in Paris, as well as those he wrote much earlier, in a Peru lost from the beginning, a feeling of loss clearly articulated in *The Black Heralds* [1918] and *Trilce* [1922]. That base is poverty, but a poverty that engenders riches without equal. In other words, a modest referent, a dazzling projection, and the imagination as an amazing foundry. Could this be a characteristic of the poetry—or culture—of Latin America? Does that indefinable Latin American flavor of Vallejo's writing consist of that capacity, which is also recognizable in other products?

In terms of the product—and this can be seen in Vallejo's case due to the high esteem in which his work was held—it can be said that it was never extinguished by his poverty and suffering. Poverty can extinguish talent, art, love, inventiveness—it does so in other areas, as for example when it holds back the development of science or engenders despotism. And yet it seems not only not to impede the imagination but in fact perhaps encourages it with the only means at its disposal. The imagination that creates from and out of poverty constitutes, therefore, "great riches," the only true capital we have at our disposal, whose potential we do not recognize or that leaves us despairing or helpless.

Perhaps this equation is the foundation of the most important thing produced in Latin America, both in terms of what these manifestations say about identity, as well as what their very structural framework can tell us, precisely because it is a structuring equation. On a cultural level this seems indisputable to me: there has been a need to invent everything, as we can see in Sarmiento or in Spanish American modernism. And so it remains today, at the cultural level (in terms of circumstances) and at the economic and political levels—culture is a way of escaping from the morass, an escape we must find to avoid suffocation; we need to invent everything from what little we actually have.

Of course, the issue is not to condemn ourselves to poverty, but rather to produce from within that poverty, which is our true condition. To deny that condition would be to condemn ourselves to insignificance, as it would also be, for example, to make ourselves believe that we have a great deal because we owe more than what we have.

I have been thinking in these terms for several years now. I wrote about it with regard to Sarmiento,[9] in whom the tension between the wasteland as a verification of reality or as a symbolic projection turns into a plan of construction—merciless, to be sure, but at least clear. Perhaps the lesson we learn from Vallejo matters more—his ill fortune, his sacrifice—in trying to visualize that to which we should aspire, or to put it another way, in trying to reclaim what would be the basic condition of truly being a culture on a par with others.

Lack and Excess in José Bianco's *Shadow Play*

From the beginning of José Bianco's intense and justly celebrated novella *Shadow Play* [*Sombras suele vestir*; 1941] certain moves stand out clearly that promise a displacement of the fantastic element evident in certain inescapable theoretical stances. Despite the evasive profile of this designation, "the fantastic" is insufficient as a category (perhaps because it is excessively affirmative) for understanding the scope of this text: saying this should be enough to reveal the possibilities and the limitations for exercising a type of criticism that I would like to call "critical work" [*trabajo crítico*].[1] Furthermore, to propose something in relation to the implied mechanism of that designation tightens the system of instrumental relationships called "literary criticism," which generally operationalizes and formulates requirements, and seeks unexpected aid from other systems destined to shed light on a different class of objects. On this occasion, I can predict that it will be psychoanalysis.

Inside and Outside the Fantastic Dimension: Argentine Realism

To begin with, and without demanding too much from the word "fantastic," which, as it were, has to do with modes of representation even if it distorts them somewhat or treads new paths, we can say that the fantastic, in this story at least, is obvious; in effect, events in the story appear normal that in reality are implausible. In other words, situations not subject to the law of causality or based in the causalities grounded in common beliefs or in other texts, are allowed in the broad spectrum of this category.[2] Here this characteristic occurs because one character lives with another who in reality is dead for everyone else. Certainly Tzvetan Todorov can help us determine more clearly into which subclass or nuance of the fantastic we could place this story without forcing it too much, as often occurs, contributing to the frequent accusation that criticism labels everything it looks at and forces it to fit into its own paradigms.

If we were to content ourselves with that determination, no doubt we would finish quickly, but we would also overlook a permanent critical requirement, one that has to do with a history—which is my history—of those who attempt criticism. That history, to put it briefly, has to do with the area of "signification," which, as seems obvious, is not only beyond apprehension and description of the evident—as is the fantastic in this case—but also surrounds, accompanies, and adds density to all verbal acts, whether or not they have fantastic intent. So, as in any other critical situation, what we will try to discern or delimit is the signification, or at least we will begin this quest, though it may prove to be beyond our abilities.

Now, since it is evident that this story is of the fantastic genre, would we not be forcing things if we brought up the question of signification? Would it not imply diminishing what the text proposes, which, undeniably, is there? Would we not be insisting on looking with our own paradigm to the detriment of other paradigms that enjoy broad support, not only by powerful traditions of genre but also by very consolidated modes of reception?

As can be seen, there is a clash of positions: one, systematic, is based on the idea that there is no text that does not manage to signify, and, as a consequence, no text escapes the process of the production of signification. The other, contingent, maintains in its analysis that the literature of the fantastic, perhaps because it so clearly presents questions about verisimilitude, is beyond all semiotic interrogations—nothing can be asked of it that does not conform to its fantastic character. In any case, it can be said as a refutation of that argument that that character, what we call "the fantastic," is nothing more than an effect of the reading or, in other words, a convention that, therefore, does not involve productive semiosis.

We could always maintain the distance between the two positions and treat this text as one of the fantastic genre, simply examining its effect in the reading. But to do that would be to condemn this and other similar and highly regarded texts to remain outside the realm of critical work, which, by definition and by choice, tries to find in all kinds of texts, in whatever category they might be placed, their key to productivity: for critical work, classifications are merely a starting point, not a limit, and this allows us to create a framework from any formulation, whatever its level and category. It is not a theory with preferences for those texts that will easily confirm it, but rather an attempt to discover categories so encompassing that as they are passed over texts, they illuminate the specificity of literary discourse, as well as and at the same time the uniqueness of the texts.

But since this is not a question of denying the evident, the problem posed here is to find the meeting point between these two positions. It is worth making clear from the beginning that at that site, the fantastic element would be a point of entry, a primary and indispensable working hypothesis, but not a limit or an end.

And so, if the fantastic is above all an "effect," what does this effect consist of in this story? One could say that, essentially, it is created by the presence of a dead woman in a representational order that should exclude her. This order is characterized by a basic verisimilitude, yet the dead woman lives with those elements (people, objects, relationships) that define her as just one more element among them, in a type of fictional verisimilitude. Put another way, this woman exists, as any other woman would exist, and participates in certain ceremonies, yet at the same time she is dead. And while the text strategically hides this discrepancy, since the anomaly is never stated, at the same time, there are clues scattered throughout that become clear to the reader at the moment of revelation (which is also the moment of consecration of the fantastic character). Expressions such as "I have the eyes of a corpse" [7], "a very clear grey" [8], "to disappear" [21], "her two loved ones, apparitions in that grayness" [4], are stated as a kind of lesson, something like "we were telling you, but you couldn't hear."

The destruction of this verisimilitude and its displacement by the fantastic are all the more jolting because the verisimilitude stems from an almost realist descriptive impulse, full of subjects that are very characteristic of social realism in Argentine literature. These include the interior space of the apartment, the girl who becomes a prostitute in order to support her family, the mentally impaired son, the decline of a lineage or the aristocracy that must come down in the world, the large family house handed down for generations, the neighborhood gossip, the world of the servants, the acquisition of wealth through financial endeavors, the journey by boat to Europe, and so on; these topics, which in social realism are "that which is told," confirm a form of Argentine literature, and up to a certain point, a paradigm that runs from Florencio Sánchez to Manuel Mujica Láinez and Cortázar.[3] In order to accentuate this characteristic even more, a certain motion that parodies characteristic discourses (for example, the discourse of biblical erudition, of the traditional story of the father's immigration, or of psychiatric opinion) must be included. And, if we talk about the paradigm as an integrated network, at least for these three powerful discourses, we must say that they are created in the naturalist moment and they forcefully define, above all, the "Argentine novel," as a designation of character all but tied to an identity. Its fundamental characteristic is the desire to "make them believe" in an indisputable referent—this would be Argentine reality—and one cannot write without reproducing it.[4]

In order to prove that in this story we are dealing with a different issue or a different dimension or, in other words, that the traditional Argentine realism does not predominate, here the fantastic element takes form from the moment of rupture or suspension of the coherence of the story told, diminishing its importance by focusing on another relationship, brought into play so as to produce an effect on the reader through identification: when Sweitzer, the verisimilar character, reads the facts, puts together the clues, and reaches the conclusion that the dead woman is there amongst them, he feels a shudder pass through him that we realize is supposed to be shared by the reader.

So, therefore, there is a series of vertiginous readings that are superimposed: that of the discursive paradigm's apparent verisimilitude; that found in a second plane, which makes its way, intratextually, into Sweitzer's reading; that of the fantastic effect; and of course, that of critical work, which tries to articulate all of these.

And, since we are talking about verisimilitude, the fantastic that takes form in this way generates a passable inverisimilitude, which we could call "familiar," since the story of the dead woman among the living is part of a well-known tradition—in ghost stories, in oral traditions, even in children's stories. Such inverisimilitude, which increases toward the end, does not break any narrative rule, so that if we call the system of rules "syntax," there can be no doubt that such inverisimilitude is simply semantic, as in fairy tales or ghost stories. This distinction is neither frivolous nor fruitless: it is related to operational systems—those that tend to break the rules produce a syntactic inverisimilitude, such as the case with Macedonio Fernández. The others, in a ritualistic way, attempt to make believable a representation that common opinion holds as unbelievable.[5]

Of course there is no accusation or reproach in this examination of *Shadow Play*. One does not ask the inverisimilitude of this story to be other than what it is, and what it is, namely, semantic, can be uncovered in the approach we are using because of the story's transitional character, that is, as the point at which the search for signification in this text—as we would search in any other—and the specificity of the fantastic gesture meet. In short, here is where the conflict is resolved between the two positions presented at the beginning as a critical-theoretical problem.

Verisimilitude/Inverisimilization: Revelation and Clues

To repeat, the inverisimilitude here consists of the fact that a dead woman is represented as cohabiting with a living man, or that he and others believe that she has lived amongst them, or that it is insinuated, via images that lead one to this conclusion, that she may have lived among them. And this representation does not have a deliberately symbolic significance; it does not imply a "however" that would follow a judgment about reality, something like "I don't believe in ghosts, but on the other hand. . . ." It is, rather, a question of an inverisimilar figuration that tends to alter textual values and open itself to other possibilities that could be found in a text and in its articulation.

But this figuration *is* fabricated, one can see, although it would be impossible to thoroughly list the productive operations. Let us say, as an example of such operations, that on the one hand there is a "revelation," and on the other, there are a certain number of clues that elicit a rereading in which the reader changes the focus of attention to things in the text that may seem gratuitous. Brief comments or details that appear unimportant take on a new light after the revelation. Now, from a particular theory of reading that does not depend on continuity and which fragments and then recombines pieces at a different level, these two cases, revelation and clues, can be connected, the connection supposing a second look and two levels of reading, one literal—that which catches the revelation, and the other evidential—that which examines the flashes of clues, that problematizes without any finality or immediate answer, that hones in on details that seem irrelevant. For its part, this trail that moves backward from end to beginning or from revelation to clues, is the inverse of what the character Sweitzer experiences—who, as he moves forward, confronts and forces us to confront the unbelievable, to confront the inverisimilitude—and ends at the revelation. In other words, he goes forward in order to understand what happened before, while we must go backward from the final point Sweitzer arrives at in the end.

We now know what the revelation consists of—Sweitzer realizes that Jacinta was dead—but the revelation also takes on its fantastic character because it proposes a violent dislocation of planes, a forced cohabitation between what seems to exist and what we finally realize exists no more. In short, the revelation is of a "lack," a word that, as soon as it appears, as soon as it is inscribed, begins to illuminate other instances in the text.

As for the clues, they are like furtive, tenuous foreshadowings, whose identification as such in the discourse is revealed only via an active retrieval, as we have indicated, not an inert one. Such retrieval is possible by the operation of a "reading memory," no doubt accumulative and preclassificatory, but, in any event, presemiotic, or in psychoanalytic terms, heedful only of the signification, with all of its inexactness and risks. We don't know what such phrases as "I have the eyes of a corpse" [7], or "her two loved ones, apparitions in that greyness" [4], or "I fear that one day you will vanish" [15], or "nobody seemed to notice her presence" [16], or "he would have liked to be consumed, . . . to disappear once and for all" [20—21], or "vague, distant, as if dispersed" [20] "mean to say," except what they say at face value. We can think of them as ambient or descriptive devices, or, in the best of cases, as metaphors, and in this sense, as concealing, although until we come to the aforementioned revelation, we don't know what they might conceal except that by concealing, they give rise to a suspicion that in itself, as a suspicion that "it means to say something else," can take us off to anywhere.

But we now know where it takes us, given that we are now acting from a rereading, and we come to see those metaphors as clues once the so-called revelation has occurred.

Now, in this instance, the phrases quoted above, and surely others as well, compose a small corpus that can be examined, presenting various possibilities. We can detect a thread that runs from the more explicit "death" to the more allusive "disappearance," and then in a subtle movement of transference, to "her two loved ones, apparitions in that greyness" [4] (a phrase that heralds the only apparition recognizable as such). This phrase in particular, without ever leaving the circuit of clues in which we can see notions of evanescence, of disappearance, of inadvertence, can be connected to another circuit that covers broader areas of the text. This can be characterized by the presence of two symbolic nuclei that communicate semantically: the "color gray" and the movement of "blurring."

If we pause for a moment in this subsystem, we cannot help but notice that gray, as a descriptive element, predominates over any other color ("gray rug" [8], "grey eyes" [7], "grey doves" [7], "greyness" [4], etc.). This undeniable presence must stem from a decision, though that does not necessarily mean it is a "deliberate choice." This repetition has, in my opinion, as much to do with stylistics as with a semiotic scope.[6] In that sense, I would say that the use springs from a need that can be linked to other registers in the text. Be that as it may, it implies not only a generalization—all depictions are gray—but also, and more important for our analysis, an image of the loss of clarity and sharpness that impedes one from seeing and perceiving the contours of things—clouds, for instance—at the moment of their impression. This effect of dissolution is equivalent to a "blurring." As can be seen, the two ideas that I alluded to earlier have been reunited.

With this idea of blurring now established, and proceeding in the same way as in previous cases so as to repeat a kind of methodical process, we can see that there is some sort of suppression of definition in what is described—a telling and not telling—so that things appear with vague and diffuse contours, contradicting or confronting a principle of precision dear to realism, classical realism as well as the Argentine version, and in this way becoming more apparent than if one were to merely follow some ideological creed. Here too there is a telling and a not telling. As one example, we can point to Stocker's description of the house and the dinner attended by his friend and associate, Sweitzer—and, evanescently, Jacinta, the dead woman. To synthesize, then, using this example, we could say that "grey" and "blurred" are connected in the formula "everything dissolved into greyness" [27], complemented by the very pertinent expression: "Jacinta felt overwhelmed by exhaustion, which blurred the traces of the man with whom she had been barely two hours earlier at María Reinoso's" [4].

Very well, the system "grey/blurred," to which we can add the notion of "traces" (clues?) as a remainder from the quotes necessary to corroborate the hypothesis, culminates in an image of dissolution. This is their base— dissolution holds up this triad. But coinciding with this same image is an evidential system in its entirety, not only because a large part of what we can consider as clues are about partial and momentary dissolutions, but also because it highlights the fundamental contents of the revelation—a death, the maximum dissolution, the supreme blurring, the implementation of absolute "lack," just as we have anticipated.

The productive character of the relationship between clues and revelation is clear, then: a dialectical relationship, if we think of each as diverse instances that interact in the text, as if they were two different places but somehow interwoven. As we indicated, this productive character, as such, stems from a reading we have characterized as "critical" and which at this time means integrative, a reading from beginning to end, set loose in turn by an internal reading of the text—that carried out by the character of Sweitzer, who is unaware of the clues we have been accumulating in our memory. Yet despite being unaware of them, something stirs in his mind, an intuition, a dissatisfaction that can never be fully satisfied because his logic is of a different sort, but his suspicion allows us to convert mere innocent phrases into clues.[7] It could be said that a certain "lack" of clues—and here the word "lack" reappears—or put another way, the state of facing a void, initiates an investigation, what we could call, borrowing from another field, "a survey," which is destined to culminate not so much in restitution but in a fullness of meaning. "His investigative spirit was alerted" [27], the text tells us, as if enabling him or authorizing him for the steps he has just begun to take.

The Letter That Is Lacking, the Letter in Excess: Vampires

Perhaps it would not be a waste of time to point out that the preceding schema has a rhetorical value, or if you prefer, one connected to a particular genre—that of the detective story. The investigation (think back to the Borgesian gesture that appears throughout *Ficciones* [1944]) tries to determine guilt or cause but always from a position of ignorance or a deficiency of information, in short, the realm of lack.[8] It is well known that such investigations can be carried out in literature (as in real life) in many ways—by conjecture, as with Poe; by reasoning, as with Doyle; by buying information, as with the police; by allowing oneself to be borne along by fleeting impressions, as with Chandler. In this story it is carried out via a process of displacement: Sweitzer leaves by taxi with Doña Carmen, the guardian of the autistic boy; he speaks with María Reinoso, the madam; and he goes to see Lucas, the servant, all after having gone to see Stocker in the sanitarium. Might this displacement be a simile of other displacements in other registers? To put it another way, if what Sweitzer carries out is something like a kind of peripeteia, there might be other homologues, but in the plane of writing, in more intimate registers, such as, for example, that of finality—determining a truth, a revelation, illuminating a semiotic process.[9]

But what is being investigated here? On Sweitzer's part, consciously and voluntarily, it is above all the truth about the lack of Jacinta. For Stocker, who was presented as living with her, she simply left, but he believes she will come back and he awaits her return. But Sweitzer knows that the investigation is about something else, it is about Jacinta's very existence, or rather, her nonexistence. In investigating this "lack," since we are on the subject, and in the powerful light of this notion, which makes us examine narrative structures in another way, we can see that he, Sweitzer, is also incomplete; he "lacks" something. Perhaps, therefore, in his search for Jacinta he is looking for something of his own that he has lost without realizing it, as always occurs when there is a disturbance in the order of the signifier. What does he lack? He is missing a letter of his surname, not a small thing if one's surname—that is, one's name—is not a signified (names, according to Frege, belong to a disturbing exception in relation to common nouns) but rather a signifier.[10] In short, he lacks a fragment of the signifier that indeed his father—the name of the father—retained. That letter is no longer, it has been lost. Where? In the customs office in Buenos Aires, when his father entered the country and, when questioned, pronounced the name correctly in his language, but which was misheard and simplified. In its original form, the name should have been "Schweitzer," but the letters *c* and *h* were dropped, and as a result of this castration, only what was left of his name remained.

If he is an investigator, therefore, it is because he is looking for something lost and unrecoverable, an impossible and unconscious search because it does not reside in the history of that suppression—he never mentions any such issue—or in the clues that have allowed us to reach that point, but rather on purely textual ground that can only be seen from outside of the text, by analysis, by virtue of a theory that sheds light on diverse objects in diverse fields.

Very well, where there is a lack, it is possible that, due to a secret law of economics, there is also a surplus. What is more, perhaps that lack appears so concretely because the surplus is so evident, just as poverty becomes obvious when it exists beside excessive wealth. That surplus, in a complementary manner, is the name to which Sweitzer's name is linked, that of his partner and friend, the character of Stocker, who lives with Jacinta, the dead woman. In his case, what exists in excess is the letter *c*, the same letter that, in a nuanced form, is missing in the other. But to show why this letter is in excess, it is necessary to construct new networks of connections.

Lack in one case and excess in the other are transferred to the characters as such, as systems of attributes—in short, as psychological representations. Characters, as we already know, are merely a function within the system we call "narration," but they are never presented as such. Instead they are invested with actions and features congruent, from the perspective of representation, with real people, in order to conform to the rules of verisimilitude.[11] These attributes are particularized, and at times, as in this case, leave a sediment, almost as if responding to the demands of the signifier. Thus Sweitzer, Stocker's partner, became such not by possessing capital, the usual route to a partnership with someone else with capital, but because he is Stocker's former trusted employee, elevated to the position of partner: there is, therefore, an evident inequality between the two, based on a lack of capital. In a different arena, both compete in the area of biblical erudition in which they are adept, but Sweitzer knows less than his partner—he lacks information that Stocker, more informed, completes. Finally, Sweitzer does not have a wife or lover—he lacks, as people are wont to say, "his other half," that is, he lacks a half. For his part, Stocker has both considerable capital and erudition in the biblical texts, and, in whatever form it was, he had a lover and still has one, although she herself is absent from the perspective of the population census. Furthermore, he has the capacity to unite what is separate and incomplete, to unify them, or at least, he is not uncomfortable with them, as is clearly underscored in the revealing comment: "[He] caressed various parts of her body without much concern for the human nexus which united them" [8].

We have shown that he can unify, that is, he controls his own unity. The question is, what does this unity consist of? One could say that his name explains this because of a double paradigm. On the one hand, since the root of his name, Stock, implies accumulation, and its final particle, -er, implies a sort of destiny; he is defined as an accumulator. In effect, as we have seen, his character traits spring from this definition. On the other hand, if we take away the excess letter, his surname would be reduced to "Stoker," the same as the author of *Dracula*, Bram Stoker, who tells the tale of dead people who live amongst, or want to live amongst, the living, and of living people who live amongst, or want to live amongst, the dead.[12] Stocker also does this; he too lives with a dead woman and wants to do so without any limitations.

At this point, a reorganization of the text continues in the sense of a possible movement toward signification. It may be that this only affects the interpretation of one character, but as perhaps we can see, what is uncovered here becomes denser and advances over what the text in its entirety is perhaps pursuing on a plane that goes beyond the mere fantastic effect. Thus, the Dracula connection explains how Stocker is revealed as a vampire in a double-faceted manner. For one thing, he lived with, and wants to continue living with a dead woman, feeding on her or feeding her, and for another, in his continuous questioning of her, it is as if he were surrounding her, imprisoning her: "I asked her questions, exasperated her" [26]. Outwardly he does not want her blood, he only wants "knowledge" of her that, no doubt, would be integrated with the rest of his knowledge that contrasts with Sweitzer's lack.

Putting it more explicitly, Sweitzer does not know very clearly what he is looking for. That uncertainty is precisely what allows us to assume that for Stocker, who has an extra letter, Sweitzer's search for the lost letter involves a seemingly inexplicable (it happens so suddenly) augmentation of a lack: "the rich man divests himself of his belongings, although not of his business acumen, and settles into a pared-down, monastic wait in a sanitarium. The only thing he retains is custody of the remnant that is the dead woman's autistic brother. Of course, in this suspended state, "he would have liked . . . to disappear" [20–21].

The inversion is total: Sweitzer ends up gaining a "knowledge," although not that of his lack because that is impossible given that everything about him is determined by that lack. And Stocker, who had and who knew everything, ends up stripped of everything; his is the paramount ignorance since he is ignorant of where Jacinta is, or rather, given that this story is presented as a simile of "Argentine realism," he is ignorant of the "truth" or reality about Jacinta.

Knowledge and Narration, Narration as Knowledge

Here, our study takes on a new twist, a deviation that tends to satisfy those first requirements that at the beginning, perhaps a bit presumptuously, we called "theoretical." What drives this change is a question: what is that knowledge gained by one and lost by the other? To begin with, this inflexion, this movement from one to the other, marks a dissociation in the plot: they can no longer continue as partners. But looking at another angle, we can argue that while that knowledge is about historical truth, it is also about "narrative" truth, to use the classic narratologic distinctions. They are, as we can see by now, two different instances.[13] Well then, the knowledge that matters is the latter, that of narration, since, according to the classic saying, the narrator is he "who knows."

In conclusion, Sweitzer is a double of the narrator, or more precisely, he embodies the narrator or is granted this mission, something Stocker himself seems to understand when he states, "Answer me in writing" [23] the last time they see each other. It is his final manifestation of knowledge, but now as the object of knowledge and no longer as its possessor or producer. In Sweitzer's case, it is an active part of the signification, and this activity is foreshadowed by phrases that could be applicable to anyone but are only applied to him as only he plans to "draft" a letter, carrying this out as would a writer: "Sweitzer took some notes in his notebook" [20]. Obviously, "draft" [*borronear*], which brings the idea of writing to the fore, is connected to "blurred" [*borroso*] which, as we have seen, has to do with the creation of inverisimilitude, which is the plane or effect that writing generates.

Thus, if this reasoning is at all valid, we can conclude that Sweitzer's name ties together a number of traces and hence could be our candidate to become the point at which the "reality" that resides in the tale told slips from the construction we are creating to an "other reality," that of textual production, which is not only the substance of what we previously called "narration" but also the key to a specific activity that overflows the explicit, beginning with the explicit itself.

As an evident result, it is only possible to establish these displacements when this supposed narrator completes his investigation and ceases to be a fictional being, a character, and becomes instead a basic function. In that moment, the narration is completed, it is "written," in the sense that all the levels that take part in the movement of the writing become objectified. In that moment, all knowledge has been transferred and a kind of fusion takes place, including a fusion between the characters: from Stocker, who felt "cold all the time like all men" [27], to Sweitzer, who, before concluding, "put on his flannel nightshirt" [33] and for whom "now it was [his] turn to be called *Don* Julio" [12].

In order to understand this scheme more clearly, we speak of "displacements." If it is a question of moving from one plane to another, the word is pertinent, but since such displacements also produce new analytic situations in the sense that new nuclei appear that must be taken into consideration, we can speak of transformations that support the text like a net. As we have seen, it is an entity unto itself, although only now do we grant it that status, that recognizes the central transformation consisting of the movement from the realist description to that of the fantastic—in short, the production of inverisimilitude that in a strange way functions not as a declaration but as a strategy, something like surrealism, where the quotidian and vulgar become imbued with the extraordinary.

In this transformation, the narrator, whose allegorical double is Sweitzer (as a fictional manifestation of the narrative function displayed in a character), maintains his unity and narrative control such that the story, as a thread or a collection of argumental sequences, takes place between constant chronological allusions such as "Lately" or "Almost every morning Jacinta went to the tenement" [12]. It is as if he wishes to show respect for a temporality that would guarantee continuity and an effective system of gaps via separate sections that would hold it together or cause its recomposition in a different place.

Contrary to what one might think at first, these two terms, "continuity" and "gaps," are not necessarily antagonistic. In a conventional logic they are dominated by temporality, but not in a narration that, as we have seen, alters conventions about verisimilitude and is established on changes in planes. Perhaps here in this movement between one and the other, the epigraph, so mysterious at first, and the title, are explained: "El sueño, autor de representaciones, en su teatro sobre el viento armado, sombras suele vestir de bulto bello" ["The dream, author of representations, in its stage built on the wind, often dresses shadows in beautiful forms"].[14]

But let us clarify something: this explains the epigraph not because the story is the story of a dream but because the approaches, the movements, the displacements, the transformations all follow the logic of dreams, where changes in register occur in uncontrolled twists, and the resignification of remainders is not only possible, but up to a certain point, normal, as the grammar would say, to paraphrase Lacan. Therefore, to interpret, the dream is "author" of representations that like this one, are imprecise in their limits, blurred (shadowy), but suggestive (beautiful).

The epigraph is taken from the poem "Varia imaginación" by Luis de Góngora. New displacements, ever simpler, ultimately form identities—for example, between "dream" and "imagination," since dreams for Góngora would be one of imagination's manifestations, and between "representation" and "writing," which would reside in the line "suele vestir" ["often dresses"]. Therefore, returning to the text, if Sweitzer embodies the narrator, we can see, now that we have been enlightened by the epigraph, that the story, or the process of its writing, begins when Sweitzer goes to bed, not because he alludes to such a thing but because, in a textual logic, the word "sleep" is the final word, with which everything concludes, and "dreaming" is the first, with which everything opens.

From sleep and dreams, representation is constructed as a displacement within a literature, from the realist appearance, which would be something like what remains by day, to the fantastic effect that, in a vampiric reminiscence, would be the nocturnal, the uncontrolled.[15]

Finale: Gazes

These transformations appear to be a fact of analysis, something that is superimposed on the text with the beneficial aim of revealing more than what it has tacitly meant to reveal. Up to a certain point this is a way of speaking, although in and of itself, analysis has such a general nature that it involves all literature and even all writing, if writing, as we believe, is to be found in signs, which, as we know, are not the same as the things they signify. However, this word could be accused of being undesirable. In order to avoid this attack, which would run the risk of causing our whole construction to crumble, we should point out that transformations are less virtual than one might think according to the textual model that has been developed. On the contrary, it can be observed that transformations function via the mediation of the gaze, a category that in the text duplicates what we have set in motion from the outside. If we have done anything at all, it is to "look at" the text—nothing else constitutes the initial moment of critical work. Well then, in the text, the gaze produces changes.

And we have examples: Jacinta is gazed upon by Doña Carmen, and from that action, textually speaking, she becomes a prostitute: "Doña Carmen conjured up an image of a degraded Jacinta" [5]. In turn, Jacinta aspires to reach understanding via the gaze: "And I wasn't even looking at them. . . . Today I am seeing them for the first time" [7], or rather, she aspires to have her gaze possess power by being able to forget the gaze of others: "Where had she seen that look?" [7]. Beings that look at each other and generate each other, like the figures that look at each other in *The Two Courtesans*, Carpaccio's painting, mentioned enigmatically as if to illustrate a narrative moment and which, remembered with difficulty, reappears later in Stocker's library, gazed at with intense curiosity by Sweitzer. If in this approach writing is the place, the space to which dreams transport representation, the painting—as another place that would schematize or illustrate or indicate what the gaze does in textual material—would allude to that writing; it would say, in a kind of invocation, that it is precisely a matter of that, of writing, that everything that can be seen is what makes writing possible.

In conclusion, then, we could say that transformation and spatiality determine writing and guide the systems through which it is carried out between the concept and the effect, leaving out something extra that always escapes.

The Suffering Narrator

For a naive or common reading (if a naive reading is still possible in a critical atmosphere that grows more and more pressing), *Goodbyes* [*Los adioses*; 1954] by Juan Carlos Onetti could be seen as quite a perverse story. Not, even for that kind of reading, because it recounts events that contradict common sense or are rejected on semantic grounds; we should keep in mind that common habits of reading today, which still predominate, accept (in the referential plane, of course) major moral outrages and even bigger monsters of the imagination without blinking an eye. Or conversely, such a reading experiences, as did readings of the past, the delicious shiver that normality experiences when confronted with imaginary horrors, while feeling nothing but repugnance when confronted with horrors that are real. If I say that this story could be perverse, it is because, in the most classic idea of what is perverse, there is a kind of permanent theft of information: that particular reading, the naive or common one—and saying that presupposes that other readings are possible—believes it will find the information, but the information escapes, like a rabbit that refuses to be caught by the hunter and that no hunter will be able to catch. In a naive reading, this creates frustration or resentment. I believe the word that leads to this uncomfortable state or that best summarizes it is "difficulty," a term that is all the more harsh applied to Onetti's text since this phenomenon of a with-drawing divergence seems to occur here not so much out of negligence but, on the contrary, out of an extreme shrewdness and is a clear indication of delibera-tion and intention.

In a reading that is immediate, naive, and common, it is understood that this occurs and that it produces certain recognizable effects that a critical reading, on a second look, perhaps forgets or does not keep in mind. The first of these effects, I believe, involves an entreaty that this kind of reader, one might con-jecture, finds annoying, and which is no doubt a sort of violence for those Macedonio Fernández calls "linear readers" ["lectores seguidos"], those who consider reading to be a smooth continuum without any surprises in its articu-lation.[1] The second effect, similarly frustrating, makes one think that the story provocatively represents an obstacle; this kind of reader may feel that it is something they must surmount, but of course the undertaking is not always successful. Most often they trip and fall, or at least fear, while reading, that this could occur. The third effect supposes the authority of an interruption that, from an ethical standpoint, should not be there (although it is difficult to avoid)—not so much because it affects an individual expectation but rather because it violates a very deeply rooted and long established principle of a continuum. This principle, as with the other two forms, exists in a cultural consciousness that finds validation in this way of reading. We can say that these three effects taken together, and viewed positively, are the indispensable pieces of a concept of narration, the how-it-is and how-it-ought-to-be of a story: no interpretation or conjecture, no confrontation with obstacles, no interruptions to endure. And so, when, due to a lack of information all of those things become manifest, we can say that the text is perverse.

However, we can also look at this another way, though still from the same position. One could imagine that a story that deals with such a concept could be, for example, about rupture. If this word legitimately enters into play, it gives rise to a different way of reading, an uncompromising approach that has no sympathy for the problems of that other approach. But there is also something else, another clarification or nuance: I believe that despite its diffusion, the concept of reading to which I have referred here is not an intrinsic part of the aforementioned cultural consciousness but rather simply established or rooted in only one level of reading. This means that there might be other levels of reading, so that we need simply to find them and avoid the trap of naturalizing the "naive" reading. In my opinion, these other levels would include that of an "evidential" reading, beyond the naive or spontaneous one, and a "critical" reading that would crown the system, as I tried to establish in *La lectura como actividad* [Reading as an Activity], whose proposals still seem useful to me.

Returning then to our point, this novella titled *Goodbyes* carries out this theft, taking away rather than providing. It makes almost no effort to fill in the blanks; it holds back instead of expanding. And only in order to rescue, out of courtesy or a calculated respect, a history that could be shattered in a dangerous fragmentation, does it resort to subterfuges or disguises to provide some kind of verisimilitude and to hide its inclination for rupture. This can be seen, it seems to me, in the climax, an important point in the story both in terms of its writing and its rhetoric. In this sense, when all of the relationships become clear and we finally find out who is who, we have the impression that each name appearing on the page acquires the exact level of agency that all classical stories aspire to. This climax gives the comforting appearance of a culmination, with its typical catharsis, as usually occurs in stories with traditional accumulative narrative structure in which everything that is told comes together and in the end erupts into a "solution." But in fact, that is not quite the way it works; in *Goodbyes* the end is just a moment, similar in intensity to all the other mo-ments. The peculiar thing about this text, therefore, is that the entire process, in all its manifestations, is an eruption, and not just the end: the fact that we finally know who all the names—or characters—are, hides a disturbing proposition, what I have called "rupture." Thinking in this way surely creates another scene and evokes another reading, which is what I will try to do here.

As we said before, this effect of informational pilferage is seen throughout the story. But to begin with, who is responsible for this? Looking at what occurs within the text, the responsibility cannot be attributed equally to all the areas or internal sections of the text, to all the characters for whom the information counts or has narrative importance. They differ in conduct and we could even say in narrative ethic, because although everything we know or forget we know (all coming from them) converges in one single voice, the voice of the story that narrates, the sources of that knowledge are diverse, and each one has its own idea about the value of the information they provide. Furthermore, they all have their own idea about the role they play in the entire narrative economy, although none of them states, and perhaps they do not even know, what that economy consists of, or perhaps it is equally important to each of them to contribute to its completion. In other words, certain characters bring information with them and become impassioned about what it means, but it does not seem as if that feeling has any purpose: they care about what occurs with the character/object of the narration, and they want, with an indifferent fervor, that this be known in the way that real beings want something to be known, either without purpose or in order to pay tribute to a moral or logical purpose. But I want to stress that there is one character who stands out from the rest, that of the shopkeeper, who besides being a member of a kind of Greek chorus, commentator on fate together with the other residents of the village in the novel, is also the narrator of history. It is he who controls the information he receives or that is produced before his eyes. For him, in contrast to the others— orderly, servant, and doctor—there is one clearly defined purpose—which has to do with narrating. That purpose makes him directly responsible for that difficult, obstacle-strewn, interrupted organization that the naive reading recognizes and condemns. He does it through self-reflective fiction: it is as if he is saying to himself the same things we see written on the page. The story that we read is, thus, the written form of what the shopkeeper would say to himself.

In principle, then, except for those characters who are watched and whose fortunes in particular constitute the details of that formless material, those about whom we try to find out (that is, the sick man and his women), there are two classes of characters who interest us in this narrative. Those who value information, who gather and sift through it with spontaneous naïveté, in particular the orderly, differ from the shopkeeper who takes in everything—what he is told and what he sees as well as what he feels, thinks, and analyzes in relation to the characters who produce the information. And while they—those who bring and take away—are real characters because they act or transmit, and because they have traits of real characters and even characteristic ways of talking or acting, the shopkeeper is not, in truth, a full character. Basically he is a capacity for collecting and reorganizing. He is the keeper not of merchandise but of information. From one moment to the next he mobilizes a productive quality that we could consider particular to the narrator; it is an attribute that he possesses and that the characters lack in every narrative economy, including this one. What then does the shopkeeper, distributor by profession, produce with all that he collects? How does he organize it?

Being a narrator would seem, before we start thinking in terms of narratology, something very obvious: how could there be narration without a narrator? No longer the "author," at most the narrator is a technical presence, or else a prolongation of the particular and characteristic presence of the enunciation, typical of all discourse: a first-person personal pronoun presented or disguised in a third person, who in turn assumes an extreme objectivity or gives in to the excess of what can be called the "omnipotence" of the narrator. To establish an important distinction, in this story the narrator is more of a "position"; he could be a character with his own history, but we can see that he sacrifices this chance in order to become a narrator. He grows as a narrator at the expense of his existence as a character. In this way he is transparent as a character, and while the others, recognizable as characters, can be defined as such because they defend their identity and their perpetuation (a character is the perfect embodiment of what Sigmund Freud called erotica, that is, the desire for "the infinite perpetuation of an I"), the shopkeeper has no other existence than the fate of those others who appear before his eyes and whose drama is concentrated by the voice he, as stated earlier, speaks to himself. And in this way he produces knowledge, that is, narration, in a perfect circle since, as we know, all narration is knowledge, whether preexisting or formed at the moment it is enunciated. It should come as no surprise, then, that in the final chapter we read: "But all of my excitement was absurd, more worthy of the orderly than of me. Because, supposing that I had guessed right when I interpreted the letter, it did not matter, with respect to the essential thing, the link between the girl and the man. She was a woman, in any case; another one" (45). The juxtaposition is clear; noting the difference between himself and the orderly (they do not compete on the same plane, as do the orderly and the maid), the shopkeeper finally recognizes what he is really doing, and although it is muddied, a truth emerges, a knowledge takes shape that the orderly, as the character he is, cannot grasp.

Thus we see that there is a narrator who comes and goes with respect to his existence as a character, and in this coming and going he is stretched thin until he disappears in the strict self-discipline of relentless observation. But, at the same time, the narrator goes on; it is he who steals the information, as if in spite of himself, through an early synecdoche—"I would rather not have seen the man, the first time he came into the store, except for his hands" [1])—a figure that reappears frequently, with stylistic stubbornness, full of echoes. And if this first appearance defines a way of seeing a character, elsewhere, such as when he says "I knew it as soon as the orderly asked, 'Do you know?' " [18], it operates in the realm of the enunciation itself, bringing into play what we call "allusion," a kind of clipping from a newspaper, although in reality it is about a struggle of suppositions. They are not the only ones: the questions that follow, such as "Is she sick? Is she going to be cured? The lungs?" [19], substitute for a complete causal discourse and call to mind that image of the "essential" with which the text ends, linked, in turn, to an economic conception of the story in which we can see elements and tendencies often discussed in criticism about Onetti.

Synecdoche, then, dominates, the narrator's gesture and has many other nuances or implications: it is a question of a broader development. For now I would simply point out two other manifestations that seem particularly notable to me. The first one involves a kind of homologizing projection of this form onto the universe: "I went to the door and spoke to her and she answered, never looking at me, her face pointed at the darkness, at the scarce, feeble lights in the mountains" [19]. It occurs to me, perhaps due to an association—returning to Mexico City one night, the lights of the city alternating with islands of shadow seemed to me to be creating a rhythm that had something to do with a grammatical figure—that that gaze, detached from the dialogical instance, found in the rhythm of the isolated lights the key to the space itself, the definition of indiscernible individual fate, which is what this text talks about explicitly. The goal of the second manifestation, "I cannot figure out if I had seen her before or if I discovered her at that moment, leaning against the door frame: a bit of skirt, a shoe, one side of a suitcase poking out into the lamplight" [16], through the same system of fragmentation and clipping with which it begins, is to complete an image, to suggest that there is something complete and homogenous that it is not necessary to transmit as such, that the play of the whole and the parts not only is licit but may also guide a decision that we would call philosophical if it weren't for the fact that we are in the literary and narrative sphere, whose scope continues to be an enigma and a challenge for the critical imagination.

And, in fact, a critical reading, resting on the answer provided by naive reading (the image of that irritating theft of information) as if this were its foundation, works through synecdoche. But this synecdoche no longer indicates a guilty theft but rather a point of departure toward a different sphere, where meanings are crossed and interwoven in a different text, one linked to what literary discourse proposes when it doesn't limit itself to determined repetition of its habits and traditions.

But, as we can see, no general consequences arise yet from an understanding of the narrator's modus operandi. We have detected his penchant for making a whole out of a part, but no "whole" appears that we could understand as anything more than the sum of this and other parts. And it will not appear; it can only be imagined as a culmination, similar to the catharsis of the story's ending. All I can say at this point is that this form of narrating, as the narrator says, tends toward the creation of a "knowledge": "I knew suddenly" [19], he declares, and later, "I knew this, many other things" [19]. This is, in truth, the goal—to know. Not, I repeat, to know about the story, merely the foundation of the intent, but rather about narrative possibilities, for the simple reason that without the creation of this knowledge, not only is there no possibility for the story but there is also no possibility for identity on the part of a character who sacrifices so much in order to gain a unique, separate position, one of pure gaze, observation, reasoning and conjecture, and also of strength. "I felt full of power, as if the man and the girl, and also the older woman and the child, had been born of my will and lived what I had determined for them" [46], he declares triumphantly toward the end.

However, as the narrator, he is isolated in the position in which he puts himself: a shopkeeper, that is, above all, a collector, even more than a recovered tuberculosis patient. He stands behind the counter, an interrupted space of exchange, as we can see in his function as postal clerk, receiving letters that he in turn passes on, but he (a mere phantasm of communication) is not trusted to handle the replies. So it is with the narrator; he can only "see" one aspect, and with that small piece he must reaffirm himself. The knowledge that he gains, then, is that of possibility itself, a hidden trace of what rationalism would call "sense," which covers up another sense, that of the gesture itself. Let me emphasize that every phrase, and even every gesture, not only says something that opens the way for communication but also states that it exists as a phrase, that there is a power that has forged it. That difference between story and plot disguises the obsolete distinction between form and content. Those terms, "story" and "plot," integrated and counterpoised in that way, would continue to be valid if by "plot" we mean a specific capacity, unique and unmistakable, linked to a specific desire that emanates from the functions of language. I am referring to storytelling, a communicative and phatic function[2] moved by a desire that is verified in the very act of transmitting a story.

A final note to this perhaps confusing accumulation of observational fragments: to see in pieces, to accumulate, involves a theory of operations for recovering partial meanings that, in turn, must take into account that something—remnants, scraps, leftovers—is left out; thus, if looking at a piece in order to understand the whole leaves in the shadows what is not seen, it could be that it is also a question of a kind of clipping, like a newspaper clipping. If this is so, the part that is discarded is relegated to some distant corner, and in principle has no purpose. I imagine that this has to do somewhere with the idea of "trash," which plays a double role: on the one hand it constitutes an attractive item for description; its presence is powerful and repeated, adding an unforgiving touch to the atmosphere: "descending through the brambles and reddish patches of bare earth to reach the hotel dump and kick around cardboard cartons, bottles, the remains of vegetables, cotton balls, yellow paper" [6]. This connects to other "squalid" atmospheric details, as Prego and Petit indicated, that are such an important part of Onetti's principal texts—in this one, the "sanitarium" and the "hotel," in others, the "brothel" or the "factory."[3] In its other role, "trash" traces a mirror image of the small, weak universe that is the material of narration: the story of "what was left" of a man, of that perishable remnant located deep below what is consecrated by the continuity of life, and which cannot be redeemed by any effort of the others, so heroic in their equally pathetic salvations.

Arguedas

Reflections and Approaches

Having listened to Professor John Murra and to Angel Rama, I feel, in relation to the figure of José María Arguedas, a bit like that Argentine from the State Department whom Murra has just described because my relationship to the work that has brought us here today is incomplete and, I would even say, sporadic. When Julio Ortega proposed that I take part in this conference, I realized two things: first, that I did not really know Arguedas, and second, that I had never managed to flesh out the image created in my mind by my reading of *Deep Rivers* [*Los ríos profundos*; 1958)] somewhere around 1960. When I read this text, I felt various things, and I think I saw various things that I promised myself I would expand upon later—and which I never did. Thus, rising to Julio's challenge to my omnipotence, but also in order to settle accounts, I decided that perhaps now was the moment to deal with what had stuck with me as a sort of carry-over. Has the moment really arrived? Today I am going to give you a few very superficial reflections that I made while rereading what I had read and reading for the first time what I had not—but that initial image, that impact from my first reading remains, and I do not want to give up the attempt to transmit it.

That image consists of what I would call the "experience of touch": it is the child touching the walls of Cuzco; it is an almost biblical image, or one of an imminence that the Bible, as well as the Mosaic moment, frequently provides. Water should spring from those walls because the child is endowed with a power, but water does not pour forth, anguish does, and that, in a more existential sense, is what the novel develops. The story presents and expands that relationship between the imminence of a miracle—which has deep roots in the history of a people—a psychological, prepsychological, almost fetal reality of loss, and an anguish that embraces or engulfs in its entirety the situation of the individual in the world, because there is nothing that the child feels that is not linked to the world as a whole. My original reading back then conveyed a solemn tone, as if I were reading something profoundly serious, solemn in the sense of rituals—not those that take place in a temple but rather those that act as memory and appeal to a plurality of instances. Curiously, what also stays with me from that first impression is the image of the top as an object that held, or should have held, some signification or played some role. I say "curiously" because Angel Rama, who spoke about orality and musicality, establishes a bridge between those two concepts and the top, which could be seen, I believe, as a concentrating object.

In the commentary I am about to make, other terms from this jargon are bound to appear, of which "concentrating object" is a foreshadowing; I ask your forgiveness in advance: at least it is good to know that some jargon is going to be used and that such jargon is not natural language.

In the superficial observations that I am going make, I have focused on what seem to me to be points of departure for considering literary aspects of Arguedas's work. The first is something quite obvious—it occurs to me that on the surface, or apparent surface, of all of Arguedas's stories, without exception, the central element or axis is the characters, which clearly seem to be the most important aspect: everything revolves around them. Very well, the importance of such centrality does not lie so much in the fact that the narrators are absorbed by the characters or, to put it another way, that they are also characters, at times acted upon, at times active, but rather in the fact that beyond that, again apparently, or superficially in the sense of what one notices immediately, there is an almost exhaustive classification of characters by means of the classic, and also most obvious, system of oppositions: those from the mountains in opposition to those from the coast, Whites in opposition to Indians with mestizos occupying an intermediary place, large landowners opposite share-croppers, feudal lords opposite poor landowners and workers—in other words, the whole gamut of societal life appears personified, or rather, characterified.

I suspect that not only in Arguedas's stories but in all stories of a similar nature (which make up the bulk of narrative wealth and even most of the narrative estate) character predominates; but in my opinion, the characters are only one element, not all of the story. If this element is seen as the sole, decisive one, then inevitably one part is seen as the whole, which has certainly lead to a type of reading that is nothing more, I believe, than a commentary on the actions carried out by the characters, or else on the psychology of the characters or on the confrontations that occur amongst them. On the other hand, even while accepting the centrality of the element of "character," I do not believe I have ever read anything that leads to a typology, in the structuralist sense of the word, and this would imply a superior level that for the moment is being drowned by the interminable commentary about conflict between subjects. In *Todas las sangres* [All Bloods; 1964], for example, we find the two brothers, two opposing personalities. This gives rise to a number of reflections about such opposition that in the end conclude with the confirmation of a very common attitude in looking at literature, that is, to see the characters as embodying realities. In fact, there are grounds for doing this, but it seems to me that we are dealing here with a trap for both reader and critic of a work such as that of Arguedas. For example, in terms of this commentary about character to the exclusion of all other elements, it is only natural that some critics find the characters contradictory, confused, ambiguous. There are also grounds for this as well if one thinks of a character such as Bruno Aragón de Peralta in *Todas las sangres;* it is not clear why he is suddenly a medieval fanatic or suddenly an adherent of Dostoevski, shot through with guilt, only to suddenly be filled with pure love for the mestizo woman, and so on. If we look at it from this perspective, characters can indeed be incongruent, confused, and ambiguous, all of which seems to me, in this case, to be of very little importance—so little, that I do not even see it as a place to start a critical study.

On the other hand, one could think that such recognizable incongruence, confusion, and ambiguity in characters' behavior is so pronounced at times that it shatters the principle of realism, that of causality, which, as we know, is a sacred principle in realist rhetoric. Thus, with the aim of pardoning the writer who has created incongruent, confused, and ambiguous characters, but who is respected and esteemed, we speak of the "intricacies" of the human soul, governed, as we know, by contradiction. Despite the fact that it is well known that love and hate are separated by a poorly established and unclear boundary, every time we suspect that a character has been poorly drawn—according to our precise idea of what would be a "well-drawn" character—and we do not wish to say so due to our cognizant respect for the work, we turn to the image of the intricacy of the human soul. We all keep a close eye on that boundary, I believe, and if we do not cross it with psychic extravagance, it is precisely in order to avoid risks and to avoid passing too quickly from love to hate and vice versa. For these obvious reasons, this way of looking at a crucial work of Latin American literature does not seem very rigorous or fruitful to me: at the most it creates duplications. Of course, this does not mean that my approach is going to be particularly rigorous: my own disability is that I am constantly moving back and forth in a game of categories, creating a jungle where I have to orient myself in order to somehow speak, despite or because of the fact that other voices, I believe, have simplified the phenomenon.

I also have the impression that if it is true that certain incongruencies in the conduct of characters rupture a causality in their creation, that rupture indirectly involves another causality, that of actions. One should look, then, not only at one category, that of the characters and their behavior with their rules of causality or congruence, but also at another, that of actions, in which, as we know, other elements come into play. Actions do not depend exclusively on the behavior of the characters, but rather, up to a certain point, are the result of a confluence (I would call it organic) of factors that are also governed by causality. If this is interrupted, the result is more important than the incongruence itself: the result is that a fracture is produced in the representation, which in turn is a central requirement of certain types of literature, as Erich

Auerbach has shown,[1] to mention only one work that focuses on this idea with rigorous historicity. Looking at it from this perspective, I can see that many of the existing studies of Arguedas establish a very direct relationship between the verbal structure presented, the text, as a specificity that we must read, and a represented reality.

Naturally, there are many things that need to be developed in this proposal, but that is not the issue, at least not for me. At this point, what I am interested in about Arguedas is not what we already know about Peruvian reality, but rather the text that Arguedas produces starting from Peruvian reality, in and against Peruvian reality. In short, I am not interested in the problem of representation in terms of accuracy or fidelity. And so, I believe that despite the fact that the fractures and incongruencies of characters and the rupture of the causality of actions, which is greater in some texts than in others (such as *Todas las sangres,* for example, which, according to some critics, Arguedas felt was one of his major works), produce a certain discontinuity from a realist perspective, that discontinuity does not keep those texts from flowing, and I can do nothing else but use an image, a powerful puff of wind, something that invades my boundaries as a reader and engages them, engaging the reading as well. Consequently, recognizing that experience, and acting with it and from it, eliminates problems for me in relation to the typical classifications such as "indigenismo," "idealism," and all those kinds of labels that function as brakes or instances of disvirtualization. For example, when you approach a text that you suspect is "indianista" but which has been presented by other readers as "indigenista," you must find a set of almost ethnographic instruments in order to resolve the superimpositions or neutralize the displacement, exactly as if facing a document or reducing the text to such. Reading from a different perspective, however, the problem disappears: I, as a reader, accept that I am driven by a reading impulse that, I believe, flows from the texts, and which immediately situates the discontinuity I spoke of earlier on another plane; it no longer would appear to be a defect in the realism, but instead would present another instance and would be one more indication of that other instance.

If, however, we were to adopt a different perspective in order to escape from this problem of ruptures, and, as if proposing a new classification, we were to say that it is a question of a "language novel," we would similarly be appealing to a quite general formula in order to escape from the predicament. In other words, we would be saying that everything we do not understand as a realist novel could be a language novel, a formula that would thus be an obvious substitute for something we do not understand. Of course, it is a language novel not only because it focuses on language but also because a clearly evident bilingual conflict serves as one of the underpinnings of the novel, as well as the function—through its undeniable use—that Quechua plays as protector of orality, song, and primitive poetry, as Angel Rama has shown. For its part, the conflict of bilingualism that is presented in these texts is posed as a problem of cultural transcendence, not simply as a relationship between two levels of language or two languages in one text, but also in the extratextual implications of the issue. To consider that these are "language novels" simply because they do not faithfully follow the realist prescriptions would be to negate the need for a more encompassing access to these texts, and, in order to find this access, I would start by defining the stated conditions as the initial ones.

First of all, we must recognize for the moment that the problem of narration itself, or, in slightly more technical terms, the problem of narrative enunciation, appears in Arguedas as a "conflict in writing," in that the writing is in no way separate from an experience of identity. The concept of "enunciation" (I, he, we) sends us to the roots of the experience of identity, the roots that are precisely expressed syntactically through the pronominal system. One indication of this dimension could be the fact that many characters, who are at the same time narrators, are also children, and as such, they deal with the issue of identity. As narrators, moreover, at the same time that these children recount what has happened to them as characters, they are also in the process of constructing, of discovering and determining, who they are. This question of identity in the narrative function has a critical point, insofar as it links narration as a discursive gesture as much to narrative attitudes and inflections as to certain recurring themes and characters. This is easily verifiable in all of Arguedas's novels; if, ideally, we could superimpose them, say by using a computer, we would see that there are indeed many themes and characters that recur, but also many literary functions, or literary-ideological functions if you prefer, that recur as well.

This would be the first level of access to these texts. At a second level, we should begin with the recognition that the external, extratextual conflict is also present, not only as an exposition of problems, but also determining the writing itself and intervening in it. Of course, it is easy to say in this sense that Arguedas writes about the new fishmeal workers (in *The Fox from Up Above and the Fox from Down Below* [*El zorro de arriba y el zorro de abajo*; 1972]); that would be the current way to examine the question of extratextuality, equivalent to saying that it "represents" real conflicts. On the other hand, what is important to realize is the way in which these new structural realities of a society such as the Peruvian one are also organizing forces, that is, how they influence the organization of writing. The third level of access to this textuality requires the recognition that something happens in the language of Arguedas's texts; after all, we must admit that the text is a language act, that is, there is a certain drama in which words act as scene and character. I emphasize this in order to support a similar idea proposed by Angel Rama, with whom it does not surprise me to find I am in agreement on this point, since we always seem to agree on these points despite the fact that we go for long stretches without seeing each other.[2]

Thus, given these three levels or possibilities, how, specifically, do we find an access to textuality? I, of course, I will repeat, have no organized or systematic process for carrying this out, although in any case this is not the time to do so, as we are in the middle of a symposium basically designed as a homage to a great writer and representative of Latin America, and to spend time on excessively systematic proposals could be tedious and not particularly pertinent unless there were sufficient time to concentrate and to discuss in depth, which is not the case. Notice that I have spoken both of the need to escape from the current way of accessing texts and of the difficulty of doing so, all of which puts me in a successive series of paradoxes from which, in the end, I will escape by recognizing that in my original reading of Arguedas, as in my reading for this event, I tended to be sensitive to the sentimental appeals, perhaps more than to other suggestions that undoubtedly also emerge from the text. The sentimental world, or the sentimental image, left a considerable impression on me, all of which kept me from proposing a more encompassing access, which, nevertheless, I believe needs to be done.

One can see that the work of the critic has its perplexities and its dramas of conscience: if on the one hand we are pulled in a certain direction by some textual nucleus, at the same time we must remain coherent within our own perspective in order to obtain some fruit from our labor. There exists the possibility, therefore, of a conflict that at some point, in some way, must be resolved. I wish to state that, despite the fact that I understand the necessity of proceeding with more precision (in which case my commentary about the behavior of the various characters is insufficient), I also recognize that what touched me the most, what got me most involved in Arguedas's texts, was their sentimental aspect: and there lies the reason for my blocked condition. Therefore, as a solution to my own conflict, I am only going to propose a few lines of thought, quite disorganized, that could provide some response to the three categories or the three necessities or the three planes of analysis that I recognize must be taken into consideration.

I believe that Arguedas's stories are undoubtedly constructed according to a model stemming from reality. In light of this, it would be possible to study these stories according to a certain logic of actions that differs very little from the logic of actions of reality itself (arrival, reception, friendship, conflict, outcome, misinterpretation, reflection, etc.). But since other instances—breaks that are fittingly notarial—make their entrance, neither obedience to nor continuation of such a model is constant, and when one is adopted, it does not imply in any way a representational attitude or a reflection of the real; on the contrary, as has already been shown, there is instead a rupture of representation. For that reason, even though it seems paradoxical because of the way this point is presented, it would be inappropriate to refer to this as a realist work. To put it another way, what I call the "model of reality" has a capacity or power for organizing the narrative structure, while "realism" is an ideology that is guided by an intention to reproduce the contents or elements understood as belonging to reality. In El sexto [The Sixth Penitentiary; 1961], this distinction as we describe it is clearly manifested in that the modeling can be seen in the structure of the story: arrival at a place, presentation of the place, exposition of conflicts, resolution of the conflicts, departure. I will insist on emphasizing that it is not a question of realism, since it is the writing that is influenced by the model, a model that includes other levels that also influence the narrative scheme. Furthermore, the scheme itself is functional and operative. I believe that Arguedas's work could be seen from this perspective and in this light.

The sentimentalism that characterized my reading cannot be mine alone: it has a permanent presence in his texts. No doubt its source must be the indigenous idiosyncrasy, although of course ethnologists have the last word about the existence and characteristics of such idiosyncrasies. In terms of its abundant presence, one way or another the sentimentality maps the work in accordance with the more or less established configurations of literary history that we refer to as "movements," "tendencies," "styles," or "schools." In this sense, Arguedas would be considered more or less a romantic, a qualification that correspondingly would be simple to make and not particularly interesting. Very well then, what I wish to show is that the manifestation of sentimentalism is not carried out through declarations, but vividly through the image of weeping. This is a consolidating image and almost always establishes a connection with certain magical categories that could belong to a certain animism. Extending this notion, I would point out that the mountains complain or threaten and the rivers roar or whisper. It could be said in this respect that there is something like a "magical realism," if you will permit me to use the expression, that is not that other realism, more or less well-known, and which could only belong to the world of the indigenous peoples, as Miguel Angel Asturias would have it.

The nationalism that we can note in Arguedas's work does not in any way make his novels simple offshoots of local color, as tempting as that idea may seem from the reading, or of indigenismo, but rather, they are, to use an image or metaphor, something like a "valorized enigma." Naturally, it would first of all be necessary to know (and I wonder if there is universal agreement about this concept) what "the nation" is, and therefore, what "nationalism" is. I think it is also important to still see it as a philosophical enigma, not a practical one, insofar as this work tends to be located in the plane of conflict and not in the plane of definition—as would be the case if it were a question of clear values, threatened and defended, or simply displayed and proclaimed. It is a conflict in relation to its identity as a nation, its development and its future, but also in relation to other nations. But there is interference by other elements in the way this issue is formed, other elements that are not able to integrate themselves and that thus continue to be discrepant. And because of this, such ever present nationalism would certainly appear as an enigma, as we have said, but "valorized," or, to put it another way, as an enigma of fundamental importance, reclaiming its past in which it would search for its inevitably traumatic origin. If as a consequence, nationalism is a polyphony between a traumatic past and a dark future, that polyphony, or crossing, gives rise to the production of the scene in which the narrative situations occur. This construction with regard to the idea of nationalism we are considering here has its parallel or its homology in the schema proposed by Arguedas's own personal history, with his traumatic past of childhood loss and a dark future, as his own suicide reveals, a suicide that was not unpredictable but rather was something that had been prepared. Therefore, there would be in this consideration a kind of linking together of very profound levels of analysis insofar as the social element that the texts connote is developed in a way that is rediscovered in the individual from the conditions of production.

As various critics have shown, *Todas las sangres* has two political events as its historical backdrop: Belaúnde Terry's[3] campaign promises and Hugo Blanco's *campesino* guerrilla actions. To state this is to assert that, besides the fact that the novel represents reality, it also has a political or ideological horizon that in some way surely determines that representation. Perhaps the motif of the mining company in the novel, which appears to be national but in truth is international or very circumscribed by international interests, is an attempt to show what was very characteristic of the Belaúnde era in such a way that that era is brought into, is incorporated into, the novel. This observation opens the way for thinking about other phenomena of that era that might have influenced the novel, although not necessarily in the form of representation, as would be the case with the mining company. For example, we could ask ourselves what role the Cuban Revolution might have played in the organization of Arguedas's thinking and in the manifestation and construction of narrative conflicts. If we look only at what the characters in his novels say about communists and *apristas*[4] and about political independence in Peru, for example, particularly phrases that appear in *El sexto* and reappear in *The Fox from Up Above and the Fox from Down Below,* we see that "action" is omitted, that is, that which a set of multiple political situations and an ideological language could have created on the basis of the articulation itself.

I would hope that this observation could overcome its own obscurity, an impression that perhaps results from the fact that we are dealing with a mere beginning notation, an intuition. To develop this further, I will look again at something that Antonio Cornejo Polar emphasizes with considerable clarity with respect to *El sexto;* he points out that at the end of the novel, the guitar whose construction is never completed and the reappearance of the songs sung by the homosexual "monsters" from downstairs allude to or imply or symbolize lack of a way out. In effect, it appears that there is no way out, all of which to me is simply indicative of the state of mind corresponding to the political era in which *El sexto* was written—that is, the dictatorship of Odría.[5] But I do not think this is what we should be looking for. Perhaps more important, in order to give you an idea of what I am trying to say, is the idea in *El sexto* that uniting all three of the prison's floors not only is possible but also contains an element of rupture, after which point the greatest dramatic tension no longer comes from the encounter of different types of people but rather from the encounter of different levels or different social positions. From then on, we can sense how the third floor acts on the first, an interaction that in fact produces the situations and generates the effects. It is here, it seems to me, and analysis can back me up, that a certain ideological force enters the text that traverses reality and that embodies a kind of thinking that began to emerge at the end of the war [World War II], the era in which *El sexto* was written. This thinking would have something to do with his arguments with Cortázar and Fuentes; it would explain his sarcasm about the structure of *Hopscotch* [*Rayuela*; 1963] and other, later works of Cortázar, and would imply, indirectly, an attack on the structuralism behind *Hopscotch* as an ideological break. He considers that these works model a literary writing and a literary attitude that differ from his own reading of such structuralism, one that views it as a theory of separate vessels, of fragments that cannot be put back together. If in this attack Arguedas does not come up with any theory to oppose that of his contenders, it does not mean that his textuality is not full of and even determined by elements similar to reality, such as, for example, the idea of the rupture of the social order.

To this I would like to add that the essence of many of the narrative situations is illuminated by poems in Quechua and not through a naturalist type of denouements. The resolutions from this tradition, in the classical sense of the word "resolution," are in effect impoverished, while the poems that elucidate a conflict, on the other hand, are rich. At the same time, although the poems are in Quechua, they appear in the novels in translated form, which supposes a certain conflict in that they take on a limit in the world of the reading. The implied musicality must be that of the original Quechua that survives in the Spanish, or perhaps that modifies or "mestizizes" the Spanish. The consequence is that in opposition to the loss of the oral referent, there is a parallel recuperation or valorization or acceptance of the written code, and in that, there is a search for just such a carefully guarded resonance, or put in broader terms, there is a permanent investigation that has to do with writing in its literary sense. At this point another aspect mentioned in the beginning is corroborated when we look at the fact that there is yet another limit on realism insofar as the text is composed of a missing thread and a dissonant chord. Furthermore, if, as is often stated, the reading forms part of the text, then the act of writing for the Spanish-speaking reader, while it could imply an abandonment of the still rare Quechua reader, does not signify abandonment of a Quechua element whose symbolic value, as well as the role that it plays in the narration, justify its being retrieved and translated, fused with an older memory.

There is something in this that deserves detailed study, not in an academic sense but in the sense of the main conflicts that, like deep rivers, run through and form Arguedas's work. I would say, complementarily, that this aspect of his work—which is linguistic in nature, an effect of translation—has a stylistic-aesthetic consequence that I would like to call "Hispano-Indian-sacred." The image I would use to describe what results is very similar to what is generally called American "baroque," like, for example, those churches in the state of Oaxaca, Mexico, that are built on a gothic model, but by indigenous artisans using an iconographic language, for which reason, due to the concentration of levels, those churches can be called "Hispano-Indian-sacred." In writing, which is what we are most interested in, this concentration is experienced as a stylistic drive that not only allows us to resolve situations, as we saw earlier, but also, in a general action, gives rise to semantic webs in which the characters are intelligible identities, though no less contradictory for that fact. We could say, in this sense, that they are generated by that stylistic drive. Looked at this way, we would be on the other side of the initial question, thinking of the characters beyond their normal conventions: the characters are not representations but rather stem from a complex necessity of writing. Bruno Aragón of *Todas las sangres,* for example, is one of the most notorious results of this drive, and thus according to this analysis, a good illustration of this aesthetic with a linguistic, or if you wish, bilinguistic, base.

All of this does not mean that there is an avant-garde destructuring in Arguedas's stories; for example, "description" appears in them quite powerfully, or, more precisely, the descriptive as a narrative channel or narrative mindset appears, with the same strength as in traditional stories, constituting their necessity and their value. His descriptions are not only of the conditions and surroundings but also move toward preparation for action, for partial confrontations culminating in collective uprisings that are, as we are all aware, simultaneously the subject of both evocation and projection, and therefore, are strongly identified with what we could call "the imaginary." This articulation is a constant, which in a certain sense implies a subterranean, or perhaps not so subterranean, epic structure with greater emphasis on the final moment, the final outburst, when the retrospective or analytical is recognized in other narrative conflicts, more defined and endowed with value. I tend to think that this is linked to another issue Rama also referred to: the shift from the individual to the collective, around which, evidently, the notion of the epic is developed. What I would like to add is that above and beyond this function, this epic structure carries consequences in the realization or concretion or formation of characters: if the Cid is a hero, and as a consequence, his actions are epic in nature, here the epic nature of the actions creates the heroes, or, more modestly, it molds them as characters. Furthermore, I would say that, as in all imaginary articulations, especially of an epic nature, literature also attempts to carry out an effective action against the outside. As for the epic nature, its value in this sense stems from the fact that not only does it gather together feats that might have been carried out, but it also attempts, in its interpretation, to assume the position of a model of reality, endeavoring to demonstrate a path for society that begins with reading. I believe that this "modeling" action is indeed involved in Arguedas's work as a possible dimension of literature for modifying reality and as a dimension stemming from modifiable reality depending on how literature might suggest this.

There is no doubt that politics are not only present in but permeate Arguedas's work: real and historical politics, that of his time. At any rate, terms that lead to immediate political proposals spring from—or perhaps the reverse, contain—the array of situations and actions: terms such as oppression, exploitation, mass movements, individual rights, and so on. Such proposals form an initial political plane, what I would call "passion." On a second plane we can place what results from the presentation-reproduction (from the mouths of characters) of well-known political discourses: Apristas, communists, independents, campesino and union leaders, Christian social activists, mystics, and so on. These discourses establish relationships among themselves, they collide, they are superimposed on one another in either an episodic or a more permanent way, all of which creates an interdiscursive web parallel to the real discursive series. In order to think on a third level, I will refer to *El sexto,* a novel I found very interesting even though it is considered a lesser work. The image I have is of a pressure cooker, as much for that kind of constant dramatic imminence as for the way politics are compressed from situation to situation—it is like an extensive, boiling metaphor from which something suddenly spills over to the outside. If Apristas and communists include each other in their discourses, beginning from the fact that they are different and even antagonistic, this could be imaginarily authorized from without, as the narrator suggests is required.

That outside is a specifically political thought structure, the "Popular Front," which acts as a real and reproducible possibility, or as a "myth of loss." I would say of such a structure that it is more than a political artifact despite being born in a very concrete historical moment—it is a way of thinking about politics and, therefore, of organizing life. It is no surprise that it primes the imaginary and spurs the production of differentiated discourses. This is what I am interested in emphasizing: in *El sexto,* the question of the subject in political discourse is reintroduced, but not in the same way as in Sartre's plays, in which someone from outside of the parties wants as much to be able to do something with them as for them to do something at all, moved to this because he feels "involved." Rather, in *El sexto,* the political subject is reintroduced as the "space" of political drama, as the effective place in which the political drama occurs. But this should not also be understood in the ethical sense of the options that are declared, as Apristas and communists do in the book, but rather precisely in the sense of the appearance of alternative characters who problematize politics in other ways, and, as a consequence, emerge steeped and saturated in politics, and ultimately are confronted with those who control preconstructed options.

This form of characterization is based on subjectivity, which would be something like the space in which the lines of reality cross and where politics are incubated or formed. I would say that this kind of subject is thought of in the manner of a post-Althusserian Marxism, which is fitting in some sense, since, as John Murra indicated, Arguedas considered himself weak in questions of political and cultural theory, which, as we know, was the object of much debate between 1960 and 1970. It is possible, in fact, that at the time that he made that statement, he was not very well versed in Marxist polemics in general or in those of Althusser in particular, since these were outside of his main areas of interest. This would indicate that a text, by insisting on this point, since it has various implications, does more than simply reproduce the world in which it is produced: it introduces the world in which it is produced in a way much richer than simple representation, a way that builds bridges to ways of thinking about the world that will be formulated much later on, through discourses that in many cases still cannot be foreseen. Getting back to the point, I would say that his subject is independent; he is free and condemned to search, but at the same time, he tries to introduce the drives that create him in objectivity. He wants to become part of that objectivity through the drives that form him, but without at the same time having to submit to that which would belong to objectivity; he is a subjective subject, but modified, and he attempts to change that objectivity from his memory, his gut, and his conscience.

Perhaps this has something to do with the initial image of *Deep Rivers*, which could be called, metaphorically, the "experience of touch": in a mythological sense one wants water to pour out of those sacred walls, but all that gushes forth is anguish. It is the desire that, although never realized, runs through, organizes, and gives form to all of Arguedas's work, like one of those deep rivers that bellow and demand, escaping at times, formulating at others, retreating at still others from what as yet cannot circulate. But that desire is not a metaphysical one; from a certain theoretical perspective it can be seen as the desire of the subject, who, desiring, constructs both his own space and the transcendent political space. Thus the political in *El sexto* is shown, in this third plane we are trying to define, as reintroducing the theme of desire and of its history whose appearance is clearly traumatic in Arguedas's work: his existence is almost interrupted at birth, but in that very moment pursues his continuity incessantly. It is the painful, conditioned childhood, the obsessive image of the mother, the always at-risk image of the father, the cultural siege, the deforming external conflict.

In all of the stories there are objects, such as the *zumbayllu* [or top] and the guitar, that function as significant objects and concentrators, as I indicated at the beginning of this piece. They deserve such qualification because a large semantic load, affective and symbolic, is deposited in them. In this way, the character who constructs or controls them or aspires to control them—since they are also objects of desire—always converges or clashes with another character in the same situation: in the convergence or clash the objects are imbued with ideological attributes that are displaced onto the characters. Thus there are those who control them better, there are those who possess the skill to construct them, there are those who can renounce them in sacrificial acts of communicative giving, and there are offerings that establish connections, ties, or exclusions. While this occurs with the guitar, we can also see it in relation to the top and to the rock that is thrown across the river with particular skill. Insofar as one person has and another wants, the object separates people into aspirants and initiates, and therefore unites them, concentrates them. Furthermore, on a second level, such objects are described with a heavy sentimental charge: when the characters come in contact with them, a situation is produced, there is a change and an emanation that "signifies" and is transported to other planes. Of course, these are objects that belong to a tradition, but they do not appear in order to reclaim it—rather, I will repeat, they appear in a narrative function. It is clear that in order for them to fulfill this role, a precise knowledge, even though erased, must have been operating in the service of the writing that presents, transforms, and produces what at the same time it leaves behind. These objects, which make Arguedas's narrative progress, help him create a living anthropology, in the sense that these stories shift from individual weeping to collective outcry, from the imminence of water to objectified anguish.

Notes on the "Holy Place" and "Otherness" in Cortázar's *Bestiary*

In light of his novel *Hopscotch* [*Rayuela*; 1963] and some of his recent stories, the eight perfect narratives published by Julio Cortázar in 1951 under the title *Bestiary* [*Bestiario*][1] have gained renewed interest. Not that they didn't stir interest when they were first published, but if Cortázar's later evolution had not occurred, the earlier stories would have run a double risk: that of being too much in the shadow of a clearly formed Borges and that of revealing an excessive desire for form, that is, to put it bluntly, an estheticist inclination, a certain evasive gratuitousness. No doubt these risks are noticed or could have been noticed by critics who found Cortázar connected, and even subordinate, to a particular literary group—the group formed around the liberal journal *Sur*—that launched a program somewhat voluntarily at the margins of reality.

Without correcting that perspective, one pertinent to a work that is unable to sever itself from its circumstances, a current examination of the stories in *Bestiary* would leave us with a few variations all the richer for being integrated into a work that has continued to develop rather than being closed off after its initial formation. In this way we will be able to determine, among other things, that while Cortázar's stories include Borges-like touches, especially in subject matter and linguistic style, they turn these ideas on their heads and end up placing them in an opposing perspective to that of Borges. We will also be able to see that processes and perfections that begin to appear here are also found throughout most of Cortázar's later work. In this way, perhaps we can confirm something considerably more human than the idea that for political peace of mind is commonly asserted—that is, that Cortázar breaks with a particular position and installs himself in a completely different one that increases its demands and resources until it breaks off from its beginnings. But no: there is an initial moment and a present moment, yet between the two is a continuity whose differential points undoubtedly respond to stimuli springing from a sociopolitical-human experience that would be the subject of another, more integral study of the varying and the unvarying elements in Cortázar's work.

To begin, we can say that it is easy to find common elements in all of the stories in this volume—they are many and varied and occur on different narrative planes. The first result of this fact is not a reiterative effect, but one of unity and complementation. Thanks to this, if we look for a moment at an isolated element, it would appear that a theme is not resolved in one particular story but is finished, completed, in another begun under a different sign. (I use the terms "theme" and "elements" in an immediate and conventional sense, as a way of lessening the distance that separates us from the text.) Thus, for example, while the "house" in "House Taken Over" ["Casa tomada"] is presented as the space where an enemy suddenly appears and expels us, in "Cefalea" the meaning of the "house" and the role that it plays in both narrations is further clarified: "Entonces la casa es nuestra cabeza" [89] ["Thus the house is our head"]. And if when the expulsion is accomplished, "house" and "enemy" are fused, it follows from this that the invading forces are inside of us, that the expulsion occurs from the moment in which we are able to objectify them and place them outside of ourselves.

Thus, in all of the stories the expulsion is expressed through something that can in fact be expelled, and what produces the expulsion—which at times is a transformation, a revelation—disrupts a state of equilibrium. It is an act of allowing the entrance, gently, I would say, of a tendency, a desire, an irrepressible something that when manifested, is confused at times with that "something" that is expelled, and at times with a characteristic of the "enemy." In "House Taken Over," it is the sudden occupants; in "Letter to a Young Lady in Paris" ["Carta a una señorita en París"], it is the rabbits vomited up by the protagonist; in "The Distances" ["Lejana"], it is the Hungarian woman; in "Omnibus" ["Omnibus"], it is the collective animosity; in "Cefalea," it is the pain; in "Circe" ["Circe"], the disposition to kill; in "The Gates of Heaven" ["Las puertas del cielo"], the image of the dead woman; in "Bestiary," the reestablishment of justice. It is a desire that resides in the actor, a tendency that defines him from the moment that tranquillity is shattered, but a desire and a tendency that, I will insist, existed in him already, contained in his being, included within him, creating a portrayal that, little by little, is revealed and takes on its completed form. That tendency and that desire demonstrate to a large extent the leap to the irrational whose appearance situates these stories in the literature of the fantastic and affiliates them with those of Borges—but with one substantial difference: Borges places the irrationality outside of the characters, out in the world; the perceiving consciousness continues to be the same—it is the facts that change. Cortázar, on the other hand, makes the opposite move: the irrationality is inside; the facts remain invariable, and the consciousness splits between its acceptance of the irrationality that is manifested and the desire to conceal this when confronted with the rationality of others.

This mechanism allows a rearrangement of the stories in this book in terms of an aspect or inflection of the story that organizes all of them—that is, the existence of a double plane whose terms are situated, resolved, or transformed in the interiority of one who suffers a sudden change in fortune. In the first place, the anecdote that forms the basis of the story is situated in the double plane, and therefore, the possibility of recounting it also lies there: the double plane *is* the form of recounting—it constitutes a fundamental structuring level. Of course this approach unifies the whole book, but in accordance with our first clarification, one should not assume that the existence of a double plane necessarily implies an opposition between irrationality and rationality, at least in the initial moment. Due to its structural quality, the double plane constitutes, above all, a formal category that functions as an axis around which the anecdote, but also all that one wishes to say, is organized. In that sense, the double plane exists in all of the stories, although in some of them, simply because it is not seen, one of the terms is not very explicit. For example, in "House Taken Over" we see the protagonists and, behind the door, we sense the others, while in "Letter to a Young Lady in Paris" we see the protagonist and, hidden from the eyes of the rest of the world but not from the one who writes, the rabbits. In "The Distances" we see Alina Reyes who writes a diary where the "other," the "miserable one" begins to appear—the "distant" form of her own being. In "Omnibus" there are the protagonists, Clara and the young man, and surrounding them in the aisles, the passengers, the conductor, and the aggressive driver, while in "Cefalea," we find the protagonists and also the "mancuspias," which become identified with pain. In "Circe," we see the protagonist, and facing him, the cockroaches in the candy as if they were a part of Delia Mañara herself. In "The Gates of Heaven," there are the protagonist and the indistinct "monsters," while finally, in "Bestiary," we find the young girl and Rema, and, as a provocative figure of otherness, the ants. Examining the two terms from the two planes, we can see that the one common to all is the protagonist or protagonists; in the other term, on the other hand, diverse antagonists appear which can be organized in a progression moving from the most elemental to the most complex in the following way:

ants	in "Bestiary"
cockroaches	in "Circe"
rabbits	in "Letter to a Young Lady in Paris"
mancuspias	in "Cefalea"
the "monsters"	in "The Gates of Heaven"
the divided "other"	in "The Distances"
the silent "others"	in "House Taken Over"
the concrete "others"	in "Omnibus"

In its totality, this circuit from ants to concrete "others" is arranged in a hierarchy based on development along a biological scale, on the one hand, and on a shift from the imaginary (or the psychotic fantasy) to the real, on the other, though in two parallel cycles. This can be clearly seen: in the first cycle, ants and cockroaches exist—they are collected and handled by the first term; the rabbits, on the other hand, are produced via an emergent mechanism of that irrepressible tendency we talked about earlier; the mancuspias, finally, are imaginary and are not even described. In the second cycle, the "monsters" are like the cockroaches—something one flees from, or like the ants, from whose organization a conflict or a decision or a personality is fashioned; the divided "other" is like the rabbits—it escapes from you even though you do not want it to; the unnamed "others" are like the mancuspias, they either advance and drive out or else encircle. The system is complete, and it completes its process of illumination in its culmination, occurring in "Omnibus," where we find the most developed of the two juxtaposed scales—that is, the "concrete others" who embody the clash, the impossibility of universalizing the eruption of irrationality or the invariability, in short, a kind of antihistoricism, a kind of Hegelianism in reverse in its final consequences found in the proposed situations.[2]

But the existence of the double plane does not exhaust the entire array of organizing elements. From the development of this idea of a tendency or desire that wells up uncontrollably, disrupting an equilibrium, we are going to extract another, around which the stories are also organized. A particular tendency arises—for example, vomiting rabbits or preparing a piece of candy with cockroaches or looking fixedly at someone with aggressive fury or escaping from the besieged house or suffering from headaches designated perfectly by the homeopathic products that relieve them. The most explicit along this line is that of vomiting up rabbits; in that act, totally fantastic, we find concretized the insinuation made in all the stories of the existence of a desire that arises without any reason and without any motives. But in "The Distances" it is even more significant: Alina Reyes sees herself whipped and beaten in Budapest, and in that vision it is as if she carried deep in the interior of something like her conscience that other miserable being, perhaps in the same way that the person who writes the final letter carries the rabbits with him, but in Alina it is more classic, less arbitrary and fantastic.

And this way of carrying another within one's own self—this way of living divided in two—illuminates all of the burdens shouldered by the characters in the other stories. We have already seen what those burdens are: to carry rabbits inside you that are going to slip out of your throat without warning, breaking with their usual schedule, caressing your throat with their fur as they go; to have gripping headaches that wait for a certain signal of disaster in order to strike; to feel that "they" have taken over the house and so we must leave; to know that the enchanting Delia Mañara, in one form or another, will prepare something that looms over her will, a will suppressed by insanity; to think that inside of one person lies something, some irregularity, that provokes and offends the "others" ("Omnibus"); to watch oneself come to a decision resulting from pure

compassion ("Bestiary"); to recognize oneself as being a witness and a protagonist, distrustful and trusting at the same time, as being capable of recognizing
the dead woman from amongst the monsters ("The Gates of Heaven").

Thus it is a general tendency: one carries someone around inside of oneself
without realizing it until a particular moment, but from that moment on, one
knows, and there is no escape. That moment marks the beginning of a sense of
discomfort, a pregnancy known for its strangeness: after all, vomiting up a
rabbit cannot be a very normal experience. All the same, the discomfort, as in
pregnancy, leads to a birth, and that which appears in embryonic form, provok-
ing the discomfort, gains ground, grows, and triumphs over that which contains it: it is ten, now eleven rabbits; it is the miserable creature that Alina Reyes
becomes; it is Delia Mañara's convulsive ecstasy as she excitedly hands the
candy with the cockroaches to her third suitor; it is the security that Clara
("Omnibus") feels thanks to the young man, in the face of what it is about her,
and now about the two of them, that provokes the "others"; it is Isabel's sobs as
she curls in Rema's arms after giving the false information about the tiger's
whereabouts; it is the sense of pride with which they lock up the besieged
"house" and throw the keys in the gutter; it is the ecstatic recognition of Celina
brought passionately back to life in the world of the "monsters"; it is the
surrendering to pain that triumphs over the "outside" in "Cefalea." Fundamentally it is the shift at the moment of ambush of a deep, well-guarded, perhaps
oppressed, interiority toward the outside; it is a "holy place" glistening at last,
which is generalized as it is transmitted, blanketing the entire existence of that
which contains it. And that holy place, beginning with the means it has chosen
in order to externalize itself, becomes impregnated with an irrationality that, by
the same mechanism, is situated inside and can only hope to slip out without
being attributed to the external world. In this reasoning we can see a marked
difference from Borges; though they share a common preoccupation with irrational elements that superficially places both in the literature of the fantastic,
Cortázar goes beyond Borges's at-this-point schematic idealism, although in
"Bestiary," all of this is still of no use—nor does he want it to be—in building a
bridge to grounds for a possible improved communicability.

There is the holy place on the one hand, the "concrete others" on the other.
Confronted with these elements, we feel as if we are barely grazing the surface of
meanings, although the essential thing is that these terms form two poles that
bring with them certain modes of narration: they fulfill, they unfulfill. But if

they do so, it is always through another organizing element, one more predictable and necessary from the point of view of the intelligibility of the story— namely the character or characters, or The Character, which is the result of an intense and at times quite technically visible fusion.

In "House Taken Over," the storyteller, who is a character in the story, declares that he himself is not important, what matters is the house and his sister. But all the same, he does not stop acting and making decisions. Furthermore, through him, all this passes into history, a history that he himself relates. Why, then, this declaration? It is as if he wished to remain blurred, indistinct, as if he valued his capacity as a mere observer and attributed some action to someone else that nevertheless, he himself is also carrying out. The complement to this tone—it is no more than this because the identities are never lost— appears in "Cefalea," where the storyteller technifies this transfer, this transference, as he states over and over "uno de nosotros, uno de nosotros" ["one of us, one of us"] did this or that. The contours of everything begin to disappear here. It would appear that what matters is the action that is carried out and not the one who executes it, but surely this is a trap. The transference is so great and so marked that the act of misleading the reader about whether there are two or three or more individuals who share that strange bond takes on enormous relevance. "House Taken Over" and "Cefalea" constitute the most extreme points of this proposal, embodied in each story in a character who interprets others through himself, deriving his identity from a group, and losing or regaining it, who knows which, in the mass of people. If we think in terms of procedures, it seems clear that in "Cefalea" the expression "one of us" is a discovery, a formula that satisfies the requirements of the idea and that also allows that idea to be developed.

This much is evident: there is a tendency to integrate the subject into a group, and this objective clearly relies on a narrative procedure, a pluralized singular, a diminished but not destroyed plural. The corresponding integrating movement is manifested in the precise moment in which the so-called holy place emerges from the interiority where it has been kept. Thus, when this pregnancy is resolved, the person who contains the projected object becomes conscious of his singularity, and the greatest isolation springs from the manifestation of his interior: at that moment he is disgusting, untouchable, privileged. The affected character thus looks for someone in a similar state, and together they constitute a group that is essentially defensive, although once formed, they do not carry out any concrete action with the intention of protecting the holy place recently brought to light. They do not carry out any action, but they still reinforce themselves in order to protect it. To confirm this, there is the final seclusion in "Cefalea" while the mancuspias howl; there is the abandonment of the house in "House Taken Over" ("I took Irene around the waist [I think she was crying] and that was how we went into the street") [7]. And there is the most clearly defined group, the one formed in "Omnibus" between Clara and the young man, the only group in the whole book that does not turn out to be ineffective, or the group in "The Distances" that is finally resolved in a transference after having produced a fundamental encounter. In another dimension, there is the group formed by Marcelo and Mauro that is created in order to see Celina in "The Gates of Heaven," or the complicity that groups Isabel and Rema together after the former provides the false information about the tiger in "Bestiary." Ineffective groups or semieffective groups, but defensive ones, constituted in order to guard the holy place certainly—but to guard it from whom?

From this question we can recover the other indicated organizing pole as a perfect articulation. This appears quite clearly in "Omnibus": the holy place must be protected from the others who do not admit its existence and from whom the protagonist withdraws, feeling in the process a sense of proud guilt that she does not want to renounce. And those elements, the holy place and the "others," are the margins between which the characters move. That action of throwing oneself—or falling—against the walls of one's own limits is what defines them and signifies them. But the narrative organization does not stop at this critical point. This back-and-forth movement engenders a struggle that is imaginarily embodied in an unequal and at times pointless conflict. Uniting the two planes, we can see the dramatic consequences that are engendered: where the attempt to fuse the group into one single character, one single organism, is most pronounced, the way out is renunciation—basically, renunciation of what is possessed and of the understanding of the other, of the other that in its turn, for what it suggests, must detest the holy place that has been revealed. To abandon the house, to shut oneself away and no longer look for food for the mancuspias implies, correlatively, to stubbornly isolate oneself in a sacred and collective way of understanding reality or to shut oneself up with pain as something secure and immutable.

These are undoubtedly renunciations, but they reach their height when the group truly cannot be formed. In "Letter to a Young Lady," the holy place and the accomplices are one and the same thing, and they form a perhaps ideal identity, but for the same reason, an intolerable and absolutely incommunicable one that is destroyed with the death of the entire group. "The Distances," whose character absolutely must form a group since her holy place is a doubling of herself, also represents a culminating point in the construction of characters by Cortázar. Her group becomes a unity that suddenly discovers itself lost, the schizophrenic who embraces her phantom, but in truth not in order to recover a unity in identity but rather to defend the existence of the phantom before the others. In order to verify the true existence of this hallucinatory creature and to calm one's fears in relation to the holy place, the group forms for an instant, just long enough to produce the transference and to accomplish the defensive action whose purpose in this case is to assure that things continue in the same way.

So, along with renunciation and suicide, we should add one other result of the development of the defensive group—invariability, the impossibility of any modification. An almost final conclusion: renunciation, suicide, invariability— at the same time that they affirm the existence of the holy place, they also emerge from the indirect triumphs of the "others," of those who embody the persecution, with whom integration is impossible, and for whom, from the holy place, there is no program to formulate. Except in "Circe." What in that story appears to be a tendency toward fusion and continuity (the third suitor following in the footsteps of the two previous ones) is broken by an act of passage into the world of the "others," a sudden and bewildered sharing of the persecution of which the fragile and frightening Delia Mañara is the object— Delia Mañara who is the confectioner of the horrible candy (and doesn't that preliminary persecution perhaps resemble that which is suddenly set loose in "Omnibus"?).

But on a more realistic plane, the scheme is confirmed in "The Gates of Heaven," whose storyteller emphasizes his divided role as observer. He has nothing to do with it, he plays with the "monsters" or those other elemental be- ings, the constantly moving ants, contemplating their communal movements; he has nothing to do with the others, he insists, including their distance. Here it is quite clear: there are two worlds. The triumphs of the holy place over the world of the "others" are ephemeral, but these triumphs are the ones that matter if we take the whole system into account. And even the defeats matter as long as they bring out the world of the "others" in sharp relief, as long as the homogeneity of those "others" (the neighborhood in "Circe," the townspeople in "Cefalea," the passengers in "Omnibus," the monsters in "The Gates," the maid in "Letter to a Young Lady") reveals their stupid, harsh, and arbitrary nature in the face of the illumination that comes with the appearance of the holy place. But there is more: the definitions formulated show, through their reasonableness, through their objectivity (just in case this is not so clear in the other stories due to the contrivances and inventions) that the world of the "others" is the "anti–holy place" without return, a verification that closes the circle whose conflicting poles are integrated in this perfectly clear game.

But the character or characters, or The Character, are presented by someone who matters. It is the storyteller, a purely technical instance in which it is worth our while to pause for a moment. Five of the stories are told in first person, the others in third person. The scheme we can draw is as follows, taking into account the role played by each storyteller:

House Taken Over	Storyteller in 1st	Storyteller is protagonist who wants to diminish his role
Letter to a Young Lady in Paris	Storyteller in 1st	Protagonist
The Distances	Storyteller in 1st	Protagonist
Omnibus	Storyteller in 3rd	
Cefalea	Storyteller in 1st	Protagonists in first
Circe	Storyteller in 3rd	
The Gates of Heaven	Storyteller in 1st	Apparent semiprotagonist, effectively is protagonist
Bestiary	Storyteller in 3rd	

It stands out that the diary of Alina Reyes, the protagonist, stops at the end and a third-person storyteller appears who explains how the story ends, taking charge of explaining that Alina can no longer write in her diary because she has indeed become a different person. Excepting a more finely honed interpretation, which I will return to later, it appears that this is a technical pitfall with no way out, something like the contrary of what happens with the unified storyteller of "Cefalea"—an excellent "out."

But looking again at the classification system, the selection of two types of narrator surely does not stem from a simple desire to vary the form of the story.

No doubt there are structural demands whose satisfaction leads to this form of narration. In my opinion, in each case one or the other type of storyteller is best suited to provide an opening for the holy place; writing in the first person makes the action emerge from inside of oneself, it makes the interiority leap out via the very experience of the person who tells us what is happening. Furthermore, it proposes inherently profound movement in the attempt to configure a group with someone similar. Writing in the third person, even more than establishing that shift, verifies it, recognizes it, admits it from an opposing perspective that moves from the outside, in. Somehow, if we keep in mind the role that the "other" and the "others" play in these stories, third-person narration implies putting oneself in the anti–holy place for one dangerous instant in order to assure that, when it is manifested, the holy place triumphs as best it can, invariably, but also a bit sorrowfully.

In "Omnibus," this point of view resides in the theme of the gaze, whose path, from the "others" to the characters, can only be observed and described from the outside, valorized even from the position of an objective storyteller who can better transmit the sense of a false bridge implied by the gaze of the others, with its initial deceptive generosity that rapidly turns into animosity, hatred, inexorable persecution, incomprehensible antagonism. In "Circe," the third-person narrator serves to fuse together the idea the "others" have about Delia with that which begins to take form in the mind of the startled third suitor: the furor at the appearance of the holy place produces its greatest significations in the act of disintegration of the probable group, an even more dramatic change of fortune when it is looked at from the outside. Finally, in "Bestiary," an objective story is necessary for the complicity to be revealed as a result of the interlinking of a series of things, and not as the result of a conscious will: the holy place emerges in this way in an almost glorious and indisputable recognition, and through it, justice itself comes forth.

But whatever function the narrator might perform, it is clear that in order to carry out the narration, he or she adopts a particular point of view and examines the substance of the story from a certain perspective. And it is not always the same perspective in all of the stories; each story's classification will allow it to determine its major significant values. In "Bestiary," for example, the story is told in third person, but the storyteller assumes the perspective of the little girl to whom things happen—a perspective that brings out her interiority. It is not that the girl is necessarily the protagonist; more than once the storyteller looks with a gaze that is not that of the protagonist, but rather subjects the protagonist to the storyteller's gaze—and in this case, this is through the eyes of the girl. Furthermore, a child is obviously a being still forming, a provisional being, and to a certain extent, still incomplete. A child sees things as more or less colored, but in any case, in outlines that adults exclude from view.

In the other stories, this distancing is not repeated in the same way, and instead, they emphasize the incomplete nature that distinguishes the characters from whose perspective the story is told. In "The Distances," Alina Reyes, incomplete by definition since she is something like a schizophrenic, must search for the miserable being that is she herself and whom she must find in order to be complete. In "Letter to a Young Lady," vomiting up the rabbits makes the protagonist (who is also the storyteller) a superabundant being, but this turns into the same thing as a kind of amputation in terms of its social effects—that is, he too is incomplete. What happens in "Cefalea" is similar to what happens in "The Distances," except that completeness has already been achieved through lack: two or more indistinct narrator-protagonists, merged into a single mass, are also incomplete due to their being conjoined; they are always already incomplete, never failing to reveal their beginning, their origin. In "House Taken Over," the lack of completeness between the brother and sister is clearly evident—they watch each other and believe that in that contemplation and the ritual of their daily tasks they can achieve the unity for which they search. Finally, in "Omnibus," the two who are being persecuted can only think of leaping off the bus—to the outside—when they sit next to each other, hold hands, and devise a plan: before, they were broken, "empty"; now they are complete and will be able to resist, if not understand. Children, incomplete beings, untouchables from whose mouths existence is expressed: here, once again, is the holy place that is impossible to bear, but also impossible not to glorify.

In "The Gates of Heaven" and in "Circe," on the other hand, the narrator adopts the point of view of an adult; all vicissitudes take the form of a rendering of judgment, a task assumed by the characters, and through them, by the storytellers, who for that reason strive to distance themselves from what they narrate. They attempt to place themselves outside of the action and to not be devoured by it, but precisely because of that, they confirm the essence of the action. They build a small bridge such that the aforementioned holy place can move from its state of isolation into a certain objectification that is not the objectivity of the other, and into a certain validation encountered at the point in which the initially extreme particularity is found, in something like a sort of recovery in terms of a limited and oppressive order—even more arbitrary in the hatred felt by the driver in "Omnibus" than in the birth of the rabbits. In light of this new function, the change of storyteller in "The Distances," which I designated earlier as a technical leap, appears, if not justified, at least imbued with meaning: what has been overturned inside can also be seen; someone functions as a bridge between a subjectivity disputed by the external world, and that external world itself in its maximum, all-embracing point of tension. That bridge is the storyteller, the most immediate manifestation of the author, his double, the one who, while wanting to establish himself in a position that has nothing to do with the author, nevertheless most quickly expresses his voice.

I have already mentioned what differentiates Borges from Cortázar; I believe we have seen how the idea of an irrationality anchored in interiority is manifested in all possible planes and levels of the literary process, of the expressive organization that constitutes a basic concern in Cortázar's work. No doubt an analysis of Borges could show how the irrational, projected to the outside, also has its own appropriate way of expressing itself. Hence, the fundamental expressive concern manifested in diverse organizing schemes in these stories of Cortázar's does not disappear in his following work, nor do the schemes that are amplified by shattering not so much their sense but rather a thematic that in "Bestiary" appears asphyxiated if not constricted in its scope. For in the end it is not necessary to invent mancuspias or vomit up rabbits in order to express a certain uneasiness in interpreting the world. Thus, the people—not the animals—in *Hopscotch* or "Meeting" ["Reunión"][3] or "The Pursuer" ["El persiguidor"],[4] without abandoning the dialectic of the holy place in opposition to alterity, have deeper resonances, encompass more varied resonators, or, if you wish, they touch feelings that are more immediate but more numerous and perhaps more complex.

The perfected survival of these stances, which engender an intensification of significations, does not exclude other elements that, for their part, propose a continuity. In order not to make these comments overlong, I will limit myself to indicating two or three instances as points of departure that he develops more completely later on. Thus, for example, in "Omnibus"—and there is only one place in the whole story where he does this—Cortázar suddenly designates certain characters by the flowers they carry: "the daisies, the gladioli, the arum lilies lined up behind them" [18]. He would go on, years later, to construct an entire story, based on this method of characterization: "The Southern Thruway" ["La autopista del sur"],[5] in which, from a certain point in the story, the characters are all designated by the models of their respective cars. The idea of the person who judges ("The Gates of Heaven": "for other people it's enough to feel that way—I have to think it" [36]), reappears in all its splendor and total misery in "The Pursuer," where observing and living constitute situational decisions that define ways of understanding reality. In the stories contained in the collection *Bestiary*, out of the opposition between what I have called "feeling" and what I have called "judging," a clear preference develops on the part of the faithful for the first term: it is the direct, enriched world of the creator, the capacity to embrace that defines true life, a fundamental feature, at last, of the holy place, still only outlined in the stories contained in *Bestiary*, though implicitly defended.

Finally, we can also uncover the moment of passage from a situation of equilibrium to another situation, that of the appearance of the holy place as something enduring that lasts for the length of the entire work. We said that there was a discomfort and, later, something like an illumination that preceded the search for the formation of a group. In the moment of passage there is a bewilderment, but almost immediately a process of familiarization begins, which is clearly evident in "Letter to a Young Lady" and in "House Taken Over": one lives with the new experience, watching it grow, we could almost say fostering it, surrounding it in a bland verbal environment more fitting of some small, common object, while at the same time always recognizing its extraordinary nature. Something similar, but with a more concrete illusionary quality, if one can say such a thing, and with an imagination less rhetorical, occurs in "Don't You Blame Anyone" ["No se culpe a nadie"],[6] in "The Southern Thruway," or in "Blow-up" ["Las babas del diablo"],[7] all from later works by Cortázar.

So we find continuity and exaltation, but also variations in this position: gradually there is less renunciation, less negation of a human perspective, that is, a historical one; little by little Cortázar discovers that the holy place is found, and not only symbolically, in all that is human, in the adventures of Che Guevara or in the martyrology of Charlie Parker—a direct relationship with things and the world, total awareness, the capacity to create. Little by little in this process, the game of incomplete beings (whose greatest systematization is perhaps reached in *Cronopios and Famas* [*Historias de cronopios y de famas*

(1962)]) tends to become diluted by an enrichment of themes or problems that exclude it. The most significant, perfectly formed glimpses that are found in *Bestiary* would have led Cortázar down a fatal path of downward spirals and narcissism if they had not produced just such a broadening process. Or perhaps not. At any rate, the important thing is not to conjecture about what might have happened, but to note what did.

I, the Supreme as Historical Novel

It could be said that counter to certain principles of reading particular to our times, in the years since 1974 when this book was published, *I, the Supreme* [*Yo el Supremo*] has been popularized as presenting a fundamental problem of rupture, perhaps overshadowing its also obvious high quality.

The fact that it is problematic, or has been considered as such, springs from two things. The first, perhaps, is its difficulty, a condition that arises in all readings of the work. The second is that it proposes multiple readings, each of which promises surprising bifurcations.

But furthermore, to the eternal perplexity of the critic, this text *appears* to contain centers that give rise to explanatory actions whose effects elusively withdraw when we try to grasp them with the aim of simplifying or reducing the problem. In all explanatory attempts we always arrive at what should be the ethic of all criticism: there is a more secret plane, a restless bubbling energy in the shadows, crouching and hidden, that criticism perceives and pursues but never reaches.

From the point of view of criticism, this text seductively tempts one to reduce it, either because of the illusion of a transcendent global significance or because of its extraordinary appeal: each fragment is a potential disturbance, requiring a boundary, as a fragment, and a certain development, and the intelligence it fosters begets a new illusion of facility. Facility that we could call "the Auerbach effect," but in his case, it was not an illusion.

In one way or another people have wished and still wish to restrain, via generalizations or dominant representations, the restless energy that emanates from this text. They have wished and still wish to control the vertigo of a reading that, in order to be so, must suspend convictions, must prohibit the very idea of meaning and of a message, in which we are accustomed to finding a guarantee we believe to be natural—the guarantee of believing something can be known. In just this way, a reading of *I, the Supreme,* which *appears* in an impressive unfolding of knowledge, pierces that knowledge, fragments it, and reconstructs it in a superior unity that clearly cannot be subjected to mere interpretation, and that evades the vigilant eye of hermeneutics, those armed forces of common sense.

One of the aspects of that unfolding concerns historical knowledge, which in the classic formulation of the historical novel appears perfectly balanced in an economic equilibrium with literary knowledge, or more precisely, that of the novel, or even more precisely, that of fiction.

We could say, in effect, that since Roa Bastos's novel appeared, numerous studies have tried to understand it as an apologia of an important historical character, related, in turn, to a kind of literary resuscitation of the figure of the dictator that has often been proposed as a way to unite various currents of Latin American literature. But its position as a historical novel was not assured: it is as if it did not quite fit the category completely because it seems that it did not meet the definitions of that subgenre, definitions that, as we know, are applied to the orthodox expressions of the nineteenth century. Or else, that position is reduced to a "variant" of the historical novel with the aim of preserving a more or less social and historical message: a recovery of the national origin of Paraguay that, through that reconstructed mythical figure, would allow us to understand the autonomous will of a country and a people. And no less complex would be the fact that the book could be alluding to the present through a complicated manipulation of a representation of the past.

But that link to the present alone is not enough to make it a historical novel. As has been known from Lukács to Eco, this genre functions, from the perspective of the predominance of what it represents, in at least three possible ways. Either it centers on an institutional issue, as we see in the work of Vicente Riva Palacio on the Inquisition,[1] for example, or it gathers together little-known or secret or quotidian aspects of a past era, as Walter Scott or Dumas did, or it recovers a particular figure, that of the representative man that in Hegel's philosophical succession was a common concern in Latin America, though not as much as in Europe. To be sure, none of these options is carried out in an exclusive, pure sense: Pérez Galdós[2] unites the first two aspects and includes the third, Roa Bastos the first and the third, although it is evident that he privileges the third but cannot escape from what the genre offers nor from what it complicates. Although it tends to be confusing, and not only in Roa Bastos, the fact that writing imposes changes—which then produce much more sophisticated texts, a dimension that the relatively simple historical novel could not even dream of—does not imply either that the genre has languished or that the renewed tendency toward that challenge should be ignored. In the last thirty or forty years, interest in this structure has increased notably and has born fruit, from Alejo Carpentier's *The Kingdom of This World* [*El reino de este mundo*] to Juan José Saer's *The Witness* [*El entenado*], including the works of Fuentes, Aridjis, and Carpentier's other works. That of Roa Bastos also does not escape from that web. All of which means that it is important to renew the idea of the "historical novel" and not abandon it.

If I refer to an "orthodox" concept of the historical novel, it is because it appears, contradictorily, to be very much present in many approaches to *I, the Supreme,* including Roa Bastos's own opinions, although in his case we find an exceptional productivity. In the 1978 Colloque de Cerisy volume on Roa Bastos,[3] and later in that of Poitiers,[4] he stated: "I did not endeavor to create a historical novel or a novelized biography, hybrid products that simulate a false verisimilitude."[5] In all of his interviews, papers, and conferences, he reiterates this assertion, the scope of which I have often wondered about. It seems to me now that it is a good way to approach the subject. Of course these two subgenres aspire to verisimilitude, and, of course, that verisimilitude is false and misleading, but denounced in this manner, its announcer seems to formulate a claim of "true" verisimilitude.

In other words, it would seem that to the extent that as a genre, as a rhetoric, all historical novels carry the stigma of false verisimilitude, *I, the Supreme*, because it seeks a true verisimilitude, is not a historical novel. Of course the disinterested and unconcerned could say that these complications are not important, that the text exists and that is enough, beyond all genre-related minutia. They could be right from the poetic perspective of literary glory; however, I believe that the topic garners as much interest as other literary topics in which the economy, surrounded by forces or tendencies, generates forms that in turn constantly renew their enigma.

Roa Bastos's words obviously suggest a fundamental problem: what is true verisimilitude? Without getting caught up in arguing about this off-track and relative tautology—because as we all know, verisimilitude is not "true"—I would say that what Roa Bastos saw in his own text is a search for, or a discovery of, a realm of truth that can be generated by a text and that has the capacity to make a revision in the area of history itself, either of a historicized preconception or of a prejudice consolidated as a historical truth. It is a question, therefore, of a revisionist objective conceived through and by mediation of a literary text. That naturally calls into question the traditional historical novel, whose objective, in contrast, could be understood as confirmational and reproducing, not contradictory, abandoning from the beginning all attempts to achieve a truth. Roa Bastos's declarations seem to follow this direction: "My novelistic project has consisted, primarily, of writing a counterhistory, a subversive and transgressive reply to the official historiography. . . . The counter-history should become an 'intrahistory,' and simultaneously, a 'transhistory.' "[6]

In short, this would be the "true verisimilitude," although two types of questions are raised by this assertion. The first type involves a strange disappearance, that of the literary object; it would appear that all efforts are essentially historical. The second type contains ideological traces.

In terms of the "strange disappearance," if I employ this formula it is because it seems to me that this text is extremely literary, if one can think in terms of levels of literariness. It is such because of its work with and in language, the richness of the discursive imagination, the constant transformation, the incessant intertextuality.

Looking at it more closely, Roa Bastos's words are not so much related to an epistemological question; rather, they reveal an intuition about the fact that the historical novel is often a commentary on the discourse of power. However, in turning to revisionism in order to attack the discourse of power, he seems to ignore—provisionally, I believe—what literary discourse itself involves as an institution, namely, how it colludes with power. In other words, if the objective is historical, it would seem that one would better attack power by not speaking about literature. Another intuition would function underneath: since literature is complicit with power, which is undeniable, the risk is to become engaged with literature and lose track of that historical objective.

In Roa Bastos's thought we can find confirmation of this idea in two cases. The first is when he alludes, in Cerisy, to what he calls "the bad conscience" of the petit-bourgeois writers: the "literary writers," stated with emphasis, search in words and in the literary institution for what they have renounced in historical facts.[7] It is a question, strictly speaking, of taking inspiration from Cesare Pavese, the act that, carried to its logical conclusion, is the revolution.

The second case confirming this idea is imaginary. It appears in the text in the constant scorn the dictator heaps on those he calls "scribes" or "scriveners" or "scribblers" [24]. This also occurs less explicitly, or in a more subtle manner, through word play and puns such as "literati/terati"[8] [51]. Through a simple process of amputation, he reveals the true character of the writer, a monster, an isolated being, surrendering to his own reprehensible logic.

In short, what Roa Bastos details is coherently manifested in the text itself, in the figures that take shape through a practiced loss of control.

The second type of question arises due to a system of evocations or associations. Keeping in mind that the book was written between 1970 and 1974 in Argentina, the concept of "counterhistory" evokes the idea of "counterideology" that circulated widely in the intellectual milieu of the time. Probably its most intense period occurred between 1965 and 1975, understood as the sphere of the possible in the ideological struggle. This usage grows, I believe, from a perspective of the alleged decline of Marxism. From the moment in which Marxism proposes a more radical type of thought, of remote possibilities (and perhaps for that reason it begins to be seen as insufficient), the expression "counterideology" allows us to understand more quickly how one can oppose power and class domination. In short, the criticism that grew out of this was created through opposition.

In the Argentine debate, that criticism revives certain classical forms, such as revisionism (constituted not so much from a distrust of Marxism as from ignorance or a total antagonism toward it), which opposed the liberal historiography considered to be the "official history." Hence we have the vindication of "the people" through opposition to "the oligarchy," although this counterideological opposition was constructed and continued to be manifested by the exaltation of the celebrated victims of liberalism. Be that as it may, those who conceived of the counterideological gesture through these new reasons found themselves face to face with classic revisionism because they had few other concrete options. In its turn, the disillusionment with Marxism was paradoxically manifested after a renaissance, via Althusser, of the structural aspects of Marxism.

Although all these aspects may appear to have little to do with a reading of the piece, it is possible to raise them and take them into consideration because, in their production, all texts are dated—their chronological stamp does not reside only in their representation. That is to say that it is not only a question of the image of Paraguay in 1840, but also a question of the process of the production of writing, for which we must keep in mind all of the various powerful influences that could have coincided such that the image of the Paraguay of 1840 could be constructed.

But it is also important to note that Roa Bastos's formula, "counterhistory," is dynamic; it does not restrict itself to a pure opposition. In short, Francia is not "revised" by opposition to what the Triple Alliance (Argentina, Uruguay, and Brazil) did in the 1860s,[9] which, on the other hand, seems to have provoked the Paraguayan trauma par excellence. Roa Bastos carries us along, or allows himself to be carried along by the writing, to an "intrahistory" that, because it supposes investigation, brings us back to the sphere of the historical novel. In effect, "intrahistory" presumes to determine the component elements of a structure, and, therefore, this gesture goes beyond mere opposition to an official or sacred image.

In turn, what results from an "intrahistorical" inward movement leads to an idea of "transhistory" that, as it is formulated, possesses a marked metaphorical character; that is to say, it unites diverse spheres and differentiated planes into one single notion. In this way, it unites a visible history, that of a man and a country, with another, secret one, that of the process of writing. Or perhaps not so secret in this book that alludes to it, problematizes it, exposes it, extracts it with dramatism and an extraordinary lucidity that becomes a driving force. But it also unfolds both *from* and *in relation to* the history of a country, in a double relationship: as reconstruction of speech and as a construction of a text.

As a consequence, these opinions, which at first seemed to reduce the field a bit, reveal a very special dynamism, very much alive, that allows a global entry into the text as if from the outside, like a gaze or a spectacle, but no less concrete for it. In other words, the steps between contra-, intra-, and transhistory show us the diversity of planes in which this text is structured, and that are articulated from and in a process of production. It is obvious that the results of this articulation will be complex, as can be easily noticed in a first reading. To put it another way, that motion through the three terms, which confronts a problem, is resolved in what we could call "the writing of a narration."

What would that narration be? Precisely that motion that carries the final metaphor to the juncture of the two histories, that of a country, as a restoration, and that of a writing, as a more problematic region, that demands or involves taking a position with respect to the situation of literature or of writing at a particular moment.

My point of departure, then, was that this text has been seen as a problem: Roa Bastos himself gives us reason to think this. But other critics also see it similarly. Rubén Bareiro Saguier insists on excluding this text from the paradigm of the historical novel: "This different categorization of events or characters separates *I, the Supreme* from the traditional historical novel and situates it in its place: the creation of an imaginary reality in accordance with social reality and certain mental schemas."[10] Similarly, Jean Andreu has observed that the text is neither a historical novel nor novelized history but an act of placing novel and history in crisis.[11]

Although I find it difficult to work with the respective arguments, I have found it useful to bring up these concepts and questions about whether it is or is not a historical novel, or what it is, or if it forms part of a particular paradigm, because, even though I get a bit lost in these discussions, the terms that they employ—creation, reality, society, cognitive schemas, textual figure—are of such a universal character that they encompass the entire problematic of this genre, with respect to which I have tried to see how permanence or continuity and modification can be reconciled. To the contrary, I do not believe we would get very far by establishing a break between this text and the historical novel. At any rate, it would be a typical way of resolving the problematic character indicated initially, canceling an entire side of the issue. In my opinion, we cannot get to the central question of its textuality this way, and that is what we need to understand. In that sense, when we disregard the relationship with the historical novel, we are following the nineteenth-century vision of the historical novel. And I believe that that hinders us from recognizing the extent of the rupture that this text has or the model of rupture that it might offer or the type of rupture in which it might be situated.

To put it briefly, that rupture would be the rupture of the limits of a genre whose basic parameters, reaching beyond the established rhetoric, are, as we said, nevertheless present in this text: documentation, investigation, reevaluation, discussions of power, the relationship with the present. These parameters, which I would like to define as operating systems, are as much at play in texts such as Riva Palacio's classic, *Monja y casada, vírgen y mártir* [Nun and Wife, Virgin and Martyr], as they are in that of Roa Bastos. The difference is that in the former the productivity stems from the affirmation, while in the latter it stems from its negation or restriction or questioning. And in order to reinforce this idea, one could say that in effect it is a question of an act of rupture because the modification in the operating system is carried out indirectly, not only in the space of the confirmed or claimed historical truths but also in that of the concrete elements of narration.

I have called this space the "writing of a narration." I can translate this concept in this particular text as a "telling," but not a *novelistic telling*, which articulates the component elements of the narration on two levels: a general one of transformation, and a particular one of construction.

In other words, the challenge of *I, the Supreme* consists of being able to leave behind the rules of the novel, leaving them floating or in a state of suspension. Thus the dictator's monologue (which has its parallel in the "Perpetual Circular," so in reality, there are two complementary structures) because of its incessance breaks with novelistic laws. Of course, since this is a question of a monologue, one could be tempted to think of "interior monologue" in the style of Joyce or of "stream of consciousness," but those concepts are more accommodating: they are quite novelistic: they "renew" the technique. Roa Bastos, on the other hand, introduces a critique from the moment he first tells of a situation or a character, establishing the conditions of possibility of this non-novelistic telling.

Here I need to articulate the categories presented. So, for example, I spoke of parameters, of a general level of transformation and a particular level of construction. These categories converge in the elements that form a narration. I will discuss only the fictional character [of the Supreme] in an attempt to describe how it takes form and how the form that it takes manifests that general sense of rupture that simultaneously creates and modifies the possibilities for the historical novel.

I will begin with something that has been discussed at length already: the displacements in the pronominal system proposed by the title itself—from an *I* [yo] to a *he* [él].[12] This move, as well as its inverse, from *he* to *I,* articulates the character; it has a productive quality. Briefly put, this is precisely what the novel narrates, the passage from one pronoun to another, from the private to the public, from the public to the private. And to show that this is nothing strange, we need only remember that this move is a leitmotif of the sense and the objectives of the historical novel: the *he* represents the region of transcendence, the *I* that of internalization, and as a consequence, is the core of the conversion of history to novel. But similar to *I, the Supreme,* this constitutes a rupture because all characters in novels, especially in historical novels, tend to be figurative characterizations, the representation of an image or of a more or less coherent figure or one whose coherence we discover or, somewhat paradoxically, whose contradictoriness we discover.

The displacements in the pronominal system create the need to develop, explain, complete, and shape—in short, the diverse situations that summon or demand writing. And if this view were to discover a confrontation with a novelistic code, the rupture would also produce an effect on the reading, which is where it can be measured. In this sense this text is unusual, although a general law could be stated according to which there is not really a reading when the relationship with a text does not provoke a suspension of all guarantees of certainty, whether the text is obscure or transparent. Of course such guarantees affect a knowledge that in an inert way attempts to reaffirm itself or that can be submitted to the demands of difference. For me, only the activity that allows that second possibility, that vertigo, can really be called "reading." And in my opinion, by its very nature this book elicits, foments, and fosters it.

But if these are the conditions for the emergence of the character, once he is formed he can be considered and examined with all his traits and abilities. Given his characteristics and his centrality—an attractive, disdainful, enigmatic, and problematic object—he constitutes a way to access the text. Going back to the words of Jacques Leenhardt, "Few works subtly extract, as does *I, the Supreme,* the axis of its centrality. Certainly the person of the Supreme seems to function as the pivot point of the work, and yet if one tries to depict him, he disappears in a multifaceted kaleidoscope. Thus one can speak of polyphony."[13]

Of course "polyphony" conjures up the image of Bakhtin, although the concept is certainly used in other senses. Be that as it may, the image is a good one: this book eliminates, in its own development, the possibility of grasping what could be its central element, that is, the very powerful main character. This idea opens up a space for reflection. For example, the first doubling, the pronominal one, *I/he* [*yo/él*] can be understood in this sense. It could be embryonic because it puts into play only two instances, but it opens the possibility of considering more abundant interplay. However, as an aside, let me mention that for critics such as Bareiro Saguier, monologuism (the fact that the dictator talks constantly, maintaining an unending conversation)[14] would be a functional attribute of the character, and, as such, an expression of another coherence, that of national integrity and the identity of a people. For Bareiro, two entities are superimposed. In my opinion, although the voice of a dictator can, under certain circumstances, embody national integrity and be the spokesperson for a people, it also, simultaneously, stifles the voice of that people.

But how is this character constructed? How does he go about taking form? Apparently his form is there from the initial moment of formation when he begins to speak. However, his complete form is a result of the whole. In other words, it is the result of a combination of ideas, of operating systems, that spring from the pronouns. On the one hand, it seems to correspond to a biological model, since the dictator is eighty-four years old when the first chapter opens, meaning that he is biologically constructed. Yet this process is not narrated, suggesting that his identity has been formed via other routes. Of course "character identity" is different from "personal identity." In short, it is not constructed through absolute representation of the historical figure but rather, in the best of cases, the representation is vague, not fixed. That is why Andreu stated that the dictator is a textual rather than historical figure.[15] The historical would, therefore, only augment that textual quality. And if for Bareiro the monologuism could be an attribute, we can now add another—the enunciative function, which to me seems dominant. The dictator is an enunciator, a giant mouth from which spring words that, besides being judgments about reality or about he himself, are also the bricks with which he constructs.

Thus, when he states "I sensed that I snored a bit during the Festival of Work, on the nineteenth" [72], the statement is so incidental that it is not really valuable in terms of understanding him as a character or a personality. On the other hand, however, the fact that he announces *everything* is valuable; his unending talk, not conversation, is his fundamental attribute.

But this attribute is not his—it is given to him by the narrator, the alter ego of a compiler. And the enunciation, for its part, is represented by a spoken monologue thinly disguised as dialogue, and by a written monologue, the "Private Notebook." We should note, in passing, that the word "compiler," as Roa Bastos himself indicated, is a kind of thief, a "com/pillador,"[16] that is, a thief who breaks in so as to rob a business or referential storehouse, and who appropriates referents, properly or improperly. His plundering is the intertextuality that, because it is created in the very cycle of the culture, cannot be subjected to any moral judgment. It is a silent and surreptitious robbery that here is revealed by an act of reconstruction of a word, similar to what he did with "literati/terati" (not through suppression, but rather through addition). This thief of referents—of texts—makes his intentioned selection, and through that, configures the depiction in a polyphonic, faceted way. But in order to fool us about what he is doing, he suggests, insidiously and surreptitiously (in an indirect, sly aside) in notes, in the tiniest of letters, betting that it will not be read, that there are corrections to this apparent figure, to what is asserted in writing of a much more legible size. In this way a musical counterpoint is established between what is stated and what is whispered. The image of polyphony returns, or perhaps to a lesser degree, that of a duet, a sonata in which the violin and the piano introduce themselves, seduce each other, correct each other constantly. In short, the compiler's notes that are corrected are the base of a musical counterpoint. But since in this correction the compiler turns out to be both a party to the case and its judge, this relationship can be seen to be legal as well as musical.

Of course the character of the Supreme is constructed around the enunciative function, but what are his particular attributes? One could say, following the previously indicated classification, that there are two types of construction: the *I* and the *he*.

As already stated, because of the relationship between the *I* and the *he*, the figure that emerges is completely the opposite of the depiction of a character, that culmination of the traditional story or its requirement of coherence. Precisely because it is not coherent, we cannot say that this is a "novel about dictators," as are Valle-Inclán's *Tirano Banderas* [The Tyrant Banderas], Carpentier's *Reasons of State* [*El recurso del método*], Asturias's *The President* [*El Señor Presidente*], or García Márquez's *The Autumn of the Patriarch* [*El otoño del patriarca*], novels that have attempted to understand a dictator in order to denounce a Latin American situation. Here there are no "dictator characters" but only "dictated instances." And if there is an insistence on the expression "dictatorship," it is the sense of a figure who is part of a spirit extending beyond the political, which is a constant. Thus, for example, a teacher, who also dictates, is a dictator. To substantiate this relationship, on page 55 it states, "This is a lesson." Because of this, but also because what we call "character" results from a system of interactions between the two pronominal instances, it is a question, as Leenhardt indicated, of a textual structure at whose center we find, instead of a character, an intellectual scribal function—that is, an evidencing of the relationship of the writer to power.

This vein could also be explored: the intellectual scribal function is, first of all, molded by power, but also, it itself functions as power. These two aspects constitute the substance of a profuse and constant contemporary debate that gives rise to numerous ideological outpourings, equivalent in a certain way to what we indicated for literature in general. In its second aspect, assuming that the first is clear and recognizable, we can ask, is the power of the writing—which is the power of the writer—abusive or legitimate? Is it fatally at the service of the powers that be, or does it confront them? This question is so diffuse that in the text in question one is aware of the power of he who dictates, but not of he who writes. The dictator who writes has power, but perhaps not Patiño, who also writes. Or is it not perhaps Roa Bastos, who holds the power, the one who writes everything that the figures in the novel say and write? And along those lines, does his instrumentality, and what he does with it in the discussion about power, matter, or is it only seen in a symbolic sense, transcended and separated from what he himself does and what he himself hopes for? In general, writers hide themselves in this question. When proposing a discussion of the power of literature, setting aside space for the characters or situations represented, they attempt to ignore their relationship to the problem, but the issue cannot be ignored: does literature constitute a power, or is it only in the service of the power or powers? The question of course is political, not in the sense of the message that one usually reads in a text, but rather in terms of the value for society of the symbolic practices, organized by the political, controlled by it, combating it.

The political nature of this work is linked to the action of dictating, which, as I already indicated, would be the trait of the dictator, although one could also say that the inherent quality of the dictator is to oppress, a perspective that corresponds to another approach. In this text, it is clear, we find the first sense: he constantly carries out the act of dictation. Thus, the inherent quality of the dictator is to dictate, something he can do through a double mechanism, that of the voice and that of language. He can dictate who has a voice and who has the language, in the linguistic sense, to use that voice. In short, the dictator becomes the person who can fully manipulate the illocutionary act. It is he who, in a privileged manner, can make words truly become actions. Therefore he becomes a teacher, and he who receives his dictates becomes a student, who on occasion, is a scribe. "As I dictate to you, you write" [19], he says a number of times to Patiño, who frequently responds with "I understand." It is the counterpart: if the dictator converts words into actions, the scribe, whose voice is forbidden (Francia tells him, "I forbid you to wallow in filth playing dirty word games" [15]), converts the actions he receives—phrases that must not be changed—into traitorous words.

But there are always holes in the scheme: he who dictates does not always do so in a clear voice; he who writes never transcribes literally what the voice dictates. Faced with this, the dictator becomes upset, for there could be betrayal in the transcription: "When I dictate to you, the words have a meaning; when you write them, another" [57]. The opposite effect of what he wants is therefore produced, and the person who appeared to be the faithful "confidential clerk" [63] becomes the unfaithful "unconfidential clerk," which constitutes a kind of allegory of literature as both limit and freedom. The space that is left between the ill-perceived voice and the impossible transcription determines the so-called literary space, the betrayal of the voice and the generation of its own, illusive splendor.

At this point we also find the political element, since the unfaithful word the dictator attempts to correct conveys a perhaps limited freedom, but one that the dictatorship attempts to repress. Here we find, in embryonic form, a theory about the limited freedom and legitimacy in literature, but also an explanation of its power.

But that power is not heard completely, and if it becomes manifest, it does so only in the area of reading, where it always formulates new protocols. And if the control of such protocols resides in the political sphere, reading would be a space of the political struggle itself. In other words, the aim of politics would be to control social reading. Correspondingly, a democratic, humane social politics would be one that sets out to alter its own control and broaden the sphere of reading. Therefore a writing that attempts to change the protocols of reading establishes itself in a political perspective. Thus, if writing, limited and with a precarious freedom, is formed from the falsification of the voice, we should not find it incongruent that the text begins by exhibiting a falsification of the writing. This is particularly important because it deals, precisely, with a beginning, the privileged incipit about which people have been conjecturing for centuries. It is the place where the rupture occurs of a previous equilibrium that might have continued. It is, therefore, the place of risk.

This falsification sets in motion the long monologue as a way of creating the conditions for determining the truth: who is the author of that falsification? The answer, one suspects, might lead to a tautology, which would make that answer insignificant. And that suggests a triple fiction, which to me seems important to emphasize. First, there is the fiction of the document as the foundation of the historical tale: all documents can be falsified. Second is the fiction of investigation as the search for the truth: what value is there in an investigation that will find, as in Chesterton's book [*The Man Who Was Thursday*], that the police who are looking for the criminal are the very criminals who provoke the police? Third is the fiction of the represented voice. If, as is suggested by the formulation, there is a questioning, it is the fiction itself, as a procedure, as a system, as a rhetoric, that is being questioned. With fiction invalidated, what survives is the writing; the only thing that can be verified is the power of the written word that, true or false, gives rise to a text.

Perhaps what this involves is, precisely, a problem of the historical novel, which, as we know, is defined as such due to the predominance of fiction. Thus, when the precariousness of fiction is brought out, the literary act is constituted between opposing signs, between falsification and its denunciation. If it becomes a historical novel, it is because it seeks something different in history from what history itself seeks. For history, the document must be verisimilar, must pass various tests. Whereas here, in denouncing fiction, the characteristics and guarantees of representation are suspended: we no longer know what is being represented.

At another level, the text appears restless and contradictory. Suddenly, the images that seem graspable encapsulate others that will dislodge the original images. This creates a vertigo; it is the condition of restlessness, and, therefore, it leads to hypotheses that are purely tentative but gradually become more complex.

Thus, synthesizing various observations, we can say that it does not seek the apologia of a historical man but rather a reconsideration of multiple influences, essentially those that concern the concept of writing or of literature. But while this question might have an epistemological dimension, the way the issues are presented has a political aspect consisting of the fact that writing—which appears as the space in which this entire conflict is organized—is presented as a productivity.

Writing questions the dominance of illustrious voices despite the dictator's defense of the voice in an attempt at self-legitimization: I am the dictator, I dictate, thus the voice is what is most important. It is clear that the power of writing is dubious, as we indicated earlier, but it is nevertheless a barrier that confronts the certainty of those illustrious voices. At the same time, those illustrious voices manifest themselves in the utopia of total knowledge that only comes from textual knowledge.

And if the text represents the utopia of total knowledge, this concept culminates in a counterutopian space that we could call "concentrational," the concentration camp. Hence the fragments about the Tevegó prison have a profound myth-making density to them: the utopia of the loss of memory and movement that call to mind that other utopia of total control called Stalinism. If this is the case, it would be another resonance that is recorded in the text. And the allusion would not be inappropriate, insofar as Stalinism can certainly be defined as the culmination of a monologuism and, given the extreme rationality of the revolution, as a reduction of rationality. That reduction, as one of the notable characteristics of the contemporary discussion, opposes the plurality of Latin American linguistic registers that, like a limit, like another kind of intertextuality, influence this text. Those registers are, precisely, the presence of the past, bilingualism and even polylingualism, the essay's least bloody hypothesis, and the error in the configuration of the political or literary or other systems. The concentrational utopia tries to imagine a world of only one voice in its victims, dissolved and lost in one lone lament.

On the one hand—and it could not be any other way, given its significance as a "historical novel"—*I, the Supreme* refers to something. On the other, as we have seen, it speaks volumes about itself as a text. What is most important for us? As far as the first point is concerned, we could carry out a moral reading, identificatory and counteridentificatory, between both attitudes. However, I believe it would be more decisive to examine the second point: what is this object that bursts, like new, into the concert of existing objects—books, ideas, things? Perhaps we cannot define it, but we can indeed capture what it is talking about when it talks about itself: it is talking about voice and about writing, about fragmentation and adulteration, about things and words, about what is and what should be. It is, furthermore, referring to a decision: to accept the order of things or lose oneself in the adventure. In that case it is not only a question of proposing "a great beyond" of the text that is within the text itself like the subconscious of language, but also an idea about history as enigma, as "the great beyond" of history itself.

Thirty Years Later

Around 1965 Buenos Aires was the scene of such cultural ferment that this is still remembered with nostalgia. It was not that everything was perfect socially and politically—far from it—but in that cultural milieu a space had taken form where creators and public, for the first time in many years, could connect without conflict. I want to remember just a few manifestations of that time: the Eudeba phenomenon[1] and the publication of *Martín Fierro*,[2] illustrated by Castagnino; the avant-garde project that spawned the Instituto Di Tella's schools of fine arts, theater, and social sciences; the keen presence of the journal *Primera Plana;* the growing influence of the University of Buenos Aires, and in particular, of the hard sciences; the sweeping development of psychoanalysis; and last but not least, the advance of literature in the public sphere, in the press, and, no irony intended, in the publishing world. In short, there was much to see, an infinity of things to learn, a great deal to read, ideas to discuss; it was a unique moment, and perhaps for that reason, to the detriment of the country, it could not continue.

What brought an end to all of this was, as we know, the military coup of 1966. A group of grim generals were able, with little discursive effort, to advance the argument that a benevolent president had committed intolerable excesses, and after they took power, not only were people's activities repressed, but also their hearts and minds. It is clear that after Onganía and his followers came to power, sadness and apathy settled definitively over a city that had previously concentrated figures, forms, and activity of unparalleled brilliance. All that interest in life emigrated—it left, as the song says, to Caracas, to Mexico City, returned to Europe, and settled in New York or Paris, places that at that time, around 1965, had not stifled the imaginary desires of Argentines so vigorously.

In the literary sphere, the major event was the so-called boom of Latin American literature, a clichéd term mentioned in all the articles. The publication of *Hopscotch* [*Rayuela* (1963)] and *One Hundred Years of Solitude* [*Cien años de soledad* (1967)] in Buenos Aires helped trigger a continent-wide process (although there had been a few premonitions before, such as the impact of *Pedro Páramo* [1955] or the growing enthusiasm for Borges's work in Europe), based on a belief that the literature produced by some Latin American writers was first-rate, so much so that it seemed the novel or short story, forms that up to then had resided in Paris, London, or New York, had settled forever in our cities, where noble texts without equal were being created. Furthermore, those works began to dazzle Europe, restored vigor to listless Spanish fiction, and opened vast imaginative experiments in the consciousness of rather ordinary readers in Germany, France, and the United States. The eruption of texts such as these confirmed a new vitality and interest, stirred passions, and promised hope.

Along with these occurrences came the interpretations; for many the sudden prominence of Latin American literature was due to the Cuban Revolution that, in elevating the possibilities for social and political change on a heroic foundation and with people determined to die if necessary for their country, drew the world's attention to a continent boiling over with problems; debates ensued over ways to solve them, whether through violence or through the imagination. Others formulated less fiery theories, such as, for example, that European and North American interest in the Spanish language and in Latin American society stemmed from the investment programs that development ideology promoted and favored, and as a consequence of such programs, departments of Latin American studies multiplied in numerous, diverse universities around the world. More metaphysical interpretations mentioned the cultural stagnation of old world cultures and the yearning for fresh and spontaneous manifestations. Europe was worn out and used up, and the imagination, together with García Márquez's yellow butterflies and guerrilla revolution, burst forth in torrents in and from the new world. More materialistic readings of the phenomenon suggested that the boom in question was purely a market phenomenon: astute editors and publicists had convinced the public, taking advantage of a real or apparent economic prosperity, that books were just as desirable and valuable as any other commercial product. And finally, I should mention the heartening idea that at last Latin America's hour had arrived, its hour of maturity and freedom of expression, with Latin Americans now free from inhibitions and foreign models, from prejudices toward an imaginary but paralyzing sense of inferiority.

All these theories are just as true as they are false, and it isn't really important which one we pick, because it doesn't matter why what erupted had so splendidly erupted. What is important, however, is to designate two classes of phenomena, one related to the present and the other to the past.

In terms of the first aspect, "the boom" is a designation that corresponds to a group of talented and successful writers from all of Latin America. I have already mentioned two of them: García Márquez and Cortázar; we also need to add Carlos Fuentes, Mario Vargas Llosa, and José Donoso, at least, as well as João Guimarães Rosa. Of course there are more who did not come to the fore in the same way but who benefited from the upsurge in reading kindled by the others. This highlights an important point: talent proliferated and burst out all over, and while many writers who became known in the sixties, seventies, and eighties did not share the same esthetic or intentions or successes of the members of the boom, it is clear they formed part of the whole, that they helped write the same brilliant page in the history of literature. Thus we should mention Manuel Puig, Rodolfo Walsh, Miguel Barnet, Salvador Elizondo, Salvador Garmendia, Elena Poniatowska, Juan José Saer, José Emilio Pacheco, Guillermo Cabrera Infante, Clarice Lispector, Jorge Enrique Adoum, and many others who, along with the aforementioned, constituted a first-rate literary army.

In truth, it was a question of a zeal for reading that was not satisfied with just a brilliant present, but that also awoke a past that could not be ignored. It was not enough to have a few people riding the crest of the wave and the crest of the numbers from the publishers, nor were those who emerged and who dazzled the world with their creations enough. Earlier figures, locally recognized but not so generally well known, rose to the surface and together formed a true Mount Olympus that made people legitimately feel that Latin American narrative not only existed but was also first-rate. We must, of course, include the incomparable Borges. Leopaldo Marechal and Adolfo Bioy Casares were rediscovered and, together with José Lezama Lima, they opened an inexhaustible vein of pleasurable though arduous reading, as did Alejo Carpentier. The mysterious and reclusive Felisberto Hernández could be compared to the equally enigmatic Juan Rulfo; and we cannot leave out Roberto Arlt or Onetti. The connections and the masters multiplied, some following in the traditions of others. Macedonio Fernández, with his power to foresee what would happen to the novel, was invoked by everyone: he was present at the creation, God the Father, the founder from whom came the most sublime orders for organizing the future.

With just such an enthusiastic vision as the lines above describe, Luis Harss and Barbara Dohlmann wrote a piece they proudly titled *Into the Mainstream* (1966) [*Los nuestros*]. This book, which consists of interviews similar to the ones Tomás Eloy Martínez produced in the journal *Primera Plana,* is the beginning of a process deriving from the ideas these writers proclaimed, but in a different frame. As was foreseeable, this book, which tried to establish a canon, or to put it another way, to indicate what should be included in Latin American literature, gave rise to a certain uneasiness and to several important questions: Would this process continue or would it be a flash in the pan? Would the same thing happen as had occurred with the modernist, naturalist, and avant-garde explosions that had created so many expectations but for which enthusiasm quickly waned? Was this new literature strong and stable or simply a mirage invented out of our need to have something to show in a competitive world jealous of the symbolic and willing to destroy anyone who dares to claim a place there?

Latin American literature continued to expand and broke through the paper curtain all over the world. The media in other countries had to take note of the phenomenon, as institutions, universities, foundations, and governmental cultural organizations had already done, all of which, since the end of the 1960s, had come to consider the texts and authors emerging from that circumstance so sonorously called the boom to be serious topics of concern. One of these media institutions was the illustrious *Paris Review,* the North American journal through whose pages marched the twentieth century in all its dimensions and intensities, via notes, interviews, and commentaries that constituted a valuable source for knowing what modernity was and above all, who the protagonists were of this intellectual and cultural epic. What the *Paris Review* considered worthy of appearing in its pages was at moments a sort of imposition, sometimes ephemeral or superficial, but at other moments the product of a close scrutiny of significant phenomena of the time, at times the development of little-known and unconventional ideas, and others a curious look at cultural issues, such as Latin American literature, that could no longer be ignored.

Precisely what this volume [*Confesiones de escritores*] gathers together are the results of that attention to Latin America, via interviews with writers whom we can immodestly recognize as triumphant—that is, those who were able to install their works in the jungle of the market and make us believe that they embodied some aspect of Latin America's vigorous culture. Deified not only in their respective countries but also on the world scene, and thus candidates for interviews at the *Paris Review,* they were simultaneously helped in consolidating that triumph by the impact that journal had, at least in North America. In a certain way, we could assume that if the *Paris Review* noticed them and sought them out, it is because each of them "signified and represented," two qualities that guarantee their existence from a critical perspective that depends on consecration of an author and on a fierce loyalty.

This volume brings together a number of these interviews; the names all resonate, forming a list in which no one is superfluous, although several people who should also be included were left out (Onetti, Roa Bastos, Rulfo, Guimarães Rosa, Arguedas, Lezama Lima, and Carpentier, for example). Their list includes Jorge Luis Borges, Pablo Neruda, Guillermo Cabrera Infante, Carlos Fuentes, Adolfo Bioy Casares, Julio Cortázar, Manuel Puig, Gabriel García Márquez, Octavio Paz, and Mario Vargas Llosa. All of these, invariably, are of major interest, and reading them illustrates a great deal about what a cultured reader, who knows their texts, would want to know about them. And if that is not a good enough reason to explore this material in Spanish, this volume also provides another motive for our interest: three decades separate it from *Into the Mainstream,* giving us reason to consider how, if Harss's book began a process, this collection, while not ending it, provides an opportunity to reflect on it. The moment seems ripe to reaffirm what occurred in these thirty years, since this collection of interviews is the other end of what burst onto the scene thirty years ago with such extraordinary force. Thus to the extent that the ones speaking here are the same ones who were speaking then, it becomes possible to establish comparisons and contrasts, to see whether or not that challenge ended in frustration and its promise in disappointment.

Around 1965, inspired by a new public, writers imagined that somehow they could transform the world of American letters, each in their own way (though some had already created their own esthetic). Now, with almost all of them securely installed in the literary institution, we can ask not only if they were able to achieve their hopes for transformation but also if they remained true to their original declarations, and even more, what scope and characteristics their esthetic has now that they are already established and no longer prey to the anxiety that accompanies such initial excitement.

This aspect of this collection, which we could metaphorically say is about "balance," is suggestive: every reader will probably think about it, not because those interviewed are famous, well-known writers, but rather, because the situation of reading in our time is unstable and precarious, and it is no longer certain that the institution consolidated in large part by the success of these writers has the strength and permanence that many of us would wish it to have. The competition literature faces with television and the overwhelming momentum of those written "products" that now substitute on an enormous scale for what not long ago were recognized as "books," combined with the cultural crisis due in part to the difficulties faced by education, not to mention by the disappearance of institutions that protected books, has created a sense of anxiety and even a lack of confidence toward reading. Be that as it may, the context now in 1995 is very different for everyone—the reading public, canonized writers, risk-taking publishers, curious critics—than it was in 1965. In the following interviews we can clearly note the changed situation.

But beyond these considerations that affected Latin American literature as a whole, and leaving aside the question of what motivated the *Paris Review* to give space to these prominent authors, reading these interviews is an experience all by itself. And, I should add, a very enjoyable one. At any rate, the interviewers all have a similar style—which must be the journal's style: they erase themselves, not competing with the interviewees; their questions appear simple, but encourage people to "open up." Of course they manipulate the answers with questions like "Don't you think that . . . ?," which lead to an appropriate answer and no doubt toward an area of interest for the average reader of the journal—the journal certainly did not wish to confront or frustrate that reader. And, of course, toward the interests of the interviewers, most of whom are distinguished members of the North American academy—university professors who teach this literature and who have to keep in mind what their students are interested in and can understand. All of the interviewers meet that description, except for our compatriot Marcelo Pichon-Rivière, in charge of the conversation with Adolfo Bioy Casares and an expert on his work. Still, they all accomplish something very difficult: the writers open and expand themselves. They are generous with their answers and even with their confessions—they discuss loves, passions, rejections, memories, obsessions, and the way they do so is fluid, congenial, competent, fascinating, as if they knew as they were talking that they would be read, an understanding that reveals their expertise, maturity, and skill in manipulating the media.

At times, however, the interviewers are frustrated in their efforts, unable to turn the writers into compliant sheep. Borges, as we know, is quite capable of pretending his interlocutor does not exist; Cabrera Infante ignores the questions and even attacks his interviewer, ridicules him, takes pity on him. More considerate writers, meanwhile, such as Bioy Casares, Cortázar, or Neruda, appear to take the questions very seriously; they act as if the interview were a solemn occasion for clearing up some of the essential issues about their work and about their relationship with the public. All of them, however, fall victim to what I would call a "reconstructive effect" consisting of accepting the previously constructed image of themselves and responding to questions having to do with that image. For example, in terms of personal anecdotes, there is Borges's blindness, García Márquez's grandmother, Cortázar's life in Paris, Bioy Casares's family and his notorious womanizing, Manuel Puig's sexual freedom, Cabrera's anti-Castroism, Neruda's political life and even his experience in the Far East, Fuentes's stint as a diplomat, the Spanish Civil War in Paz's writings, and so on. But let's be clear: it's not that they want to talk about these familiar issues; they are interviewed about them and they generally respond with a confident air, accepting them as a challenge.

One could ask about their respective esthetics, despite the fact that none of the interviewers touches on that question; it is a thorny subject and only very indirectly mentioned. The interesting thing is that there are common or shared elements or perspectives, despite the fact that the interviews were carried out during very different periods. One of those issues is the idea that "creativity" does not follow a plan, and that when writing, they do not know just what they seek or where they are going. Yet this does not mean that they are following surrealist inspiration or automatic writing. For Cabrera and for Vargas Llosa, it is a question of some event or observation that suddenly strikes them as a possibility to develop, the rest being pure diligence. Almost none of them express any admiration for literary criticism, and all for similar reasons. Rather than fearing it, they feel that the literary criticism of which they have been the object has failed to touch upon the central meaning of their works—something that, on the other hand, they all consider to be impossible to grasp. (Puig, however, complains of being ignored, of the critics' indifference to him.) Concurrently, they also state that writing, as Neruda says explicitly, grows out of an internal need that if ignored leaves a terrible emptiness, an unbearable illegitimacy.

Since all of the writers in this volume have been the object of numerous interviews—it is claimed that Borges has logged over fifteen hundred worldwide—we can confirm that characteristic themes or preoccupations can be found in the material in this volume. For example, Octavio Paz (and it is delightful to read that in the Far East he learned to "distrust the I") returns to the fundamental question about literature in relation to politics to which he was faithful throughout his career, as do García Márquez and Vargas Llosa. There are many commonalities among these three authors in their way of looking at this issue. For the same reason, it does not surprise us to find that Puig talks about sex and Cortázar about the difference between assuming social and political commitments and writing literature of the fantastic. Fuentes in turn remains faithful to that reasonable tone I have observed in almost all of his presentations, whether oral or written, which allows him to approach with great equanimity the most serious and acute contemporary problems.

In short, one can find much varied and passionate material in this volume. Furthermore, the careful and complicated translation—since the dialogues were originally rendered into English from the Spanish and now from the English into Spanish—makes these great writers available to a public that not only loves them but has also found in them for some time a source of enjoyment, of spontaneous and vehement texts, never miserly in their expression or ideas. To the contrary, they are full of very intelligent proposals and very natural and brilliant formulations.

Notes

All endnotes by the translator are enclosed in brackets throughout. All translations of titles and text are by Susan Benner unless otherwise noted.

Complex Feelings about Borges

1 [From Hernández, *El gaucho Martín Fierro/The Gaucho Martín Fierro*, 176–177. English translation by C. E. Ward.]

2 [Borges, *El "Martín Fierro"* (first published in book form in 1953).]

3 [See Jitrik, "Otras inquisiciones."]

4 [The article, entitled "Poesia argentina entre dos radicalismos," can also be found in Jitrik, *Ensayos y estudios de literatura argentina*, 200–221.]

5 Macedonio Fernández (1874–1952) was an Argentine avant-garde writer and poet known for his metaphysical tendencies.

6 [Jitrik, "Estructura y significado en *Ficciones* de Jorge Luis Borges." The article was also published under the same title in *Cuadernos Americanos* 53 (1969): 50–62.]

7 Juan Carlos Onganía (1914–1995) was head of the Argentine Army from 1962–1965, he led a military coup against the president of Argentina, Arturo Umberto Illia, in 1966, and ruled the country as dictator until he himself was toppled in a coup in 1970.

8 [In Spanish America, *criollos* are those who are of European (usually Spanish) descent but who were born in Spanish America. As an adjective, *criollo* has come to describe something "traditional" or deeply rooted in Spanish American traditions.]

9 José López Rega (1916–1989) was personal assistant to Perón during his exile and minister of social welfare under the second Perón government; he was known as "el brujo," or "the wizard," in part due to his belief in astrology and occult practices.

10 [A reference to: Pedro Orgambide, *Borges y su pensamiento político* (Borges and his Political Thought).]

11 Jorge Rafael Videla (1925–) was the leader of the military coup that toppled Perón's widow, Isabel Perón, in 1976 and head of the military junta that took power; he was named president of Argentina and held that post until 1981. Thousands of Argentines were killed, tortured, or disappeared under his reign of terror.

12 Alfonso Reyes (1889–1959) was a Mexican writer, poet, journalist, and diplomat, considered to be one of the most important Mexican writers of the twentieth century.

13 [In *The Order of Things*, Foucault quotes Borges as mentioning a particular Chinese

encyclopedia, "The Celestial Emporium of Benevolent Knowledge," in which animals are divided into a "bestiary" organized into fourteen categories.]

14   This is a reference to a satirical piece written by Quevedo in which he makes fun of his rival, Góngora. Popularly known as simply "Aguja de navegar cultos" (A ship's compass for fools), the complete title of this works is "Libro de todas las cosas y otras muchas más con la aguja de navegar cultos." It can be found in Quevedo, *Obras Fiestas.*

15   Leopoldo Lugones (1874–1938) was a famous Argentine poet and writer considered to be one of the great Latin American modernists. As a young man, Lugones was considered a socialist, but he became increasingly conservative over the years, eventually supporting militarism and dictatorship.

16   [See "Conjectural Poem" in Borges, *Selected Poems,* 158–161, trans. Alistair Reid. The original Spanish poem was first published in *La Nación* in 1943.]

17   ["Soy," originally in Borges, *La rosa profunda*; English translation ("I Am") by Alistair Reid in *Selected Poems,* 356–357.]

18   [In Borges, *A Universal History of Infamy.* Original Spanish version (*Historia universal de la infamia*) published in 1935.]

19   Saúl Yurkievitch (1931–) is an Argentine experimental poet, writer, and literary critic who has focused on Latin American avant-garde poets. David Viñas (1929–) is an Argentine critic and novelist.

20   It is important to emphasize here that this piece was written around 1980—not only in light of changes in Borges's thinking since then, but also in light of my own way of seeing things, perhaps in short cycles.

21   Charles Maurras (1868–1952) was a French neoclassical writer and ultraconservative nationalist politician. Gabriele D'Annunzio (1863–1938) was an Italian poet, novelist, dramatist, and soldier who supported Mussolini and fascism.

22   [Julio Argentino Roca (1843–1914), president of the Argentine Republic from 1880 to 1886 and from 1898 to 1904).]

23   In my forgettable article on *Adán Buenosayres* [Jitrik, "*Adán Buenosayres*"] written in 1955, it seemed to me at the time that this was the case. But later, the relationship between Marechal's idealism and Peronist "doctrine" struck me as being more complicated than this, or at least, they did not seem so useful to each other.

Between Being and Becoming

1   [Juan Manuel de Rosas (1793–1877) was the governor of the province of Buenos Aires from 1829–1832 and again in 1835–1852, and leader of the federalist movement of the time. He became a repressive and ruthless dictator who controlled much of the country until he was ousted in 1852.]

2   [Lucio Mansilla (1831–1913) was an Argentine journalist, soldier, politician, and

writer. Cacique Baigorrita (1837–1879) was a legendary *cacique*, or leader, of the Ranquel Indians of the Argentine Pampas.]

3   [Antonio López de Santa Anna (1794–1876) was a Mexican general who ruled Mexico under dictatorial leadership from 1832 to 1836 and again from 1841 to 1844 and 1846 to 1855.]

4   [The Unitarians were a liberal political group that supported centralized power based in Buenos Aires and uniting the country as a whole beneath one central government.]

5   [Bernardino Rivadavia (1780–1845) was a progressive Unitarian Argentine politician and cabinet minister from 1811 to 1814 and 1820 to 1824.]

6   [The panopticon was a prison design created by Jeremy Bentham, in which there was a central observation booth or tower surrounded by prison cells around the perimeter.]

7   [The prison of Lecumberri, Mexico, was infamous as a prison for political prisoners; it was later converted into Mexico's General Archive (Archivo General de la Nación) and a museum.]

8   ["¡Que me importan los desaires / Con que me trate la suerte! / Argentino hasta la muerte / He nacido en Buenos Aires." Trans. Susan Benner. From "Trova" by Carlos Guido y Spano (1827–1918). The poem can be found in Perrone, ed., *La poesía argentina*, 30–32.]

9   [In 1872 in a wave of anti-immigrant sentiment, a group of armed gauchos killed dozens of immigrants in the town of Tandil; many of those killed were Basques, although the victims included immigrants from several different countries.]

10   [A group of progressive and literary intellectuals in Argentina, started by Marcos Sastre in 1837.]

Echeverría's "The Slaughter House"

1   Friedrich Kainz, *Estética*.

2   See José Enrique Etcheverry, *Horacio Quiroga y la creación artística*. He quotes various texts: "I struggled to ensure that the story had one single line, drawn by a hand that never shook, from beginning to end" ("Ante el tribunal" (1930) [Before the Court]); "Do not start writing without knowing from the first word where you are going" ("Decálogo del perfecto cuentista" (1927) [Ten Commandments for the Perfect Short Story Writer]). [Both texts can be found in Quiroga, *Todos los cuentos* ("Ante el tribunal," 1206–1207; "Decálogo del perfecto cuentista," 1194–1195).]

3   In *Ojeada retrospectiva*, chapter 8 [*Dogma socialista de la Asociación de Mayo: precedido de una ojeada retrospectiva 79*], Echeverría sets up a classification of his friends' work that confirms this idea. I will quote here the stated principles: first— "Later, in *La Moda* [Alberdi], under the pseudonym 'Figarillo,' leads us to expect an American Larra. We are quite sorry that Mr. Alberdi has completely abandoned this

form of manifesting his thought, perhaps the most efficient and advantageous in these countries." Second—"Mr. Mitre, scientific artillery man, soldier from Cagancha and in the location of Montevideo, has, despite being quite young, acquired many titles as a prose writer and a poet. His muse can be distinguished from that of his contemporaries by the manly freedom of its movements and by a certain martial tone of voice that reminds us of the robust tone of Callimachus and of Tyrtaeus. He is presently occupied in historical works that will, without a doubt, earn him new laurels" [ibid. 82., trans. Susan Benner]. Third: "His muse [that of José Mármol], reflexive and enthusiastic, stands out among his contemporaries for its originality and the nerve of his expression. . . . He has had two plays put on stage, 'El Poeta' and 'El Cruzado,' which have gained the approbation of the public. What stands out in particular in these works is his lyric inspiration and the lively color-fulness that characterizes his pen" [ibid. 83–84, trans. Susan Benner].

4 [This volume of short poems, originally published in 1834, can be found in Eche-verría, *Obras completas*, 715–749.]

5 [Also called "Cantos a Avellaneda" [Cantos for Avellaneda] this long poem origi-nally published in 1849, can be found in Echeverría, *Obras completas*, 519–583.]

6 Certainly there are lyric passages in *La cautiva* [The captive] [see Echeverría, *El matadero/La cautiva*], both in the descriptions of nature and in the expressions of emotion. Does this contradict the radical unity of the poem? The romantic concept consists precisely of diversity within homogeneity, the interference of the objective by the subjective. For classic art, on the other hand, this interpenetration, cohabita-tion, or "mixing" was impossible.

7 See Echeverría, "Fondo y forma en las obras de imaginación, estilo, lenguaje y ritmo" [in Echeverría, *Obras completas*, 341–345]. The reader might also find inter-esting the article by Emilio Carilla, "Ideas estéticas de Echeverría."

8 [All translations of the story here, except for the one line indicated in note 13, come from Angel Flores's translation, "The Slaughter House," in *The Oxford Book of Latin American Short Stories*.]

9 See the issue of *Communications* 11 (1968) dedicated to "Le vraisemblable."

10 See Estebánez Calderón, *Escenas andaluzas*.

11 [The dictatorship and cult of Juan Manuel de Rosas.]

12 See Pierre Martino, *Parnasse et symbolisme*.

13 [The original line, "En fin la escena que se representaba en el matadero era para vista, no para escrita" (*El matadero* 103), was not included in Angel Flores's translation.]

14 Noël Salomon relates this phrase ["the scene at the slaughter house"] to Echever-ría's belief in lithographs and illustrated books. But we could wonder about the basis of this belief. Without a doubt there is an attitude there before which it is possible for a word to dare to be visual. Naturally, the space left open when that becomes impossible will be filled in with paint.

15 See *Primera Lectura del Salón Literario*: "The truth is that the Spanish of that time

were the most backward of the European nations, and we, with regards to progress, thanks to their paternal government, found ourselves in even worse condition." [The original Spanish can be found in Echeverría, *Obras completas* 101.] Also in *Ojeada*, in a letter to Alcála Galiano, we find this reiterated: "Furthermore, it can be seen that one facet of this movement is the complete divorce from everything colonial, or what is the same thing, from everything Spanish, and the *foundation of beliefs* about the democratic beginnings of the American revolution." [Echeverría, *Dogma socialista de la Asociación de Mayo,* 108].

16   See Roland Barthes, "The Reality Effect."

17   But for the same reason, it is fascinating for a romantic who, developmentally speaking, has just broken various barriers that kept him from understanding the world. We can see this above all in the style. Nevertheless, there are holdover values that subsist in the mix—do not think that the equilibrium is perfect and the result unique. See Noé Jitrik, "Soledad y urbanidad," in *Boletín de Literatura Argentina*.

18   [A member of the liberal, progressive group that had supported the Unitarian constitution of 1826, and that opposed the Federalists and the dictatorship of Juan Manuel de Rosas. Unitarians supported centralized power, while the Federalists sought to have power distributed among the provinces.]

19   See Claude Brémond, "La logique des possibles narratifs," in *Communications* 8.

20   See Jean-Paul Weber, *Génèse de l'oeuvre poétique*.

21   This issue springs from two problems. On the one hand, it is evident that in transcribing the speech of the "butcher," Echeverría wants to highlight the linguistic "barbarism" of that world, a clear expression of extreme barbarism. It is barbarism in his eyes and in the eyes of his audience, whose gaze is, at the same time, that of the civilized, transcendent conscience. Here we find an esthetic elaboration—it is the "realism" that demands verisimilitude, fidelity, rigor, conciseness, etc. But on the other hand, when the narrator becomes contaminated with this speech and adopts it in order to describe everything related to that barbaric world, something other than a realist elaboration occurs; the language he employs is the most appropriate, it is the one that "corresponds" to the thing described. There in the narrator's component, there would be an uncontrolled level in which is deposited a considerable load of intentionality.

22   [See Francisco Ayala, "Sobre el realismo en Literatura," in *Experiencias e invención: ensayos sobre el escritor y su mundo:* "It would behoove us, then, that in order to attempt to clarify this concept [realism], we begin to examine it there where for the first time it becomes formulated in such a way as to express a certain artistic and literary theory. It is generally agreed that realism emerged in France around 1840 . . . already in 1842, Balzac, in his preface to the *Comédie Humaine,* had established a new literary precept."]

23   [The poem *El ángel caido* can also be found in Esteban Echeverría, *Obras completas,* 587–710.]

24   Here I am employing the concept of verisimilitude as something positive, but I am

also conscious of the risks involved, especially in light of the works of Genette ["Vraisemblable et motivation"] and Barthes ["The Reality Effect"]. However, I do not contradict them since they apply this to realist aspects, that is, those where what is verisimilar is only slightly different from what is real. In classic rhetoric, on the contrary, inverisimilitude in narrative was judged very harshly, though inverisimilar aspects were accepted if they occurred in real life.

25   It might be helpful here to remember his clumsy, idle scribblings about the guitar, those nebulous stories from his youth. According to his biographers (see Alberto Palcos, *Historia de Echeverría*), the poet engaged in his experience of "the masses" at an age when he was guided by desperation. Is it not reasonable to believe that some of that experience left an impression on him, and that somehow his emotional world was shaped by that experience?

26   [Throughout these essays, the terms "America" and "American" are used in the Latin American sense that refers to *all* of the Americas, north and south, not only the United States. The term "North American" is used to designate phenomena particular to the United States.]

27   See Félix Weinberg, *El Salón Literario*.

28   I am trying to highlight as precisely as possible the existence of a second level enfolded within the text, a second text that we can only read now, and that could not have been read in Echeverría's time, neither by he himself nor by his contemporaries. This reading, which unites the two texts, reveals a kind of vitality. If we were able to read nothing more than the original reading of the time, Hamlet would be an entertaining aficionado of paradoxes, Don Quixote a madman, and the Unitarian in "The Slaughter House" an ideal hero.

Canon and Margin

1   [Antonio Porchia (1886–1968): Argentine poet born in Italy but residing in Argentina most of his life, known for his fragmented, aphoristic poetry. Some of his best known work has been translated into English by W. S. Merwin in a volume titled *Voices*.]

2   [Mexican novelist (1864–1939), strongly influenced by French naturalism.]

3   [On the one hand, Fuentes (*Valiente mundo nuevo: épica, utopia y mito en la novela hispanoamericana* [1990]) ritually contrasts "tradition" and "modernity," but on the other, in a more inclusive view, he states that "the pact of civilization consists of recognizing that we are a polycultural space, owners of an enormous variety of traditions from which we can choose elements to create a new model of development, without any reason to remain wedded to only one solution" (15).]

4   The editor Lemerre asked Mallarmé for a sonnet with certain characteristics; from this request/instruction came the famous "Sonnet in X," which followed all the norms, but at the same time, proposed a radical transgression in subject matter, nothing less than "emptying." ["Sonnet in X" or "Sonnet in YX" is the unofficial

title of the sonnet whose first line is "Ses purs ongles très haut dédiant leur onyx" / "The onyx of her pure nails offered high." Mallarmé, *Oeuvres complètes*. For the translation, see Mallarmé, *Selected Poetry and Prose,* ed. Mary Ann Caws, 49.]

5   So-called literary criticism is less and less important in the observance of canonical rules; such criticism is limited to grumbling dissension, which must be justified by invoking norms or canons. Little attention is paid to literary criticism except when it upholds values that can or will be useful in market terms. For academic or university criticism, the overseeing of adherence to norms has become a cause for archeological speculation: to determine, for example, if such-and-such texts or authors have been true to their own canons.

6   [Estridentistas were members of the Estridentismo movement, which began in Mexico around 1921. Mostly poets, the estridentistas were an avant-garde group (with ties to the Italian futurists) that focused on an immediate present and on social issues of the time.]

7   [José Manuel Estrada (1842–1894) was an Argentine writer, historian, and politician who was named secretary of foreign relations by Sarmiento during the latter's presidency.]

8   With respect to the boom, the implications of the support provided by the journal *Primera Plana* from Buenos Aires, *Mundo Nuevo* from Paris, or *México en la cultura* should be investigated.

9   See Jacques Leenhardt for a discussion of avant-garde art and the creation of a public.

10   Columbus's diary of his voyage begins as a traditional ship's log, but bit by bit, it moves into another realm; it turns into a space for questions and answers that normal logbooks would certainly not have included.

11   [Bernardino de Sahagún (1500?–1590) was a Spanish Franciscan missionary who came to Mexico in 1529 and who chronicled many aspects of Aztec life and culture and his experiences in the new world.]

12   [Bernardo de Balbuena was a sixteenth-century priest who later became archbishop of San Juan, Puerto Rico. His famous poem, written in 1604, is entitled "La grandeza mexicana."]

13   Here we should mention in this respect the case of writers such as the Inca Garcilaso or Juan Ruiz de Alarcón, who follow in the footsteps of Peninsular literature although they preserve, especially the former, semantic traces of an original American experience.

14   [A fifteenth-century (1402–1472) poet-king of the Texcocan tribe of what is now Mexico.]

15   [See Picón Salas, *A Cultural History of Spanish America.*]

16   [Popular late-eighteenth-century Argentine *sainete,* or farcical play, of unknown authorship, written in approximately 1787. See *El amor de la estanciera,* ed. Mariano Bosch.]

17   [Eugenio María de Hostos (1839–1903) was a Puerto Rican writer who wrote pas-

sionately in favor of independence from Spain. José Vasconcelos (1882–1959) was a well-known Mexican writer, philosopher, and politician. Juan Montalvo (1833–1889) was an Ecuadorian writer and political essayist.]

From History to Writing

1   Estuardo Núñez, "Lo latinoamericano en otras literaturas," in César Fernández Moreno, ed., *América Latina en su literatura*, 93–120 [translated into English in a condensed version (Moreno, Ortega, and Schulman, eds., *Latin America in Its Literature*) that does not include Núñez's essay]. For Voltaire, there was *Candide* (1758), and for Marmontel, *Les Incas* [*The Incas, or, The Destruction of the Empire of Peru*] (1777), along with other examples by Madame de Graffigny, Marivaux, John Dryden, etc.

2   [Ricardo Rojas, introduction to *Historia de la literatura argentina* 1:25–66.]

3   [*Antonelli* can be found in Echeverría, *Obras escogidas*, 9–52.]

4   Pierre Martino, *Parnasse et symbolisme.*

5   Juan Luis Guerrero, *Tres temas de filosofía en las entrañas del Facundo.*

6   [*Enriquillo* has been translated into English by Robert Graves, in Galván, *Manuel de Jesús Galván's Enriquillo/The Cross and the Sword.*]

7   Julio Leguizamón, *Historia de la literatura hispanoamericana,* chap. 15.

8   Alberto Zum Felde, *La narrativa en Hispanoamérica,* chap. 2.

9   Jean Franco, *Historia de la literatura hispanoamericana,* chap. 2.

10   Jacques Leenhardt, "La dictée de Gaspar de Francia."

11   [Pedro Díaz Seijas, "De la realidad al mito en *El siglo de las luces,*" 125.]

12   Maurice Blanchot, *La part du feu.*

13   Emilio Carilla, *El romanticismo en la América hispánica,* chap. 12, 2:59–86.

14   György Lukács, *The Historical Novel.*

15   Vicente Fidel López, "Carta Prólogo," *La novia del hereje* (1846), Buenos Aires, 1917; cited by Emilio Carilla, op. cit. [*El romanticismo*].

16   [Antonio Castro Leal, prologue, *Monja y casada, virgen y mártir,* by Vicente Riva Palacio, ix.]

The Latin American Avant-garde

1   [Salvador Novo (1904–1974) was a Mexican writer and member of the literary movement "los Contemporáneos." Pedro Henríquez Ureña (1884–1946) was a Dominican linguist and prolific essayist. Salomón de la Selva (1893–1958) was a poet who was born in Nicaragua, raised in the United States, and lived for many years in Mexico.]

2   ["La Semana de Arte Moderna" (Modern Art Week) was a festival and exposition that took place in São Paulo, Brazil, in February 1922. It included art of all kinds—

visual arts, literature, music—as well as numerous conferences and confrontations, with the intent to break with traditional esthetics and create a new artistic language and approach.]

3   [Héctor Libertella, *Nueva escritura en Latinoamérica*, 19–20.]

4   For example, the frequent attacks on futurism that in particular have been made by surrealism; consider César Vallejo's rejection of surrealism and even of creationism.

5   [Julio Ortega, "La escritura de la vanguardia," 196.]

6   Julia Kristeva, *Revolution in Poetic Language*.

7   [Jaime Concha, "Huidobro: fragmentos," 30.]

8   See Jean Van Heijenoort, *De Prinkipo à Coyoacán: sept ans auprès de Léon Trotsky*.

9   Renato Poggioli, *The Theory of the Avant-Garde*.

10   [Héctor Libertella, *Nueva escritura en Latinoamérica*, 28.]

11   [See Tynianov, "De l'évolution littéraire."]

12   See Philippe Lacoue-Labarthe and Jean-Luc Nancy, *The Title of the Letter: A Reading of Lacan*. These authors further develop Lacan's ideas on the concept of "strategy."

13   [See Larrea, "Vicente Huidobro en Vanguardia."]

14   [See Tzara, "Note on Poetry," *Seven Dada Manifestos and Lampisteries*, 75–78.]

15   See Jean Cohen, "La comparaison poétique: essai de systématique"; Gerard Genette, "La rhétorique restreinte"; Cedomil Goic, "La comparación creacionista."

16   [See, e.g., Larrea, *César Vallejo*.]

17   See Jean Pierre Faye, "Montage, production."

Beneath the Sign of the Baroque

1   [Fray Cayetano Rodríguez (1761–1823).]

2   [*Conceptismo* was one of the branches of the Spanish baroque literary style that emphasized the use of conceits, concepts, and complex relationships among concepts for understanding and expressing reality.]

3   [Trans. Susan Benner.]

Argentine Nationalism

1   [Augustín Irusta (1902–1987), Roberto Fugazot (1901–1971), and Lucio Demare (1902–1981).]

2   [Carlos Gardel (1895–1935) was a famous Argentine singer, song-writer, and actor, particularly well known for his characteristic tangos.]

3   [This novel has been translated into English as part of a Ph.D. dissertation. See trans. McKay, *The Mad Toy*.]

4   See Noé Jitrik, "Entre el dinero y el ser. Lectura de *El juguete rabioso*," in *La memoria compartida*, 74. For more on Iturri, see Carlos Páez de la Torre, *El canciller de las flores*.

5   Noé Jitrik, "1926: año decisivo para la narrativa argentina," in Noé Jitrik, *El escritor argentino: dependencia o libertad*, 83–88.

6   [Argentine sainete refers to a comedic one-act farce satirizing everyday life.]

7   [See Borges's essay "Las alarmas del doctor Américo Castro" (1941), in Borges and Clemente, *El lenguaje de Buenos Aires*, 37–48.]

8   Note that we approach these linguistic observations not in the sense of a "national language," an idea that supports and sustains nationalistic declarations that would have annoyed Bakhtin (*Speech Genres and Other Late Essays*), but rather in the sense of usage and creativity that, referring to a "belonging," suggest that a national identity is generated and regenerated; it cannot be determined forever, except for ideological mechanisms. See Ramón Alvarado, "Nacionalismo, lenguaje e identidad colectiva."

9   [Mariano Moreno (1779–1811) was an Argentine revolutionary involved in organizing the Republic after independence. Bernardo de Monteagudo (1786–1825) was a Peruvian revolutionary involved in the fight for independence and one of the authors of the Peruvian Declaration of Independence. Juan José Castelli (1764–1812) was an Argentine revolutionary involved in the fight for independence.]

10   [The Unitarian movement supported centralized power based in Buenos Aires and opposed the regionalist Federalist movement, which sought to have power distributed among the provinces.]

11   See Félix Weinberg, "La Generación del 37."

12   [Bartolomé Mitre (1821–1906) was an Argentine writer, soldier, politician, and political philosopher who became Argentina's first president (1862–1868).]

13   See Juan Balestra, *El noventa*. Also see Noé Jitrik, *La revolución del 90*.

14   See Emilio Fermín Mignone, "Los católicos y la revolución de 1890."

15   [Radicalism as a political movement takes its name from the group that promoted it, the Unión Cívica Radical or Radical Civic Union.]

16   [Leandro Alem (1844–1890) was an Argentine politician aligned with Adolfo Alsina's Autonomist Party. Alem co-founded and led the Unión Cívica Radical.]

17   However, according to Julio Irazusta (*Balance de siglo y medio*, 91–92), Victorino de la Plaza, in his final message in 1916, had already formulated a "nationalist program": depend on the country's own strengths, reduce public expenditures, improve the collection of custom taxes and popular savings, utilize the country's own raw materials and labor, produce goods that had previously been imported, encourage industrial development, and so on.

18   See Luis V. Sommi, *La revolución del 90*.

19   The first approach emerges with *El payador* (1916), and the second with "La hora de la espada" (1924), which begins a series composed of *La Patria Fuerte* (1930), *La Grande Argentina* (1930), and the articles published in *La fronda*, beginning in 1931.

20   [The "tragic week" (*semana trágica*) occurred in Buenos Aires in January 1919 under the government of Yrigoyen. A strike that started in one factory grew into a city-wide general strike that was then viciously repressed by the army. The event

marked a turning point both in terms of the development of the labor movement in Argentina and in terms of increasing military repression against popular
movements.]

21   [See Alain Rouquié, *Poder militar y sociedad política en la Argentina*. The quotation
from Manuel Carlés's speech of May 4, 1919, reads: "The Patriotic League is an
association of peaceful, armed citizens who stand guard in order to keep watch over
society and defend it from the foreign plague" (Library of the Patriotic League,
1919).]

22   See Juan V. Orona, *La revolución del 6 de septiembre*.

23   However, Raúl Scalabrini Ortíz, a crucial member of FORJA, surfaced during the
war collaborating with pro-Nazi publications financed by the German embassy.
And he is not the only one.

24   In Alain Rouquié's book, op. cit. [*Poder militar y sociedad política en la Argentina*],
there are exhaustive descriptions of this realization on the part of the military.

25   See Félix Luna, *Alvear*.

26   See Raúl Scalabrini Ortíz, *La política británica en el Río de la Plata*.

27   [Published in the Buenos Aires newspaper *Crítica*.]

28   Félix Luna, in *Alvear*, discusses a "formal, folkloric nationalism that had protected
the old Argentine aristocracy so that they could differentiate themselves from the
immigrant flood" (189). The Legión Cívica [Civil Legion], Legión Colegio Militar
[Military School Legion], and the Liga Republicana [Republican League] are some
of the initiatives he mentions, all connected to the leaders of military coups.

29   See Marcelo Sánchez Sorondo, *Argentina por dentro*.

30   Ernst Gellner would have appreciated this example from Argentina. See *Naciones y
nacionalismo*.

31   See Robert Potash, *Documentos del G.O.U.*

32   [Lunfardo is a slang dialect particular to the Río de la Plata region, which developed
in the underworld from a combination of Italian and Spanish but soon became
generalized to the population as a whole. It is very commonly used in the lyrics of
tangos.]

33   A particularly picturesque and amusing example was the code developed to replace
Lunfardo words in tangos; for example, the more expressive term *chorra*, from the
tango of the same name, was replaced with the more acceptable "ladrona" [thief],
much to the delight of the perpetual mavens of the absurd.

34   See Marcelo Sánchez Sorondo, *La Argentina por dentro*.

35   See Perón's speech, "La nación en armas," from January 1944, given in the city of La
Plata. In *Doctrina peronista* (Buenos Aires: Subsecretaría de Informaciónes, 1951).

36   [Maté or *yerba mate* is a plant used to create a tea commonly drunk in the Río de la
Plata region, thus symbolizing something indigenous to the area and belonging to
all classes, as opposed to imported whiskey.]

37   [*Alpargatas* are hemp sandals commonly worn at the time by the working classes,
so a similar chant in English might be "Up with boots, down with books."]

38   During 1993 there was much talk of the archives from the first period of Peronism, in which is found all of the information on the flight of the Nazis to Argentina. See Tomás Eloy Martínez, "Perón y los nazis."

39   [The Chapultepec Accords (Actas de Chapultepec) were created during the Pan-American conference held in Chapultepec, Mexico, in 1945, during which the participants agreed to provide mutual support in the event that the independence of any of the American nations was threatened.]

40   [In 1926 the Mexican government expelled a number of foreign priests and enacted a series of laws that severely limited the activities of the Catholic Church. After failing to get the government to rescind the laws, an uprising developed called the Cristero War, led by priests and their followers, which lasted from 1926 until 1929 when an agreement was signed between the government and the church.]

41   [Eduardo Lonardi (1896–1956), Pedro Eugenio Aramburu (1903–1970), and Isaac Francisco Rojas (1906–1993).]

42   See Julio Irazusta, "La sociedad mixta, 'sistema económico de una revolución,' " in *Balance de medio siglo*, 185–199.

43   For a discussion of the "Protocols of the Elders of Zion" and anti-Jewish aspects of nationalism, see Norman Cohn, *The Myth of the Jewish World Conspiracy and the Protocols of the Elders of Zion*.

44   [The original lines read "¡Que me importan los desaires / Con que me trate la suerte! / Argentino hasta la muerte / He nacido en Buenos Aires." From the poem "Trova" by Carlos Guido y Spano (1827–1918), in Perrone, ed., *La poesía argentina*, 30–32.]

45   [In 1872 in a wave of anti-immigrant sentiment, a group of armed gauchos killed dozens of immigrants in the town of Tandil; many of those killed were Basques, although the victims included immigrants from several different countries.]

46   For literature previous to this, see authors such as Ignacio B. Anzoátegui, Federico Ibarguren, Julio Menvielle, Santiago de Estrada, Leonardo Castellani, Marcelo Sánchez Sorondo, Mario Amadeo, and Fermín Chávez, among others, whose books develop the principal themes of the nationalism that existed between 1940 and 1960.

47   ["La hora de la espada" is the title of a speech given by Lugones in the Circulo Militar in Buenos Aires in 1924 on the anniversary of the battle of Ayacucha, in which Lugones threw his support behind the military and called on them to raise their swords once again. See Lugones, *La hora de la espada y otros escritos*.]

48   See the chapter entitled "Maurras" in Julio Irazusta, *Actores y espectadores*, 131–144. [This essay was removed from later editions of this volume, but can also be found with the title "Maurras y su *Encuesta sobre la monarquía* traducida al castellano" in Irazusta, *Estudios histórico-políticos*, 165–172.]

49   See Adolfo Prieto, ed., *Proyección del rosismo en la literatura argentina*.

50   [See, e.g., Scalabrini Ortiz, *Petróleo e imperialismo*.]

51   [In August 1947 a congress of radical groups, with Frondizi at the head, met in

Avellaneda to reassess and reaffirm their position. In this meeting they developed the Declaración de Avellaneda (Declaration of Avellaneda), stating their basic principles.]

52   [A right-wing extremist paramilitary organization responsible for numerous assassinations, disappearances, and other acts of violence.]

53   [The military dictatorship that took power in 1976 referred to itself as "el Proceso de Reorganización Nacional" (the Process of National Reorganization), which was shortened by both the military and the public to simply "el proceso" (the process).]

54   See Comisión Nacional sobre la Desaparición de Personas, *Nunca más* [Never Again]: *The Report of the Argentine National Commission on the Disappeared.*

55   [On assuming power after a military coup on June 28, 1966, the military junta, headed by General Juan Carlos Onganía, promulgated new laws seriously censoring Argentine universities. Many universities and their faculty and administrators resisted this repression, and on July 29, 1966, police and military raided various departments of the Universidad de Buenos Aires. Numerous students and professors were rounded up and arrested, many of them being seriously beaten in what then became known as "la noche de bastones largos."]

56   For Elie Kedourie (*Nationalism*), nationalism is "a doctrine invented in Europe at the beginning of the nineteenth century" (9). And for Anthony Smith (*National Identity*), it is "an ideological movement for attaining and maintaining autonomy, unity and identity on behalf of a population deemed by some of its members to constitute an actual or potential 'nation'" (73).

Sarmiento and the Origins of Argentine Literature

1   [Both works in Spanish appear in *Recuerdos de provincia, precedido de Mi defensa* by Sarmiento. A small selection of sections of *Recuerdos de provincia*, trans. Grummon, appears under the title "Selections from Provincial Recollections" in *A Sarmiento Anthology*.]

2   [A reference to Sarmiento's famous text *Facundo: Civilization and Barbarism* (*Facundo, o civilización y barbarie*; 1845).]

3   [Sarmiento, "De las biografías," 129.]

4   [Fray Felix Aldao was an Argentine priest who left the church to become a caudillo in the civil wars in the interior of the country in the 1820s and 1830s. Sarmiento wrote a short biography of him titled *Apuntes biográficos sobre el General Fray Félix Aldao*.]

5   [*Recuerdos de provincia*, 53.]

6   [*Recuerdos de provincia*, 164.]

7   ["Provincial Recollections," in *A Sarmiento Anthology*, 50, trans. Grummon.]

8   [Portions of this work by Sarmiento have been translated into English under the

title *Travels, a Selection*, trans. Muñoz, which contains vols. 1 and 3 of the original work. Selections from vol. 2 have been translated as "Travels in the United States in 1847" in *A Sarmiento Anthology*, trans. Grummon.]

9   [See Borges, prologue to *Recuerdos de provincia.*]

10 [*Recuerdos de provincia*, 121.]

11 [*Recuerdos de provincia*, 70.]

12 [Jitrik refers here to his prologue to the 1977 Biblioteca Ayacucho edition of *Facundo:* Jitrik, "El *Facundo:* la gran riqueza de la pobreza," published in English as Jitrik, "*Facundo:* The Riches of Poverty." The Sarmiento reference is to Sarmiento, *Facundo*, ix–lii.]

Autobiography, Memoir, Diary

1   [See, e.g., Goambrowicz, *Diary.*]

2   [See Paz, *Memorias.*]

3   [See, e.g., Sarmiento, *Recuerdos de provincia, precedido de Mi defensa.*]

4   [See, e.g., Mansilla, *A Visit to the Ranquel Indians* or *Entre-nos, causeries de los jueves.*]

5   [See, e.g., Posadas, *Memorias de Gervasio Posadas;* Oliver, *Mundo mi casa,* and *La vida cotidiana;* Mansilla, *Entre-nos* and *A Visit to the Ranquel Indians;* Ocampo, *Autobiografía.*]

6   ["The May Revolution" of 1810 was the beginning skirmish of Argentina's wars of independence. "The Revolution of '90" (1890) was an uprising against the corrupt and autocratic government of Juárez Celman in July of that year.]

7   [See, e.g., Belgrano, *Autobiografía.*]

8   [See, e.g., Dickman, *Recuerdos de un militante socialista,* and Repetto, *Mi paso por la política: de Roca a Yrigoyen,* and *Mi paso por la política: de Uriburu a Perón.*]

9   [See Aráoz Alfaro, *Crónicas y estampas del pasado,* and Aráoz, *El recuerdo y las cárceles.*]

10 [See Gálvez, *Memoria de la vida literaria argentina.*]

11 [See, e.g., Lanusse, *Protagonista y testigo,* and *Mi testimonio.*]

12 [See Camps, *Caso Timerman.*]

13 [See Guido y Spano, *Autobiografía.*]

14 [See Cané, *Juvenilia.*]

Martí in the Latin American Library

1   [See Ette, "La polisemia prohibida."]

2   [Many of Martí's newspaper articles can be found translated into English in Martí, *Inside the Monster.* The *Declaración de Montecristi* can be found in an English translation in Marti, "Manifesto of Montecristi," trans. Elinor Randall, in *Our America*, 390–400.]

The Riches of Poverty Revisited

1 [See Vallejo, *Crónicas 1915–1938,* prologue and notes by Ballón Aguirre.]

2 Similar obsessions with money can be found in the letters that José Clemente Orozco sent to his wife while he was in the United States creating the murals he was contracted to paint. There is one difference, however: Orozco's preoccupation is more precautionary—it does not have the same sense of anguish we can find in Vallejo (see José Clemente Orozco, *Cartas a Margarita*). In all of this there remains a possible topic for future research—the role money has played for Latin American artists, not in their representations but, rather, semiotically.

3 [Vallejo, *Poemas humanos/Human Poems,* trans. Eshleman.]

4 [From "O bottle without wine! O wine that widowed from this bottle!" in *Poemas humanos/Human Poems,* 161.]

5 [From "Paris, October 1936" in *Human Poems,* 79.]

6 [From "Two Anxious Children" in *Human Poems,* 251.]

7 ["Today a splinter has entered her," in *Human Poems,* 273.]

8 ["How much suffering" is from "The Nine Monsters," *Human Poems,* 259–262.] There is a temptation here to comb through his poems looking for his most eloquent lines: "The enormous quantity of money it costs the poor being" [from "Ultimately, without that good repetitive aroma," *Human Poems,* 33], "want pulls me out from between my own teeth" [from "The Starving Man's Rack," *Human Poems,* 19], "I still buy / 'du vin, du lait, comptant les sous'" [from "Alfonso, I see you watching me," *Human Poems,* 207], "Let the millionaire walk naked, barebacked!" [from "Let the millionaire walk naked, barebacked!," *Human Poems,* 291].

9 [Jitrik, "*El Facundo*: la gran riqueza de la pobreza."]

Bianco's *Shadow Play*

1 I refer to these distinctions in my book *Temas de teoría: el trabajo crítico y la crítica literaria.*

2 In terms of the "fantastic," see Tzvetan Todorov's book *The Fantastic: A Structural Approach to a Literary Genre.* Although he does discuss it, the author of this well-known book takes issue with the idea of a "fantastic genre" as proposed by Northrop Frye (*Anatomy of Criticism*).

3 Roberto Arlt takes up these same topics but twists them, forces them into new forms, and converts them into something else, although he does not put an end to them. Bianco himself resumes them in his excellent later novel, *La pérdida del reino* [The Loss of the Kingdom].

4 This position began with Echeverría and *The Slaughter House* [*El matadero* (1871, posthumous publication)]; it began to take shape in the project and work of Cambaceres, continuing with Gálvez and later, in a more covert form, it appears in Robert Arlt's work to then be continued in whomever nuances the techniques,

but always guided by similar referents—Marechal, Sábato, Cortázar, Viñas, Dal Masetto, Castillo, Soriano, Rivera, etc.

5   In a piece on "inverisimilitude" in Raymond Roussel, Julia Kristeva places herself in the purely semantic plane, following the most successful instructions of the structuralists (see Julia Kristeva, "La productivité dite texte"). It is possible to conceive of "syntactic inverisimilitude," such as I have postulated in terms of the attempt by Macedonio Fernández (see Noé Jitrik, "La 'novela futura' de Macedonio Fernández," in *El fuego de la especie*, 151–182). There are differences between the one and the other, including differences in their thinking.

6   Here I employ the concept of "stylistics," recalling Amado Alonso, José Moreno Villa, Raimundo Lida, and those who used this term in all of its richness in the twenty years from 1930 to 1950, principally following the German school of Leo Spitzer and Helmut Hatzfeld.

7   In terms of the notion of "critical reading" I refer you to my book *La lectura como actividad*. There is a possible classification of readings based on the "position" of the reading in which the "critics" would culminate in a group that contained both the "literal" camp and the "evidential" camp.

8   Here I am harking back to my study "Estructura y significación en *Ficciones*, de Jorge Luis Borges," in *El fuego de la especie*, 129–150.

9   "Peripeteia" means a sudden change of fortune, an unexpected occurrence. Although they do not have the same origin, if we force the meanings a bit, this word might have something in common with "peripatetic," a certain intimate movement, a certain displacement.

10 In Michael Dummett, *La verdad y otros enigmas;* see "La filosofía de Frege" and "La distinción fregeana entre el sentido y la referencia."

11 This idea also appears in "Una categoría básica, el 'personaje', desde la perspectiva del trabajo crítico," in Noé Jitrik, *Temas de teoría: el trabajo crítico y la crítica literaria*, 133–147.

12 At least this is the interpretation of Francis Ford Coppola in his film, as difficult as it may be to accept; I am referring to the attraction those beautiful women in the film feel for the classic cadaver.

13 It is Tzvetan Todorov who formulated this idea in this way in "Analyse du récit," in *Littérature et signification*: "it is easy to see, in particular, that the opposition between the referential aspect [history] and the literal aspect [the story] of an utterance corresponds to what Frege does with *Bedeutung* and *Sinn* ["reference" and "sense"] [51].

14 [From "Varia imaginación, que en mil intentos," no. 74 of Góngora's "Sonetos amorosos," originally written in 1584. In Luis de Góngora y Argote, *Sonetos*, 262.]

15 Reasoning that might stem from surrealist doctrines, but which is also found in certain mystics such as Mircea Eliade. In "Mircea Eliade: enigma y parábola" (in Adolfo Castañón, *La gruta tiene dos entradas*, 140), Castañón develops this idea: "The fantastic adopts the mask of the natural," states Eliade, and Castañón adds:

"That transmutation of the fantastic into the natural and of the sacred into the quotidian . . . but also in the opposite direction: the quotidian universe as a door opening into the great beyond, history as a sign of another history, an interior one, transcendent, 'elapsing' outside of time."

The Suffering Narrator

1   [See Fernández, *Museo de la novela de la eterna*, 29–34.]
2   [Jitrik refers here to Jakobson's article on the six functions of communication, "Linguistics and Poetics," in Jakobson, *Language and Literature*, 62–94.]
3   [See Prego and Petit, *Juan Carlos Onetti.*]

Arguedas: Reflections and Approaches

1   [A reference to Auerbach's *Mimesis.*]
2   Now, here toward the end of 1983, I cannot say how long it will be until we see each other again. That will depend now on when I myself die.
3   [Fernando Belaúnde Terry (1912–2002) was president of Peru from 1963 to 1968 and again from 1980 to 1985. In 1968 he was toppled from his first presidency by a military coup in part due to his reluctance to expropriate U.S.-controlled oil fields.]
4   [Members of the socialist-leaning Peruvian political movement APRA (Alianza Popular Revolucionaria Americana, or the American Popular Revolutionary Alliance), established in 1924.]
5   [Manuel Odria (1897–1974) was a Peruvian dictator who seized power in a military coup in 1948. He was legally elected president in 1950 but continued to use often brutal dictatorial methods to rule the country. He allowed elections in 1956 and lost to Manuel Prado.]

Notes on Cortázar's *Bestiary*

1   [Six of the original eight stories in *Bestiario* have been translated into English and are included in the collection *Bestiary* by Cortázar ("House Taken Over," "Letter to a Young Lady in Paris," "Omnibus," "Circe," "The Gates of Heaven," and "Bestiary"). The story "Lejana" in the original collection has also been translated into English as "The Distances" in Cortázar, *Blow-up and Other Stories*, 17–27. "Cefalea" has not been translated. Page numbers here for the seven translated stories refer to pages in the English translations mentioned in this note. Page numbers for "Cefalea" refer to Cortázar's original Spanish version.]
2   The same scale, the same stages were imagined by Hegel to explain the highest levels of humanity, but with a negative sign. From the cockroaches to the "concrete others," the motion would seem to give meaning to the circuit.
3   [An original Spanish version of this story, "Reunión," was included in Cortázar,

Todos los fuegos el fuego, 68–86. An English translation, "Meeting," appears in Cortázar, *All Fires the Fire and Other Stories,* 49–64.]

4   [An original Spanish version of this story, "El persiguidor," was included in Cortázar, *La autopista del sur y otros cuentos,* 100–151. An English translation, "The Pursuer," appears in Cortázar, *Blow-up and Other Stories,* 182–247.]

5   [An original Spanish version of this story, "La autopista del sur," appears in Cortázar, *La autopista del sur y otros cuentos,* 162–184. An English translation, "The Southern Thruway," appears in Cortázar, *Bestiary,* 182–198.]

6   [An original Spanish version of this story, "No se culpe a nadie," appears in Cortázar, *Final del juego,* 13–18. An English translation, "Don't You Blame Anyone," appears in Cortázar, *Bestiary,* 110–113.]

7   [An original Spanish version of this story, "Las babas del diablo," appears in Cortázar, *La autopista del sur y otros cuentos,* 86–99. An English translation, "Blow-up," appears in Cortázar, *Blow-up and Other Stories,* 114–131.]

I, the Supreme as Historical Novel

1   [A reference to Riva Palacio's novel *Monja y casada.*]

2   [Benito Pérez Galdós (1843–1920) was a Spanish writer who was influenced by Balzac's realism and wrote on historical and religious themes.]

3   [Leenhardt, ed., *Littérature latino-américaine.*]

4   [Centre de Recherches, *Seminario sobre* Yo el Supremo.]

5   [Roa Bastos, "Réflexion auto-critique," 141.]

6   [Roa Bastos, "Réflexion auto-critique," 141–142.]

7   [Leenhardt, *Littérature latino-américaine,* 139.]

8   [This is a play on words combining "literati" with the Greek prefix "terato," meaning "monster"—the writer as monster.]

9   [This is a reference to the bloody war fought between Paraguay and the Triple Alliance of Argentina, Uruguay, and Brazil from 1864 to 1870, which resulted in the decimation of the Paraguayan people and the redrawing of the country's borders.]

10   [Bareiro-Saguier, "Niveaux sémantiques de la notion de personnage," 174–175.]

11   [Andreu, "Modalidades del relato en *Yo el Supremo.*]

12   [Jitrik is playing on the double meaning of the word *el,* the definite article in Spanish akin to the English "the," but which, when used with an accent mark, *él,* is the third-person singular pronoun equivalent to "he." Thus the original title in Spanish, *Yo el Supremo* ("I, the Supreme") moves from *Yo* ("I") to *el* ("the"/"he"). In the novel, the dictator ruminates frequently on the "I"/"he" split. See for example, *I, the Supreme,* 45 and 92.]

13   [Leenhardt, "La dictée de Gaspar de Francia," 51.]

14   [Bareiro Saguier, "La Historia y las historias en *Yo el Supremo.*"]

15   [Andreu, "Modalidades del relato en *Yo, el Supremo.*"]

16   ["Compiler" is *compilador* in the original Spanish, and *pillador* in Spanish means

one who pillages or plunders; the *com* would suggest commerce or business—
comercio in Spanish.]

Thirty Years Later

1   [The Eudeba "phenomenon" was a project carried out by the Editorial Universitaria de Buenos Aires (Eudeba), a publishing house created in 1958. Under the
direction of Boris Spivacow, director of the institution from 1958 to 1966, it under-
took a project to make Argentine literature broadly available to the general public
by publishing popular, inexpensive editions of Argentine literature that were sold
in popular venues and neighborhood kiosks on city streets. The project was successful in popularizing and widely disseminating many literary works.]

2   [Hernández, *El gaucho Martín Fierro*.]

Works Cited

Acevedo Díaz, Eduardo. *Ismael*. 1888. Montevideo: Editorial Alfa, 1966.

Alvarado, Ramón. "Nacionalismo, lenguaje e identidad colectiva." *Versión* 2 (April 1992): 141–162.

El amor de la estanciera. Edited by Mariano Bosch. Buenos Aires: Imprenta de la universidad, 1925.

Ancona, Eligio. *La cruz y la espada*. 1864. Mérida, Mexico: Maldonado Editores, 1950.

———. *Los mártires del Anahuac: novela histórica*. 1870. Mexico City: Editora Nacional, 1956.

Andreu, Jean. "Modalidades del relato en *Yo el Supremo* de Augusto Roa Bastos: lo Dicho, el Dictado y el Diktat." In *Seminario sobre* Yo el Supremo *de Augusto Roa Bastos*, edited by Centre de Recherches Latino-Américaines de l'Université de Poitiers. 61–113. Poitiers: Centre de Recherches Latino-Américaines de l'Université de Poitiers, 1976.

Aráoz, Rodolfo. *El recuerdo y las cárceles: memorias amables*. Buenos Aires: Ediciones de la Flor, 1967.

Aráoz Alfaro, Gregorio. *Crónicas y estampas del pasado*. Buenos Aires: El Ateneo, 1938.

Arguedas, José María. *Deep Rivers*. Translated by Frances Horning Barraclough. Prospect Heights, Ill.: Waveland Press. 2002. Translation of *Los ríos profundos*, 1958.

———. *The Fox from Up Above and the Fox from Down Below*. Translated by Frances Horning Barraclough. Edited by Julio Ortega. Pittsburgh: University of Pittsburgh Press. 2000. Translation of *El zorro de arriba y el zorro de abajo*, 1972.

———. *El sexto*. 1961. Lima: Editorial Horizonte, 1987.

———. *Todas las sangres*. 1964. Lima: Editorial Horizonte, 1987.

———. *Yawar Fiesta*. Translated by Frances Horning Barraclough. Prospect Heights, Ill.: Waveland Press, 2002. Translation of *Yawar fiesta*, 1941.

Arlt, Roberto. *El juguete rabioso*. 1927. Madrid: Cátedra, 2001.

———. *The Seven Madmen: A Novel*. Translated by Naomi Lindstrom. Boston: Godine, 1984. Translation of *Los siete locos*, 1929.

Asturias, Miguel Angel. *The President*. Translated by Francis Partridge. London: Gollancz, 1963. Translation of *El señor presidente*, 1946.

Auerbach, Erich. *Mimesis: The Representation of Reality in Western Literature*. Translated by Willard R. Trask. Princeton: Princeton University Press, 1953. Translation of *Mimesis; dargestellte Wirklichkeit in der abendländischen Literatur*, 1946.

Ayala, Francisco. *Experiencias e invención: ensayos sobre el escritor y su mundo*. Madrid: Taurus, 1960.

Bakhtin, Mikhail Mikhailovich. *Speech Genres and Other Late Essays*. Translated by Vern

W. McGee. Austin: University of Texas Press, 1986. Translation of *Estetika slovesnogo tvorchestva,* 1979.

Balestra, Juan. *El noventa.* Buenos Aires: Fariña, 1959.

Bareiro-Saguier, Rubén. "Niveaux sémantiques de la notion de personnage dans les romans de A. Roa Bastos." In *Littérature latino-américaine d'aujourd'hui. colloque de Cerisy,* edited by Jacques Leenhardt. 165–180. Paris: Union Générale d'Éditions, 1980.

Barthes, Roland. "The Reality Efffect." In *The Rustle of Language,* translated by Richard Howard. 141–148. Berkeley: University of California Press, 1989. Translation of *Le bruissement de la langue,* 1984.

Belgrano, Manuel. *Autobiografía.* Buenos Aires: Editorial Universitaria de Buenos Aires, 1966.

Beruti, Juan Manuel. *Memorias curiosas. 1942–1946.* Buenos Aires: Emecé, 2001.

Bianco, José. *La pérdida del reino.* Buenos Aires: Siglo XXI, 1972.

——. *Shadow Play; The Rats: Two Novellas.* Translated by Daniel Balderston. Pittsburgh: Latin American Literary Review Press, 1983. Translation of *Sombras suele vestir,* 1941, and *Las ratas,* 1943.

Bilbao, Manuel. *El inquisidor mayor, novela escrita.* Buenos Aires: Imprenta, litografía y fundicion de tipos, de la Sociedad anónima, 1871.

Bioy Casares, Adolfo. *The Invention of Morel.* Translated by Ruth L. C. Simms. New York: New York Review of Books, 2003. Translation of *La invención de Morel,* 1940.

Blanchot, Maurice. *La part du feu.* Paris: Gallimard, 1993.

Borges, Jorge Luis. *Discusión.* 1932. Buenos Aires: Emecé, 1996.

——. *Dreamtigers.* Translated by Mildren Boyer and Harold Morland. Austin: University of Texas Press, 1989. Translation of *El hacedor,* 1960.

——. *Evaristo Carriego: A Book about Old-time Buenos Aires.* Translated by Norman Thomas di Giovanni. New York: Dutton, 1984. Translation of *Evaristo Carriego,* 1930.

——. *Ficciones.* Various translators. New York: Knopf, 1993. Translation of *Ficciones,* 1944.

——. *El idioma de los argentinos.* 1928. Buenos Aires: Seix Barral, 1994.

——. *In Praise of Darkness.* Translated by Norman Thomas di Giovanni. New York: Dutton, 1974. Translation of *Elogio de la sombra,* 1969.

——. *El "Martín Fierro."* 1953. Madrid: Alianza Editorial, 1999.

——. *Other Inquisitions, 1937–1952.* Translated by Ruth L. C. Simms. Austin: University of Texas Press, 1995. Translation of *Otras inquisiciones,* 1952.

——. *El otro, el mismo.* Buenos Aires: Emecé, 1969.

——. Prologue to *Recuerdos de provincia* by Domingo F. Sarmiento. 9–10. Buenos Aires: Emecé, 1944.

——. *La rosa profunda.* Buenos Aires: Emecé, 1975.

——. *Selected Poems.* Edited by Alexander Coleman. New York: Viking Penguin, 1999.

——. *A Universal History of Infamy*. Translated by Norman Thomas di Giovanni. New York: Dutton, 1972. Translation of *Historia universal de la infamia*, 1935.

Borges, Jorge Luis, and Adolfo Bioy Casares, eds. *Poesía gauchesca*. Mexico City: Fondo de Cultura Económica, 1955.

Borges, Jorge Luis, and José E. Clemente. *El lenguaje de Buenos Aires*. Buenos Aires: Emecé, 1963.

Brémond, Claude. "La logique des possibles narratifs." *Communications* 8 (1966): 60–76.

Breton, André. *Manifestos of Surrealism*. Translated by Richard Seaver and Helen Lane. Ann Arbor: University of Michigan Press, 1969. Translation of *Les manifestes du surréalisme*, 1947.

Cambaceres, Eugenio. *En la sangre*. 1887. Buenos Aires: Ediciones Colihue, 1988.

Camps, Ramón J. A. *Caso Timerman: punto final*. Buenos Aires: Tribuna Abierta, 1982.

Cané, Miguel. *Juvenilia*. 1884. Buenos Aires: Centro Editor de América Latina, 1967.

Cárcano, Miguel Angel. *La fortaleza de Europa*. Buenos Aires: Guillermo Kraft, 1951.

Cárcano, Ramón J. *Mis primeros 80 años*. Buenos Aires: Editorial Sudamericana, 1943.

Carilla, Emilio. "Ideas estéticas de Echeverría." *Revista de Educación* 3.1 (1958): 1–13.

——. *El romanticismo en la América hispánica*. 1958. 2 vols. Madrid: Editorial Gredos, 1975.

Carpentier, Alejo. *Explosion in a Cathedral*. Translated by John Sturrock. Minneapolis: University of Minnesota Press, 2001. Translation of *El siglo de las luces*, 1962.

——. *The Kingdom of This World*. Translated by Harriet de Onís. New York: Noonday Press, 1989. Translation of *El reino de este mundo*, 1949.

——. *Reasons of State*. Translated by Francis Partridge. London: Readers and Writers, 1977. Translation of *El recurso del método*, 1974.

Castañon, Adolfo. *La gruta tiene dos entradas*. Mexico City: Vuelta, 1994.

Castellanos, Rosario. *The Book of Lamentations*. Translated by Esther Allen. New York: Penguin Books, 1998. Translation of *Oficio de tinieblas*, 1962.

Centre de Recherches Latino-Américaines de l'Université de Poitiers. *Seminario sobre Yo el Supremo de Augusto Roa Bastos*. Poitiers: Centre de Recherches Latino-Américaines de l'Université de Poitiers, 1976.

Cerretani, Arturo. *Matar a Titilo*. Buenos Aires: Siglo Veintiuno Argentina Editores, 1974.

Chesterton, G. K. *The Man Who Was Thursday: A Nightmare*. 1908. New York: Modern Library, 2001.

Cohen, Jean. "La comparaison poétique: essai de systématique." *Langages* 12 (1968): 43–51.

Cohn, Norman. *The Myth of the Jewish World Conspiracy and the Protocols of the Elders of Zion*. London: Serif, 1996.

Comisión Nacional sobre la Desaparición de Personas. *Nunca más: The Report of the Argentine National Commission on the Disappeared*. New York: Farrar, Straus, Giroux, 1986. Translation of *Nunca más: informe de la Comisión Nacional sobre la desaparición de personas*, 1984.

Concha, Jaime. "Huidobro: fragmentos." *Revista Iberoamericana* 106–107 (1979): 29–36.

Cortázar, Julio. *All Fires the Fire, and Other Stories.* New York: Pantheon Books, 1973. Translation of *Todos los fuegos el fuego,* 1966.

——. *La autopista del sur y otros cuentos.* 1951. New York: Penguin Books, 1996.

——. *Bestiario.* 1951. Buenos Aires: Editorial Sudamericana, 1979.

——. *Bestiary: Selected Stories.* Translated by Alberto Manguel, Paul Blackburn, Gregory Rabassa, Clementine Rabassa, and Suzanne Jill Levine. London: Harvill Press, 1998. Partial translation of *Bestiario* (with other selected stories included), 1951.

——. *Blow-up and Other Stories.* Translated by Paul Blackburn. New York: Pantheon Books, 1985.

——. *Cronopios and famas.* Translated by Paul Blackburn. New York: New Directions, 1999. Translation of *Historias de cronopios y de famas,* 1962.

——. *Final del juego.* 1964. Buenos Aires: Editorial Sudamericana, 1976.

——. *Hopscotch.* Translated by Gregory Rabassa. New York: Pantheon Books, 1987. Translation of *Rayuela,* 1963.

——. *Todos los fuegos el fuego.* 1966. Buenos Aires: Editorial Sudamericana, 1970.

Díaz Seijas, Pedro. "De la realidad al mito en *El siglo de las luces.*" In *La gran narrativa latinoamericana.* 123–164. Caracas: Monte Avila, 1992.

Di Benedetto, Antonio. *Zama.* 1956. Buenos Aires: Adriana Hidalgo Editora, 2000.

Dickman, Enrique. *Recuerdos de un militante socialista.* Buenos Aires: Editorial La Vanguardia, 1949.

Drumont, Edouard Adolphe. *La France juive: essai d'histoire contemporaine.* Paris: Marpon and Flammarion, 1886.

Dummet, Michael. *La verdad y otros enigmas.* Mexico City: Fondo de Cultura Económica, 1990.

Echeverría, Esteben. *Dogma socialista de la Asociación de Mayo: precedido de una ojeada retrospectiva sobre el movimiento intelectual en el Plata desde el año 37.* 1846. Buenos Aires: Editorial Perrot, 1958.

——. *El matadero; La cautiva.* 1871, 1837. Edited by Leonore Fleming. 5th ed. Madrid: Cátedra, 1997.

——. *Obras completas.* 1951. Edited by Juan María Gutiérrez. Buenos Aires: Antonio Zamora, 1972.

——. "The Slaughter House." Translated by Angel Flores. In *The Oxford Book of Latin American Short Stories,* edited by Roberto González Echevarría. 59–72. New York: Oxford University Press, 1997. Translation of *El matadero,* 1871.

Echeverría, José Antonio. *Obras escogidas.* Havana: Dirección General de Cultura, 1960.

Estébanez Calderón, Serafín. 1847. *Escenas andaluzas.* Madrid: Confederación Española de Gremios y Asociaciones de Libreros, 1995.

Etcheverry, José Enrique. *Horacio Quiroga y la creación artística.* Montevideo: Universidad de la República, 1957.

Ette, Ottmar. "La polisemia prohibida: la recepción de José Martí como sismógrafo de la vida política y cultural." *Cuadernos Americanos* 2.32 (1992): 196–211.

Faye, Jean Pierre. "Montage, production." *Change* 1 (1968): 5–13.

Fernández, Macedonio. *Museo de la novela eterna (primera novela buena)*. Buenos Aires: Ediciones Corregidor, 1975.

Fernández de Lizardi, José Joaquín. *The Itching Parrot*. Translated by Katherine Anne Porter. Garden City, N.Y.: Doubleday, Doran, 1942. Translation of *El periquillo sarniento*, 1816–1830.

Fernández Moreno, César, ed. *América Latina en su literatura*. Mexico City: Siglo Veintiuno Editores, 1972.

Fernández Moreno, César, Julio Ortega, and Iván A. Schulman, eds. *Latin America in its Literature*. Translated by Mary C. Berg. New York: Holmes and Meier, 1980. Partial translation of *América Latina en su literatura*, 1972.

Filloy, Juan. *Op Oloop*. 1934. Buenos Aires: Losada, 1997.

Flaubert, Gustave. *Salammbo*. Translated by A. J. Krailsheimer. New York: Penguin, 1985. Translation of *Salammbô*, 1862.

Foucault, Michel. *The Order of Things: An Archaeology of the Human Sciences*. London: Routledge, 2001. Translation of *Les mots et les choses*, 1966.

Franco, Jean. *César Vallejo: The Dialectics of Poetry and Silence*. Cambridge: Cambridge University Press, 1976.

Frías, Heriberto. *Tomóchic*. 1893–1895. Mexico City: Porrúa, 1979.

Frondizi, Arturo. *Petróleo y política: contribución al estudio de la historia económica argentina y de las relaciones entre el imperialismo y la vida política nacional*. Buenos Aires: Raigal, 1955.

Frye, Northrup. *Anatomy of Criticism*. 1957. Princeton: Princeton University Press, 2000.

Fuentes, Carlos. *The Death of Artemio Cruz*. Translated by Sam Hileman. London: Secker and Warburg, 1977. Translation of *La muerte de Artemio Cruz*, 1962.

———. *Valiente mundo nuevo: épica, utopia, y mito en la novela hispanoamericana*. Mexico City: Fondo de Cultura Económica, 1990.

Gallegos, Rómulo. *Doña Barbara*. 1931. Translated by Robert Malloy. New York: Peter Smith, 1948. Translation of *Doña Bárbara*, 1929.

Galván, Manuel de Jesús. *Manuel de Jesús Galván's Enriquillo: The Cross and the Sword*. Translated by Robert Graves. Bloomington: Indiana University Press, 1954. Translation of *Enriquillo*, 1882.

Gálvez, Manuel. *El diario de Gabriel Quiroga*. 1910. Buenos Aires: Taurus, 2001.

———. *El mal metafísica*. 1916. Buenos Aires: Espasa-Calpe, 1943.

———. *El solar de la raza*. 1913. Buenos Aires: Ediciones Dictio, 1980.

———. *Memoria de la vida literaria argentina*. Buenos Aires: Editorial Kapelusz, 1977.

García Márquez, Gabriel. *The Autumn of the Patriarch*. Translated by Gregory Rabassa. New York: Harper Perennial, 1991. Translation of *El otoño del patriarca*, 1975.

———. *Chronicle of a Death Foretold*. Translated by Gregory Rabassa. New York: Knopf, 1990. Translation of *Crónica de una muerte anunciada*, 1981.

———. *One Hundred Years of Solitude*. Translated by Gregory Rabassa. New York: Knopf, 1998. Translation of *Cien años de soledad*, 1967.

Gellner, Ernst. *Naciones y nacionalismo*. Mexico City: Editorial Patria/Conaculta, 1991.

Genette, Gerard. "La rhétorique restreinte." *Communications* 16 (1970): 158–171.

——. "Vraisemblable et motivation." *Communications* 11 (1968): 5–21.

Gerchunoff, Alberto. *The Jewish Gauchos of the Pampas*. Translated by Prudencio de Pereda. New York: Abelard-Schuman, 1959. Translation of *Los gauchos judíos*, 1910.

Gilimón, Eduardo G. *Un anarquista en Buenos Aires, 1890–1910*. Buenos Aires: Centro Editor de América Latina, 1972.

Goic, Cedomil. "La comparación creacionista." *Revista Iberoamericana* 106–107 (1979): 129–139.

Gombrowicz, Witold. *Diary*. Translated by Lillian Vallee. Evanston: Northwestern University Press, 1988. Translation of *Dziennik*.

Gómez de Avellaneda y Arteaga, Gertrudis. *Guatemocín*. 1846. Havana: Editorial Letras Cubanas, 1979.

Góngora y Argote, Luis de. *Sonetos*. Madison, Wisc.: Hispanic Seminary of Medieval Studies, 1981.

González, José Luis. *La llegada: crónica con "ficción."* 1980. Mexico City: Alfaguara, 1997.

Guerrero, Juan Luis. *Tres temas de filosofía en las entrañas del Facundo*. Buenos Aires: Elevación, 1945.

Guido y Spano, Carlos. *Autobiografía*. Buenos Aires: Ediciones Troquel, 1966.

Guzmán, Martín Luis. *The Eagle and the Serpent*. Translated by Harriet de Onís. Garden City, N.Y.: Dolphin Books, 1965. Translation of *El águila y la serpiente*, 1928.

Halperin-Donghi, Tulio, Ivan Jaksic, Gwen Kirkpatrick, and Francine Masiello, eds. *Sarmiento: Author of a Nation*. Berkeley: University of California Press, 1994.

Harss, Luis, and Barbara Dohmann. *Into the Mainstream: Conversations with Latin-American Writers*. New York: Harper and Row, 1966.

——. *Los nuestros*. Translated by Luis Harss, Paco Porrúa, and Sara Porrúa. Buenos Aires: Editorial Sudamericana, 1966. Translation of *Into the Mainstream: Conversations with Latin-American Writers*, 1966.

Hiriart, Hugo. *Galaor*. Mexico City: Joaquín Mortiz, 1972.

Hernández, José. *El gaucho Martín Fierro/The Gaucho Martín Fierro*. Bilingual edition. Translated by C. E. Ward. Albany: State University of New York Press, 1967. Translation of *El gaucho Martín Fierro*, 1872–1879.

Hugo, Victor. *Hernani*. 1830. Lanham, Md.: University Press of America, 2001.

——. *Les orientales, et Les feuilles d'automne*. 1829, 1831. Paris: Librarie Générale Française, 2000.

——. *Preface de Cromwell and Hernani*. 1827, 1829. Chicago: Scott, Foresman, 1900.

Huidobro, Vicente. *Ecuatorial*. 1918. Santiago: Editorial Nascimiento, 1978.

Irazusta, Julio. *Actores y espectadores*. Buenos Aires: Ediciones Dictio, 1937.

——. *Balance de siglo y medio*. Buenos Aires: Theoría, 1966.

——. *Estudios Histórico-Políticos*. Buenos Aires: Ediciones Dictio, 1973.

Jakobson, Roman. *Language and Literature*. Cambridge: Harvard University Press, 1987.

Jitrik, Noé. "*Adán Buenosayres:* la novela de Leopoldo Marechal." *Contorno* 5–6 (1955): 38–45.

——, ed. *Las armas y las razones: ensayos sobre el peronismo, el exilio, la literatura.* Buenos Aires: Editorial Sudamericana, 1984.

——. *El balcón barroco.* Mexico City: UNAM, 1988.

——. *Confesiones de escritores. Los reportajes de* The Paris Review: *escritores latinoamericanos.* Buenos Aires: El Ateneo, 1996.

——. *El ejemplo de la familia.* Buenos Aires: Eudeba, 1998.

——. *Ensayos y estudios de literatura argentina.* Buenos Aires: Editorial Galerna, 1970.

——. *El escritor argentino: dependencia o libertad.* Buenos Aires: Del Candil, 1967.

——. "Estructura y significado en *Ficciones* de Jorge Luis Borges." *Actual: Revista de la Universidad de Los Andes* 2.3–4 (1968–1969): 72–86.

——. "El *Facundo:* la gran riqueza de la pobreza." Prologue to *Facundo, o Civilización y barbarie,* by Domingo Faustino Sarmiento. ix–lii. Caracas: Biblioteca Ayacucho, 1977.

——. "*Facundo:* The Riches of Poverty." Translated by Ann Gatschet, Lisa Bradford, and Janet Greenberg. In *Sarmiento: Author of a Nation,* edited by Tulio Halperin-Donghi, Ivan Jaksic, Gwen Kirkpatrick, and Francine Masiello. 169–192. Berkeley: University of California Press, 1994.

——. *El fuego de la especie.* Buenos Aires: Siglo XXI, 1971.

——. *Historia e imaginación literaria: las posibilidades de un género.* Buenos Aires: Biblos, 1995.

——. *La lectura como actividad.* Mexico City: Premiá, 1984.

——. *Línea de flotación: ensayos sobre incesancia.* Mérida, Venezuela: Ediciones El Otro, El Mismo, 2002.

——. *La memoria compartida.* Buenos Aires: Centro Editor de América Latina, 1987.

——. "Otras inquisiciones." *Revista Centro* 2.4 (1952): 35–37.

——. "Papeles de trabajo: notas sobre la vanguardia latinoamericana." *Revista de Crítica Literaria Latinoamericana* 15.8 (1982): 13–24.

——. *La revolución del 90.* Buenos Aires: Centro Editor de América Latina, 1970.

——. "Sentiments complexes sur Borges." *Les Temps Modernes* 420–421 (1981): 195–223.

——. "Soledad y urbanidad." *Boletín de Literatura Argentina* 2 (1966): 27–61.

——. *Suspender toda certeza: antología crítica (1959–1976).* Buenos Aires: Biblos, 1997.

——. *Temas de teoría: el trabajo crítico y la crítica literaria.* Mexico City: Premiá, 1987.

——. *La vibración del presente.* Mexico City: Fondo de Cultura Económica, 1987.

——. *Vertiginosas textualidades.* Mexico City: UNAM, 1999.

Joly, Maurice. *The Dialogue in Hell between Machiavelli and Montesquieu.* Translated by John S. Waggoner. Lanham, Md.: Lexington Books, 2002. Translation of *Dialogue aux enfers entre Machiavel et Montesquieu, ou La politique de Machiavel au XIXe siècle,* 1864.

Joyce, James. *Ulysses.* 1922. New York: Modern Library, 1992.

Kainz, Friedrich. *Estética.* Translated by Wenceslao Roces. Mexico City: Fondo de Cultura Económica, 1952. Translation of *Vorlesungen über Ästhetik, 1948.*

Kedourie, Elie. *Nationalism.* London: Hutchinson, 1960.

Kristeva, Julia. "La productivité dite texte." *Communications* 11 (1968): 59–83.

———. *Revolution in Poetic Language.* Translated by Margaret Waller. New York: Columbia University Press, 1984. Translation of *La révolution du langage poétique,* 1974.

Lacoue-Labarthe, Philippe, and Jean-Luc Nancy. *The Title of the Letter: A Reading of Lacan.* Translated by François Raffoul and David Pettigrew. Albany: State University of New York Press, 1992. Translation of *Le titre de la lettre,* 1973.

Lanusse, Alejandro Agustín. *Mi testimonio.* Buenos Aires: Lasserre Editores, 1977.

———. *Protagonista y testigo (reflexiones sobre 70 años de nuestra historia).* Buenos Aires: M. Lugones Editores, 1988.

Larrea, Juan. *César Vallejo: o, Hispanoamérica en la cruz de su razón.* Córdoba, Argentina: Publicaciones del CEFYL, Universidad Nacional de Córdoba, 1958.

———. "Vicente Huidobro en Vanguardia." *Revista Iberoamericana* 106–107 (1979): 213–273.

Larreta, Enrique. *La gloria de don Ramiro.* 1908. Madrid: Espasa-Calpe, 1970.

Lastra, Bonifacio. *Bajo el signo nacionalista: escritos y discursos.* Buenos Aires: Editorial Alianza, 1944.

Leenhardt, Jacques. "La dictée de Gaspar de Francia." In *Littérature latino-américaine d'aujourd'hui: colloque de Cerisy,* edited by Jacques Leenhardt. 51–64. Paris: Union Générale d'Éditions, 1980.

———, ed. *Littérature latino-américaine d'aujourd'hui: colloque de Cerisy.* Paris: Union Générale d'Éditions, 1980.

Leguizamón, Julio. *Historia de la literatura hispanoamericana.* Buenos Aires: Editorial Reunidas S.A., 1945.

Lezama Lima, José. *Oppiano Licario.* 1977. Madrid: Cátedra, 1989.

———. *Paradiso.* Translated by Gregory Rabassa. Austin: University of Texas Press, 1988. Translation of *Paradiso,* 1966.

Libertella, Héctor. *Nueva escritura en América Latina.* Caracas: Monte Avila, 1977.

Lopez, Vicente Fidel. *La novia del hereje, o La inquisición de Lima.* 1846. Buenos Aires: La cultura argentina, 1917.

Lukács, György. *The Historical Novel.* Translated by Hannah Mitchell and Stanley Mitchell. Lincoln: University of Nebraska Press, 1983. Translation of *A történelmi regény,* 1947.

Lugones, Leopoldo. *La grande Argentina.* 1930. Buenos Aires: Editorial Huemul, 1962.

———. *La hora de la espada y otros escritos.* 1924. Buenos Aires: Perfil, 1998.

———. *La patria fuerte.* Buenos Aires: Taller Gráfico de L. Bernard, 1930.

———. *El payador.* 1916. Buenos Aires: Editorial Huemul, 1972.

Luna, Félix. *Alvear.* Buenos Aires: Libros Argentinos S.R.L., 1958.

Mallarmé, Stéphane. *Oeuvres complètes.* 1945. Paris: Gallimard, 1970.

———. *Selected Poetry and Prose*. Edited by Mary Ann Caws. Various translators. New York: New Directions, 1982.

Mallea, Eduardo. *History of an Argentine Passion*. Translated by Myron Lichtblau. Pittsburgh: Latin American Literary Review Press, 1983. Translation of *Historia de una pasión argentina*, 1937.

Mallea, Narciso S. *Mi vida, mis fobias*. Buenos Aires: Imprenta Mercatali, 1941.

Mansilla, Lucio. *Entre-nos: causeries de los jueves*. 1889–1890. Buenos Aires: Editorial Universitaria de Buenos Aires, 1964.

———. *A Visit to the Ranquel Indians, una excursión a los indios ranqueles*. Translated by Eva Gillies. Lincoln: University of Nebraska Press, 1997. Translation of *Una excursión a los indios ranqueles*, 1870.

Marechal, Leopoldo. *Adán Buenosayres*. 1948. Buenos Aires: Editorial Sudamericana, 1970.

Mármol, José. *Amalia*. Translated by Helen Lane. Oxford: Oxford University Press, 2001. Translation of *Amalia*, 1855.

Marmontel, Jean François. *The Incas, or, The Destruction of the Empire of Peru*. Alston, England: John Harrop, 1808. Translation of *Les Incas, ou La destruction de l'empire du Pérou*. 1777.

Martel, Julián. *La bolsa*. 1891. Buenos Aires: Editorial de Belgrano, 1981.

Martí, José. *Inside the Monster: Writings on the United States and American Imperialism*. Translated by Federico de Onís, Luis A. Baralt, and Elinor Randall. New York: Monthly Review Press, 1975.

———. "Manifesto of Montecristi." Translated by Elinor Randall. In *Our America: Writings on Latin America and the Struggle for Cuban Independence*, edited by Philip S. Foner. 390–400. New York: Monthly Review Press, 1977.

———. *Simple Verses/Versos sencillos*. Translated by Manuel A. Tellechea. Houston: Arte Público Press, 1997. Translation of *Versos sencillos*, 1891.

———. *Versos libres*. 1913. Havana: Editorial Puebla y Educación, 1997.

Martínez, Tomás Eloy. "Perón y los nazis." *El Periodista de Buenos Aires* (in two installments) 48 (9–15 Aug. 1985): 25–27; vol. 49 (16–22 Aug. 1985): 23–25.

Martino, Pierre. *Parnasse et symbolisme*. Paris: Librairie Armand Colin, 1958.

McKay, Ellen Michele Gracey. *The Mad Toy: A Translation of Roberto Arlt's* El juguete rabioso *with critical introduction*. Ph.D. diss. University of Texas at Austin, 1998. Doc. no. 9838046, Ann Arbor, Mich.: UMI, 1998.

Mendoza, María Luisa. *El perro de la escribana, o, Las piedecasas*. Mexico City: Joaquín Mortiz, 1982.

Mignone, Emilio Fermín. "Los católicos y la revolución de 1890." *Revista de Historia* 1 ("La crisis del 90") (1957): 56–60.

Mitre, Bartolomé. *Soledad*. Buenos Aires: Imprenta de la Universidad, 1928.

Novo, Salvador. *Antología de la poesía norteamericana moderna*. Mexico City: El Universal Ilustrado, 1924.

Núñez, Estuardo. "Lo latinoamericano en otras literaturas." In *América Latina en su literatura*, edited by César Fernández Moreno. 92–120. Mexico City: Siglo xxi, 1972.

Ocampo, Victoria. *Autobiografía*. Buenos Aires: Ediciones Sur, 1979.

Oliver, María Rosa. *Mundo mi casa: recuerdos de infancia*. Buenos Aires: Falbo Librero Editor, 1965.

———. *La vida cotidiana*. Buenos Aires: Editorial Sudamericana, 1969.

Onetti, Juan Carlos. *Body Snatcher*. Translated by Alfred Mac Adam. New York: Pantheon Books, 1991. Translation of *Juntacadáveres*, 1964.

———. *Goodbyes and Stories*. Translated by Daniel Balderston. Austin: University of Texas Press, 1990. Translation of *Los adioses* (and other selected stories), 1954.

———. *Farewells; and, A Grave with No Name*. Translated by Peter Bush. London: Quartet Books, 1992. Translation of *Los adioses,* 1954, and *Para una tumba sin nombre*, 1959.

Orgambide, Pedro. *Borges y su pensamiento político*. Mexico City: Comité de Solidaridad con el Pueblo Argentino, Casa Argentina, 1978.

Orona, Juan V. *La revolución del 6 de septiembre*. Buenos Aires: Imprenta López, 1966.

Orozco, José Clemente. *Cartas a Margarita*. Mexico City: Biblioteca Era, 1987.

Ortega, Julio. "La escritura de la vanguardia." *Revista Iberoamericana* 106–107 (1979): 187–198.

Ortega y Gasset, José. *The Dehumanization of Art, and Other Essays on Art, Culture and Literature*. Translated by Helene Weyl. Princeton: Princeton University Press, 1968. Translation of *La deshumanización de arte*, 1925.

Pacheco, José Emilio. "Nota sobre la otra vanguardia." *Revista de Literatura Iberoamericana* 106–107 (1979): 327–334.

———. *You Will Die in a Distant Land*. Translated by Elizabeth Umlas. Coral Gables, Fl.: North-South Center, University of Miami, 1991. Translation of *Morirás lejos*, 1978.

Páez de la Torre, Carlos. *El canciller de las flores*. Tucumán: UNT, 1992.

Palcos, Alberto. *Historia de Echeverría*. Buenos Aires: Emecé, 1960.

Payno, Manuel. *Los bandidos de Río Frío*. 1889–1891. Mexico City: Editorial Porrúa, 2000.

Paz, José María. *Memorias*. 1855. Edited by José Luis Lanuza. 4 vols. Buenos Aires: Editorial Schapire, 1968.

Pérez Galdós, Benito. *Trafalgar*. 1873. Madrid: Cátedra, 1996.

Perrone, Alberto, ed. *La poesía argentina*. Buenos Aires: Centro Editor de América Latina, 1979.

Picón Salas, Mariano. *A Cultural History of Spanish America: From Conquest to Independence*. Berkeley: University of California Press, 1962.

Piglia, Ricardo. *Artificial Respiration*. Translated by Daniel Balderston. Durham: Duke University Press, 1994. *Translation of Respiración artificial*, 1980.

Poggioli, Renato. *The Theory of the Avant-Garde*. Translated by Gerald Fitzgerald. Cambridge: Belknap Press of Harvard University Press, 1968. Translation of *Teoria dell'arte d'avanguardia*, 1962.

Porchia, Antonio. *Voices.* Translated by W. S. Merwin. Port Townsend, Wash.: Copper Canyon Press, 2003 (1969). Partial translation of *Voces,* 1943.

Posadas, Gervasio. *Memorias de Gervasio Posadas, Director Supremo de las Provincias del Río de la Plata en 1814. memorias de un abanderado (Nueva Granada 1810–1819).* Madrid: Editorial América, 1920.

Potash, Robert. *Documentos del G.O.U.* Buenos Aires: Editorial Sudamericana, 1984.

Prego, Omar, and María Angélica Petit. *Juan Carlos Onetti, o, La salvación por la escritura.* Madrid: Sociedad General Española de Librería, 1981.

Prieto, Adolfo. *La literatura autobiográfico argentina.* Rosario: Facultad de Filosofía y Letras, 1966.

——, ed. *Proyección del rosismo en la literatura argentina.* Rosario: Universidad Nacional del Litoral, 1959.

Quevedo, Francisco de. *Obras fiestas.* Madrid: Castalia, 1981.

Quiroga, Horacio. *Todos los cuentos.* Edited by Napoleón Baccino Ponce de León and Jorge Lafforgue. Nanterre, France: Allca xx; Madrid: Fondo de Cultura Económica, 1993.

Rebolledo, Efrén. *Salamandra.* Mexico City: Tallere Gráficos del Gobierno Nacional, 1919.

Repetto, Nicolás. *Mi paso por la política; de Roca a Yrigoyen.* Buenos Aires: Santiago Rueda, 1956.

——. *Mi paso por la política; de Uriburu a Perón.* Buenos Aires: Santiago Rueda, 1957.

Riva Palacio, Vicente. *Monja y casada, virgen y mártir.* 1868. Mexico City: Editorial Porrúa, 1974.

Roa Bastos, Augusto. *I, the Supreme.* Translated by Helen Lane. New York: Knopf, 1986. Translation of *Yo el Supremo,* 1974.

——. "Réflexion auto-critique à propos de *Moi, le Supréme,* du point de vue sociolinguistique et idéologique: Condition du Narrateur." In *Littérature latino-américaine d'aujourd'hui: colloque de Cerisy,* edited by Jacques Leenhardt. 136–149. Paris: Union Générale d'Éditions, 1980.

Rojas, Ricardo. *Historia de la literatura argentina: ensayo filosófico sobre la evolución de la cultura en el Plata.* 1924–1925. 9 vols. Buenos Aires: Guillermo Kraft, 1960.

——. *La restauración nacionalista: crítica de la educación argentina y bases para una reforma en el estudio de las humanidades modernas.* 1909. Buenos Aires: A. Peña Lillo, 1971.

Rouquié, Alain. *Poder militar y sociedad política en la Argentina.* Buenos Aires: Emecé, 1981.

Rulfo, Juan. *Pedro Páramo.* Translated by Margaret Sayers Peden. Austin: University of Texas Press, 2002. Translation of *Pedro Páramo,* 1955.

Saer, Juan José. *Nobody Nothing Never.* Translated by Helen Lane. London: Serpent's Tail, 1993. Translation of *Nadie nada nunca,* 1980.

——. *The Witness.* Translated by Margaret Jull Costa. London: Serpent's Tail, 1990. Translation of *El entenado,* 1983.

Sánchez, Florencio. *La gringa*. 1904. Rosario, Argentina: Ameghino Editora, 1999.

Sánchez Sorondo, Marcelo. *Argentina por dentro*. Buenos Aires: Editorial Sudamericana, 1987.

Sarmiento, Domingo Faustino. *Condición del extranjero en América*. Buenos Aires: Editorial Luz del Día, 1953.

———. *Conflicto y armonía de las razas en América*. 1883. Caracas: Universidad Central de Venezuela, Facultad de Humanidades y Educación, Comisión del Bicentenario del Nacimiento del Libertador, 1983.

———. "De las biografías." In *Obras completas* (53 vols.), 1:129–131. San Justo, Argentina: Universidad Nacional de La Matanza, 2001.

———. *Facundo, o, Civilización y barbarie*. 1845. Caracas: Biblioteca Ayacucho, 1977.

———. *Facundo: Civilization and Barbarism*. Translated by Kathleen Ross. Berkeley: University of California Press, 2004. Translation of *Facundo, o, Civilización y barbarie*, 1845.

———. *Recuerdos de provincia, precedido de Mi defensa*. Buenos Aires: Sur, 1962.

———. *A Sarmiento Anthology*. Translated by Stuart Edgar Grummon. Edited by Allison Williams Bunkley. Princeton: Princeton University Press, 1948.

———. *Travels: A Selection*. Translated by Inés Muñoz. Washington, D.C.: Pan American Union, 1963. Partial translation of *Viajes por Europa, África y América, 1845–1847, 1849*.

———. *Viajes por Europa, África y América, 1845–1847*. 1849. Madrid: Allca xx and Fondo de Cultura Económica, 1996.

Scalabrini Ortiz, Raúl. *El hombre que está solo y espera*. 1931. Buenos Aires: Plus Ultra, 1983.

———. *La política británica en el Río de la Plata*. Buenos Aires: FORJA, 1936.

———. *Petróleo e imperialismo: el ejemplo de Méjico y el deber argentino*. Buenos Aires: Fuerza de Orientación Radical de la Joven Argentina, 1938.

Scott, Walter. *Ivanhoe: A Romance*. 1791. New York: Modern Library, 2001.

Seijas, Pedro Díaz. "De la realidad al mito en *El Siglo de las luces*." *La gran narrativa latinoamericana*. 1976. Caracas: Monte Avila, 1992.

Smith, Anthony D. *National Identity*. Reno: University of Nevada Press, 1991.

Sommi, Luis V. *La revolución del 90*. Buenos Aires: Ediciones Pueblos de América, 1957.

Soriano, Osvaldo. *A Funny Dirty Little War*. Translated by Nick Caistor. New York: Readers International, 1986. Translation of *No habrá más penas ni olvido*, 1980.

Stoker, Bram. *Dracula*. 1897. New York: Doring Kindersley Publishing, 1997.

Todorov, Tzvetan. *The Fantastic; A Structural Approach to a Literary Genre*. Translated by Richard Howard. Cleveland: Case Western University Press, 1973. Translation of *Introduction à la littérature fantastique*, 1970.

———. *Littérature et signification*. Paris: Larousse, 1967.

Torres, José Luis. *La década infame*. Buenos Aires: Editorial Freeland, 1973.

Tynianov, Iouri. "De l'évolution littéraire." In *Théorie de la littérature*, edited by Tzvetan Todorov. 120–137. Paris: Seuil, 1965.

Tzara, Tristan. *Seven Dada Manifestos and Lampisteries*. Translated by Barbara Wright. London: Calder Publications, 1992. Translation of *Sept manifestes Dada, lampisteries*, 1963.

Valle-Inclán, Ramón del. *Tirano Banderas*. Madrid: Espasa-Calpe, 1978.

Vallejo, César. *The Black Heralds*. Translated by Richard Schaaf and Kathleen Ross. Pittsburgh: Latin American Literary Review Press, 1990. Translation of *Los heraldos negros*, 1918.

——. *Crónicas 1915–1938*. Edited by Enrique Ballón Aguirre. 2 vols. Mexico City: UNAM, 1984.

——. *Poemas humanos/Human Poems*. Translated by Clayton Eshleman. New York: Grove Press, 1968. Translation of *Poemas humanos*, 1939.

——. *Trilce*. Translated by Clayton Eshleman. Hanover, N.H.: University Press of New England, 2000. Translation of *Trilce*, 1922.

——. *Tungsten: A Novel*. Translated by Robert Mezey. Syracuse, N.Y.: Syracuse University Press, 1988. Translation of *El tungsteno*, 1931.

Van Heijenoort, Jean. *De Prinkipo à Coyoacán: sept ans auprès de Léon Trotsky*. 1978. Paris: Lettres nouvelles, M. Nadeau, 1988.

Varela, Félix. *Xicoténcatl: An Anonymous Historical Novel about the Events Leading Up to the Conquest of the Aztec Empire*. Translated by Guillermo I. Castillo-Feliú. Austin: University of Texas Press, 1999. Translation of *Jicoténcal*, 1826.

Vigny, Alfred de. *Cinq-Mars: or, A conspiracy under Louis XIII*. Translated by William Hazlitt. Boston: Little, Brown, 1907. Translation of *Cinq-Mars, ou Une conjuration sous Louis XIII*, 1826.

Voltaire, François Marie Arouet. *Candide*. Translated by Tobias Smollett. Franklin Center, Pa.: Franklin Library, 1979. Translation of *Candide, ou L'optimisme*. 1758.

Weber, Jean-Paul. *Genèse de l'œuvre poétique*. Paris: Gallimard, 1960.

Weinberg, Félix. "La Generación del 37." *Todo es historia* 242 (1987): 86–88.

——. *El Salón Literario*. Buenos Aires: Hachette, 1958.

Wilder, Thornton. *The Bridge of San Luis Rey*. 1927. New York: Perennial Classics, 1998.

——. *The Ides of March*. 1948. New York: Perennial, 2003.

Zola, Émile. *The Masterpiece*. Translated by Thomas Walton. Ann Arbor: University of Michigan Press, 1968. Translation of *L'oeuvre*, 1886.

Zum Felde, Alberto. *La narrativa en Hispanoamérica*. Madrid: Aguilar, 1964.

Index

Noé Jitrik was born in 1928 in Rivera, Argentina. He is the director of the Instituto de Literatura Latinoamericana at the University of Buenos Aires. He has taught at universities in Argentina, Mexico, the United States, Puerto Rico, France, and Venezuela. Jitrik is the author of many works of literary criticism and more than a dozen books of fiction and poetry. He is currently editing a twelve-volume history of Argentine literature.

Daniel Balderston is a professor of Spanish at the University of Iowa. He is the author of books including *El deseo, enorme cicatriz luminosa: ensayos sobre homosexualidades latinoamericanas*; *Borges, realidades y simulacros*; and *Out of Context: Historical Reference and the Representation of Reality in Borges* (also published by Duke University Press).

Susan Benner is a lecturer in the English department at Iowa State University. She is a coeditor and co-translator of *Fire from the Andes: Short Fiction by Women from Bolivia, Ecuador, and Peru*.

Library of Congress Cataloging-in-Publication Data
Jitrik, Noé, 1928–
[Essays. English. Selections]
The Noé Jitrik reader : selected essays on Latin American literature / Noé Jitrik ; edited by Daniel Balderston ; translated by Susan Benner.
p. cm. — (Latin America in translation/en traducción/em tradução)
Includes bibliographical references and index.
ISBN 0-8223-3533-6 (cloth : alk. paper) — ISBN 0-8223-3545-x (pbk. : alk. paper)
1. Spanish American literature—History and criticism. 2. Argentine literature—History and criticism. I. Balderston, Daniel, 1952– II. Benner, Susan E. (Susan Elizabeth), 1957– III. Title. IV. Series.
PQ7081.J523 2005
860.9'98—dc22
2004028254